Praise for *America[...]*

"Studded with fascinating tidbits. . . . Th[...]
interesting and his conflicting view of Freudianism well worth absorbing."
—*The New York Times Book Review*

"A thorough yet concise history of the talking cure. . . . A capable explanation of a complicated field."
—*Kirkus Reviews*

"An authoritative, readable book, this is highly recommended for large general libraries and collections in health and social science."
—*Library Journal*

"Engel's *American Therapy* is an important and necessary book for anyone wishing to review either the landscape of contemporary Americana, or the disposition of contemporary therapy in America."
—James Hollis, Ph.D., Jungian analyst and author, most recently of *What Matters Most: Living a More Considered Life*

Jonathan Engel holds a Ph.D. in the history of science and medicine from Yale and has written extensively about the historical development of U.S. medicine and health policy. His previous books are *Doctors and Reformers: Discussion and Debate over Health Policy 1925–1950*, *Poor People's Medicine: Medicaid and American Charity Care since 1965*, and *The Epidemic: A Global History of AIDS*. A professor of health care policy at Baruch College, CUNY, he lives in New Jersey.

American Therapy

The Rise of Psychotherapy
in the United States

Jonathan Engel

GOTHAM
BOOKS

GOTHAM BOOKS
Published by Penguin Group (USA) Inc.
375 Hudson Street, New York, New York 10014, U.S.A.

Penguin Group (Canada), 90 Eglinton Avenue East, Suite 700, Toronto, Ontario M4P 2Y3, Canada (a division of Pearson Penguin Canada Inc.); Penguin Books Ltd, 80 Strand, London WC2R 0RL, England; Penguin Ireland, 25 St Stephen's Green, Dublin 2, Ireland (a division of Penguin Books Ltd); Penguin Group (Australia), 250 Camberwell Road, Camberwell, Victoria 3124, Australia (a division of Pearson Australia Group Pty Ltd); Penguin Books India Pvt Ltd, 11 Community Centre, Panchsheel Park, New Delhi–110 017, India; Penguin Group (NZ), 67 Apollo Drive, Rosedale, North Shore 0632, New Zealand (a division of Pearson New Zealand Ltd); Penguin Books (South Africa) (Pty) Ltd, 24 Sturdee Avenue, Rosebank, Johannesburg 2196, South Africa

Penguin Books Ltd, Registered Offices: 80 Strand, London WC2R 0RL, England

Published by Gotham Books, a member of Penguin Group (USA) Inc.

First trade paperback printing, November 2009

1   3   5   7   9   10   8   6   4   2

Gotham Books and the skyscraper logo are trademarks of Penguin Group (USA) Inc.

The Library of Congress has cataloged the hardcover edition of this book as follows:
Engel, Jonathan.
American therapy : the rise of psychotherapy in the United States / by Jonathan Engel.
p. ; cm.
Includes bibliographical references.
ISBN 978-1-592-40380-6 (hardcover)   ISBN 978-1-592-40491-9 (paperback)
1. Psychotherapy—United States—History. I. Title.
[DNLM: 1. Psychotherapy—history—United States. 2. History, 20th Century—United States.
3. Psychoanalysis—history—United States. WM 11 AA1 E57a 2008]
RC443.E54 2008
616.89'14—dc22
2008023517

Printed in the United States of America
Set in Bembo   Designed by Ginger Legato

For my mother, Diana Engel,
married to a psychiatrist for forty-three years

Contents

PREFACE • IX

1 • FREUD • I

2 • ORTHODOXY AND PRAGMATISM • 19

3 • A CRYING NEED • 43

4 • THINKING • 76

5 • ALCOHOL • 109

6 • PSYCHOLOGICAL SOCIETY • 132

7 • NARCISSISM • 167

8 • NARCOTICS • 195

• PSYCHOANALYSIS IN DECLINE • 218

10 • BIOLOGY • 240

AFTERWORD • 255

ACKNOWLEDGMENTS • 263

NOTES • 265

BIBLIOGRAPHY • 307

INDEX • 341

Preface

In the early 1970s, Daniel Irving, a psychiatrist and psychoanalyst in Washington, D.C., was treating one of his first patients. Three months into the patient's treatment, Irving offered his first grand insight into her condition—a classic case of penis envy. The woman, a teacher in her twenties, resisted the diagnosis. "Who are you to tell me I have penis envy?" she demanded of the analyst, and quit shortly after.[1]

Irving was very much an "orthodox" analyst—a psychoanalyst who closely adhered to the teachings and methods of Sigmund Freud and his circle of followers. The holder of an M.D. degree from an accredited medical school in the United States, in addition to his four years of psychiatric residency he had completed seven years of training in psychoanalysis, during which he attended seminars, underwent a training analysis of some 800 to 1,000 hours, and analyzed several patients under the supervision of an analyst based at a training institute. Upon completion of his training, he was certified to bill himself as a psychoanalyst, join the local psychoanalytic society, and begin treating patients in individual psychoanalysis. The treatment, dispensed four or five days per week in fifty-minute sessions, allowed Irving to elicit information about his patients' psychic states through free association and to offer interpretations as to the hidden motivations, desires, and fears that had driven them to a state of neurotic unhappiness. In the case of the schoolteacher, he had obviously offered his insight before she was receptive to it.

Today, only the faded remnants of psychoanalysis survive in the United States. A few hundred analysts practice in the nation's larger cities, each treating one or two patients who can afford the time required as well as the out-of-pocket costs running around $40,000 per year— often for five years or more. These analysts tend to supplement their incomes with other patients whom they treat in psychoanalytically oriented psychotherapy. Unlike the analytic patients, the therapy patients come only once per week, usually for a period of months, during which they subject their psyches to the same analytic investigations as the analysis patients, albeit often while sitting up and facing the analyst. For both types of patients, the analyst tries to help the patient recall difficult and painful thoughts and feelings that have been stored in the deep recesses of memory, in an effort to grant the patient insight into his own emotional makeup and perhaps grant him psychic peace. At best, the patients emerge from the process less depressed and anxious, more aware of their own flaws and foibles, and better able to live life on their own terms rather than follow paths laid down for them by family or societal expectations, or by unacknowledged fear of failure. At worst, they emerge unchanged, unhappy, bereft of several thousand dollars, and perhaps cynical about the utility of all talk therapy.

Psychoanalysis has largely died, yet its legacy remains. Millions of Americans who daily engage in psychotherapy benefit from concepts and ideas wrought by the few thousand psychoanalysts who dominated mental health care in the 1950s and 1960s. Ideas such as the unconscious, repressed thoughts, Oedipal feelings, cathartic insights, and sexualized dreams survive from these decades when psychoanalysts dominated the nation's departments of psychiatry, and when psychoanalytic ideas percolated into the nation's social work curricula, psychology training programs, and psychiatric ferment. Even as many mental health practitioners have aggressively cast off psychoanalytic modes of inquiry, the legacy of Sigmund Freud, the progenitor of psychoanalysis, remains firmly rooted in our everyday vernacular. Hardly an American lives today who has not heard references to "Freudian slips," "unresolved baggage," and "fixations" of one type or another. Knowingly or not, we have absorbed the lessons of psychoanalysis.

But Americans seeking mental health care today have moved on from Freud. More Americans than ever are now engaged in psychotherapy, and a growing proportion of the therapy is decidedly un-Freudian. Most Americans in therapy today attend sessions once per week for two or three months. During those sessions they speak face-to-face with the therapist, who is rarely a psychiatrist or a doctorally trained psychologist. The therapist, often a social worker, a licensed therapist, or a pastoral "counselor" whose training was originally theological, conducts sessions using insights from more practical schools of therapy such as cognitive behavioral, interpersonal, or rational emotive. Some draw on the intellectual legacy of Freud as they deliver "psychodynamic" psychotherapy, meaning that they continue to seek clues to their patients' afflictions in childhood experiences and in repressed memories.

Patients come to therapy for a variety of reasons. Some are depressed, some phobic, some anxious. Many have had difficulty creating satisfying intimate relationships, or have repeatedly found themselves attracted to destructive mates. Some are pathologically shy; others compulsive; and still others simply unhappy with their lives. Most function at a reasonable level insofar as they are able to maintain employment, attend school, and generally comport themselves according to the mores of polite society. Some, the very sickest, can do none of these things.

Psychotherapy works. Multiple studies conducted over the past half century have demonstrated that two-thirds of people who engage in psychotherapy improve. Their depressions lift; their anxieties lessen; their neurotic behaviors depart. Success rates are similar for patients using every type of therapist, and even some nontherapists.

Psychotherapy has its horror stories. The practice of therapy has attracted its share of kooks: some well intentioned, others less so. Court records give testament to an array of charlatans who have abused their positions as therapists to seduce patients, "treat" them sexually, discover memories that never existed, and swindle them out of their savings. Some therapists have created cultlike auras surrounding their treatment and later fled the country. Others have simply disappeared shortly before being exposed as fraudulent. And every therapist, no matter how legitimate and well intentioned, has had his detractors. One eminent psychiatrist in the 1940s explained that his catatonic patient had "split herself off from the world of reality" and had made a "regression to an infantile state." As the psychiatrist left the room, the patient, who had not spoken in three years, lifted her head and said, "Did you ever hear such damn nonsense in all your life?"[2]

Of late, psychotherapy has faced challenges from biological psychiatry. A series of miracle drugs discovered over the past fifty years— Thorazine, reserpine, Valium, Xanax, Elavil, Prozac, Wellbutrin—have produced extraordinary results in millions of patients. Donald Klein, a longtime professor of psychiatry at Columbia University, recalled treating hospitalized World War I veterans during his training days in the 1950s. Some had scarcely spoken in decades; others spent their days frozen and immobile. Upon being administered Thorazine, however, they recovered like latter-day Rip Van Winkles. "Doc, when am I getting out of here?" asked one patient who, moments before, had sat staring at the wall.[3] Thirty years later, patients being treated with Prozac and other newer drugs that regulated levels of chemicals in their brains, not only recovered from chronic depressions, but proclaimed themselves "better than well."[4] One patient tried to explain to her mystified husband that on Prozac she felt more like herself than she ever had before. Peter Kramer, a psychiatrist in Rhode Island who noted many such cases with Prozac, suggested that the efficacy of the new drugs had actually reshaped his entire conception of what constituted mental illness. If idiosyncrasies responded to Prozac, they may have actually been symptoms of underlying disorders rather than tics of the personality.

Some psychotherapists were initially worried that the wonder drugs would gradually displace them, but the fears have proved to be unfounded. Research shows that most patients improve more thoroughly, and experience fewer relapses, when they are treated with a combination of medication and therapy. While medication corrects the underlying neurochemical imbalances that may have laid the foundation for psychological disorders, habits of the mind develop over years and still need to be corrected by slow retraining. If we compare medication to an artificial hip implanted to replace an aging and useless natural joint, then psychotherapy is like the rehabilitation therapy that teaches the patient how to use his new limb and learn to walk again without a physical barrier. Moreover, millions of patients seeking mental health care eschew medication entirely, finding psychotherapeutic intervention to be more acceptable and less ominous. And often, the therapy alone works. Drugs can be an enormous boon for those who are deeply unhappy or have tried psychotherapy to no avail, but most patients still seem to prefer working with the brain chemistry they were born with rather than seeking a new mixture. A comparison to plastic surgery is not inapt. Plastic surgery can spell salvation for those who have been deeply scarred through injury or ill luck, but most people stick to cosmetics and moisturizers, and make the best of their natural endowments.

Psychotherapy emerged from the long shadow of Freud as a more targeted, short-term, educational process. Rather than an extended exploration of the soul, today it is a treatment tailored to specific diseases, disorders, and situations. Sufferers of alcoholism, narcotics addiction, depression, bipolar disorder, pathological insecurity, and phobias turn to therapy not for understanding but for cure. Couples approach their therapists to repair their broken relationships, while the traumatized and haunted seek relief from their demons. And millions of Americans, generally dissatisfied with their own responses to life's challenges, seek advice and direction in therapy, in hope that new insights into their own functioning will bring opportunities for change. As far back as 1948, Kenneth Appel of the department of psychiatry at the University of Pennsylvania wrote, "Parliaments are for society what the psychiatrist's consulting room is for troubled, sick individuals. Troubles can be thrashed out in both places."[5]

Psychotherapy emerged from the 1970s sullied by its own excesses. Primal scream therapy, est, rebirthing therapy, and other bizarre approaches to mental health brought scorn upon the endeavor, and reinforced the popular notion that psychotherapy did little more than allow narcissists to indulge in their favorite pastime. Conservative clergymen, long skeptical of the godlessness of the Freudian enterprise, felt vindicated in their suspicions and tried to steer their flocks back to church. But in the past twenty years, therapy has recovered its honor. Clerics from many churches are now among its strongest supporters, offering their congregants premarital and personal growth counseling in a setting that looks remarkably psychotherapeutic. Most seminaries of all denominations now offer training in counseling, and many of the most popular self-help groups—among them both Alcoholics Anonymous and Narcotics Anonymous—demand that their adherents accept a "higher authority." For millions of Americans, psychotherapy has now become a stepping-stone on the path to spirituality.

The history of psychotherapy in the United States, a field just 100 years old, is a classic American tale of discovery, entrepreneurship, and self-promotion. Money plays a role, but so, too, do science, suffering, and the healing arts. Americans, those eternally optimistic people who seem constantly to reinvent themselves, have long looked to therapy as a conduit to new lives and improved selves. Nowhere else in the world do people explore their deepest and most intimate secrets with total strangers with such alacrity and enthusiasm. No other society in the world challenges its people with quite the degree of freedom and choice as does the United States, but such freedom necessitates guidance, and psychotherapists have become the guides of choice for millions of Americans. In 1978 Hans Strupp, an eminent psychology researcher at Vanderbilt University, wrote, "Psychotherapy, assuredly, cannot be all things to all people, but if it can be some things to some people, there is no need for its proponents to feel defensive or ashamed."[6] Psychotherapy, in fact has been much to many—in odd ways both more and less than it has promised.

CHAPTER I

Freud

O f course you have to start with Freud. To start anywhere else would be to engage in academic quibbling. Freud was the dominant psychological figure of the twentieth century, towering over psychotherapy the way Beethoven cast a shadow upon nineteenth-century musical composition. For most of the century after Freud presented his theories to the world, virtually all subsequent contributors to psychotherapeutic thought would preface their ideas by explaining how their insights differed from those of the master: either extensions, rebuttals, or technical tweaks. Men and women who claimed to have founded whole new *schools* of psychology— Adler, Jung, Horney, Klein, Sullivan, Alexander—upon close examination proved to be little more than cantankerous acolytes fighting for the meager rays of light that could penetrate the dense branches of the master's reputation. Decades after psychopharmacologists, ardent feminists, and experimental psychologists had disproved the theoretical basis, the essential *legitimacy*, of the Freudian enterprise, psychological theorists would continue to painstakingly explain how their work related to or failed to relate to it. The 100-year-old opus still represented the pathway to mental health for so many afflicted souls.

He was a great man. That was recognized early and often. As early as 1926, a mere fifteen years after Freud's first visit to the United States,

William McDougall, professor of psychology at Harvard, wrote, "Freud has done more for the advancement of psychology than any student since Aristotle."[1] A decade later, Abraham Myerson, a prominent psychiatrist in Boston, reflected to the great Adolf Meyer, paterfamilias of the Johns Hopkins psychiatry department, "First, I am a great admirer of Freud....I measure greatness by the influence a man has upon the thoughts and deeds of his time, and measured by this standard Freud is a great man and, I believe, an honest man."[2] And after another decade, a half century after Freud's initial exposition of his work, Karl Stern would write in *Commonweal*, "There is no doubt of the genius of Freud. Probably no single individual has contributed more to the knowledge of human psychology."[3] Such praise suggested that Freud belonged to the very small pantheon of individuals whose mere thoughts were so profoundly discomfiting as to have changed the world. Augustine, Copernicus, Locke, Darwin, Marx—it is hardly bathos to include the discoverer of the unconscious among them.

Sigmund Freud was born in 1856 in Moravia, a province of the Hapsburg empire. At age four he moved with his family to Vienna, where he would live for nearly all of the rest of his life. In 1873 he began medical studies at the University of Vienna, and following his graduation in 1881, he continued in neurological training in Paris and Berlin before returning to Vienna in 1886. For the following decade Freud treated patients with the meager tools then available to specialists in nervous diseases: hypnosis and electrotherapy.

Both techniques had come to neurologists of the day by way of the eighteenth-century Viennese physician Franz Anton Mesmer (he of "mesmerize"), who had had his patients swallow iron, after which he exposed them to magnets in an effort to modulate humors and fluids in the body and thereby render cures of whatever hysterical symptoms ailed them. Mesmer coined the term "animal magnetism" and dictated a series of twenty-seven postulates by which animal bodies interacted with electricity, celestial bodies, and the Earth. Nervous symptoms were caused by misalignments of these various forces and bodies, and realignment through magnetic and electrical stimulation could bring relief. Commencing a long history of psychotherapeutic immodesty which continues today, Mesmer claimed, "One will notice by the facts, according to the practical rules which I establish, that this principle can immediately cure illness of the nerves and 'mediately all others."[4]

Mesmerism had its day in the early nineteenth century. The mesmeric technique could cure rheumatism, epilepsy, depression, menstrual cramps, deafness, and blindness, in addition to ordinary hysteria.[5] Hundreds of aspirants adopted Mesmer's techniques, and thousands of satisfied customers sang his praises. Mesmerism, indeed, was the rage in a Europe taken with all things modern. It combined two phenomena of au courant society, psychic manipulation and electricity, and exploited them to advance the condition of mankind. The Montgolfier brothers' pioneering hot-air balloon—the rage a half century earlier—could hardly make such claims to progress. The balloon, after all, had only gone up and down.

Freud was interested in the mesmeric tradition of electrical stimulation (electric shocks seemed to do something to nervous patients, even if the exact effect could be neither described nor explained), but was even more interested in the technique of hypnosis, which descended to him through the same channels. Mesmer and his disciples had noticed that patients placed in a state of enforced relaxation could become susceptible to the power of suggestion. They seemed to descend into an intermittent state of consciousness that lay somewhere between deep sleep and true wakefulness: A condition often termed "catalepsy." This cataleptic state was intriguing to students of the mind. Patients were capable of comprehending articulated suggestions, yet seemed to respond from a point of mind beyond their usual state of consciousness. Some were impervious to pain in this state; others were capable of remembering incidents and situations that had been lost to their usual memory channels. Such a state seemed to promise entry to deeper truths that lay locked in the patient's hidden persona.

Freud practiced neurology for a decade, the nascent medical specialty addressing diseases and dysfunction of the brain and nervous system, and even published a few papers in the area. He drew on his own early anatomical explorations of the spinal cords of fishes, as well as human brain stems, and treated what patients he could through electrotherapy and hypnotism. He soon concluded that classic electrotherapy "was of no help whatever," and that the most widely used textbook on the technique, authored by eminent German neuropathologist Wilhelm Erb, "had no more relation to reality than some 'Egyptian' dream-book, such as is sold in cheap book-shops."[6] Hypnosis, however, was a different matter. The cataleptic state into which patients descended under hypnosis was real and observable, and seemed to offer a vehicle by which to explore the mind's nature. Traveling to the French city of Nancy in 1889 to perfect his technique, he observed a master hypnotist's work on hospitalized mental patients, and hypothesized the "possibility that there could be powerful mental processes which nevertheless remained hidden from the consciousness of men."[7] He returned to Vienna recharged, and in the next five years turned from clinical medicine to scientific research.

Freud's magnificently original and comprehensive theory of the mind's structure, and his proprietary curative approach dubbed "psychoanalysis," was articulated and refined in dribs and drabs over the succeeding forty-five years. Freud's own writing on the subject, compiled years later in the authoritative *Standard Edition*, fills some twenty-two volumes. The emendations of his followers and detractors fill many times that many. And the secondary literature on Freud's opus since penned by historians, psychologists, psychiatrists, philosophers, biographers, literary theorists, and various post-Freudians fills a good-sized library. Since Freud's life and work is merely the starting point for this study of American psychotherapy, I will describe the theory and its development here in only its barest essence. The interested reader is referred to the bibliograpy at the end of this volume for further exploration.

Shortly after Freud graduated from medical school, he became acquainted with a prominent Viennese family physician named Josef Breuer. Breuer, already well established in his career, took an interest in the young neurologist and served him as somewhat of a professional mentor. The senior physician provided Freud entrée to Viennese medical society and possibly helped him out financially as well during his early years when he was struggling to develop a practice.

Breuer worked with numerous well-to-do patients who appeared to suffer from "nervous exhaustion," the catchall term at the time for mood disorders that rendered patients inexplicably tired, melancholy, and generally unable to engage in life with vitality. When Freud returned to Vienna after his early training sojourns in Paris and Berlin, Breuer told him of a patient—a young woman of "unusual education and gifts"— whom he had hypnotized repeatedly, and in so doing he had managed to expose and negate psychic roots of her exhaustion that had previously been inaccessible. Freud described Breuer's technique thus:

A chance observation showed her physician that she could be relieved of these clouded states of consciousness if she was induced to express in words the affective phantasy by which she was at the moment dominated. From this discovery, Breuer arrived at a new method of treatment. He put her into deep hypnosis and made her tell him each time what it was that was oppressing her mind. After the attacks of depressive confusion had been overcome in this way, he employed the same procedure for removing her inhibitions and physical disorders. In her waking state the girl could no more describe than other patients how her symptoms had arisen, and she could discover no link between them and any experiences in her life. In hypnosis she immediately discovered the missing connection. It turned out that all her symptoms went back to moving events which she had experienced while nursing her father; that is to say, her symptoms had a meaning and were residues or reminiscences of those emotional situations.[8]

Freud was fascinated with a number of components of this story, and in many ways he spent the remainder of his life creating and revising a theory of the mind to explain what Breuer had observed. The theory was complex, but rested on four fundamental assumptions: (1) that there were components of the patient's mind and memory that were unavailable to her in a normal waking state, which Freud dubbed the *unconscious*; (2) that disturbing thoughts, feelings, and emotional reactions lying dormant in the unconscious were capable of creating mischief within the conscious realm of the brain without the patient's knowledge; (3) that the very frightfulness of these thoughts and feelings had forced the patient to *repress* them—that is, to drive them into the unconscious; and (4) that only through bringing these unconscious thoughts forward into the realm of consciousness could anxieties be resolved, neuroses salved, and depression alleviated.

In 1895, Freud and Breuer together published their pathmark work, *Studies in Hysteria,* which laid out their experiences with the initial patient, as well as subsequent similar patients who suffered from symptoms of anxiety and depression. Shortly after, in a move which foreshadowed a lifetime of intolerance for intellectual and organizational challengers, Freud broke with Breuer and proceeded to turn his full energies to unlocking the mysteries of the unconscious, and to developing a technique for resolving the anxiety-producing tensions harbored within.

One of the first questions Freud asked was where the unconscious memories and feelings had come from. Over the course of seeing patients during the following decade, he concluded that the bulk of the anxiety-producing memories were based in infantile and childhood ex-

periences, and often revolved around sex. Either the infant had witnessed a sexual encounter between his parents or had actually felt
sexually drawn to a parent. The conjecture that an infant was capable of
sexual yearnings later became one of the centerpieces of Freud's theory
of psychological development, and he ultimately refined it into a sort
of cookie-cutter prescription of normal infantile sexual development,
wherein a child went through various sexual stages in his early years
(oral, anal, genital), felt intensely attracted to the parent of the opposite
sex (the famous *Oedipus complex*), resolved mentally to harm or remove
the same sex parent, and ultimately repressed these sexual feelings as he
entered a lengthy period of sexual *latency*, which lasted roughly from
age three to the onset of puberty.[9]

Freud tweaked the theory many times over the ensuing decades. In
such works as *Three Essays on a Theory of Sexuality* (1905), *The Ego and
the Id* (1923), *The Interpretation of Dreams* (1900), and *The Psychopathology
of Everyday Life* (1901), Freud expounded on several unresolved questions, such as whether or not the infant had actually seen parental sexual
activity or had merely conjectured it; to what degree dreams revealed
the hidden desires and fears of the unconscious; and whether or not all
infants proceeded lockstep through the three phases of infantile sexual
development, and what happened if they did not. (He ultimately concluded that homosexuality and sexual perversions were the frequent results of interrupted sexual development.) Freud also created a physical,
or possibly metaphysical, model of the mind in which infantile urges resided in the *id*, while the sorts of conscious impulse controls that society
expected of a healthy adult resided in the *ego*. (He later added a third
layer, the *superego*, representing a sort of über parental instinct that inces-
santly impelled the ego toward responsible action.) Much of the maturation process consisted of the growth and strengthening of the ego to
grant it the authority to suppress the id, and many of society's more
dysfunctional artifacts and pathologies—war, violence, taboos, myths,
organized religion—were either mass expressions of iditic impulses or

societal efforts to restrain these impulses and thus promulgate civilization. In Freud's view, everybody was a potential rapist and rioter, and only through the constant enforcement of social controls could people's egos be strengthened enough to resist the ever-present infantile impulses that lay locked beneath the surface.

Freud considered *repression* and *anxiety* the two foundation points of his theory. Repression of uncomfortable, frightening, or socially unacceptable thoughts was ubiquitous, and perhaps necessary. If people were to grow into mature sexual beings, and ultimately into productive and contributing members of society, confusing and discomfiting infantile sexual feelings needed to be removed from the consciousness, lest they overwhelm the developing child. Similarly, Freud later posited that details of traumatic events associated with violence and sex were also often repressed in a sort of survival coping mechanism promulgated by the ego. Anxiety (as well as depression) was the inevitable result of repressed thoughts and feelings struggling to be heard from the unconscious. Since everybody had been an infant, and since all infants were cognitively incapable of making sense of the multitude of situations they were exposed to and feelings they experienced, anxiety was the essential tension. Anxiety was not necessarily bad. Anxiety was what compelled people to work hard, better their lot, build societies, and seek happiness within the confines of societal norms. Freud accepted this arrangement as inevitable and possibly desirable. No social rebel himself, he maintained impeccable habits, engaged in socially acceptable pastimes (hiking, intellectual discourse, the collecting of antiques), and was rarely seen without suit and tie freshly pressed, hair combed, beard trimmed, and a hat carefully adjusted—the picture of the nineteenth-century gentleman.

Anxieties, however, could turn destructive. Left to fester, with no outlet for resolution, and inadequately contained by an incompletely developed ego, anxiety could saturate the psyche and render the sufferer miserable. As Freud turned toward a new treatment of nervous ailments after 1895, he consulted with a steady stream of patients complaining of overwhelming depression and nervousness, strange personality tics, and growing alienation from friends, family, and society at large. They had become phobic and reclusive, incapable of engaging in life, and no longer able to be happy or enjoy everyday pleasures. These patients, predominantly upper-middle class or wealthy, and disproportionately female and Jewish, sought relief from symptoms that had simply become intolerable. And as Freud turned his full attention to relieving these patients of their *neurotic* symptoms (a catchall term invoked by Freud to describe precisely those symptoms he deemed consequences of unresolved repressed impulses), he quickly realized the limits of Breuer's hypnotism approach to the problem.

Breuer had claimed some success with hypnosis on his early hysterics, and initially Freud adapted the hypnosis approach as well. But hypnosis had its limitations. Not all patients could be hypnotized; under hypnosis not all patients were able to recall repressed ideas; and even those patients who could be made aware of repressed ideas under hypnosis did not always, upon awakening, experience the resolution and peace of mind Breuer had described in his own patients. A new way must be found to bring these repressed unconscious thoughts into consciousness, and one which kept the patient awake and aware so that he or she could process the uncomfortable thoughts using the full powers of adult insight and judgment that the patient had gained through maturation.

What Freud ultimately developed was the technique he termed *psycho-analysis* (now spelled without the hyphen). In psychoanalysis, the patient lay on a couch (the infamous couch!) four or five days per week for an hour, with the analyst sitting out of view behind her head. In this relaxed position, the patient simply allowed her mind to wander and spoke whatever thoughts came into her head, however odd, embarrassing, vexing, or socially unacceptable. Through this enforced regimen of *free association*, the analyst gained access to patterns in the patient's thoughts, and ultimately to the unconscious level of thought as well.

Then, through analyzing the patterns and inconsistencies in the stream of talk, the analyst would make suggestions to the patient regarding the meaning of her thoughts and what they implied about the repressed memories hidden in her unconscious. Through this iterative process of free thought, speaking aloud the thoughts, and interacting with the analyst, the patient would gradually gain access to the repressed thoughts lying in her unconscious, bring them to the realm of the conscious, and resolve the decades-old fears and anxieties within a sensible adult framework.

One of Freud's early observations was that patients inevitably began to project feelings that they had had for other individuals in their life onto the analyst himself. This *transference* phenomenon became one of the most important tools in the analyst's arsenal, for as the patient began to retarget past reactions and feelings onto the analyst, the analyst gained great insights into the nature of these feelings. By carefully using the transference process, the analyst could gain a privileged post within the ferment of the patient's mind, and thus more ably leverage his own suggestions to the patient. That is, the analytic encounter became more than simply an unusually intense and honest conversation; it became a unique sort of conversation in which the analyst became both guru and confidant to the patient, while retaining his position of utter aloofness.[10]

Several points are worth noting here. First, while much of the technique later became codified into a rigid orthodoxy, Freud himself remained somewhat flexible during his own years as a practicing analyst, varying the length and frequency of sessions, and regularly modifying his own theory to accommodate new observations from the consulting room. Second, while Freud believed that he had stumbled on a new psychological technique of great promise, he recognized its limitations. Not all patients benefited from the process, and Freud ultimately admitted that severely mentally ill patients were simply not susceptible to the beneficial insights of analysis.[11] In a work penned late in his life, *An*

Outline of Psychoanalysis, Freud admitted, "It is true that we do not always succeed in winning, but at least we can usually recognize why we have not won.... The future may teach us to exercise a direct influence, by means of particular chemical substances, on the amounts of energy and their distribution in the mental apparatus. It may be that there are other still undreamt-of possibilities of therapy. But for the moment we have nothing better at our disposal than the technique of psychoanalysis, and for that reason, in spite of its limitations, it should not be despised."[12] That is, Freud was justly proud of having the first word in his own psychological revolution, but he was willing to admit that he probably would not have the last.

Had Freud been content merely to develop his theory and treatment technique within the confines of a private clinical practice, and publish his observations in periodic treatises, he would have been an influential figure in psychology, though probably not the object of near adulation of future generations of acolytes. But Freud was also an institution builder, and he cemented his influence by creating a psychoanalytic organization. By 1902 a handful of interested physicians had begun to meet regularly with Freud to discuss theory and technique, and share clinical experiences. These doctors—Otto Rank, Hans Eitingon, Carl Jung, Sándor Ferenczi, Karl Abraham, and Alfred Adler—constituted the core of the nascent Vienna Psycho-Analytical Society, which by 1908 had seeded the international Psycho-Analytical Congress. Within a few years, these early followers of Freud spread through Europe and North America to disseminate the psychoanalytic gospel, setting up psychoanalytic societies in Berlin (Abraham and Eitingon), Zurich (Jung), Budapest (Ferenczi), Toronto (Ernest Jones), and New York (A. A. Brill). Representatives from the various societies and institutes gathered at annual congresses to share clinical results and argue over theory, and the congresses in turn gave rise to several journals, including the *Yearbook for Psycho-Analytic and Psychopathologic Research*, and the *International Journal for Medical Psycho-Analysis*. In 1912, Otto Rank and another early psychoanalyst, Hanns Sachs, founded *Imago*, which attempted to reach a broader nonmedical audience with news of psychoanalytic developments.

Although Freud stridently argued that psychoanalysis was not a "system" and that his method was open to exploration, extension, and improvement from outsiders, his actions suggested otherwise. Within five years of the first international congress, Alfred Adler and Carl Jung broke off to found their own psychological societies, having differed with the master over specifics of analytic theory and technique. Adler placed more emphasis on the individual's will to dominate ("masculine protest"), while Jung overlaid a mystical theory of societal archetypes and symbols on to dream theory, and conjured up a quasi-Indian social force that underlay the id's essential motives.[13]

Freud's reaction was swift and hostile. Not only did he sever all professional and scientific relations with the two men, he deemed their work and discoveries fatuous and contemptible. "Everything that Adler has to say about dreams," wrote Freud in 1914, "is equally empty and unmeaning."[14] Similarly, Jung's work was "so obscure, unintelligible, and confused as to make it difficult to take up any position on it."[15] In Freud's mind, the two movements were wholly incompatible with psychoanalysis itself, and indeed barely even merited mention. Adler's system had not furnished "a single new observation," concluded Freud. "I fancy I have made it clear that it has nothing to do with psycho-analysis."[16]

Freud's reaction to his detractors was emblematic of his need for absolute control, which later translated into a rigid dogma guiding the work of the leaders of the world's various psychoanalytic societies. Adler and Jung had done little beyond offering minor modifications to Freud's system. They had both retained the essential cornerstones of repression, resistance, and transference, and both agreed with Freud that regular therapeutic sessions with a trained analyst, in which free associations were discussed to better bring repressed thoughts to light, were the most promising path to resolution and peace. They were psychoanalysts, albeit ones who had overlaid a few novel ideas on the original Freudian structure.

But the fact that Freud was unwilling to accept criticism from these two detractors exposed, despite his protests, his essentially antiscientific attitude. Enlightenment philosophy had clarified the essential difference between science and dogma as being one of proof; scientific assertions had to successfully test against empirical data, while religious assertions did not. Anybody engaged in an enterprise deemed scientific needed to submit his assertions and tests to the scientific community to be further tested, disproved, improved, or discarded. Science was open and communal, and no postulate or theorem could be privileged above another unless it could stand up to empirical testing.[17] Yet Freud, by so quickly and antagonistically dismissing his early critics, established a quasi-religious tone to the enterprise. Freud did not claim omniscience, but he did retain a privileged place for himself in the new science of psychoanalysis. He believed that his writings defined the principles and parameters of a new science, and any deviations from those principles were to be viewed with extreme skepticism. Even in the United States, the country that ultimately received Freud's teachings with the greatest enthusiasm and codified them through the most powerful and influential of the world's psychoanalytic societies, analysts did not cleave firmly enough to Freud's texts to satisfy him. He noted, when writing in 1925, that in the United States psychoanalysis had "suffered a great deal from being watered down," and that "many abuses which have no relation to it find a cover under its name."[18]

The dogmatic tone of psychoanalysis that Freud established so early in its history would plague the enterprise for much of its life and would ultimately be its undoing. For while Freud was certainly a psychological revolutionary—his assertion of the centrality of sex, his conception of an unconscious realm of the mind, and his "discovery of the unconscious" were all radical breaks with prevailing notions of sanity and mental health—he could not foresee the extraordinary advances that psychology and psychiatry would make in understanding brain chemistry, psychosocial development, and the nature of mental illness.[19] While the psychoanalytic establishment rigidly stood by the Freudian canon for decades after Freud's death, the rest of the brain sciences would forge ahead. A small group of Freudians would survive into the following century, but they resembled nothing more than a fanatical Essene sect, living apart in the wilderness where they could continue to seek truth in the master's writings.

Freud's reception in the United States was oddly warm compared to the initial hostility that had greeted his work in Europe. Freud himself was always uncomfortable in the United States, and viewed the nation and its inhabitants as somewhat barbaric. He would make only one visit to the country, in response to an invitation to speak at Clark University in 1909, and after that had no desire to return. And even as young psychiatrists flocked to the early American psychoanalytical institutes for training, Freud was largely dismissive of the growth of his science in America, considering its form there adulterated and overly professionalized.

Ironically it was American society's general openness to heresy and innovation, in contrast to Europe's fierce loyalty to established institutions and ideas, that made it so receptive to psychoanalytic theory. Although Freud viewed the United States as anti-intellectual and uncultured, the nation's general dismissiveness of tradition and convention left it open to the best new ideas, the best new problem-solving approaches. Several of the most eminent American psychologists and psychiatrists—G. Stanley Hall at Clark, James Jackson Putnam at Harvrd, Adolf Meyer at Johns Hopkins, and Smith Ely Jelliffe at Harvard—became early enthusiastic students of Freudian theory, in marked contrast to their academic counterparts on the continent. Meyer, for example, was willing to hear the new truths being promulgated by Freud and his followers, as he was willing to hear any new ideas or approaches that might advance psychiatry. Meyer's approach to psychiatry was deeply pragmatic: a "nonadherence to any theory in particular," in the words of two of his colleagues.[20]

As Meyer went, so went America. Meyer had emigrated from Zurich in 1892 to teach neurology at the University of Chicago. From there he became medical director of the state psychiatric hospital in Kankakee, Illinois, and later held the same position at Worcester State Hospital in Massachusetts, before being recruited to the new psychiatry department at Hopkins. At Worcester, Meyer had begun to establish his reputation as the foremost teacher of psychiatrists in the country, using his keen eye for symptoms and a predilection for description and classification to train his young residents in the many distinct symptoms and syndromes that could be discerned as mental illness. Too nuanced and erudite a man to ever fully commit to one school of treatment, he nonetheless saw in Freudian theory a valuable set of insights and theoretical structures that could possibly serve psychiatrists well in their understanding of neuroses. This openness to Freud was passed down to his residents at Worcester and Hopkins, who spread throughout the nation to take up prestigious positions in other medical schools, teaching hospitals, clinics, and institutes. Meyer's reach within American psychiatry was so broad that at the time of his death, in 1950, though he had neither written books nor established a "school" of psychiatric thought, he was broadly considered the most influential figure in American psychiatry.[21]

Through the influence of Meyer, Hall, Putnam, and their students, Freudian theory quickly permeated mainstream American psychiatric thought. Psychoanalytic institutes were established in Baltimore, Washington, Boston, Chicago, St. Louis, and San Francisco, in addition to the initial one in New York. While analytically trained psychiatrists never constituted a majority of the profession, by mid-century they did constitute a majority of academic psychiatrists and psychiatric directors at major teaching hospitals. Analytic training for psychiatrists would never quite become the norm, but it would become sort of an elite standard for the profession, rather than a marginal enterprise as it was in Europe. In part this was due to its early adoption by Meyer and his colleagues, and in part it seemed to be compatible with an underlying strain in the American zeitgeist. Psychoanalysis's oddly significant influence on American psychiatric thought would persist for decades, long after empirical evidence suggested that it should be abandoned.

One of the oddities of psychoanalysis in the United States was its appropriation by physicians. Where Freud suspected that medical training was an unnecessary prerequisite to analytic training (in 1926 he proposed that the United States train social workers in analytic technique and turn them into a "band of helpers for combating the neuroses of civilization"), Abraham Brill and other early American analysts attempted to exclude all non-M.D.s from membership in the New York Psychoanalytic Institute.[22] While American psychoanalysis was never entirely the province of physicians, it did become medicalized in a manner not foreseen by Freud. As a result, psychoanalysis in the United States became predominantly a clinical technique for treating illness, rather than an educational technique for increasing self-knowledge. Moreover, given the disproportionate influence Freudian psychiatrists had within the American psychiatric establishment, it became the treatment technique without peer. While many board-certified psychiatrists over the succeeding half century would never undergo analytic training, and fewer than half would ever practice orthodox analysis during their careers, virtually no psychiatrists trained in American medical schools or in American residency programs up through the 1970s could fully escape its teachings. American psychiatry from 1945 to 1980 was essentially Freudian psychiatry, even if many of its practitioners would not openly describe themselves that way. By contrast, European psychiatry over the same period tended to relegate psychoanalysis to a more fringe status: one of many tools to be used in treatment of the mentally ill.

The medicalization of psychoanalysis in the United States pushed the nascent enterprise from one of scientific inquiry to one of treatment. Freud himself was always cautious about whether psychoanalysis could effectively alleviate pain; he famously stated that the process could not guarantee happiness, but could merely return the patient from a state of "hysterical misery to ordinary unhappiness."[23] For Freud, psychoanalysis was always as much a process of discovery as it was a viable therapeutic technique. Self-knowledge was a goal worthy of pursuit, not so much for the increased happiness it could potentially bring, but for the mere fact that clarification of truth was the worthiest of life's goals. If psychoanalysis could bring one closer to the truth about one's own makeup, then that alone justified its existence.

But men and women who came to control access to analysis in America, through leadership of the analytic institutes and control over the training regimens, had come to the science from the vantage point of medicine. Their predilection was not to inquire but to cure. Their analysands were patients, first and foremost, and as such demanded relief first, and knowledge second. This did not compel an adulteration of Freudian orthodoxy, but it did impose on the enterprise a certain consumerist attitude natural to medical practice. Patients were customers, as all doctors knew, and thus their wants needed to be satisfied. Patients who sought psychoanalytic treatment usually desired alleviation of their symptoms, or at least the ability to live in a generally happier state.

But if Freud viewed himself as a scientist, it was a very strange science he was promulgating. The science of psychoanalysis contained theories and hypotheses, but it lacked a method of empirical observation. Patients' statements in free association were said to represent precisely what the analyst said they represented—no more, no less. And since the precise moment of free association for a specific patient could not be re-created by other analysts, the interpretations were untestable, or in the word of philosopher Karl Popper, "unfalsifiable."[24] This initial flaw was huge and ultimately fatal, for when taken to its logical end it meant that virtually everything that Freud said and wrote, and all that his acolytes wrote as well, was pure speculation. The early analysts *had* spent tens of thousands of hours listening to the free association of their patients, but none of their interpretations of those associations were subject to outside verification. If an analyst said that a patient's neurotic fear of cats was related to his infantile sexual fantasies about his mother, then it was thus; empirical testing of the interpretation was simply impossible.

Certain skeptics were aware of the methodological flaw. Adolf Meyer, though one of the founding members of the American Psychoanalytic Association, ultimately disassociated himself from the enterprise precisely for its dogmatism and lack of scientific support. His colleague Abraham Myerson felt similarly. In 1937 Myerson wrote to Meyer, "Apparently the Freudians know nothing at all about control experiments. They assume the validity of their postulates and seek to prove them, which is a most vicious way of operating.... The whole theory of sex has been built up on the most slender possible basis." And while Myerson admitted that "on the whole there had been some good accomplished" by psychoanalysis, "it had definitely hindered some of the younger psychiatrists from studying man objectively and with the instruments of present-day science."[25] Psychoanalysis, already a drag on scientific psychology in 1937, would continue to hinder empirical inquiry into the workings of the mind for decades to come.

CHAPTER 2

Orthodoxy and Pragmatism

From the beginning, Freud's system of understanding the mind gave rise to followers who adhered with increasing rigidity to his stated precepts. This practice, described as "orthodoxy" in Freudian circles, ran counter to the general patterns of scientific evolution. While many prominent individuals within the history of science were ultimately recognized as scientific "revolutionaries," inevitably their work was superseded by that of their disciples, who took the original revolutionary breakthrough as only a point of departure from which to advance their own research and discoveries. Among Freudians, however, a very different pattern of development ensued. Convinced of the overarching rectitude of Freud, zealous Freudians devoted their lives not to moving beyond the initial Freudian conjectures, but rather to reaffirming Freud's conjectures and models through case studies, tortured theorizing, and sometimes by simple bombastic insistence.

Divorced from any empirical grounding, the first generation of Freudian acolytes felt free to take various Freudian conjectures to a theoretical extreme. Different analysts focused on various components of Freud's theory as more or less important, but in each case the result was to take an initial theoretical construct and build an increasingly Byzantine and bizarre edifice upon it. If Freud suggested that dreams held symbolic clues to the true proclivities of the mind, some analyst or another could, at will, decide the true meaning of a dreamy recollection of running water, a relative, a friend, a teacher, a dead celebrity, falling, drowning, or most anything else. If Freud had suggested that a certain sort of neurotic tic was rooted in, say, the oral phase of psychological development, an overly zealous theoretician would build an entire psychology based on oral fixations and retarded psychosocial developments. And because the essential "proof" of all such theories lay in the analyst's own interpretations of the free associations that only he or she was privy to in private therapeutic sessions, there was no possibility for an outside observer to prove or disprove the validity of the assertions. Psychoanalysis was a world unto itself, replete with its own internal logic.

The exemplar of this extreme tendency toward orthodoxy was Melanie Klein, a London-based analyst who focused on treatment of children. Born in Vienna in 1882, Klein had survived the tragic early deaths of a brother and sister, and suffered bouts of depression for much of her life.[1] After moving to Budapest in 1910 with her husband, she sought analysis with Sándor Ferenczi, after which she embarked on her own analytical practice, largely focused on work with children. In 1924 she underwent a second analysis, with Karl Abraham, who died before the analysis could be completed. Facing increasing opposition from the Berlin analytic establishment, she relocated to London in 1927, where she spent the remainder of her life and career.

Klein's work centered around play therapy with children. Bringing children as young as two and a half into her consulting room, she would give them dolls, toys, construction materials, and puppets with which they could engage in free play, in a childhood version of Freud's free associations. By observing the manner in which the children interacted with the toys, and through what limited conversation the children were capable of, Klein would interpret their play as manifestations of neurotic blockages, and thereby grant the children access to the cathartic resolution at the center of the Freudian experience.

And what interpretations they were! Klein was obsessed with sex in

all iterations, and assumed that sexual fears, confusions, desires, and misunderstandings lay at the root of virtually all childhood unhappiness. A
child, aged two and three-quarters, who was brought to her for excessive naughtiness and moodiness, was deemed to suffer from "a neurotic
working over of her Oedipus conflict." The fact that the child demanded
to be tucked into bed each night was interpreted as the child's wish to
be prevented from getting out of bed to impose her aggression against
her parents, or possibly as defense against fear of nocturnal attacks. "The
attacks were to be made, for instance, by the 'Butzen' [her father's penis],
which would injure her genitals and bite off her own 'Butzen' as a punishment for wanting to castrate him."[2] Klein asserted quite confidently
that the Oedipus complex began as early as the sixth month of life, "at
the same time the child begins to build up its super-ego," and that the
preponderance of everyday play could constructively be viewed as manifestations of unresolved Oedipal feelings.[3] This particular child's doll,
for example, "would sometimes stand for a penis, sometimes a child she
had stolen from her mother, and sometimes her own self. Full analytic
impact can only be obtained if we bring these play-elements into their
true relation with the child's sense of guilt by interpreting them down
to the smallest detail."[4]

Another patient, aged three and three-quarters, had the habit of lift-
ing up the rug on Klein's consulting couch, which Klein interpreted as
the child wanting to "look inside her mother's bottom for the 'Kakis'
(feces), which signified children to her." This child, who had a history of
bed-wetting, was cured when Klein interpreted the bed-wetting as "attacks upon her parents copulating with each other." The child had
"wanted to rob her pregnant mother of her children, to kill her and to
take her place in coitus with her father." The bed-wetting, and puta-
tively these aggressive desires, had begun when the child was two.[5]

In Klein's world, no childhood impulse or activity was too pedestrian to be asexual. The most mundane naughtiness could have at its
roots some convoluted tension involving fear, anger, aggression, feces,

phalluses, Oedipal impulses, fratricidal longings, or latent homosexuality. One patient, a boy aged three and three-quarters, had been brought to Klein for treatment purely as a prophylactic measure, for there had been other cases of neuroses in the family. When the boy grew frustrated with a doll he could not make stand up and a toy car that apparently did not function as he had wished, Klein's interpretation was thus:

> In the analytic session just described, Peter has been depicting the following things: the toy man, the deer, etc., which kept falling down, represented his own penis and its inferiority in comparison to his father's erect member. His going to pass water immediately after was done to prove the contrary to himself and to me. The motor-car which would not stop moving and which aroused both his admiration and anger was his father's penis that was performing coitus all the time. After feeling admiration for it he became enraged and wanted to defecate. This was a repetition of his passing stool at the time when he had witnessed the primal scene. He had done this so as to disturb his parents while they were copulating and, in phantasy, to harm them with his excrement. In addition, the lump of stool appeared to the boy as substitute for his inferior penis.[6]

Klein asserted that through this tortured interpretation, she was "able to gain access to Peter's very strong passive homosexual attitude."[7] All of this in a child not yet four years old, who had not even exhibited any neurotic tendencies!

Another child, aged six, was brought to Klein because of poor sleeping and thumb-sucking behaviors. The mother had noticed that the child, between six and nine months, had evinced "evident sexual pleasure" at having her genitals and anus washed. "The over-excitability of her genital zone was unmistakable," reported Klein. These feelings underlay the child's "desire to be seduced," which Klein could deduce through the child's paper cutouts in her consulting room. When the child tore the head off one of her paper figures, Klein identified "oral-sadistic, urethral-sadistic, and anal-sadistic phantasies." When the child pretended to feed a powder to one of the dolls, Klein realized that "the fluid and the powder represented urine, faeces, semen and blood, all of which, according to Emma's phantasies, her mother put inside herself in copulation through her mouth, anus and genitals."[8] Alas for the child, treatment was broken off after 575 hours of treatment, at which point Klein did not consider the analysis "by any means complete."[9]

Why is Klein an exemplar of Freudian orthodoxy? Although she had been dismissed from Berlin analytical circles as "unorthodox," this accusation merely meant that she had distanced herself from the hierarchy of the Berlin Psychoanalytic Society and had dared to venture away from the established child analytic techniques of Anna Freud, the master's daughter.[10] In fact, Klein had taken Freudian conjectures regarding infantile psychosexual development to an extreme degree. Convinced of her own rectitude and her own interpretational infallibility, she took license to view virtually all childhood behaviors as potentially neurotic, and to find root causes of said neuroses in anything sexual, phallic, or fecal.[11] Refusing to establish baselines of wellness, Klein could find mental illness wherever she looked, merely by defining it so. And although Freud himself had expressed some doubt toward the end of his life that his techniques and understandings were truly correct, Klein felt no such reservation. She asserted that psychoanalysis had led to "the creation of a new child psychology," and that her conclusions had been gained by "direct observations of children" and "confirmed and supplemented by the analysis of small children."[12] It is this certainty of rectitude, untestable and unfalsifiable, and divorced from the context of objective definitions of psychological health and wellness, that identifies Klein as orthodox, and led some of her most esteemed contemporaries to place her work at the pinnacle of the "classical Freudians."[13] She had the faith and confidence of the believer, rather than the skepticism of the scientist.

Klein manifested a classic symptom of orthodoxy of any type in viewing alternative explanations not merely as scientific challenges, but as actual threats to her influence. Science is essentially a collaborative enterprise, which is why publication of research is so central to the effort. No one person, no matter how brilliant or insightful, can solve all of the universe's secrets. Rather, scientists tend to add to the corpus of knowledge through incremental contributions, which are thereby assimilated into the scientific ferment (or "paradigm," as Thomas Kuhn, the noted historian and philosopher of science, so famously termed it) and built on further by other scientists, or else wisely discarded if proven to be unsustainable. No scientist welcomes attacks on his or her theoretical contributions, but all understand that a dynamic scientific community is central to vital science. Not so Klein. When émigré Jewish psychoanalysts, escaping Hitler's Germany, landed in London through the 1930s, Klein viewed their arrival with fury. Their own understanding of psychoanalysis differed from hers, and their presence in London complicated her own claims to analytic dominance. Angry with her colleague Ernest Jones for having facilitated their immigration, she accused him of "having done much harm to psychoanalysis," despite knowing that deprived of Jones's efforts, most would have died in Nazi gas chambers.[14] How different was the reception of the émigré physicists, also escaping European fascism, who were welcomed by their English and American colleagues as a fortifying force in the physics enterprise.[15] But the physicists' colleagues, unlike Klein, were practicing science.

By contrast, psychoanalysis in the United States veered gently right. Even as Freudian theory found a receptive audience among some elite neurologists and psychiatrists in Eastern cities, some well-regarded American psychiatrists expressed skepticism about the cultlike aura surrounding Freudian institutes and psychoanalytic societies. Adolf Meyer, while interested in psychoanalysis, distanced himself from the movement as he learned more about it, and insisted through his career that analysis must remain merely a tool in the armament of psychiatry, and not vice versa.[16] Similarly, William Alanson White, chief psychiatrist of the federal government's St. Elizabeth's mental hospital in Washington, D.C., remained skeptical of the grandiose claims of the orthodox Freudians, even while he himself used some of the Freudian tools of extended talk therapies in treating patients.

The transitional figure in bringing Freudian theory to pragmatically oriented American psychiatrists was Harry Stack Sullivan, founder of the Washington School of Psychiatry, a widely published author on psychiatric theory, and one of the most influential psychiatrists in the country for the two decades between 1930 and his death in 1949. Sullivan was unquestionably a Freudian, in the sense that he ascribed a good deal of importance to the experiences of early childhood and believed that young children, even infants, experienced periods of anxiety over parental miscues and simple misunderstandings that could become the basis of troubling neuroses later in life. While he never underwent a training analysis, he did participate in several hundred hours of analysis with his close colleague Clara Thompson after she returned from training with Sándor Ferenczi in Budapest in 1933.

But unlike the orthodox Freudians', Sullivan's understanding of neurosis did not end with infantile sexual mix-ups. Rather, through his work at Sheppard Pratt Hospital outside Baltimore, and later in private practice in New York City, Sullivan developed an "interpersonal theory" of psychological development, in which he viewed the essential human urge not toward sexual aggression, but rather toward intimacy. And in Sullivan's view, intimacy did not require sex. Rather, intimacy was the culmination (frequently unrealized) of a life spent seeking social connections and social placement. Sullivan viewed happiness and psychic equilibrium not as a cathartic reaction of insights and understanding, but as natural consequences of fulfilling relationships, intimate friendships, love, and social standing.

Sullivan developed his theory to some degree in response to an understanding of the root causes of his own unhappy periods. Born to a poor immigrant Irish family in upstate New York, he attended Cornell University on scholarship, but failed out in his second year either as a result of excessive drinking or possibly due to some sort of psychological break resulting from a homosexual episode.[17] He returned the following year to complete his bachelor's degree at Cornell, and two years later matriculated at Chicago College of Medicine and Surgery, completing the program without incident.

Sullivan was homosexual, introverted, and an alcoholic. He maintained a long-term relationship with a man several years his junior, whom he introduced variously as a life partner or an adopted son. Raised a Catholic amid anti-Catholic sentiment in Norwich, New York, he had no close friends as a child or as an adolescent, and by all accounts few in college as well. His drinking, which pervaded both his personal and social life, seemed a necessary precondition for normal social intercourse. By the end of his life his social awkwardness had evolved into full-blown misanthropy. His colleague Leslie Farber described him as "a lonely, bitter, hardened cynic, a pretender who preached pretending, a con who counseled cons, a democrat whose egalitarian credentials were that he despised all men equally."[18]

But Sullivan's own general unhappiness, indeed his probable nervous breakdown during college, gave him unusual insight into the very nature of happiness. Through his life he viewed true friendship as perhaps the greatest single antidote to depression. While he never fully dismissed the Freudian focus on infantile anxiety, he added within his own theoretical construction a new phase of preadolescence that he viewed as equally important, insofar as it was the period during which psychologically healthy individuals made their first true friendships independent of parental influence. Failure to progress fruitfully through this period presaged further failures in adolescence and adulthood to establish progressively more intimate friendships and relationships, which ought to culminate in full-blown adult love. Sullivan summarized his observations in his "theorem of tenderness," which he viewed as the necessary prerequisite to love.[19]

Sullivan's most original work was conducted in his seven years at Sheppard Pratt Hospital, in which he served as a chief on a ward of largely psychotic patients. His great practical breakthrough came in granting the psychiatric nurses on the ward unusual latitude in attending to patients as they sought fit, rather than dictating tight medical directives to them. Sullivan found that the nurses' inherent powers of empathy and kindness seemed as effective in treating the patients as advanced psychiatric techniques, if not more so. He claimed that he was able to nurture in a nurse a "lush crop of self-respect from the good accomplished with the patients," and that a nurse was able to draw upon "that intuitive grasp of personal totalities that was once her property in common with all preadolescents."[20] Moreover, Sullivan concluded that because nurses tended to be drawn from an economic class similar to that of the patients they were treating, they were better able to establish a rapport with the patients, which facilitated healing. A doctor, by contrast, was "so detached from a 'natural' grasp on personality that it usually takes him from 12 to 18 months residence on the staff of an active mental hospital to crack his crust."[21] In other words, not only were nurses better than physicians at establishing healing relationship with the patients, it was the fact of their lack of a formal elite education that enabled them to empathize with the patients. His biographer, Helen Swick Perry, concluded that while Sullivan may have initially chosen to work with staff who were "low on the totem pole" to ease his own sense of social insecurity, he ultimately concluded that the patients experienced diminished anxiety with "lower-echelon staff."[22]

To some degree, Sullivan's work presaged the movement toward humanistic psychology later espoused by Carl Rogers and others during the decades following World War II. Grounding his ideas on mental health in the ability of people to emotionally connect with those around them, including their healers, he dispensed with the Freudian ideal of the aloof and dispassionate psychoanalyst, and cleaved instead to a vision of the patient-analyst relationship as one built on kindness, empathy, and tenderness. With his colleague Clara Thompson, he propounded a therapeutic approach grounded in love and acceptance as the surest path to mental health.[23]

Like any good Freudian, Sullivan focused on anxiety as the prime cause of neurosis, but distinct from Freud he found the roots of anxiety in social uncertainty. Certainly infants experienced anxiety, but not because of the aggressive Oedipal sex drives that Klein discerned. Rather, infants, like adults, experienced anxiety in response to the changes in moods of those around them. In adults as well, Sullivan understood anxiety to be a natural response to disapproval or dislike by one's peers.[24] Thus, for Sullivan, friendship in all guises—professional, social, sexual— was the key to mental health, and friendship was as necessary between patient and analyst as it was between preteens.

Sullivan's focus on social interactions led him to both sociology and social activism in the latter half of his career. Fascinated with the work of anthropologists Ruth Benedict and Edward Sapir, he began to define himself as a "social psychologist" in his forties, and in his last decade he came to believe that broad improvement in mental health was not possible without a radical restructuring of society to a more Marxist ideal. In 1933, he wrote that progress in societal mental health required "the personal necessity of interest in the general welfare," and that humanity needed to "take stock in time to save our civilization from destruction by the mob violence of unhappy folk ignored too long by those given the leisure to work a remedy."[25] And in his final and most influential tome, *The Interpersonal Theory of Psychology,* Sullivan wrote: "Thus as psychobiology seeks to study the individual human being, and as cultural anthropology, which has been a powerful tributary to social science, seeks to study the social heritage shown in the concerted behavior of people making up a group, so psychiatry—and its convergent, social psychology—seeks to study the biologically and culturally conditioned, but *sui generis*, interpersonal process occurring in the interpersonal situations in which the observant psychiatrist does his work."[26]

However, free thinker though he was, Sullivan never broke with Freud on many fundamentals. While distancing himself from notions of the unconscious, he accepted the ideas of repression and infantile roots for at least some anxiety. And although he emphasized the need for a radically different relationship between therapist and patient than that which Freud espoused, he retained the ideas of transference and, perhaps more important, of countertransference—the involuntary feelings that the analyst began to project on the patient during the course of analysis, through which intimate bonds could be established. Moreover, like Freud, he felt confident in imposing his interpretations of the patient's free associations upon the analytic situation. And in a step that Freud had decisively rejected, Sullivan brought severely psychotic patients into analysis while at Sheppard Pratt, interpreting their silence during the analytic sessions as a healthy part of the transference process, and understanding social rejection to be, in part, the cause of their illness. Like Freud, he arrogated to himself the privilege of understanding the mental processes without external review or validation of his insights. The Freudian privilege was alive and well in Sullivanian interpersonal psychiatry.

Sullivan had a despicable side that undermined his credibility, and ultimately his influence on American psychiatry. Aside from his ever-present drinking and misanthropy, he was conceited and at times cruel. Young psychiatrists training under him were subjected to withering and destructive critiques that often needed to be rectified by further training and analysis after they left Sullivan's tutelage. One psychiatrist wrote of having to "pick up the pieces after Sullivan countless times with men who left Washington battered by him and came to New York to continue their training."[27] He had a sadistic side, which led him to frequently abuse colleagues, and periodically patients. In one case, he prescribed a course of regular rectal manipulation for a man with anal-centered phobias, which nearly led the man to a psychotic break. "No, this man was bad news," wrote a colleague familiar with Sullivan's career. "All the more so because like most psychopaths he could also wear a smooth and seductive front."[28] Sullivan would die under mysterious circumstances at age fifty-six in a hotel room in Paris, alone and probably drunk.

Further extending the humanism and pragmatism of Sullivanian psychoanalysis was Karen Horney, a contemporary and colleague. Horney was born outside of Hamburg, Germany, in 1885, and showed early academic promise. She received her medical degree from the University of Berlin in 1911, and took further training in psychiatry at Urban Hospital in Berlin and at Lankwitz-Kuranstalt at Charite. She underwent a training analysis with Karl Abraham at the Berlin Psychoanalytic Society, where she also taught until emigrating to the United States in 1932. During this time she had met and married Oskar Horney, given birth to three daughters, suffered the deaths of both parents within a year of each other, and divorced Horney after finding the marriage untenable. Small wonder that the focus of her psychological research was loss and emotional conflict, and that her medical school thesis was titled "A Casuistic Contribution to the Question of Traumatic Psychoses."[29]

Horney began to break with Freudian orthodoxy almost immediately upon completing her analytic training. Like Sullivan, she found roots of neuroses not only in infantile trauma but also in lifelong experiences of isolation and alienation. She, too, attributed neurosis to a misfit between individual and society, suggesting (albeit less radically than Sullivan) that societal pressure to behave in certain conforming manners ("the tyranny of the should," in Horney's words) could separate a person's conscious behavior from subconscious or unconscious drives. That is, in striving to conform, a person could be denying her genuine self by spending too much psychic energy trying to be something she was not.[30]

Horney is often called the first feminist psychologist. From the onset of her career, she rejected many of Freud's sexual constructs, suggesting that much of the phallic symbolism in Freudian psychosexual theory was simply off, and that both girls and boys experienced traumatic early fright and yearnings not from coveting a metaphysical phallus, but from desiring intimate and protective love from parents, which may or may not have been forthcoming. Horney wrote extensively on women's life experiences—pregnancy, motherhood, marriage, and divorce—and attributed significance to all of these events and experiences. And unlike Freud, she insisted that people had the potential for lifelong psychological growth. Profound psychological experiences did not, in Horney's view, end when a child entered the period of sexual latency at age three.

Horney made important contributions to the realm of interpersonal psychology, which would rise to dominate therapeutic technique decades later. She hinted in her later work that *thinking* as much as feeling had a role to play in mental health, and that through analysis and retraining of thought patterns patients could begin to tame their psychic demons.[31] By emphasizing the importance of thinking through problems, or "cognition," Horney was coming close to wholly breaking with the Freudian idiom, for an essential tenet of psychoanalysis was that problems and solutions lay in unconscious memories rather than in conscious cogitation. Such thinking was truly American in its outlook: pragmatic and proactive. Horney's psychology was, above all, optimistic—that quintessential American characteristic.

But Horney never really left psychoanalysis. Even after being banished from the New York Psychoanalytic Society in 1941, she started the rival American Institute for Psychoanalysis with Sullivan, Clara Thompson, and Erich Fromm (who themselves split from her a few years later). Though her theories were informed by humanism, empathy, and tenderness, and were based on the potential for people to grow through life, she nonetheless remained convinced of the central role of

early experiences in the formation of neuroses; of the essential importance of the unconscious; and of the role of free association and transference in the analytic experience. She had pushed Freudian technique
and theory to new frontiers, but she had not dispensed with it wholly.
Rather than being the mother of a new psychology, she was an extender
and embellisher of an existing paradigm, albeit in a uniquely American
mold. She and Sullivan had laid an American patina on the Freudian
creation, but had left it largely intact.

Child Guidance

As Sullivan and Horney were gradually transforming the imported
Freudian enterprise to a more Americanized form, an alternative and
even more pragmatic form of psychotherapy was developing on its own
in the United States, from genuinely American roots. The movement,
which came to be known as "child guidance," had its genesis in the
good-government ethos of progressive America: the utopian impulse
toward self-improvement that could take place only in the ahistorical
and classless matrix so unique to the new world. While temperance
groups were busy ridding the world of "demon gin" and other vices,
and while suffragettes fought to further extend the vote to the nonvot-
ing half, a few idealistic psychologists looked to the childhood roots of
delinquency and dysfunction, and began a mental hygiene movement
intended to cleanse people of unhealthy habits of the mind.

Although most large-scale social movements tend to have multiple
roots, child guidance can reasonably be traced to the vision of just one
man, Lightner Witmer, the world's first clinical psychologist.[32] Witmer
studied the nascent brain science of psychology at the University of
Pennsylvania in the 1880s and received a Ph.D. in the discipline from
the University of Leipzig (Germany). At the time, psychology was a science grounded in psychometrics—the measurement of the mind. Using

interviews and testing, psychologists sought to measure variables of the human mind on a variety of axes—cognition, intelligence, social aptitude, emotional maturity, pathological predisposition—and find predictable patterns in both the causes of these characteristics and the likely life courses that individuals with certain measurements would take. The reputation of psychometrics today has been marred by accusations of racism and eugenical impulses, but at its onset it was an honest effort to measure various components of mental functioning.[33] Witmer's interests were always more applied than theoretical. Not content to simply measure and report, he wished to effect change in those individuals whom testing designated as psychologically impaired. Upon returning from Leipzig in 1892, he took a position at the University of Pennsylvania as director of its psychological laboratory, but only four years later he established the nation's first psychological clinic.

Witmer's clinic focused on children who were generally referred by the surrounding Philadelphia schools because of problematic behavior and academic performance. Upon admission, the children were subjected to a range of both physical and psychometric tests to establish a diagnosis, or at least a baseline measurement. After a diagnosis was made, various interventions were applied in an effort to thwart the child's further slide into educational deficiency and behavioral delinquency. In placing such substantial emphasis on diagnosis, Witmer situated himself comfortably in the nineteenth-century mania for measurement and classification of all things physical and mental. While medicine, generally, was still substantially ineffective at intervening in the course of disease, it had greatly improved over the previous hundred years in its ability to accurately describe disease states, and thus could offer accurate prognoses, if not therapeutic intervention. Scientists and physicians interested in diseases of the mind aspired to similar status.[34]

Most of Witmer's contributions to mental hygiene came as a result of his pragmatic approach to emotional problems. Utterly opposed to doctrinaire theories of psychosocial development, Witmer preferred to attack problem cases with whatever tools he had at his disposal. While studying at the University of Pennsylvania, Witmer had taught prep school in Philadelphia, and on at least two occasions observed children who were falling behind their peers. One child's reading problems were rectified simply by fitting him with glasses, while another had probably suffered minor brain injuries from an accident at an early age, which had left his speech slurred and thereby impeded his social development. In each case, Witmer realized that diagnosis and early intervention, with either glasses or speech therapy, would have rectified the deficiency much earlier, and would have allowed each boy to reach his academic and social potential. Witmer's conclusion from these observations was that mental faults and blockages could have very pedestrian causes, and that the appropriate remedy might be quite simple. His other conclusion was that prophylactic mental hygiene was the preferred ideal; most problems were easier to rectify earlier than later, by which point resulting pathologies may have multiplied.[35]

Witmer's treatment model made use of a team consisting of a psychiatrist, a psychologist, and one of the new clinical social workers being produced by the social work schools at Smith College and at the New York School of Social Work.[36] The approach was holistic. Like the work of Sullivan and Horney, it grounded mental health in interpersonal dynamics, but went further in viewing the sum of mental health as being one of psychosocial fit. While Horney and Sullivan would not embrace the tools of anthropology and sociology until the 1930s, Witmer understood from the beginning of his career that the individual is, above all, a product of his social context, and thus any meaningful sort of psychological intervention must attack the social context of mental disease.

Witmer's team approach was designed to confront the many challenges facing the individual in a complex society. The psychologist would draw upon his extensive training in psychological testing, measurement, and observation in an effort to tease out where, precisely, the malfunction was rooted. The social worker would work to better the fit between the patient and his social setting, visiting with parents, teachers, clergy, and other individuals prominent in the child's life to both understand the social context of the patient's pathology and change it when possible. And the psychiatrist, being a trained physician, would diagnose both the physical and neurological roots of any maladaptions present. Psychotherapy would be applied, initially by the psychiatrist, but later by either the social worker or even the psychologist to help east the "fit" between the patient and his surroundings. Witmer's innovative use of psychologists as active clinical agents is part of the reason why he is frequently viewed as the founder of clinical psychology.[37]

What type of psychotherapy was being applied in Witmer's clinic?[38] It bore scant relation to the analytic approach which Brill, Putnam, and other early Freudians were importing to the United States. Above all, it was eclectic and pragmatic. Children brought to the clinics did not suffer from the self-described neurotic alienation of Freud's upper-class Viennese patients. Rather, they had been brought to the clinic for the most prosaic of reasons—misbehaviors such as disobedience, truancy, and stealing, and personality problems such as nervousness, shyness, and an inability to focus. Often, the children were experiencing tensions at home resulting from poverty, divorce, or the cultural alienation common to recent immigrants.[39] As such, they generally needed help in adjusting to both their social situation and the important individuals in their lives.

Therapists at the clinics generally focused on the relationship between the child and the adults around him. Sometimes, the most constructive approach was simply to change the child's milieu. If a social worker found that the child seemed to be having a particularly bad response to a school situation, she might try to transfer the child to a different school, or at least a different class. If certain adults in the child's life (usually parents) were found to be barriers to emotional health, the social worker might try to work directly with the parents to change

their behavior and parenting style. (One early report on the child guidance movement noted that "psychotherapy is by no means confined to
the child; usually the more toxic factors in the situation are found in the
adult environment.")[40] And if transfer or parental counseling were not
realistic options, than the child was counseled on ways to better adapt to
his insalubrious situation.

Psychotherapy in the child guidance movement was radically different from that practiced by psychoanalysts, in that it rejected the existence of the unconscious. Or perhaps it is more accurate to say that
child guidance counselors were never aware that the unconscious had
been discovered in the first place. Therapy was, above all, an effort to
teach the child new skills to cope with his or her difficult environment
("coping mechanisms" in modern parlance). The patient was assumed
to be an emotionally conscious actor who was capable of understanding
her own impulses and predilections. Therapy could assist the child in
solving her problems only insofar as she desired to improve her state
and make necessary changes in her behavior. The goal of all such therapy was to help people to live optimally within their own milieu and
within the limitations of their own emotional capacity. Notably, such
therapy was termed "realistic psychotherapy."[41]

With the advantage of hindsight, it appears that both the child guidance movement and the more Americanized Freudians ultimately arrived at the same place—one of situating mental health within an
interpersonal and social context. Both Horney and Sullivan (and others
of their circle, such as noted analyst Erich Fromm) looked to anthropology late in their careers to try to understand the manner in which social
forces and context mold the psyche in ways both healthy and ill. But
the path to such realizations, and the theoretical underpinning of the
approaches, differed substantially. The interpersonal psychoanalysts arrived at their conclusions through a slow evolution away from Freudian
orthodoxy, by coming to understand that not all of their patients' problems seemed susceptible to treatment through free association and in-

terpretation. Rather, all too frequently, the patients simply refused to get well, even after lengthy analyses, and social forces from beyond infancy arose too frequently in the analytic process to be simply dismissed. At the same time, neither Sullivan nor Horney could ever dismiss Freud entirely. As discussed above, each clung to the analytical model of treatment—one patient, one analyst, talking and listening, through a process designed to foster psychological insight concerning the genesis of the patient's persona.

By contrast, child guidance grew out of the very untheoretical experiences of social workers, whose training was with people rather than thoughts. Although over the course of the 1930s and 1940s psychiatric social workers would gradually distance themselves from their more community-focused colleagues, the psychiatric social workers remained grounded in the understanding that people lived and grew within a specific place, surrounded by specific people, whose malfeasance, ineptitude, and incompetence could bar the path to mental health. A child growing up in poverty and violence, surrounded by filth and hopelessness and subjected to insensitive teachers and derelict, alcoholic, or absent parents, could hardly be expected to attain emotional equanimity. The wonder was not that America's slums produced maladjusted children; the wonder was that intact children emerged from the insalubrious milieu as frequently as they did.

The psychotherapy of mental hygiene was not a voyage of self-discovery. Such an effort was too indulgent, too fatuous, an approach considering the compelling needs of the children. Rather, it was a way of teaching survival skills, using whatever tools were available. Given the magnitude of the challenges they faced, psychiatric social workers in the clinics did not have the luxury of cleaving to a particular ideology, or of dismissing one approach over another for failing to abide by a specific technique. Social entrepreneurs that they were, they learned from their mistakes and gleaned techniques where they could. The Commonwealth Fund's 1934 report on the state of the child guidance movement emphasized that child guidance was "eclectic, in that it adopts facts and hypotheses from various fields of research and methods from all three of its component professions and from various schools of thought within those professions. It is an open-minded attempt to solve concrete problems as presented. Its methods have already changed materially in a quarter-century and will no doubt change still further."[42] Writing of the movement in 1931, psychologist William Burnham succinctly stated that the aim of child hygiene was really no different from the aim of good education: "normal healthful development and the acquisition of habits of healthful activity, physical and mental."[43]

Sociometry

The evolution of psychoanalysis to a more interpersonal emphasis, coupled with the pragmatist's emphasis on a milieu and adjustment, found expression in Jacob Levy Moreno's pioneering work in sociometry in the 1930s. Moreno was born in Romania in 1892 and graduated from the University of Vienna Medical School in 1917. Rejecting psychoanalysis at an early stage in his career, he drew instead on his lifelong love of theater to pioneer a new sort of therapy in which he asked individuals in a group to take on dramatic roles. He hoped that through identifying with a character and acting out emotions in a variety of contrived scenarios, the participants would begin to expose aspects of their own psychopathology that could then be examined, and perhaps resolved, by the group. Although this sort of nascent "group therapy" would not really find popular acceptance for another two decades, Moreno's early efforts laid the groundwork for greater emphasis on interpersonal dynamics in the therapeutic effort.

At the same time as he was developing this early form of group therapy, Moreno undertook a five-year research effort at the New York

State Training School for Girls in Hudson, New York. The school was populated by some 500 girls sent there by courts from around the state to be rehabilitated, or sometimes simply held, until they were of legal age. In a modern idiom we would deem them to be girls "at risk" of failing, with a high potential for truancy, early motherhood, criminal behavior, and impoverishment. Moreno realized that as the girls arrived at the training school with nonexistent social networks and no family support, the school provided the ideal social laboratory for observing the formation of social networks and for gaining insight into patterns of social interactions.[44]

From 1932 to 1938 Moreno administered numerous sociometric tests to the school's residents in an effort to discern the roles they took on within the school's sixteen separate residential cottages. Each cottage had a resident house parent, a kitchen officer, and a dining hall. During social and educational activities the girls were brought together, but for the domestic aspects of life they remained segregated in their cottages. To determine the roles that the girls played within the artificial cottage communities, and the manners in which their individual personalities dictated social orders both within and between the cottages, Moreno asked them questions concerning which girls they would choose to associate with, be friends with, or actively exclude from various activities and from their social networks.

Moreno observed that some girls were consistently chosen for inclusion and others rarely so. Some girls bonded together into pairs or triplets, and others were free agents. Some girls (whom Moreno described as *introverts*) preferred to include girls from within their own cottages, while others (described as *extroverts*) looked across the entire spectrum of choices within the school to create bonds. Seventy-five of the 505 resident girls were never chosen, while some girls were chosen more than forty times. Some girls drew from their complete panoply of choices to accept or reject; some drew from only a small roster; and others ("indifferent" girls) failed to register choices at all, or listed choices that were inconsistent with the attractions and rejections listed by others in relation to them. Moreno followed up this initial round of tests with subsequent ones to more precisely elicit the girls' preferences regarding socializing and living. He then went about modeling the ideal cottage communities.

Moreno's most significant insight was that girls living in cottages with a disproportionate number of extroverts—that is, with a large number of girls whose social networks were focused outside the cottage rather than inside—were at a much greater risk for running away from the school. That is, regardless of a girl's initial attitude and predilection upon being assigned to the school, membership within a tight cottage-bound social network meant that there was a greater chance that she would successfully complete the term. By changing the living arrangements of the girls to reflect the mapped social preferences, Moreno significantly reduced the rate of runaways. Moreover, the mere fact of participating in the numerous role-playing tests that Moreno administered seemed to raise the success rate of the school's residents. In a recap of Moreno's work, psychologist Paul Hare reflected: "By the time a new girl made her way through the situational tests, from entrance to exit test, she had presumably become quite familiar with role-playing and the fact that Moreno was trying to make her stay at Hudson as productive as possible. She must have received the message that she was important and her social atom was important. She had learned how to adjust her behavior in interactions with different persons in different situations. She was learning the social skills that she had presumably lacked when she was sent to the school for 'training.' "[45]

Moreno's work foreshadowed the rise of group therapy as a major treatment modality in the 1960s and 1970s, but perhaps more important it reinforced the American trend toward a more pragmatic, societal-based conception of mental health and treatment. Although exposed to the Freudian ferment in his training years in Vienna, Moreno had actively discarded such a theoretical conception of psychological development, and chose instead to pursue a far more empirically based approach to a study of the mind and a treatment of its pathologies. Moreno's work at Hudson is notable for its lack of a theoretical basis. Rather, seizing the opportunity to explore relationships that had developed among a sizable group of girls isolated from their formative social milieus, he discovered the power of natural social proclivities, and the price of failing to recognize those impulses. And in an utter rejection of ego-based psychology, he based his "fix" not on self-exploration and knowledge, but on rearranging living situations and on imparting social coping skills to girls who had hitherto lacked them. Such pragmatism reflected a divergent impulse within American therapy, and foreshadowed future work on fixing broken bonds, re-acclimating people to normal social intercourse, and on educating rather than analyzing.

Moreno may have been following his own instincts, but his work reflected a growing recognition by at least some American psychiatrists that the initial burst of enthusiasm for Freud had led them awry. Uncomfortable with psychoanalysis's overly theoretical to psychology, these psychiatrists turned to the ongoing work of the child guidance clinics, the research emerging from the nation's social work schools and psychology departments, and the dissident views of some members of the profession who had joined the newly formed American Orthopsychiatric Association (AOA) for direction. Frederick Allen, president of the AOA and director of the Philadelphia clinic, who had grounding in both psychology and psychiatry, admitted in a 1933 speech that psychiatry had failed to "contribute to an understanding of the social conditions through which we have been passing" and had become "too enmeshed in the intricacies of individual psychology" while neglecting "large social forces."[46] Although Allen never fully disavowed the Freudian stress on the past—"the phantasies and unconscious desires of the child"—he was far more willing than other early analysts to dismiss the importance of transference and to see the therapist's role as one of educator. "The influences that are helpful in therapy are not essentially different from the influences in normal life," Allen wrote. The goal of the therapist, in working with a child, was to help him "utilize" his experiences in the "management of his own life, and in the relations he establishes with others."[47]

By the end of the 1930s, divergent strands in American psychotherapy strived either to further formalize the Freudian enterprise through newly created societies, institutes, training regimens, and prerequisite degrees (particularly the M.D.) or to move in an almost entirely opposite direction, to embrace the growing discoveries of social work and psychology, sociometry and child guidance. Not all mental health professionals fell neatly into one camp or another. Many luminaries such as Meyer, Horney, and Sullivan remained deeply influenced by Freud and his followers, while looking beyond Freudian techniques for new tools by which to move their patients and clients forward. Others broke more radically with the fold, or failed to embrace it in the first place. Neither camp had really gained preeminence in the years before the United States entered World War II, and it would be another two decades before the therapeutic profession solidified into a hierarchy of prestige and influence.

CHAPTER 3

A Crying Need

World War II changed everything. Before the war, psychotherapy had been a marginal treatment delivered by a few psychiatrists and psychologists in either private practices or in child guidance clinics, almost entirely within the nation's major cities. Few physicians opted for psychiatric training; few social work graduates embarked on careers in psychiatric social work; and almost no psychologists viewed psychotherapy as a reasonable career track. The public perceived nonpsychotic mental illness with only the haziest understanding, when it bothered to acknowledge its existence at all. As late as 1943, an army colonel inspecting shell-shocked troops at a psychoneurotic hospital in North Africa spoke for many when he contemptuously dismissed the official diagnosis of psychoneurosis. "Nuts," he said. "Somebody has thought up a new two-bit word for being yellow."[1]

But if the troops were simply yellow, there were suddenly an awful lot of them. Forced conscription of troops began after the Pearl Harbor attack of December 1941, and almost immediately army induction officers began discovering extraordinary numbers of men who were mentally unfit to serve in the armed forces. Young men in the prime of physical health and fortitude showed up at induction stations with severe anxieties, depression, antisocial demeanors, uncontrolled anger, and generally unstable psychic presentations. They were bed-wetters, drop-outs, drunkards, and chronic misfits. The army's doctors were reluctant to allow them onto ships, into infantry divisions, or even into support branches. They feared that as many as 25 percent of the inductees presented intolerable psychological risk profiles, and by 1943 the Veterans Administration successfully lobbied Congress to define "psychoneurosis" as a line-of-duty ailment qualifying those so designated for full disability benefits if discharged.[2]

Ultimately, the army was forced to acknowledge the magnitude of the problem. The army medical corps appointed William Menninger, one of the cofounders of the famed Menninger Psychiatry Clinic in Topeka, Kansas, as chief psychiatrist of the armed forces, elevated psychiatry to equal rank with medicine and surgery, placed trained psychiatrists in all 108 induction centers and in all of the army's 65 domestic and 217 foreign general hospitals, and created 10 specialized army hospitals purely devoted to the treatment of neuropsychiatric disorders. Psychiatrists were assigned to basic training camps to help ease civilian recruits' transition to combat life, to all large transport and hospital ships, and to disciplinary barracks and army rehabilitation centers for military prisoners. The army expanded its convalescent hospitals to accommodate the influx of psychoneurotic patients coming off the combat lines, who by war's end composed 30 to 50 percent of all recuperating soldiers. Eight psychiatrists served in the inner circles of the surgeon general's office, and 2,400 army physicians served in neuropsychiatry through the war.[3]

The findings of these psychiatrists and the general physicians serving alongside them were dismaying. From January 1942 to December 1945, 1,875,000 men were rejected from military service for neuropsychiatric reasons, constituting 12 percent of all inductees and 37 percent of all those rejected for medical reasons. During the same period, approximately 1 million soldiers suffering from neuropsychiatric disorders were admitted to army hospitals, representing 6 percent of all wartime admissions. Nearly two-thirds of the admitted patients fit within the diagnostic range of neurotic, suggesting that rather than being congenitally "crazy" or psychotic, they were reasonably healthy men who simply lacked the emotional fortitude to withstand the horrific experience of combat without undergoing a psychological break. By the end of the war, 380,000 men had been granted discharge for psychiatric reasons, representing nearly 40 percent of all medical discharges. Including the 137,000 men who had been discharged for "personality disorders," nearly half a million men had been discharged from the army during the war years for reasons related to mental disorders.[4]

There had been some fraud in the ranks, however, and at least a few of the psychiatric symptoms had been contrived explicitly to earn their sufferers early discharges. Upon inspecting a group of 2,800 soldiers exhibiting suspicious psychiatric symptoms during transport to battle theaters in either Europe or the Pacific, General Elliot Cooke concluded that many were simply cowards with "gangplank fever." Some had purposely injured themselves in an effort to win discharge. Others had enrolled in brief seminars to learn how to behave so that they could be classified as psychoneurotic. "If that's the best you have, keep them at home and we'll win the war without any help," one infantry officer had told Cooke, after observing the malingering soldiers.[5]

The vast majority of psychoneurotic complaints were legitimate. Infantry soldiers in Europe were being pushed to the limits of human endurance, often serving between 40 and 80 days on the front lines without a break. Psychiatrists estimated that most men reached their psychological limit after 200 days of combat service, by which point they were so nervous and jumpy as to undermine the morale and efficacy of their units.[6] John Appel, an army neuropsychiatrist observing the combat situation in Italy in spring 1944, feared that for lack of replacement troops, "no man is removed from combat duty until he has become worthless as a fighter."[7] While shell shock had been observed in American troops during World War I, the short period during which

American troops had actually engaged in frontline combat during that war, coupled with generally less destructive armaments (particularly from the air), had rendered the syndrome relatively unimportant to army physicians. In contrast, the much broader military draft for World War II, coupled with longer tours of duty, longer stints on the front lines, and greater exposure to more destructive combat ordnance, commonly induced psychic breaks in combat soldiers. E. A. Strecker, consultant to the surgeon general, concluded that the greater numbers of psychoneurotic cases meant that "deeper emotional recesses have been penetrated…that we have come perilously close to the saturation point of human emotions, and that while there may be no limit to the resources of engineering genius in perfecting machines of war, there is a limit to the capacity of human emotions to survive the psychic devastation and degradation which are produced."[8]

The army's experience with psychoneurosis during the war had led it to two sobering conclusions. The first was that even the most psychologically healthy men would almost inevitably break down after long-term exposure to the horrors of modern battle. An investigation by the army's surgeon general's office in 1945 concluded that six months of continuous fighting was the maximum that even the "sturdiest and most stable soldier" could endure without breaking. That is, the process of psychological breakdown was actually a *normal* response to the highly abnormal conditions of combat. The report quoted one damaged soldier who pithily explained, "It finally got me, the noise and all. Never used to bother me, but I've been slipping for a month. I guess I'm through."[9]

But perhaps more troubling was the 12 percent rejection rate of physically healthy inductees. The World War II draft was the first total draft in the nation's history, and as such provided unprecedented information regarding the general health of the nation's young men. And while the pitiful state of physical health of many of the young men— missing teeth, untreated abscesses and sores, uncorrected vision problems, uncorrected skeletal deformities, untreated chronic infections—would later galvanize the nation into enlarging its physician workforce and facilitating rural access to modern medicine, the 12 percent rejection rate for mental illness stood alone for its shock value. Neither mental health professionals in government planning agencies nor those in academic research departments had come close to projecting the high prevalence of mental illness nationally. While the United States, like all nations, had long been treating the severely mentally ill (asylums had existed to house the insane in the United States beginning in the eighteenth century, and in Europe from the Middle Ages), it had taken comfort in the knowledge that this class of its citizens was a small and stable minority. In 1945, the total inpatient population of all of the nation's state and private insane asylums and psychiatric hospitals had climbed to just under a half million, or about a third of 1 percent of the population. The sudden realization that mental illness, in some form or another, might affect one in ten Americans, rather than one in three hundred, was shocking and deeply sobering.[10]

A New Awareness

Whether rejected initially, treated and returned to battle, or dismissed, servicemen who encountered mental health professionals while in uniform returned home somewhat better informed about the potential for mental health professionals to help them live fuller lives. They passed on these insights to family and friends who had also been exposed to new ideas surrounding psychotherapy while maintaining the home front during the war. Popular journals, too, as part of generally broader coverage of scientific and medical developments during those years, began to report with greater frequency developments coming from the mental health professions. In many ways, the nation was moving toward greater acceptance of the role of psychotherapy in everyday life. Psychiatry, in short, was not just for treating the hospitalized insane anymore. In 1946, the venerable *Saturday Evening Post* announced, "This war, even more than the last one, gave psychiatrists an opportunity to prove themselves in the troubled world outside of the locked hospital ward."[11]

At the same time, journalists and social scientists began to better document the pervasiveness of mental illness throughout the country. Rural life, rooted in small communities and farm work, and previously assumed to be psychologically salubrious, turned out to be quite the opposite. An Ohio government study of rural Miami County found that the incidence of mental illness among inhabitants was in fact higher than that found in urban areas; that between 10 and 20 percent of the residents probably needed to see a psychiatrist; that one in five children was maladjusted; and that one of every twenty-three inhabitants of the county would spend part of his life in a mental institution. The study's author wrote that "many...live miserably, and at a level far below their real capacity."[12] The broad phenomenon of mental illness received wide exposure in a report, *Where Do People Take Their Troubles?*, published in 1945 by Lee Steiner, an investigative journalist. Steiner described the mentally troubled as unextraordinary: "young people who were loaded down with ambitions they could not fulfill, unmarried people in their thirties or forties who were having disturbing love affairs, or those who were disturbed because they had no love affairs...people who had troubles with in-laws or relatives...drug addicts, shop-lifters, students on the verge of suicide."[13]

Americans were also becoming more familiar with the practice of psychotherapy, and that most arcane and urbane of pursuits, psychoanalysis. Freudian terms such as "inferiority complexes," "repressions," and "frustrations" were appearing in movies and in popular novels. *Time* magazine devoted its cover story to Freud and psychiatry in October 1948, and summarized for its readers the jargon of the master: "The theory is that if the patient talks enough about his troubles, he will finally get 1) the relief any confession brings; 2) a somewhat less sentimental view of himself; and 3) a realization that he too can be a grown-up."[14] William Menninger, still the chief psychiatrist of the army, noted in an interview that year that "people are beginning to see that damage of the same kind can be done by a bullet, bacteria or mother-in-law."[15] And Franz Alexander, a well-regarded professor of psychiatry at the University of Chicago, noted (perhaps self-servingly) in 1946, "A visit to a psychiatrist is no longer fraught with opprobrium and anxiety but is becoming as acceptable as consultation with any other specialist in the field of medicine."[16]

Awareness led to optimism. Whereas neurotic tics had long been seen as simply immutable components of the personality, many Americans began to wonder if perhaps the "brain boys" had it in their power to fix some of these idiosyncrasies.[17] While people had long been aware that some of their friends and family were morose or melancholy, hyper or manic, or simply impetuous and unpredictable, now for the first time some began to ask whether these troubling personality features could perhaps be ameliorated through psychotherapy. Karen Horney published a book of collected reflections on therapy in 1946 aimed at making psychoanalysis less threatening. Titled *Are You Considering Psychoanalysis?*, it contained numerous suggestions, including that idea that analysis could "help man get in touch with the darker reaches of his life and learn the deeply hidden sources of his strengths and weaknesses."[18] Alexander predicted that the next target of analytically oriented psychotherapy was the "simpler cases," with the "expectation of being ultimately able to prevent psychoneuroses."[19]

At the same time, large numbers of Americans maintained their skepticism. Even as millions of Americans became aware of the potential of psychiatry to heal, many millions of others resisted the notion that talking to strangers about sensitive and private topics such as sexual yearnings, unresolved fears, and bizarre fantasies could possibly help one achieve greater happiness or satisfaction with one's lot. And many physicians in other fields stood ready to reinforce these biases with their own suspicions of their standoffish psychiatric colleagues. Psychiatrists were a "queer bunch," in the words of one popular magazine writer, and even medical luminary Alan Gregg, medical director of the Rockefeller Foundation, accused them of speaking "a dialect, a special lingo more productive of resentment than comprehension by their medical brethren."[20]

Even if psychiatry could successfully heal emotionally afflicted patients, was this necessarily advisable? Many Americans perceived, correctly, that psychiatry was devoid of morality, and that psychotherapy aimed to absolve guilt without demanding repentance. Some clergy were out-and-out hostile to the enterprise, with Monsignor Fulton Sheen of Kansas accusing it of harboring "materialism, infantilism, hedonism, and eroticism."[21] Rudolf Allers, a professor of psychology at Catholic University, wrote an impassioned attack on psychotherapy, claiming that the stated goal of getting a patient to better "adjust" was possibly morally bankrupt. "Adjust to what?" he wrote. "If morals become a hindrance to adjustment and (apparent) individual well-being, then morals must be changed. This has been declared openly to be the talk of psychiatry."[22] Even William Menninger admitted that there were times when a clergyman might be the more appropriate counselor than the psychiatrist, given that some guilt was grounded in real misdeeds which required not psychic clarification, but moral clarification. "Remember," Menninger implored. "The minister...deals with...a real guilt over transgressing explicit moral laws, not the irrational guilt of the emotionally disturbed patient."[23]

Such resistance underlay general skepticism of the psychiatric enterprise. Were "mental health," "adjustment," and "catharsis" unmitigated goods? What if they entailed forfeiting one's essential being, soul, or moral grounding? At what point were doctors curing an illness, and at what point were they attempting to reshape an individual's personality? Many of the most creative and ingenious individuals throughout history had suffered from crippling depression and anxiety, and possibly such suffering was the source of their genius. Greer Williams, a widely read magazine writer, spoke for many when he wrote, "Psychiatry, in probing the mind, toys with the meaning of life itself, and the resistance to its crusade for wider probing is understandably strong."[24] And even those who admitted the potential efficacy of therapy sometimes wondered if some troubled souls would not, perhaps, be better left alone. "Before we decide to screen them out," warned Frederick Dershimer, a psychiatrist for Dupont, "we need to give serious consideration to the fact that the inventor of nylon was a known psychiatric case for years."[25]

Despite the presence of such skepticism, research indicated that there was a crying need for more, rather than less, psychotherapy. An influential study conducted in 1946 tracked 150 known neurotic patients as they interacted with the medical establishment, and found a startling panoply of misdiagnoses and ineffective interventions. The general conclusions of the study were that most patients with emotional or psychiatric indications who sought care from internists or general practitioners would not receive optimum care, or even adequate care. "The result is a tremendous army of maladjusted persons going from doctor to doctor and receiving illogical medical and surgical therapies that only aggravate their problems," the primary investigator wrote. One researcher who commented on the report concluded that "the misdiagnosis and mismanagement of the so-called functionally ill patient is the medical scandal of the day."[26]

The study had focused on only 150 patients, but there was a growing recognition that many Americans, particularly those that had returned mentally scarred from the war, were simply being ignored and their psychic wounds allowed to fester. Survivors the world over were discovering that psychic injuries did not automatically heal when the shelling stopped. Once the war was over, civilians who lived in countries that had been occupied by the Axis powers needed to relearn norms of social interaction now that they were no longer living in fear of physical danger or attack. French intellectuals spoke of a condition in these populations known as *asthenie*, the "inability to react normally to a given situation, explosive emotion, anxiety, hypersensitivity to noise...a collective inferiority complex, especially in young people...a phenomenon of collective castration."[27] American psychiatrists observed a similar syndrome in the returning U.S. soldiers. In the words of Karl Bowman, president of the American Medical Association, they had become "embittered, distrustful, irritated" and harbored a suspicion that they had been "wasting their time defending such a country."[28]

Some Americans, of course, felt that the solution was to simply buck up and bear it. The colonel who suspected that neurosis was really just a "two-bit word for being yellow" continued to speak for a broad swath of Americans, who simply accepted that psychic pain and unhappiness were normal, perhaps necessary, components of life. Americans who had conquered the frontier a generation or two earlier had endured extraordinary hardships, including illness, loneliness, hunger, and deprivation, and they frequently lost children, spouses, and siblings along the way. Had they stopped after each setback and loss to complain or to indulge in self-pity, the West would not have been won, and the wilderness would have gone untamed.

But a growing number felt that this attitude was obsolete. People did not choose to suffer depression; they suffered it because they had no choice. With breakthroughs in the worlds of psychiatry, psychology, social work, and psychiatric nursing, the nation stood on the brink of a new era in which mental illness might be cured and unbearable misery alleviated. Martin Gumpert, a New York physician and author, called for a national commitment to building a "system of mental hygiene" and a "thorough investigation of social behavior by scientific psychological methods."[29] William Menninger urged Americans to find hope in medicine's "Cinderella, psychiatry" which offered its "therapeutic effort to a world full of unhappiness and maladjustment."[30] And even some elected representatives began to wonder whether the government should have a substantially larger role in bringing modern mental health care to the American people.

Training Psychiatrists

The largest barrier to making psychotherapy more available to Americans was the shortage of trained professionals. Psychiatrists—medical doctors who had undergone advanced formal training in psychiatry to the point of board certification—were so scarce as to be an oddity. Fewer than half of the nation's medical schools had a full-time psychiatrist on faculty, and the total time devoted to psychiatric education in the general medical school curriculum was probably fewer than six hours.[31] In 1946, the American Psychiatric Association had under 4,300 members, and of these, as many as half worked full-time in administrative positions in state psychiatric hospitals, leaving them unavailable to treat patients. While there were 1,200 residency openings for training in psychiatry, William Menninger deemed many of these training programs, perhaps a third, to be "woefully inadequate," leaving only 900 viable spots in the three-year programs. This meager number of annual graduates of psychiatry programs could barely replace those psychiatrists lost each year to death or retirement, much less provide the material for future growth. "This psychotherapeutic reality is, indeed, grotesque," Martin Gumpert wrote in 1946. "Millions of people need treatment, and only a few thousands can get it—at an exorbitant price and a tremendous sacrifice of time."[32]

How many psychiatrists did the country really need? Nobody knew for sure. Neither the profession nor the government had yet been able to produce a reliable figure for the true number of neurotic Americans needing treatment, nor was there agreement over the best way to combine professional expertise to produce the best clinical benefit. Did

every neurotic need to see a psychiatrist, or could a psychologist or social worker handle certain cases if closely supervised? Did psychiatrists
need to undergo analytic training, which entailed a further three to four
years beyond completion of residency? And did patients really need
to see their therapists for the standard 300 to 500 hours dictated by
the Freudians, or could they get reasonable results with fewer hours
of engagement? These questions weighed on the minds of mental
health planners in the years after the war, and well-intentioned professionals had a hard time reaching consensus. Psychiatric leaders
thought between 15,000 and 20,000 psychiatrists would be adequate,
but the National Health Advisory Council thought that 40,000 might
be optimal. [33]

Some trends were already moving in an upward direction. The number of medical school graduates choosing psychiatric training had grown
sharply during the World War II rising from 3 percent to 7 percent of all
new doctors. [34] The U.S. Congress intervened in 1946 by passing the
National Mental Health Act, which appropriated $7.5 million for in-
creased research in mental illness and for increased training of both psychiatrists and psychologists. [35] And the Veterans Administration (VA),
faced with hundreds of thousands of discharged soldiers badly in need
of counseling, psychotherapy, and general psychological support in re-
adjusting to civilian life, substantially increased its own training efforts
in the mental health professions. Many VA hospitals established training
relationships with nearby medical schools in the years after the war, with
the specific intention of creating psychiatry residency slots and training
opportunities for clinical psychologists. By 1950, VA hospitals had established five times as many psychiatric residency positions as had existed
in the system in the years preceding World War II. [36]

One question that arose frequently was the appropriate level of training for effective psychiatric practice. The standard in the late 1940s was
a two-year internship in general medicine, followed by a three-year res-

idency in psychiatry. (And these five years followed an initial four years in medical school to earn the M.D. degree.) The most hard-core Freudians, of course, insisted that this was only the barest minimum, and that any physician who attempted to practice psychotherapy without having undergone a complete training analysis was condemned to clinical incompetence, if not outright negligence. Frieda Fromm-Reichmann, for example, who made her career at the analytically oriented Chestnut Lodge in Rockville, Maryland, declared that "unless the psychiatrist is widely aware of his own interpersonal processes so that he can hide them for the benefit of the patient in their interpersonal therapeutic dealings with each other, no successful psychotherapy can eventuate." Such awareness, in Fromm-Reichmann's opinion, could come about only through analysis. She admitted to her readers that she had been relieved when she became "acquainted with the tools furnished by Freud," and that prior to Freud's discoveries, "psychiatrists had been in the dark both to the detriment of their patients and to the disadvantage of their professional self-respect."[37]

The Menninger Clinic, the Menninger brothers' psychiatric hospital in Topeka, Kansas, trained virtually all of its residents in Freudian technique, and subjected them to extensive psychological screening before admitting them to the program. The clinic's medical directors began to question their own strict psychological standards, however, when a VA-sponsored study showed that their initial screening tests did not predict whether a resident would complete the training program or thereafter be able to maintain a successful psychiatric practice. Many students who tested well later dropped out or upon completion of training proved ineffective in their professional work. VA researchers suggested that a broader spectrum of applicants should be accepted to the program, with one wag pointing out that some major contributions to psychoanalysis had been made by "distinctly abnormal people."[38]

But others, including William Menninger, questioned the analytic orientation entirely. Even as his eponymous clinic continued to preach the benefits of orthodox analysis, Menninger questioned the morality of persevering in an enterprise that could treat only six to eight patients per day when so many hundreds of thousands were going untreated and the shortfall of professionals was so great. Transformed by his wartime experiences, the most famous psychiatrist in the country derided himself and his colleagues for "talking our jargon and accepting the trickle of all comers for our ranks." In a major piece in the profession's flagship organ, the *American Journal of Psychiatry,* he urged his colleagues to devote their efforts to "helping the average man on the street." The war had exposed an "international psychosis" which had nothing to do with the Oedipus complex, and the profession needed to turn its attentions to "individual struggles, community needs, state and national problems."[39]

Menninger felt that psychiatry, rather than burrowing into an increasingly arcane and insular world of abstract concepts and jargon, needed to become more accessible and welcoming. Since the nation could never possibly train all of the psychiatrists it would need, it needed to better teach basic psychiatric diagnosis and treatment to general physicians, so they could either collaborate with trained psychiatrists or offer first-line treatment on their own. Students in medical school needed to be introduced to psychiatric ideas so that they could enter their careers better informed about the psychiatric components of ordinary health and disease. Menninger spoke urgently to his colleagues: "We must clarify our concepts; we must overcome our isolation from medicine and surgery; we must develop a system and a role in medical school that encourages the better students to become identified with us."[40]

Others agreed. Peter Denker, a psychiatrist at Bellevue Hospital in New York, examined 1,500 cases of crippling neuroses treated by a mixture of psychiatrists, psychologists, and general practitioners. To his surprise he detected no difference in success rates posted by the three groups. If anything, the general practitioners had been slightly more successful, reporting that 65 percent of their cases were "apparently cured" versus only 63 percent of the cases treated by psychiatrists. According to his study, the most important variable was the individual physician's personality and effort rather than a particular school of thought or type of training.[41] And no less an authority than Franz Alexander, a professor of psychiatry at the University of Chicago and one of the most eminent figures in postwar American psychiatry, considered the possible deleterious effect of analytic treatment. He reasoned that if the intensity of the analytic relationship fostered "anxious dependence" upon the analyst, a less intensive therapeutic modality might actually accelerate cure.[42]

The problem with these conjectures was that virtually none were backed by data. Denker's study relied on the physicians themselves reporting results, and it was quite possible that the lower success rates reported by the psychiatrists simply reflected their own higher criteria for what constituted a successful treatment. Similarly, Fromm-Reichmann's insistence on the centrality of analytic training to effective psychotherapy practice reflected her own experience, which may well have been real. What was needed was a set of standards, verified by a disinterested third party, that psychiatrists could use to grade neuroses and establish baselines at both the beginning and the end of treatment. But in 1947 none of the mental health professions had produced a standard set of symptoms by which to diagnose and grade psychiatric patients, and certainly none had established criteria and systems by which to reliably measure results. Many individuals within the mental health community who had treated shell-shocked victims of the war understood that the developments of psychiatry in the 1920s and 1930s were wholly inadequate to address the magnitude of the challenges that lay before them in the next decade.

Psychiatric Social Workers

Social work, too, had been transformed by World War II. As had happened during World War I, social workers were pressed into service to calm terrified soldiers, help reacclimate shell-shocked veterans to civilian life, and generally assist psychiatrists in their work treating the war's psychological victims. Military psychiatric social workers invented their own roles in World War II, "fumbling as to their place" but committed generally to the ideals of helpfulness and kindness in a world which seemed to lack both.[43] Social workers sometimes did little more than simply listen, but for battle-weary soldiers, this may have been the most welcome of gifts. "Perhaps for the first time since the soldier has been in the Army, he has an opportunity to talk to a sympathetic listener and be recognized as an individual," reported one social worker returning from the front.[44] And in an urgent effort to recruit new psychiatric social workers to serve recently discharged veterans, the American Red Cross proclaimed in its newsletter that for these men "only the shooting is over." The psychiatric social worker, by virtue of her training, could spell the difference between an alienated, shell-shocked veteran and a productive citizen. "A discharged veteran may return home recalcitrant and maladjusted but her [the social worker's] skill can help him take his place as a useful and happy citizen in a land for which he fought so hard."[45]

The war provided an opportunity for a nascent and still pliable profession to coalesce around several clearly defined principles and goals. The first psychiatric social workers were drawn from the ranks of graduates of Smith College's School of Social Work and prompted by the school's directors Mary Jarrett and Dr. Elmer Southard to undertake internships at the Boston Psychopathic Hospital in the years from 1907 to 1910. With support from the Russell Sage Foundation of New York, several of these early psychiatric social workers engaged in further training in hospitals and child guidance clinics, while graduates of the New

York School of Social Work began to pursue similar opportunities.[46] William Allan Neilson, president of Smith College, noted of these early participants, "It was clearly understood from the beginning that we were not making half-doctors. These women were to be aides to experts … intelligent cooperators with the psychiatric doctors."[47]

From the beginning, psychiatric social workers viewed themselves as adjunct to psychiatrists, either in the form of support staff or as independent ancillary professionals who could complement the ego-focused work of analytically trained psychiatrists. With several social work schools incorporating mental hygiene classes into their curricula in the 1920s, social work students learned that the psychological instability of the individual was as important a component of social disharmony as poverty, deprivation, ignorance, and general filth. And while the early psychiatric social workers in no way saw themselves practicing psychotherapy, they did understand that therapy for certain individual clients was probably an important part of the social adjustment.[48]

Adolf Meyer's efforts after 1915 to move psychiatry toward a more holistic understanding of mental health and hygiene inadvertently opened up mental health to social work. Social work's roots were in community aid, having started as part of the effort to integrate new immigrants into American life, and social workers played an essential role in strengthening communal life, particularly in urban areas. Meyer's argument that psychiatrists should "trace the plain life history of a person" and thus create "a record of the main events of the life of the whole bundle of organs, that is, 'the individual as a whole,'" was a clarion call for social work to become more intimately involved in mental hygiene, and by association in psychotherapy.[49]

But the problem for psychiatric social work was how to define itself. It was not psychiatry; that much was certain. Psychiatrists, after all, were medical doctors who specialized in diseases of the mind, whereas social workers were, well, what exactly? At the genesis of the profession, social workers were just that: concerned people who worked with others

within a *social* context, teaching people how to get along with one another—within their families, neighborhoods, cities, churches, and countries. They taught life skills, counseled new immigrants on the basics of
comportment, deportment, cleanliness, manners, temperance, and life
habits. Grounded in morality, social work arrived in tandem with the
great social improvement movements of the early twentieth century
such as temperance and YMCAs.

But *psychiatric* social work implied an emphasis on the individual
rather than the community. Psychiatric social workers through the
1930s struggled to find the right role for themselves in working within
a psychiatric setting without become junior psychiatrists, leading to several decades of professional ambivalence. "We have been confused in the
area of our job and its relationship to psychiatry and the patients with
whom we deal, reluctant to think alone, not sure that we have enough
to give that may be accurate or pertinent to our field," Leona Hambrecht, president of the American Association of Psychiatric Social
Workers, wrote in 1940.[50] And if the social work president could not
define precisely what her colleagues did and did not do, nobody else
could either. Mildred Scoville, an earlier president of the association,
could assert little more than that psychiatric social work consisted of
"social case work established within psychiatric agencies," and even
more vaguely, that psychiatric social work was "social case work in
whatever field whose practitioners have at their command an adequate
working of mental hygiene."[51]

So what were they doing, exactly? They were dealing with "clients"
(as opposed to patients), usually as an adjunct to a psychiatrist. Initially
they facilitated the client's entry to a mental hygiene clinic or child
guidance clinic, sometimes doing little more than filling out the correct
forms or making sure that the client was placed with the correct psychiatrist. But soon they began speaking at length with the clients, trying
to understand what sort of environmental conflicts were blocking the
clients' ability to live fully within the constraints of their surroundings.

And conversations about social conflicts inevitably led to conversations about fears, anxieties, disgust, remorse, and the whole panoply of feelings which psychiatrists tended to discuss with their patients when conducting psychotherapy. While not trained in psychotherapy, many social workers, like Sullivan's psychiatric nurses, possessed intrinsic interpersonal skills which allowed them empathize with their clients and be taken into their confidence. In short, psychiatric social workers were turning into psychotherapists.

As early as the mid 1930s, psychiatric social workers began to acknowledge that they were, in fact, practicing psychotherapy, albeit perhaps not with the same degree of expertise as trained psychiatrists. "In an ideal relationship between psychiatrist and psychiatric social worker," Sarah Swift of the Institute for Child Guidance wrote, "the work of the two would be so closely integrated that the client could accept both as sources of help without making one or the other the sole focus of his emerging emotional needs."[52] Such an assertion blurred the lines between social worker and psychiatrist, and indicated the desire of at least some social workers to erase the line entirely. "As social case work is more vitally related to psychiatry, the line of demarcation between the two becomes less clearly defined," Swift offered.[53] Other social workers tried without success to maintain some boundary between the two professions, for fear of forfeiting the integrity of the social work profession or, perhaps, in a calculated move to assuage psychiatrists' turf concerns and disclaim any ambition to displace the psychiatrists. Social workers participating in a roundtable discussion in the late 1930s, for example, explained that "exploration of the inner world" of the patient was the exclusive domain of the psychiatrist, and that the social worker should avoid approaching the patient on this level in an effort to "avoid injuring the transference."[54]

By 1947, however, some social workers had grown weary of the farce. Psychiatric social workers were psychotherapists, plain and simple, and the tortured explanations of why they were not carried as much weight as the Flat Earthers arguing their worldview in the age of Galileo. "Again the problem with labels comes up," wrote the social work committee of the Group for the Advancement of Psychiatry (GAP). "For example: If the p.s.w.er works with the patient (child)—it's called psychotherapy; if the p.s.w.er works with the mother—it's not called psychotherapy; if the psychiatrist works with the mother—it's called psychotherapy. In other words: what the doctor does is always psychotherapy; what the p.s.w.er does may or may not be."[55] In another session of the GAP group, social workers concluded that the profession had "grown into" its present role, and that a social worker might "perform all work done with the child and parent, except a very neurotic child 'who needs close to analytic therapy.' "[56] Social workers could do everything that a psychiatrist could do except for traditional psychoanalysis. Notably, the analytic training institutes in 1947 continued to exclude all but a very few non-M.D.s from their training ranks.

Some social workers went as far as suggesting that social workers might be *better* than psychiatrists at conducting psychotherapy. Participants at a conference on social work therapy at the Southard School in Boston concluded that for psychotherapy with children, where the ability to understand the child's world was central to understanding the sorts of emotional conflicts he might be experiencing, social workers were more empathetic, more "ready to participate in the child's environment." Social workers were more likely to try to help the child adapt to his environment (over which the child presumably had little control), whereas psychiatrists tended to try to change the environment itself—a frequently futile undertaking.[57]

In fact, given the progressive strain in American psychiatry as articulated by Sullivan, Horney, and their colleagues, an ability to conceive the whole of the patient's life experience, including social networks, cultural context, and life trajectory, necessitated a psychotherapist with a more holistic orientation. As early as 1929, Marion Kenworthy, director of the department of mental hygiene at the New York (later Columbia)

School of Social Work, had written that social workers needed to "develop a capacity to view the intellectual growth and educational experience of the individual as a continuous and progressive process."[58] Social workers were trained, above all, to listen and to empathize, and to try to understand the relationship of the patient to his or her social context. They were, after all, *social* workers. Psychiatrists, by contrast, grounded their training in a medical model; there was health and there was sickness, and sickness tended to have a pathogenic cause. Even when psychiatrists had undergone psychoanalytic training, they still tended to view a patient as just that: a patient, whose lack of health must be rooted in a cause that could be discovered and potentially negated. "The social case worker deals with a wide range of social and personal problems ... unemployment, poor housing, need for money, need for medical care, need for help in planning care of children, need for help with disturbing inter-personal relationships," declared GAP's social work committee in 1948. The effective social worker must therefore "know the tension in their lives" if she was to be of any use.[59]

Was this psychotherapy? Freud had strenuously resisted the notion that psychoanalysis was simply an ordinary conversation, albeit one characterized by unusual candor. In Freud's view, the analytic relationship was a unique one, predicated on the absolute aloofness of the analyst, who alone could induce the transference phenomenon so vital to analytic success. For Freud, psychoanalysis was supposed to be devoid of context, the only relevant facts being those buried in the unconscious. And even as psychoanalysis was transformed under the onslaught of American pragmatism, it maintained its orientation toward transference, repression, and catharsis. Sullivan was willing to acknowledge the usefulness of kindly psychiatric nurses, and Horney admitted that life events beyond infancy could play significant roles in the formation of repressed traumas in the unconscious, but no psychoanalysts by 1947, and few analytically oriented psychiatrists, were willing to admit that psychotherapy was simply an empathetic conversation.

The social workers, by contrast, were suggesting that empathy was the major precursor to successful therapy. While the unconscious might or might not exist, and while transference might or might not happen, the social worker could produce results by *understanding* the patient and his world. The director of the Wilder Child Guidance Clinic in St. Paul wrote in 1948 that the problems of most children treated in clinics were not the "material studied in psychiatric hospitals." Rather, they were problems resulting from "home, school, neighborhood," because of "poverty, stupidity, cruelty, neglect, prejudice, and disease."[60] Marion Kenworthy had presciently warned in her 1929 treatise that effective casework could transpire only when the client felt that his "intimate personal affairs are safe," and that those who could "convey this impression" to their clients "had the beginnings of leadership."[61] But by 1948, data about comparative success rates posted by social workers and psychiatrists was still scarce and unreliable. A war of words was beginning, but one in which neither side had good empirical evidence to fall back on.

Psychologists

Clinical psychology, too, got a pop from the war. Like psychiatric social work, the profession had been ambiguously defined through the 1930s, but was forced to remake itself as a viable clinical profession by the military's dire need for mental health professionals during the war years. Like psychiatric social work, it struggled to define itself in the shadow of psychiatry, but unlike social work it started from the terra firma of scientific grounding, doctoral level preparation, and an established history of professional standards and academic rigor.

Psychology was already fairly old at the time of America's entry to World War II; William James had been appointed the nation's first professor of psychology at Harvard University in 1876, and over the subsequent fifty years the discipline had carved out an academic expertise for itself in measuring and studying mental function. The academic discipline turned into a viable profession in the early decades of the twentieth century as a variety of clients—school systems, the army, the U.S. government, employers, the court system—called upon psychologists to conduct testing of potential recruits, employees, immigrants, and prisoners.

Unlike social work, which had always rested on vague professional underpinnings and morphed quickly and easily into new roles as the situation demanded, psychology was more clearly defined. Psychologists went to nationally known universities for training at the doctoral level, published their extensive research in a variety of academic journals, and established professional norms for administering, scoring, and interpreting psychological tests. If quantification was the gold standard for admission to the lofty club of "hard" sciences, then psychology, more than any other social science, achieved that standard. By 1920, the profession drew on a dizzying variety of instruments to measure intelligence, emotional stability, professional proclivity, life outlook, and cultural orientation. Such tests as the Stanford-Binet and Wechsler-Bellevue intelligence tests, and the Rorschach personality test, all in wide use by 1920, would come to exemplify the profession's work for a half century.

The Rorschach test would prove to be a catalyst for a profession poised at the edge of clinical intervention. Invented in 1911 by Hermann Rorschach, a Swiss psychiatrist, the test consisted of ten amorphous inkblots, each symmetrical about a vertical axis. The tester would show the inkblots to the client, who would interpret each image without any prompting or feedback. Psychologists were trained to interpret the response so as to gain insight into the psychological orientation and health of the subject. These interpretations were then used to judge the patient's suitability for a particular job or a particular psychiatric treatment.

The Rorschach test was pivotal to the profession of psychology because it required interpretation. While other tests, particularly the intelligence tests, produced clear numerical scores, the Rorschach tests required that the tester, in most cases a psychologist, actively interpret the subject's responses to produce a score. Such interpretation drew the psychologist from his aloof scientific post and required him to make independent judgments about his subject's emotional health and makeup. This act of interpretation pulled psychologists into a more dynamic relationship with their subjects and placed them a step closer to providing clinical intervention.

A few psychologists began conducting psychotherapy during the 1930s, particularly within child guidance clinics, but they remained a distinct minority. In 1939, psychologists listed psychotherapy as only their sixth most frequent activity in child guidance clinics, and over a third of such psychologists failed to list it entirely. A survey a year later of the 2,739 members of the American Psychological Association revealed that only 272 held positions which they described as predominantly clinical. In a historical appraisal, Sol Garfield, a clinical psychologist based in St. Louis, remarked of the profession that when he was practicing clinical psychology in the 1930s, the profession's future "did not look particularly bright," and that its involvement in psychotherapy was "unpredictable."[62]

A few psychologists, among them Carl Rogers of the University of Chicago, wrote influential treatises on clinical technique during the 1930s, but clinical activity remained a marginal activity for psychologists until after World War II, when the Veterans Administration faced an overwhelming influx of psychoneurotic veterans and a significant shortage of clinical professionals trained to treat them. Paul Hawley, the chief medical director of the VA, lobbied for expansion in all of the mental health professions, despite his own psychiatric background. While addressing the American Psychological Association in 1946, he admitted, "We cannot hope to do it adequately unless we have the active help of all sciences and professions which can make contributions."[63] At that time, the VA was treating 44,000 psychiatric patients, but only 30,000 patients of all other types.[64]

Hawley's great contribution lay in recognizing that not only could the VA system employ clinical psychologists to help ease its shortage of trained therapists, but it could train them as well. In the same 1946 speech he pledged to create a "nation-wide training program in clinical psychology" to be closely allied with Ph.D. programs and medical schools around the country. The program would place graduate students into supervised internships and residencies, similar to the postgraduate medical training model, and would ideally employ some of its more talented graduates upon completion of the program. Within a decade of the announcement, the VA system was employing 600 clinical psychologists and a further 65 vocational psychologists. This was three times the number of self-described clinical psychologists in existence in the country in 1940.[65]

From 1945 until 1950, clinical psychology struggled to define itself as a profession distinct from psychiatry and psychiatric social work. With its roots in experimental psychology, it had a firmer foundation from which to draw its parameters, yet the danger was that it would be overwhelmed by the psychiatric inclination to use talk as a vehicle to get at the unconscious. One astute watcher noted the similarities between clinical psychology and optometry (of all things), writing that "in some respects their cases are similar. Both function in fields that are adjacent to medical practice."[66] Although psychologists wished to distance themselves from their medical brethren, they strongly declined joining forces with their co-therapists in social work. Quantitative psychologists saw social work as too loose, too undisciplined, and too feminine a pursuit, yet they could hardly avoid the fact that in day-to-day practice, the techniques of the two professions appeared suspiciously similar. The defensive psychologists sought to distinguish themselves with an appeal to scientific rigor: "The psychiatric social worker is trained to accept assumptions about human behavior whereas the clinical psychologist is taught to question almost any assumption," stated one psychologist in the late 1940s.[67] But such sweeping generalizations were born more of hope than observations as psychologists struggled to define their field.

The clinical psychologists were carving out their own niche. Their training substantially differed from that of either psychiatrists or social workers, laden with courses in statistical and experimental methods and requiring an extended independent research project. The psychologists tended to be much more firmly grounded in theories of the mind ("personality and psychodynamics") and theoretical structures of the psyche based at least in part on decades of quantitative studies.[68] They rejected psychiatry's increasing reliance on analytical ideas and constructs, and instead insisted on practicing a more hands-on, pragmatic sort of therapy. Psychologists were trained in *measurement*, and the Freudian approach to therapy was simply not compatible with objective outcomes research. Language, the primary tool of psychotherapy, was too amorphous to satisfy the psychologists with their quantitative rigor. "If you are helping an adult to overcome a speech defect, you do not try to regress him to a speechless infantile level and then retrain his speech from the beginning," Laurence Shaffer, a psychologist at Columbia University's Teachers College, said in 1947.[69] At a gathering of clinical psychologists in 1947, Shaffer stressed the importance of forging their own therapeutic approach: "Only by understanding therapy, as well as by practicing therapy, can clinical psychology meet its new opportunities and its new obligations to serve human welfare."[70]

Not surprisingly, many psychiatrists viewed psychology's movement into therapy with hostility. They not only worried about more competition for a limited pool of private patients, but they held a certain contempt for psychologists, who had not gone through the same long years of medical school and residency training in preparation for using psychotherapy to treat patients. The fact that psychologists actively sought to distance themselves from the medical and Freudian idioms added insult; at least if the psychologists were going to poach psychiatric patients, they should have the decency to mimic psychiatric practice. As early as 1930, long before clinical psychologists treated significant numbers of psychotherapy patients, Karl Menninger, brother of William and a prominent psychiatrist in his own right, derided clinical psychologists as mere intelligence testers: "When they discovered tests a few years ago which in a general way measured the amount of intelligence a person has, and began applying these tests to people far and wide, they found out that many people had fewer brains than had been supposed. Accordingly they began to suspect that a person who got into trouble did so because he hadn't enough brains to keep out of trouble."[71]

Other prominent psychiatrists were equally dismissive. Daniel Blain, chief of the neuropsychiatry division of the VA, stated in 1946 that "very few psychologists can be found with the competence to do therapy on their own responsibility," and that while a psychologist could be a "valuable team member," he was "least trained and experienced" in giving psychotherapy.[72] William Menninger, despite his enthusiasm for expanding the ranks of mental health clinicians of all types, regarded clinical psychological training as second rate compared to psychiatric training, and further felt that many clinical psychologists had simply "picked up" their skills in haphazard fashion. Nonetheless, Menninger warned his fellow psychiatrists in 1947 that a very large percentage of the clinical and social psychologists were "*doing* treatment."[73]

By the early 1950s, psychiatrists had become more aggressive in defending their turf, which was being rapidly encroached upon. They accused psychologists of lacking the requisite medical training to understand the organic roots of many mental illnesses (a marked turn from Freudian orthodoxy, which tended to discount the organic and elevate the psychological), lacking the proper therapeutic perspective to interact empathetically with patients, and lacking the "total therapeutic armamentarium" of physicians.[74] In late 1952, the psychiatrists tried a new tactic and lobbied heavily for a proposed bill in the New York legislature that defined medicine as "diagnosis and treatment of all physical and mental conditions," which, if written into law, would allow psychiatrists to sue psychologists for practicing medicine without a license. The bill died in committee, though the strategy would be used for decades by psychiatrists.[75]

How different were psychiatrists and psychologists when practicing psychotherapy? Little data exists for the late 1940s for therapeutic approaches broken down by professional orientation, though we know that the preponderance of American psychoanalysts at that time held the M.D. degree. Medical school was very different from graduate programs in psychology, being highly oriented toward anatomy, physiology, and pharmacology, while psychology maintained its roots in quantitative measurement and analysis. Residency training for psychiatrists, too, was quite different from the supervised therapeutic sessions of the young psychological intern, as it tended to be based in hospitals and focused on psychoses. We do not know whether or not psychiatrists and psychologists really worked differently once they entered the private practice of counseling functional neurotics. Studies suggest that neither profession could claim a significantly greater success rate, but success itself was defined by the practitioners and not checked by disinterested observers.

We do know, however, that in 1946, psychiatrists could do several things which psychologists could not. They could prescribe medication and shock treatment. They could admit patients to the hospital. And in a few drastic cases, they could perform surgery on the brain. In later decades, after pharmaceutical companies had developed multiple effective antidepressive and antipsychotic medications, these distinctions would have profound effects on the two competing professions. In 1946, when the first antidepressant and antipsychotic agents were still a decade away, the distinction was less significant, though still important in the areas of shock treatment and, to a lesser extent, psychosurgery.

Shock and Surgery

Psychiatrists had been aware for some time that schizophrenic patients afflicted with epilepsy improved after a seizure. In 1934 Ladislas Meduna, a Hungarian neurologist, induced a seizure in a psychiatric patient using metrazol, a highly potent convulsive agent, and thus introduced the practice of convulsive-irritative therapy. Two Italian psychiatrists, Ugo Cerletti and Lucino Bini, refined the technique in 1937 by placing two electrodes on a patient's temples and passing an electrical current through his brain. At almost the same time, Manfred Sakel induced convulsions in a patient by injecting him with a high dose of insulin, thus producing a hypoglycemic coma. All three methods were first performed in the United States in the late 1930s, first on schizophrenics and later on depressives. By 1945, the insulin and electroshock procedures were in wide use in American psychiatric hospitals.[76]

Psychiatrists were ambivalent about the rise of shock therapy. Most recognized, from an early point, that it was potentially beneficial in some cases. "Only a stupid person would decry shock therapy," offered Charles Burlingame, a psychiatrist at the Institute for Living in Hartford, Connecticut.[77] When it worked, the therapy worked quickly and left few side effects. There was some danger in the actual administration of the therapy—the convulsions, if too strong, could lead to broken bones and teeth, a bitten tongue, sore muscles—but this simply demanded research in dosage and application techniques. A few patients complained of some memory loss, though this usually appeared to be short-term. Many patients, particularly those who had suffered severe, prolonged, and crippling depression, improved dramatically.

On the other hand, the treatment did not seem particularly effective in cases of schizophrenia, and early skeptics criticized Sakel for proclaiming it so. Winfred Overholser, a prominent psychiatrist in Massachusetts, wrote in 1937 that "this is another instance in which a form of treatment which has been effective in some cases, has been popularized and prematurely hailed as a panacea," while Burlingame hastened to temper his enthusiasm with the warning that "one should not condone [its use] for everything from an ingrowing toenail to baldness."[78] The biggest problem with shock therapy was that nobody understood how it worked, or even had any reasonable theory to explain it. Clearly it "rewired" the brain in some manner, but since neither psychiatry nor neurology at the time understood the basic anatomical structure of the brain, much less the biochemical basis of mood, the phenomenon was a puzzle. Moreover, the utter physicality of the regimen undermined virtually all working hypotheses regarding the basis of mood, from Freud's theory of the unconscious to Sullivan's theory of interpersonal frustrations. The idea of a completely physiological basis of mood was so radical as to be risible, yet nobody could explain the efficacy of shock therapy without it.

Far more troubling, and controversial, was the advent of psychosurgery. In 1935, Egas Moniz, a Portuguese neurologist, developed a surgical technique to separate the thalamus from the prefrontal cortex of the brain. Initially called a *leucotomy*, the operation was intended to destroy small areas of the frontal lobes in an effort to alleviate horrendous symptoms of anxiety, obsessiveness, and schizophrenia. Moniz based his work, in part, on observations of soldiers who had sustained brain injuries during World War I. Those who had sustained particular damage to the frontal lobes often acquired an odd set of behaviors characterized by "hilarity, euphoria, and childishness," in the words of Jack Pressman, a historian of psychosurgery.[79] The procedure, while drastic, seemed to promise some hope to the most insoluble of cases. While it did compromise the patient's intellectual functions and dim the patient's emotional responses, it brought relief in some cases. "Even after the extirpation of the two frontal lobes there remains a psychic life which, although deficient, is nevertheless appreciably better than that of the majority of the insane," Moniz wrote.[80]

Moniz's work was seized upon by an American neurologist named

Walter Freeman. After purchasing a leucotome (the ice pick–like instrument that Moniz had used to perform his early procedure) from a French instrument maker, Freeman performed the first American leucotomy on a middle-aged woman who had complained of agitating, obsessional, and suicidal thoughts, and growing distress, in 1936. When the patient waked four hours later, she described herself as no longer sad, and as incapable of remembering her old fears. Freeman wrote, "I knew from the first that there was a stroke at the fundamental aspect of the personality, that part that was responsible for much of the misery that afflicts man."[81] Within a month, Freeman had performed five more such procedures, and within a year a dozen more. Gathering professional momentum, he modified the procedure, invented new tools, and began to travel the country in search of patients on whom he could deliver relief, eventually taking to working in a traveling surgical van and at one point demonstrating his ability to perform leucotomies (or *lobotomies*, as Freeman's modified procedure was called) on both sides of the brain at once, grasping a leucotome in each hand. By the end of his career, he had performed 2,500 lobotomies, and declared lobotomy to be the "method of choice in institutional practice."[82]

Most psychiatrists and neurologists were appalled. The procedure seemed crude and destructive, "not an operation but a mutilation," one surgeon observed. Loyal Davis, one of the preeminent neurosurgeons in Chicago (and later, Ronald Reagan's father-in-law), noted that Freeman's description of his work "gives one's surgical conscience a slight twinge."[83] While the procedure did offer relief to some agitated depressive patients, it did not offer much relief to schizophrenics, as had first been claimed. Out of 228 hospital patients in West Virginia who had undergone the procedure in a flurry of surgical activity in 1952, only 86 were discharged, and most of these to supervised living situations.[84] One psychologist in California responded furiously to lobotomists' claims of emptying hospital beds: "Decapitation, I submit, is equally effective in emptying hospital beds and every bit as much of a 'cure.' "[85]

Both shock and psychosurgery raised troubling issues for psychiatry. The profession regarded itself as superior to social work and psychology in counseling mental patients, due to its grounding in the medical sciences, rather than the social sciences. Unlike practitioners from its two competing professions, psychiatrists could medicate, hospitalize, and perform surgical procedures. Yet faced with two of the more promising, if controversial, medical innovations, the profession responded with ambivalence. The mysteriousness of shock and the crudeness of lobotomy gave pause to a profession immersed in ego-centered and interpersonal theories of the mind and psyche, yet it was precisely these types of treatments (though not necessarily these two specific treatments) that in theory elevated psychiatry to a privileged perch in mental health care.

The situation demanded more research. In 1947, the nation was investing scarcely any funds in psychiatric research: approximately one penny for every $65 invested in medical research. Although the recently enacted National Mental Health Act promised to greatly increase this sum (in part through the establishment of the National Institute of Mental Health), the scientific discoveries would not be forthcoming for some time. In the empirical vacuum, no one mental health profession could credibly claim superiority over the other two, and nor was any one fully comfortable explaining what, exactly, set it apart. For all that social workers claimed a *social* grounding and psychologists claimed a *psychometric* grounding and psychiatrists claimed a *medical* grounding, nobody was sure exactly how this played out in the counseling room. Did the professions really provide psychotherapy differently, and if so, did it make a difference in outcomes and success? Early data suggested not, but there was so little, and it was so unreliable that it could scarcely be relied upon. Moreover, nobody knew how closely the therapy provided in private sessions actually comported with the claimed techniques of the practitioner. One therapist could claim to be an orthodox Freudian, another an empathic humanist, another a facilitator of interpersonal growth, but no one knew for sure whether the three actually interacted differently with their patients. Franz Alexander noted a few years later that all knowledge of psychological processes during treatment had been derived from the records and recollections of the therapist, "who, as a participant observer, cannot hope to be objective about his own reactions."[86]

Mental health professionals did find a few areas of agreement in 1949: There ought to be more trained therapists treating patients; they ought to be brought in earlier in the life of a mental patient rather than later; they ought to work together in some sort of modified team approach; and professionals in all fields could benefit from more research. Beyond that, the ever-growing psychotherapy professions could find little common ground.

CHAPTER 4

Thinking

Humanism

The growth of psychotherapy after the war brought about a cascade of new ideas in the following decade. Hundreds of newly trained psycho-therapists from a variety of training backgrounds experimented with their own different therapeutic techniques and began to create new "schools" of therapy. Although many of these approaches differed little from existing techniques, a few stood out for their far-reaching implications in delivering treatment: One new technique emphasized cognitive processes over emotional processes, for example, and another required behavioral interventions instead of psychological interventions. Some of these new schools would die off as soon as their founders lost interest, but others would attract broad ranks of followers who would perpetu-ate the ideas and teachings of the school long after the founder had moved on or had passed away.

One of the most prominent new approaches to arise in the early 1950s was Carl Rogers's "client-centered therapy," the forerunner of a number of closely related therapeutic approaches that described them-selves as "humanistic." Client-centered therapy required the therapist to reduce his role in the therapeutic relationship to one of sympathetic and nonjudgmental listener, whose greatest contribution to the mental health of the client was to "hear" him, or in Rogers's terms, to make sure that the client "experienced himself as *received*."[1] For Rogers, the primary goal of the therapist was to reassure the client that his feelings were valid, and this was best achieved through careful listening, repeatedly restating the client's articulated feelings, and reassuring him as to the *reality* of these feelings. In Rogers's scheme, feelings were neither good nor bad, they simply existed, and neuroses were caused primarily by the client's perception that his feelings were unwelcome by family, friends, and society generally. In hiding these invalidated feelings, the client denied a crucial aspect of himself and thus lived a reduced and compromised life.

Rogerian therapy was rooted in empathy, understanding, and acceptance. He wrote of his approach, "I have spent many hours listening to recorded therapeutic interviews—trying to listen as *naively* as possible."[2] Rogers viewed judgment as the source of much psychic harm and eschewed the Freudian penchant for analysis and interpretation (which implied judgment). In an interview in 1957, he insisted that he and his team "treat the client as a person, not as an object to be manipulated," and that they related to the client "not as scientist to an object of study...but as person to person."[3] It was this person-to-person quality of the therapy that set it apart and democratized it. If traditional psychotherapy, rooted in Freudian models, implied an asymmetry between therapist and patient (one aloof and omniscient, the other regressing toward infantile helplessness), Rogerian therapy proposed the symmetry of mutually sympathetic friends sitting down to chat. In modern parlance, Rogers assumed more than anything that people just wanted to feel heard.

Although very different from orthodox Freudian analysis, client-centered therapy did retain certain aspects of its continental precursor. For one, the process looked much the same as analysis. Although the client usually did not lie down, he did talk a lot in a very unstructured and rambling manner, resembling nothing so much as Freudian free association. And while the humanistic therapist did not try to impose analytical readings of the free associations onto the patient, he did listen carefully and at length to the ramblings in an effort to tease out previously unspoken feelings, after which he could validate them as real and meaningful. The therapist might not root his client's feelings in infancy, but the validating quality of the exchange did not differ so vastly with that offered by psychoanalysts. In both therapies, feelings were dominant, and thoughts secondary. Edward Shoben, Jr., an academic psychologist writing in the late 1940s, noted that humanistic psychology, above all, insisted that the "proper content of counseling contacts is the 'feelings' of the patient rather than his overt behavior or his intellectualized beliefs."[4]

The problem with the Rogerian approach was that beyond obviously exhibiting a deep empathy for the client (Rogers avoided the word "patient"), it was not clear precisely what the psychologist was supposed to do in these sessions. Rogers himself was most unhelpful in this regard, offering dreadfully vague and convoluted explanations of his theories and techniques in his extensive writing through the 1940s and 1950s. For example, in his widely read book *Client-Centered Therapy*, which he published in 1951, Rogers offered this description of his efforts to train new counselors in his technique:

> So it is with the counselor. As he finds new and more subtle ways of implementing his client-centered hypothesis, new meanings are poured into it by experience, and its depth is seen to be greater than was first supposed. As one counselor-in-training put it, "I hold about the same views I did a year ago, but they have so much more meaning for me."[5]

It is left to the reader to make sense of that! In another emphatic but vague description, Rogers offered this advice for those who desired to follow in his path:

The counselor says in effect, "To be of assistance to you I will put aside myself—the self of ordinary interaction—and enter into your world of perception as completely as I am able. I will become, in a sense, another self for you—an alter ego of your own attitudes and feelings—a safe opportunity for you to discern yourself more clearly, to experience yourself more truly and deeply, to choose more significantly."[6]

The passion in these passages is clear, but the technique is less so. Rogers followed firmly in the social work tradition of empathy, but dropped the traditional social work grounding in social functioning and admonition. More than anything, he had dropped shame from the menu of constructive human emotions. If Freud viewed much of the central human psychic drama as the triumph of the civilizing ego over the primitive id, Rogers believed that the superego of society endlessly squelched all in its path, driving people to become compromised and false. Clients did not need their therapist to expose the unconscious tensions underlying their neurotic selves; they needed, instead, to be taught to celebrate their uniqueness as individuals. The successful therapy client, in Rogers's telling, spoke thus: "Is it possible that I can really want to take care of myself, and make that a major purpose of my life? That means I'd have to deal with the whole world as if I were guardian of the most cherished and most wanted possession, that this I was between this precious me that I wanted to take care of and the whole world.... It's almost as if I loved myself—you know—that's strange—but it's true." The therapist sat by and applauded the insight.[7]

Rogers's philosophy of self-love may have been rooted in the austere Puritanism of his youth and the suppressive atmosphere in his home in turn-of-the-century Chicago. His father was a civil engineer, his mother a woman of "strong puritanical convictions," in the words of his biographer. They were supportive, but "masters of the art of subtle and loving control," and firm adherents to the Protestant work ethic.[8] Enrolling first in the agricultural college at the University of Wisconsin, Rogers migrated to history, theology, and ultimately to psychology, in which he earned his doctorate at Teacher's College in 1928.

Client-centered therapy seemed to contradict Rogers's roots in a psychology department within a school of education. Instead, his technique was a natural extension of the empathetic school of therapy promoted within social work schools (and applied in child guidance clinics), striving to accept each client on his own terms within the reality of his own life. It broke from social work, however, insofar as it refused to place mental health within a social context. While social workers aimed to help the client adjust to the realities of his situation, Rogerian therapists aimed to help the client adjust to the realities of his inner being, regardless of the social demands placed upon him. It was a therapy born of utopian optimism, "a pull toward wholeness," in the words of one Christian theologian, resting on an assumption of "our basic goodness."[9]

Non-Rogerians were contemptuous. One psychoanalyst in Chicago dismissed Rogerian therapy as "unsystematic, undisciplined and humanistic. [He] doesn't analyze and doesn't diagnose....To Rogers, that is fine."[10] Furthermore, Rogers promised effective therapy in far less time, at a far lower cost. Holding treatments to forty to fifty interviews (rather than the hundreds common in analysis), Rogers asked his clients at his clinic on the South Side of Chicago to pay what they wished—which was usually between $5 and $17 per hour. In later years, Rogers experimented with even shorter therapy regimens, capping treatment at twenty sessions, and ultimately he ventured into group therapy in the 1970s.

Rogers was only one of a number of humanistic psychologists who came to prominence in the 1950s, though he was probably the most forceful proponent for the movement. His most influential colleague, Abraham Maslow, emerged from the very different milieu of the immigrant-dense Lower East Side of New York City, although he also trained at both the University of Wisconsin and at Teachers College. Closely allied with

Horney and Fromm early in his career, as well as the behaviorist J. B. Watson, Maslow ultimately broke with both schools of thought to create a modified sort of humanistic psychology based in human potential rather than in psychic limits.

Maslow is best known for his theory of "self-actualizing" individuals: people who have reached their full potential in all spheres of achievement, including the social, intellectual, emotional, and moral. Like Rogers, Maslow was an optimist who viewed the essential human endeavor not as one of sexual conquest or territorial expansion, but as one of human achievement and fulfillment of needs. In his best known work, *Motivation and Personality*, published in 1954, he arranged human needs in a hierarchy of urgency starting with basic physiological needs and progressing to the highest, most abstract sorts of human endeavor, such as moral integrity, spiritual peace, and intellectual satisfaction. Self-actualized people had achieved at the highest possible levels.[11]

Unlike most of the psychologies that have been, or will be, discussed in this book, humanism was a political as well as therapeutic movement. Emerging in the zeitgeist of postwar antifascist sentiment, humanism attempted to elevate the individual at the (implicit) expense of society. Whereas both psychoanalysis and child guidance situated the patient or the client within a social structure, and to a certain degree reinforced that structure, humanistic psychology perceived the genuine individual as stripped of that structure, nakedly pursuing higher levels of achievement. Moreover, the underlying philosophy indicted most social structures as undermining human freedom and impairing human potential. Allan Buss, a psychologist at the University of Calgary, categorized Maslow's work as the "embodiment of the liberal frame of mind," emphasizing "optimism, pluralism, individual freedom ... and the gradual development toward perfection."[12]

As a politically motivated movement, humanism was fated to fade quickly. The movement was so vaguely defined as to be incapable of perpetuating itself vigorously, and seemed to invite converts to its ranks more than aspiring students. While Rogers did evaluate his clients for the success or failure of their treatment, the evaluations could not be exploited to further refine the counseling technique. A therapy based entirely on supportive listening seemed incapable of making critical insights into the malfunctions of the psyche. Ultimately, it would prove to be a detour in the history of American therapy, more than a milestone.

Behaviorism

Behavioristic therapy arose concurrently with humanistic psychology, but the approach stood in direct opposition to humanism, interpersonal psychology, psychoanalysis, and indeed nearly every type of psychodynamic therapy that had come before. Grounded in the pathbreaking work of Ivan Pavlov and his famous dogs, behaviorism started with the understanding that the only observable component of psychology was the behavior of the subject; all else was conjecture. In this world of the concrete and physical, the idea of the unconscious had no more place than the Christian idea of a soul, and all nonbehavioristic psychologies were really nothing more than forms of a "subtle religious philosophy," in the words of John Watson, one of the founders of the field.[13]

Behaviorists were extreme anti-intellectuals, but they were anything but antiscientific. They based their work on some of the oldest and firmest psychological research, going back to Pavlov's famous observations of dogs that salivated in response to a dinner bell, as well as an influential study by Watson and his assistant Rosalie Rayner in which they taught a one-year-old baby to fear warm, furry animals by making a loud, clanging sound behind the child every time he picked up a white laboratory rat.[14] Multiple studies through the 1920s indicated that many behaviors could be learned or unlearned through reward and punishment regimens in a controlled setting. The most fervent adherents of the movement concluded that all behaviors were learned, and that these learned behaviors constituted an individual's personality.

Behaviorists were the polar opposites of humanists. Rather than emphasizing empathy, client-therapist relationships, and the uniqueness of each individual's relationship with his milieu, they examined the conscious learned habits and activities of people and concluded that what had become habit could be reversed with proper education. It was an oddly cold approach to psychology: one which elevated observable behaviors to the exclusion of all other aspects of human existence. Watson wrote in 1930: "Behaviorism…was an attempt to do two things: to apply to the experimental study of man the same kind of procedure and the same language of description that many research men had found so useful for so many years in the study of animals lower than man."[15] The approach was taken even further by Watson's colleague, B. F. Skinner, who dismissed the relevance of any psychological model based on the existence of unobservable mental structures. When asked what was wrong with a colleague's approach to psychology, Skinner famously replied "too much theory."[16]

Watson and Skinner's ideas were introduced into clinical work through behavior therapy, the general term for a variety of therapies created in the 1950s which used rewards, punishments, aversions, and conditioning to teach or train subjects to behave differently than they had in the past. Behavioral therapists utterly rejected traditional psychotherapy as useless, preferring instead to focus on the very observable and measurable changes wrought through *operant* conditioning (in Skinner's term). Hans Eysenck, an English behavior therapist, described the various ways in which behavior therapy superceded traditional psychotherapy, starting with the accusation that psychotherapy was based on "inconsistent theory" that had never been properly formulated, whereas behavior therapy was based on "consistent, properly formulated theory leading to testable deductions." Not surprisingly, Eysenck accused psychotherapy of replacing old symptoms with new ones, whereas behavior therapy led to "permanent recovery."[17] While psychotherapy might cure, at most, two-thirds of neurotics, behavior therapy was reportedly successful in 90 percent of cases.[18]

Behavior therapists were uninterested in self-knowledge, psychic growth, adjustment, maturation, or any of the other stated goals of traditional psychotherapy. Rather, they understood neuroses to be simply the existence of behaviors that led to distress for those who performed them, and their aim was to halt the behaviors without concern for understanding their underlying causes. If a woman consistently found herself dating men who brought her grief, then success would be achieved by getting her to stop dating such men, regardless of the underlying psychic conditions that led her to engage in destructive relationships. While most any psychotherapist—Freudian, Sullivanian, interpersonal, or the like—would see personal exploration and growth as a necessary precursor to changing behavior, behaviorists assumed that if the behavior could be changed, the underlying misery would resolve itself. "It is small comfort to tell a patient whose neurotic anxieties remain undiminished after treatment that he is cured because his personality has matured," Joseph Wolpe and Arnold Lazarus, two noted behaviorists, wrote in 1966.[19]

Behavior therapists used several different techniques to treat their patients. In aversion therapy, perhaps the most notorious, patients were made physically uncomfortable through the use of electric shocks or powerful emetics while being exposed to stimuli that they had previously found attractive. By forcing the patient to associate extreme discomfort, nausea, and physical pain with the objects of their desire, they learned to avoid the object. The technique, made famous in the movie *A Clockwork Orange*, was used successfully on delinquents, thieves, vandals, and other miscreants. One early experiment involved applying electrodes to an infant, aged eleven months, who had persisted in vomiting frequently shortly after eating. When the therapist detected that vomiting would begin, he applied an electrical shock to the baby at the start of vomiting and applied follow-up shocks once per second during the vomiting. After six sessions, the vomiting ceased.[20]

Many of the patients treated by aversion therapy were sex fetishists who wished to be cured of their peculiar attractions. One patient treated in 1954, for example, had been strangely attracted to baby prams and women's handbags. Over the previous ten years he had repeatedly tried to damage the handbags of strange women by cutting them, scratching them, or smearing them with mucus. Far worse, he felt compelled to damage prams by crashing into them with his motorcycle, splattering them with mud, squirting oil on them, or setting them on fire. The object of his fascinations appeared to be the prams and handbags, and not the babies within or the women holding them. He admitted that he had had the urge to damage prams and handbags since age ten, and that both represented to him "symbolic sexual containers," which were often the object of his masturbatory fantasies. His wife testified that he was a good husband and father to their two children.

The patient was treated through classic aversion therapy: He was injected with apomorphine to produce powerful feelings of nausea while nurses surrounded him with prams and handbags. After five days of this treatment he admitted to no longer feeling the old attractions. After further treatment, during which he was surrounded by prams and handbags in bed while being given further doses of emetics, he was found "sobbing uncontrollably" and begged to the nurses to "take them away."[21] He thereupon surrendered to the nursing staff the photographs of prams he had long carried in his wallet. Nineteen months later, his wife reported that he no longer required the objects to have sex, nor did he fantasize about them while masturbating.

In a similar case, a thirty-three-year-old transvestite was treated by being asked to dress in women's clothes while admiring himself in a mirror. Therapists placed electrodes in the bottom of the shoes he was wearing, and administered shocks to him at various points during his undressing and dressing ritual. The shocks were administered once per minute and were continued for five hours per day over six days. Six months after the therapy, the patient reported no desire to wear women's clothes. His relationship with his wife had improved, and he reported that sexual urges, previously satisfied by transvestism, could now be sated only through masturbation or intercourse with his wife.[22]

In stimulus satiation therapy, behaviorists used a reverse approach, rewarding a patient's urges by inundating him with the objects of his desire, in the hope that a saturation point would be exceeded, after which the patient would begin to reject the object. In a typical such case, a patient in a psychiatric hospital was known to hoard towels, often accumulating two dozen or more towels in her hospital room before nurses could remove them. During the therapy, nurses would continually stop by to offer the patient new towels, seven per day at first, going up to sixty per day by the third week. At first the patient enjoyed the bounty and thanked the nurses for their largesse. But by the third week, when the woman had more than six hundred towels in her room, she began to tell the nurses to stop giving her more and actually began to remove them from her room. By the sixth week she begged, "I can't drag any more of these towels, I just can't do it!" Thereafter, nurses stopped giving her new towels. All hoarding behavior ceased after that; a year later she was found to have only one to five towels in her room at any one time.[23]

A variant form of therapy was reciprocal inhibition, in which two competing stimuli were administered at the same time in the hope that one would dominate the other. This could be used to help alleviate phobias, such as a case of terrible cat phobia in which the patient awoke each morning so terrified that she anticipated each juncture during the day when she might confront a cat. Virtually a prisoner in her house, the woman could no longer tend her garden, visit with friends, sit next to someone wearing a fur coat, or watch television, for fear of seeing a cat. She was treated by gradually introducing her to catlike objects (pieces of velvet and fur, toy kitties, pictures of cats) in a controlled setting. After mastering a series of catlike objects, she was shown a small kitten. When she was able to approach and touch the kitten, she was exposed to a full-sized cat. Within three weeks she reported feeling significantly more relaxed and capable of walking within ten yards of a cat. She was then given a kitten to hold, and upon successfully holding and petting it she described the experience as "one of the greatest days of my life."[24]

These cases typified behavior therapy insofar as in each case the therapy was quick and successful. Behaviorists pointed to their successes in arguing against psychodynamic models of neuroses, claiming that habits had the tendency to "lead to their own reinforcement."[25] Thus, even if a patient could be given the insight to understand the initial reasons why she had adopted such odd behaviors, such knowledge might not necessarily allow her to stop. The two therapists who treated the cat-phobic woman described above noted that a patient with neurotic symptoms who was treated with insight-oriented psychotherapy would almost certainly develop them again if exposed to the same environmental stimuli.[26] To eliminate neurotic behavior, what was required was not insight but re-habituation, to thwart the initial habits reduction that had proven to be maladaptive.

Behaviorists were pragmatists, above all, and were willing to experiment with a variety of drugs and stimuli to produce either relaxation and pleasurable responses in patients to reward good behaviors, or tension and nausea to punish offending ones. Therapists used massage, warm baths, gentle voices, emetics, shocks, oxygen inhalation, muscle relaxants, hallucinogens, and antianxiety drugs.[27] They treated stage-frightened dancers, obsessive-compulsives, fetishists, rapists, phobics, blocked writers, and a host of other neurotics, all of whom displayed maladaptive behaviors. Treatments generally took a few days to a few weeks and tended to rely on commonsense approaches. All presumed that habits and behaviors were learned, and therefore could be unlearned.

Not all the therapies worked. Behavioral efforts to treat homosexuality were notably unsuccessful. In one infamous effort, gay men were given emetics while being shown pictures of nude men, and synthetic testosterone while being show pictures of nude women. While the efforts did periodically dissuade the patients from engaging in homosexual relations, they did not induce them to become heterosexual. Rather, the patients either became virtually asexual or continued with their previous lifestyle. Out of sixty-seven patients treated this way, only three reported that they had converted to a heterosexual lifestyle.[28]

Behaviorists, in their own way, were as dogmatic as the orthodox Freudians. Having been successful at attacking neurotic symptoms without recourse to dynamic therapy, they dispensed with the older approach entirely. Feelings, for behaviorists, were simply irrelevant to mental health. Insofar as patients were depressed or anxious, the remedy was to change the behavior that was causing the depression or anxiety, rather than trying to understand the underlying tensions that may have led to the development of such behaviors or feelings to begin with. Early success using strictly behavioral approaches reinforced the conceit and encouraged them to further discount the contributions and insights of traditional therapists.

But like all therapists who cleaved too closely to a strict orthodoxy, behaviorists undermined themselves. All research by 1960 indicated that patients responded positively to many different types of therapy, although patients with certain sorts of complaints tended to respond better to some types of treatment than to others. The relationship between the therapist and the patient was important, as was empathy, insight, practicality, the ability to know the patient within his or her environment, and the ability to listen carefully. All of these new therapies had added to the array of tools available to the therapist, and the behavioral approach, rather than displacing all previous approaches, was better seen as one more addition. Behaviorists were no more humble than so many of the therapists who had come before. Fortunately, a new type of therapist, who would take seriously the discoveries of the behaviorists but extend them further into the centers of thinking itself, was just appearing.

Thinking

Behaviorism was a substantial and innovative break from psychoanalysis, but had it gone too far? Grounded in the concept of *learning*, behaviorism posed as its central truth that just as maladaptive behaviors had once been learned, they could also be unlearned. But by focusing exclusively on behavior, to the exclusion of emotions, behaviorists dismissed a third sphere of human experience: *thinking*.

Psychoanalysts had long dismissed thinking as a marginal neurological endeavor. Obsessed, as they were, with visceral responses to early childhood experiences, analysts had rarely paused to consider how those experiences and feelings were processed by the infant. Rather, they had assumed that cogitation—the aspect of brain functioning unique to human beings—was largely absent at the early age when many of the most psychologically significant events were experienced. Infants saw, heard, reacted, and ultimately repressed, but they did not mull and analyze. Buried in the unconscious as early as infanthood, these repressed experiences played havoc with the patient's psychic equilibrium until they could be resuscitated and defused.

But starting in the late 1950s, several psychoanalysts began to question the wisdom of dismissing the role thinking played in neuroses. The most famous of these early thinking revolutionaries was Albert Ellis, a classically trained psychoanalyst who observed early in his professional practice that many of his patients were simply not improving. Many patients did improve considerably in the early sessions of an analysis, but they seemed incapable of learning to use psychological insights gained from their sessions toward relieving their anxious symptoms long-term.

Ellis described the typical patient saying to him, "Yes, I see exactly what bothered me now and why I was bothered by it; but I nevertheless still am bothered. Now, what can I do about that?"[29]

Ellis's great breakthrough was to take the insight of behavioral therapists—that maladaptive behaviors could be both learned and unlearned—and apply this insight to thinking. For Ellis, feeling was just another sort of thinking, albeit a type of thinking that was emotionally highly charged. And just as maladaptive behaviors could be unlearned, so too could maladaptive thoughts, which in turn could help undo the destructive feelings that defined neurosis. In a profound break from Freudianism, Ellis and other early thinking psychologists began to believe that one could learn new constructive styles of thinking without necessarily discovering and analyzing the origins of the bad thinking habits. Aaron Beck, another early and important *cognitive* therapist (as these types of therapists came to be known), summarized the essential breakthrough of Ellis as assuming that a patient who had learned poor reaction patterns could unlearn them "without the absolute requirement that he obtain insight into the origin of the symptom."[30]

Ellis considered a neurosis to be simply a specialized case of poor thinking, or in his pithy words, "stupid behavior by a non-stupid person."[31] Ellis presented an example, now well known, of two people confronted with a piece of partially moldy bread. The person thinking clearly, understanding that the moldy part was not good to eat, cut off the moldy part and ate the rest. But the neurotic, reacting highly emotionally to the mold, threw the whole piece of bread away and ate nothing. "Because the thinking person is relatively calm, he uses the maximum information available to him—namely, that moldy bread is bad but non-moldy bread is good," Ellis wrote. "Because the emotional person is relatively excited, he may use only part of the available information—namely, that moldy bread is bad."[32]

Ellis concluded from this example, and many others that he observed in his practice, that his neurotic patients were more than emotional;

they were consistently failing to think clearly, which in turn was further feeding their neuroses. Unable to apply powers of reason to their confrontations with reality, they consistently overreacted, misperceived threats and danger, failed to appreciate love and support, saw failure (or success) where it did not necessarily exist, and generally reacted to the world with "disordered, over- or under-intensified, uncontrollable emotion." The disproportionately emotional reaction was a result of "illogical, unrealistic, irrational, inflexible, and childish thinking."[33]

The critical difference between Ellis and Freud was in viewing poor thinking as the locus of neuroses. For Freud, clear thinking about neuroses was impossible, for neuroses were caused by thoughts and memories not available to the conscious mind. For Ellis, neurotic thinking was wholly conscious—it was simply bad thinking. So that while the corrective for Freud was to help people unveil the origins of their bad thinking, the operative remedy for Ellis was to teach people how to think better. While both men were curious as to how patients originally "became illogical," Ellis took the process two steps farther in asking, "How do they keep perpetuating their irrational thinking?" and "How can they be helped to be less illogical, less neurotic?"[34] Thus, Ellis felt that the critical role of the therapist was not simply to guide the patient to inner discovery; it was to teach the patient how to think.

While Ellis noticed that patients brought their own unique illogic into therapy sessions, he also noticed that patients with illogical thinking sequences began to fall into one of twelve fairly predictable patterns. While no patient exhibited all twelve patterns of sloppy thinking, most patients exhibited one or more. These erroneous ideas were as follows:

- That it was necessary to be universally loved rather than winning specific approval and affection;
- That certain acts were "wicked" rather than merely inappropriate;
- That when life did not proceed as planned, it was "catastrophic,"

rather than that not all things in life were controllable, and that therefore one should not try to control everything;

- That unhappiness was born of external events, rather than internal disequilibria;
- That one should avoid difficult situations rather than facing them squarely;
- That an unhappy event or idea could permanently mar one's life, rather than that grief fades and that most people are able to regain happiness, even after suffering terrible tragedies;
- That one has no control over one's emotions, rather than that one can control one's emotions "if one chooses to work at controlling them."[35]

To counter these misperceptions and wrongheaded ideas about life, Ellis taught that the therapist needed to serve as a "frank counter-propagandist," chipping away at the patient's belief system born of a lifetime of inner propaganda. The therapist must "keep pounding away, time and again, at the illogical ideas which underlie the client's fears."[36] He must point out to the patient when he was "catastrophizing"—viewing a situation in the worst possible light. He must allow a patient to express his fears and then show him why these fears were probably unfounded, or better yet, show him that even if these fears came to pass, the result would probably not be nearly as bad as he expected. In Ellis's view, "Clear thinking... leads to sane emoting."[37]

A case from Ellis's practice is helpful for illustrating the technique. A patient who had long had difficulty with sexual relations with women came to Ellis for treatment. Ellis discerned that the man was very frightened of rejection, to the point of paralysis, and attempted to teach him the folly of his thinking. Asked why it would be so terrible to be rejected by a girl, the man responded: "Because—uh—I—I just thought the world would come to an end if that would have happened." The dialogue continued:

Ellis: But why? Would the world really have come to an end?

Patient: No of course not.

Ellis: Would the girl have slapped your face, or called a cop, or induced all the other girls to ostracize you?

Patient: No, I guess she wouldn't.

Ellis: Then what would she have done? How would you— really—have been hurt?

Patient: Well, I guess, in the way you mean, I wouldn't.

Later in the conversation, Ellis emphasized the point again:

Ellis: Suppose you actually did ask a girl for a kiss, or something else; and suppose she did reject you. What would you really lose, thereby, by being so rejected?

Patient: Really lose? Actually, I guess, very little.

Ellis: Right: damned little. In fact, you'd actually gain a great deal.

Patient: How so?

Ellis: Very simply: you'd gain experience. For if you tried and were rejected, you'd know not to try it with that girl, or in that way, again. Then you could go on to try again with some other girl, or with the same girl in a different way, and so on.

Patient: Maybe you've got something there.

Notice that in the sequence, Ellis did not emphasize the source of the man's sense of inadequacy and fear of rejection. Although in earlier sessions Ellis had elicited information about the man's childhood, including evidence that suggested that a hypercritical father had probably taught the man, when young, to unreasonably fear failure and rejection, Ellis did not feel satisfied in simply exposing the *source* of the man's anxiety. Rather, he felt that the truly useful component of the therapy began when he could *teach* the man how to think in a new, more realistic and constructive way. Incidentally, in this case, the man did eventually ask a girl out, persevered after initially being rejected, and was eventually able to win her over, in spite of what he described as her history of frigidity.[38]

Ellis called his therapeutic approach rational emotive therapy (RET) because he felt that the constructive processes lay at the nexus of thinking *and* emotions. While other cognitive therapists would make advances in future years toward cognitive behavioral therapy, which combined elements of RET and behavioral therapy, Ellis cleaved throughout his career to the idea that rational thinking was the best tool available to reform troublesome emotions. Clear emotions led to clear actions, which led to untroubled lives, and clear emotions were the product of rigorous thinking. People who thought rigorously and rationally learned to recognize when their emotions were unconstructive, and what they could change about their actions and situations to better their lot. The most mature thinkers learned, as well, when to accept the status quo.[39]

Ellis was trained in scientific psychology, having received his Ph.D. in the discipline from Columbia University in 1949. He completed a full training analysis and embarked on a practice of traditional psychoanalytically oriented psychotherapy. Only after a decade of practice did he begin to develop his rational emotive approach, by which time he had collected a substantial number of case records of patients who had been treated using the different approaches. Drawing on his statistical training, he studied the efficacy of each type of treatment and found that of patients treated with orthodox analysis, 50 percent showed little improvement and 50 percent showed either "distinct" or "considerable" improvement. Of those treated with psychoanalytically oriented therapy, 37 percent showed little improvement and 63 showed either distinct or considerable improvement. Of those treated with rational emotive therapy, only 10 percent showed no improvement, and 90 percent showed distinct or considerable improvement. Furthermore, nearly three times as many patients treated with the rational technique showed "considerable" improvement in comparison to those treated with either of the psychoanalytic techniques.[40]

The statistics were suspect, insofar as Ellis, deeply committed to his new brand of rational therapy, had an incentive to overstate the success of the patients treated rationally, and to understate the success of the patients treated with traditional approaches. And even Ellis admitted that most of his patients treated with RET did not discard all of their irrational behaviors (though most discarded some). Nonetheless, for the right sorts of patients—"not too psychotic...fairly intelligent...and reasonably young," who showed a "willingness to work, intellectual curiosity, and a willingness to accept direction from the therapist"—the new approach appeared quite promising. Moreover, the number of sessions necessary for producing good to excellent results was vastly fewer than that required by traditional psychoanalysis. The breakthrough carried with it substantial promise. Oddly, it would remain a marginal approach among psychotherapists for another two decades.

Drugs

Behavioral and cognitive therapies were a significant departure from Freudian approaches to mental healing, yet they all shared a continuing reliance on psychological models of mental illness. All three continued to look to the *mind* as the source of emotional and cognitive functioning, and devised therapies to alter the mind's habits, responses, and understandings of itself. Talk was the basis of such approaches, and it was seen as the primary avenue of access into the mind, though behaviorists relied on reteaching physical behaviors.

Organicists, however, took an entirely different tack. Rooted in the centuries-old sciences of anatomy and physiology, organicists viewed mental health as simply an extension of physical health, and the mind as merely a product of the physical structure of the brain. Gene Marine, a science journalist, reported that many scientists agreed "that the physical study of mental illness might ultimately make the adjective 'mental' completely superfluous."[41] And while in 1946, when the federal government first began to fund mental health research, little was known about the organic basis of mental illness, by the late 1950s a great deal of knowledge had been garnered.

Some of the first indicators of the connection between anatomy, physiological processes, and the mind grew out of sex research on animals. Rudimentary understanding of the endocrine system went back to the late nineteenth century, and by 1950 researchers had come to observe the remarkable physical and behavioral effects of applying male and female sex hormones to chicks, rats, and embryos of all sorts. Injecting testosterone into a female chick, for example, could not only induce the growth of a cock's comb, but could spur the chick to crow like an adult cock and to make involuntary male-like copulatory motions. By contrast, a female rat caged with another female rat in estrus would begin to display aggressive male sexual behavior. Further, this behavior would cease rapidly upon the removal of the rat's cortical glands.[42]

Neuroanatomist Nathan Winkelman made the first breakthrough in understanding the organic basis of some mental illness in the late 1940s, when he autopsied the brains of recently deceased schizophrenics and observed a decrease in ganglion cells. While Winkelman had no explanation regarding how these observed changes could cause, or perhaps have been caused by, schizophrenia, his observations suggested that schizophrenic symptoms might actually be the manifestations of an underlying physical disease or malformation, rather than a psychological tic as had been previously thought. Skeptics, on the other hand, noted that all of the patients had been subjected to multiple rounds of electroshock therapy, which perhaps had been the cause of the structural changes.[43]

Counterintuitively, major advances in the understanding of brain structure and chemistry over the following decade came largely from observing the effects of new drugs upon the mentally ill. Lithium, for example, a naturally occurring metallic element, was discovered by John Cade of Australia to have remarkable sedating effects on manic-depressives, though he had come to this discovery by accident while experimenting with lithium salts on guinea pigs. Even more intriguing, lithium did not seem to have any effect on any other sorts of behavior, nor did it sedate healthy patients, nor did it reduce manic behavior in non-manic-depressive patients. The drug's narrow action implied that manic-depressive illness was caused by a highly specific physical malfunction in the brain, though whether it worked by restoring missing lithium or by intervening in some other misfiring chemical pathway could not be determined. The specificity, the "one-drug/one-disease model" so beloved by pharmacologists, was the first tangible evidence that mental illness was perhaps simply illness.[44]

Several other drug breakthroughs in that decade furthered physiological understanding, or at least hypothesizing, about mental illness. Iproniazid, the first of a class of antidepressants that later came to be called monoamine oxidase inhibitors (MAOIs), was discovered in the early 1950s and briefly prescribed widely. Imipramine, the first of the tricyclic antidepressants, was discovered later that decade. Both drugs had their drawbacks—iproniazid could cause high blood pressure, severe headaches, and brain hemorrhages, while imipramine seemed to affect a number of brain chemicals that had little to do with depression—but even so, they and their biochemical descendants were prescribed widely throughout the 1960s and 1970s. Many patients improved dramatically on the drugs, though few escaped without side effects. As a result, many doctors remained reluctant to resort to their use.

Even more exciting were two new tranquilizing drugs discovered at almost exactly the same time. The two drugs, chlorpromazine and reserpine, were derived quite differently—chlorpromazine was created in the

Rhône-Poulenc pharmacology labs in Switzerland, while reserpine, long used in India, was an extract of the snakeroot shrub—but both had near miraculous effects on severely ill schizophrenic patients. While neither drug actually cured the disease, both substantially calmed patients, to the point of their being either amenable to psychotherapy or reasonable candidates for discharge. Doctors described the drugs' results as "dramatic" and "incredible."[45] Patients who had been confined to near-prison conditions, shackled to beds, or forced to wear straitjackets were now allowed to roam freely through the hospitals. Other patients who had lived in psychiatric hospitals for a decade or more could now be released. Chlorpromazine, known as the "drug which emptied the hospitals," seemed particularly promising. Psychiatrists at state hospitals were stunned by the drug's effects: Stories circulated about excited psychiatrists investing in the stock of SmithKline (the company that produced its American form, Thorazine) and retiring soon thereafter.[46] The drugs, while not cure-alls, "dried out the soggy patient material and made it combustible," in the words of George Brooks of the Vermont State Hospital.[47]

The advent of the new drugs, however imperfect, caused a reckoning within psychiatry. Clear evidence of an organic basis to certain mental disorders severely challenged the assumptions of psychoanalysis, as well as most psychoanalytically oriented therapies. The fact that depression, anxiety, and manic behavior could be corrected, or at least partially alleviated, by a pill suggested to many psychiatrists that these illness were caused by a simple physical malfunction of the brain. Even if scientists and physicians did not yet know precisely what that malfunction was—anatomical, biochemical, or something else—many had no doubt that they someday would know. In 1957, Linus Pauling, who had recently been awarded the Nobel Prize in Chemistry (he would win a second Nobel, in peace, in 1964), undertook a major five-year study of mental illness and announced to the American Psychiatric Association his confidence in knowing that "most mental disease is chemical in origin, and that the chemical abnormalities involved are usually the result of abnormalities in the genetic constitution of the individual."[48]

By the late 1950s, not only had some psychiatrists become organic in their approach to mental illness, they had begun to argue that psychiatrists who refused to move to this orientation and refused to exploit the newly available medications were practicing medicine unethically. Physicians, they argued, had an obligation to patients to make use of all tools at their disposal to cure and heal, and the active rejection of large classes of treatments for ideological reasons constituted a betrayal of the physician-patient trust. An anonymous psychiatrist wrote an impassioned two-part article for the *Atlantic Monthly* in 1954 accusing psychoanalysts of cleaving to "rigidly held beliefs concerning a metaphysical psyche." He declared to readers that were he to retrain in psychiatry, he would focus on "biochemistry, neurophysiology, and electronics" rather than psychology, and he implored his colleagues to first, "demonstrate our abilities to cure our patients" before venturing to advise them on their "numerous everyday problems."[49]

That psychiatrist was perhaps overly optimistic, suggesting that the medications and procedures then available were more effective and reliable than in fact they were. He suggested that lobotomies could reduce anxiety without "any impairment of the patient's intelligence," and that the 10,000 such procedures in England had already allowed a third of that nation's inpatient psychiatric population to go home. And he wrongly asserted that insulin comas (a competing form of shock therapy) could effectively cure schizophrenia (later research demonstrated it most effective in treating chronic unipolar depression). Nonetheless, he trumpeted the new research, promising that even though it might be another century before true knowledge of the brain's functioning was discovered, "I would not change my present line of work because we are only at the very beginning of its possibilities, rather than near the end of an already overexplored and dogma-ridden field."[50]

The general psychiatric establishment also began to move, slowly, toward the organic approach. By 1962 both the American Psychiatric Association and the Group for the Advancement of Psychiatry had permanent committees on biological psychiatry, whose job it was to create policy and practice standards surrounding pharmacology, surgery, and shock therapy for the profession. While initially these recommendations were tentative and almost marginal, as early as 1961 Robert Felix, president of the American Psychiatric Association, implored psychiatrists to consider themselves physicians first, and to not diminish the importance to their work of physical causes of disease. The following year, GAP's committee on medical education released a report and recommendations on psychiatric training all but accusing non-organic psychiatrists of negligence and malpractice. The report read: "By refusing either to carry out physical and neurological examinations themselves or to arrange for them, by emphasizing emotional factors in illness to the point of neglecting organic diagnostic work, by delaying medical procedures, and by failing to keep up his fund of essential medical knowledge, the psychiatrist affects a 'do as I say, not as I do' attitude."[51]

Organic psychiatry received support from an assortment of Americans. Close relatives of chronically ill psychiatric patients took solace in knowing that they had not caused their relative's illness, but that it was simply a physical dysfunction, probably congenital and genetic.[52] Friends and family members of patients who were benefiting from antidepressants, or one of the recently released tranquilizing medications such as Miltown and Equinil, expressed relief at the newfound mental and emotional stability and congeniality of their loved ones. One enthusiastic nurse lauded her newly tranquilized patients, who had become calm, pleasant, and accommodating. "I had never been able to work with [Mr. White] before, but this morning everything seemed to work out very well," she wrote. Members in her patients group could even tell if a fellow patient was or was not on medication. "What's the matter, did you run out of pills?" they would ask somebody being particularly difficult that day. The answer was often yes.[53]

A third group rested in between. Open to the promise of the new drugs, this group nonetheless assumed that psychotherapy would still play a role in treating mental illness, either alone or in conjunction with the drugs. While the antidepressants actually seemed to treat depression, other drugs were less successful. Chlorpromazine and reserpine didn't actually cure the hallucinations and fractured cogitations of schizophrenics; rather, they only removed the agitation that accompanied the symptoms and which made the patients so difficult to control or to treat. Many analysts and therapists were willing to acknowledge the benefits brought by the drugs, but continued to assert that therapy could still help in ordering the mind of a patient, teaching new thought patterns or reshaping behaviors. If many neurotic symptoms were in fact learned, then removing the underlying biochemical and physiological causes alone would not necessarily cause the patient to unlearn the poor thinking and behavioral patterns that defined his life. Those habits would need to be exorcised through slow, methodical therapy, even with the best of medications. *Consumer Reports* magazine, which studied the new drugs in 1955, concluded that chlorpromazine would not eliminate the need for psychotherapy, but would make psychotherapy easier for patients whose agitation and anxiety were "so severe as to interfere with the emotional rapport between doctor and patient."[54] Heller Azima, a professor of psychiatry at McGill University, accepted that the drugs "facilitate psychotherapeutic exploration" in cases of overwhelming anxiety, but could also possibly block effective therapy when the absence of anxious symptoms might have been the galvanizing force inducing the patient to embark on therapy.[55]

This last point bothered psychoanalysts particularly. Even of those therapists who accepted that drugs brought symptomatic relief to some patients, some still refused to accept that the process was benign. In classic Freudian theory, anxiety was essential to the analytic process. It was the great driver pushing patients to persevere in the hard work of analysis, to establish a transference with the analyst, and to search the painful and often traumatic memories that lay buried in the unconscious. Removing anxiety through chemical means could only blunt the urge toward self-exploration. While this dulling of the senses might be desirable for a patient locked in an unavoidably dreadful reality (a prisoner, a terminal cancer patient), for most patients it blocked progress toward cure.

The new drugs proved divisive while at the same time exposing various therapists' true understanding of mental illness. The most orthodox and conservative of analysts and therapists viewed them with suspicion, or even total dismissal; others viewed them as a godsend; and the bulk took a wait-and-see attitude. This last group was probably the most realistic, and certainly the most pragmatic. Focused on helping people get well, they were willing to seize what tools were available to them, while refusing to imbue the tools with powers they did not possess. The drugs were problematic. They were chemically dirty and biochemically incomplete. They produced headaches, heart palpitations, sweating, strokes, shakes, shimmies, stooped gaits, slurred words, and depressed countenances. They failed to work on many patients, and on other patients they appeared to stop working after a time. Many patients who improved on the drugs never made recoveries complete enough to live independently, and many patients stabilized enough to leave mental hospitals showed up at the admitting desks weeks or months later having failed to maintain their drug regimens. One could see why many therapists believed that the drugs showed promise, while still cleaving to psychotherapy as a primary intervention.

Still, optimism was in the air. Linus Pauling, on winning a large grant from the Ford Foundation to study brain chemistry, stated, "I foresee the day when many of the diseases that are caused by abnormal enzyme molecules will be treated by the use of artificial enzymes."[56] And Abraham Myerson of Boston Psychopathic Hospital wrote in 1948, "If I were asked to predict the status of psychiatry 25 years from now, I would state without hesitation that biochemistry, biophysics, [and] pharmacological therapeutics will hold the center of the state." Not everybody was quite so optimistic, but few could deny the beginning of a revolution.

Outcomes

What worked? As healers of all types debated the merits of their various therapies, psychiatric investigators began to conduct research on the success rates of the therapies in an effort to discern their effectiveness. Such research was hard, however. Although the American public had been sold on psychotherapy as a product of science, most of the claims that therapy could be backed up by science had come from the therapists themselves.[57] A few psychiatrists and psychoanalysts had begun to express doubts about their own usefulness by the mid-1950s, although their reactions were largely unscientific. Clarence Oberndorf, a psychoanalyst in New York City, had noticed that although early in his career he had experienced some success in treating patients with short-term therapy, by 1945 the profession had moved to substantially longer analyses (five to seven years) despite lacking evidence that prolonging the treatment led to improved outcomes. He proposed that all analysts submit to outside review after two years of analyzing a patient, but the suggestion was rejected by the profession.[58] Conversely, but to a similar end, Clara Thompson, Harry Stack Sullivan's longtime colleague, noted that when psychoanalysts were forced to shorten treatments during the war to three times per week, or sometimes even twice or once per week, their success rates did not seem to fall significantly. "In actual duration of treatment in terms of months and years," she wrote, "the patient going five times a week takes about as long to be cured as the patient going three times."[59]

Lawrence Kubie, another prominent American analyst in the late 1940s, similarly observed a spate of unsatisfactory analytic outcomes. Writing to Edward Glover, his own mentor, he admitted that he could

no longer explain away such failures as due to "either inadequate training or inferior analytic ability," but rather had to accept that such failures were the "result of certain basic inadequacies in the therapeutic
leverage of even the best and most skillful analysts."[60] Kubie and Oberndorf's observations were further validated in 1946 when Peter Denker,
another psychoanalyst in New York, tracked five hundred psychoneurotic patients who were treated with nothing beyond "sedatives, tonics,
suggestion, and reassurance," and found that 72 percent recovered.[61] And
yet another psychoanalyst in New York, Joseph Wilder, surveyed several
thousand patients who had undergone analysis, some for years, some
only for weeks, and found little improvement in outcomes after the first
thirty to forty sessions.[62]

These early studies all had flaws. Either they were conducted by the
same analyst who had actually treated the patients (meaning that he had
a substantial preexisting bias in finding success); or the sample size was
too small; or the criteria by which "success" had been defined was ambiguous. Moreover, it was very difficult to know, when comparing successfully treated patients with those who had gotten better on their
own, if they had started at the same level of illness, since no therapist in
1950 had good standards for measuring the status of a patient's mental
health at either the beginning of the treatment or the end. Behaviorists
and cognitive therapists, for example, tended to measure success by ces-
sation of symptoms and the patient's return to regular habits, whatever
they might be. Thus, when simple dysphoria was ameliorated, a cure
was recorded. But the most orthodox of Freudians had never aspired to
simply bring the patient to a state of happiness; rather their goal had always been profound psychological change in the most hidden recesses
of the unconscious. A psychoanalyst in Berlin, Otto Fenichel, who conducted some of the earliest outcomes studies on analytic patients, in the
1930s, stated that he was not looking for "merely the disappearance of
symptoms," but rather the "manifestation of analytically acceptable per-

sonality changes."[63] By contrast, a team of psychologists trying to evaluate outcomes in 1956 simply looked to "restore the patient to his previous level of *comfort* and *efficiency*."[64]

The first broad study designed to examine the effectiveness of psychotherapy across many patients and many physicians was conducted by Hans Eysenck, a London-based psychologist, in the early 1950s. Eysenck used what is now called a *meta-analytic* approach to his work, meaning that rather than collecting original data, he aggregated results from a number of existing studies and generated statistics describing the full set of data. His conclusions, based on 8,053 cases presented in 24 separate studies, were damning to psychotherapy: He found that about two-thirds of all patients in any kind of psychotherapy improved after two years, but that about two-thirds of neurotics who received no treatment also improved after two years. The finding challenged the essential integrity of the psychotherapeutic enterprise.[65]

But Eysenck, a committed skeptic of psychoanalysis, harbored his own bias. Eysenck's work drew on studies conducted as early as the 1920s, continuing right up to a year before he published. In general, he did a good job of representing the efficacy of different types of therapy. For example, he found that many of the more orthodox psychoanalysts produced successful outcomes in half or fewer of their patients, while the more eclectic and pragmatic therapists were able to push their rates of cure as high as 75 percent. However, several investigators who studied his results in the following decade found that he had overstated the spontaneous remission rates of the untreated neurotics, and that probably fewer than one-third got better on their own, instead of the two-thirds he had reported. Moreover, a number of neurotics who initially claimed to have recovered without treatment had in fact sought out both formal and informal treatment, and many had received some treatment (though they often left before finishing). If, as the early research showed, a great deal of improvement could be garnered in the first few

weeks and months of treatment, then many of these patients had probably benefited from their truncated interactions with professional therapists.[66] Critics of Eysenck believed that he had used the ambiguity of
the data to discredit psychoanalysis—and, to a lesser degree, verbal
psychotherapy.[67]

Some of the studies that Eysenck drew on had shockingly few cases
in the sample; one had four patients and another had six.[68] This alone
would have weighed against including them in the meta-analysis, as
studies of very small populations were prone to misinterpretation. But
far more problematic was the difficulty of establishing similar standards
for patients from different studies being compared to one another. No
matter how researchers tried to quantify the degree of psychiatric distress or illness, they were left with the problem of interpretation: At
some point, a fallible human being had to rate a patient along a non-
quantifiable scale to establish the level of his or her illness, and every researcher used a slightly different scale by which to rate the patient.
Researchers tried to get around this problem by creating multiple discrete criteria by which to judge patients' health—anxiety level, self-
directed aggression, externalization, level of psychosexual development,
anxiety tolerance, insight, ego strength, motivation, quality of interpersonal relationships—but they could not dispense entirely with human
judgment.[69] One well-known psychiatrist observed sadly, "I think it is a
distressing property of this field that different people can interpret the
same data not orthogonally but diametrically."[70] In other words, biased
psychiatrists could read into a situation exactly what they wished and
interpret data in completely opposite ways.

A further troubling finding surrounded the phenomenon of informal therapy. Psychiatrists knew that many Americans sought counseling
from nonprofessional counselors: clergymen, physicians, marriage counselors, or even athletic coaches. While many of these counseling sessions
were ad hoc and lasted little more than a few minutes, some were more
formal and might unfold over several weeks or even months. The prob-

lem for professional psychotherapy was that many Americans who used these informal networks for counseling reported being highly satisfied with the outcome. Seventy-eight percent of people who had consulted with a member of the clergy, for example, testified that the experience had either "helped" or "helped a lot." Seventy-six percent of people who had consulted with a physician reported the same (versus only 59 percent of people who had consulted with a psychiatrist), and perhaps most disquieting, 77 percent of people who had discussed at length their personal problems with a lawyer reported being satisfied.[71]

Who knew what to think? One thing everybody seemed sure of was that talking your problems over with somebody was probably helpful. A certain number of people who suffered at length from either excessive anxiety or depression seemed to get better on their own after a year or two, though this number was probably closer to one-third than to two-thirds. About two-thirds of people who saw any sort of counselor, whether medical, psychological, clerical, or even legal, seemed to get better. Of course, nobody had a good definition of what it meant to get "better," much less "cured." Moreover, nobody knew if the patients seeking professional therapy were sicker to begin with than the patients who went at it on their own. It looked as if most improvement took place early in the therapeutic process: some time in the first thirty to fifty sessions, and perhaps sooner. It also seemed that the precise orientation of the therapist, as well as his or her technical training, was largely irrelevant to success.

As for drugs and shock therapy, these too seemed to work. Many patients who had undergone shock therapy got better; many patients medicated on Miltown, chlorpromazine, or iproniazid improved; and even a few who had been lobotomized seemed happier, more independent, and less worried. A major problem with almost all of these observations was that nobody had established a clear standard by which to evaluate the patients before treatment. Presumably, patients who never sought any professional help were never as sick as patients who had lived in a state hospital for a decade a more, so it was not surprising that the hospitalized patients might require far more invasive measures to get well. In fact, one could hypothesize that patients self-sorted quite efficiently, bringing themselves to the lowest, least-invasive, and least-formalized sort of therapy that could restore them to a basic level of functioning. The least sick toughed it out on their own; those a little sicker consulted with their minister, doctor, or sometimes lawyer; the next group sought psychotherapy; the ones after that psychoanalysis; then drug treatment, shock, and in the worst, most insolvable cases, lobotomy. Not surprisingly, then, each therapeutic approach seemed to claim roughly similar cure rates.

Outcomes research would eventually get better, but it would take decades. In the meantime, the field was open for different therapists to claim superiority of approach and philosophy, and it was up to the bewildered patients to make sense of it all.

CHAPTER 5

Alcohol

P roblem drinking in the United States was hardly new, but social concerns over it rose markedly in the decade after World War II, in part in response to an increase in drinking, and in part in response to a change in drinking habits and patterns that threatened to undermine certain social structures. Actual intake of alcohol rose nearly 30 percent per capita from 1940 to 1950, and the increase was particularly marked among women. The public became attuned to the problem with the 1949 publication of *The Problem Drinker* by Joseph Hirsh, which described the substantial rise in Americans who drank at all, drank socially, and drank heavily. Trying hard not to be alarmist, Hirsh pointed out that modernity placed new stresses on broad classes of people that could drive many of them to drink. In a "world of acute tensions and violence," people reached for alcohol to self-medicate.[1]

By 1955 there were over 4 million problem drinkers in the country and an additional 8 million habitual drinkers.[2] The distinction was necessarily vague; habitual drinking turned problematic when the drinker could no longer control its frequency and intensity. Americans who had once comfortably denounced drunks—"If a drunkard is in the gutter, that is where he belongs," William Summer, a sociologist, had written in 1910—now recognized that those drinking might be the very people on whom their companies, churches, and marriages depended.[3] These drinkers were imperiling their own lives and livelihood, as well as those of the 20 million close friends and relatives who depended on their continued functioning. Ralph Habas, who authored *How to Live Without Liquor* in 1955, wrote that these people had "no more business drinking than a diabetic has indulging his taste for sweets."[4]

The costs of problem drinking, or alcoholism as it was becoming known, were immense. Drinking destroyed marriages, broke careers, harmed children, and fractured communal ties. John Thomas, a Catholic priest in St. Louis, found drinking to be the single greatest cause of marital breakdown in his study of 7,000 Catholic divorces. One group estimated that drinking was costing the U.S economy $1 billion per year in absenteeism, and $750 million per year in extra medical costs for treating the health problems associated with drinking. Karl Menninger pronounced that within psychiatry, "nothing looms so large on the horizon as the drug people prescribe for themselves."[5]

Most troubling, for many observers, was the rise in female drinking. Before the prohibition era, only one in twenty-five alcoholics had been female; in the years before World War II it was one in six; and by 1955 it was one in four. Marvin Block, a physician in Buffalo who closely observed alcoholic behavior, felt that even that last statistic greatly undercounted women drinkers, whom he felt might actually constitute the majority of alcoholics if you could include the many "hidden cases" who drank exclusively at home and alone.[6] Increases in women's drinking frightened alcohol researchers for its promise of social breakdown. While a man's drinking could, conceivably, be shielded from the home, a woman's drinking would inevitably undermine family ties and ultimately damage the next generation. Habas wrote, "For while a man can frequently go on drinking for years without being unduly concerned about the effect it is having on his children, the alcoholic woman with a family is commonly tormented by the feeling that she is an 'unnatural mother.'"[7] Feminists, not surprisingly, chafed at the double standard.

Bertha Schwartz, a New York City councilwoman, demanded to know why women "should be singled out" and why drinking should be viewed as "a reflection on womanhood."[8]

What constituted problem drinking? Was it how much you drank or how frequently or with whom? It seemed to have something to do with losing control, although a certain amount of cutting loose at parties seemed acceptable. Employers easily measured the problem by how frequently it bled over into the workplace. By 1957, several large companies had begun to implement workplace alcohol programs in an effort to help their wayward employees who were missing work because of drinking, and bring them back to the productive workforce. Harold Vonachen, director of the medical department at Caterpillar Tractor Company, was not worried about the "social phenomenon of martinis before dinner or drinking one too many on Saturday nights." Rather, he worried about "absenteeism...irritability, sloppy appearance."[9] Corporate alcohol programs, designed to help curtail problem drinking before it got out of control, were designed to save money and grief. Henry Mielcarek of Allis-Chalmers estimated that his company's alcohol program saved the company $80,000 in recovered absenteeism.[10]

Problem drinking went far beyond missed work, however. The line between social drinking and problem drinking was hazy, but it had something to do with crossing the line between the *desire* to drink and the *need* to. Of course, most alcoholics claimed that they drank only from desire, not from need, and that they could stop whenever they wished, but psychologists and social workers began to record certain patterns indicating a compulsive relationship with alcohol. Robert Seliger, a psychiatrist in Baltimore and an authority on alcohol abuse, posed a telltale test in 1955, which included the following questions:

- Do you need a drink at a definite time every day?
- Do you prefer to drink alone?
- Is your drinking harming your family in any way?

- Is your drinking hurting your reputation?
- Has it made you careless of your family's welfare?
- Has your drinking made you harder to get along with?
- Is it making your home life unhappy?
- Is it jeopardizing your job, or hurting your business or professional career?

While no one yes answer indicated alcoholism with finality, any yes answer was a "red light warning to put on the brakes" and indicated the potential to become a problem drinker.[11]

While drinking was obviously widespread, and transcended wealth, education, class, and race, it was not evenly spread throughout the country. Sociologists and social workers had noted since the 1920s that different immigrant groups had different drinking habits, and the World War II draft confirmed these observations with strong data. Jewish draftees in Boston, for example, exhibited virtually no alcoholism, while Irish Catholics substantially outdrank their Yankee co-recruits.[12] A study in 1958 conducted by the Yale Center of Alcohol Studies confirmed these wartime observations, showing that rates of alcoholism were 25.6 percent for those of Irish descent, 7.8 for Scandinavians, 4.8 for Italians, 4.3 for the English, 3.8 for Germans, and .5 for Jews.[13] While genetics might play some role in these differences, social and cultural norms were probably the primary culprit, with different ethnic groups using alcohol in different styles to facilitate social discourse, release tension, and ease bonding. In part, too, different groups acculturated their young into drinking patterns in very different way. More Jews, for example, actually drank *at all* than people from any other group (that is, the fewest teetotalers), but almost always in a tightly controlled religious setting while taking food.

What was it to be a "problem drinker"? How did one differentiate the social drinker from the occasional drinker from the binge drinker,

the heavy drinker, or the drinking addict? And at what point did drinking go from being simply a pleasant diversion to a soul-shattering vice?

Those who suffered alcohol's worst scourges knew the true evil of
the habit. To be locked inescapably in an embrace with alcohol was a
"living nightmare, conceived in the shades of hell," in the words of one
sufferer.[14] Alcoholics inevitably declined, going from high-class bum to
skid-row derelict, and few crawled out on their own. Typically a man in
a downward alcoholic spiral started in the flophouse, moved next to the
mission, then to the streets. As he ran through his funds, he regressed
from cheap bars to fortified wine, to vanilla and lemon extract, and
worst, to the alcoholic extracts of canned heat (Sterno), which he
squeezed through a cloth into a cup and mixed with water. Meals could
be had for little more than the price of singing some hymns or listening
to a sermon; sometimes all they required was testimony of religious
epiphany. Such a pledge, often made on bent knee, was known as "taking a nose dive."[15]

Many more alcoholics kept up some semblance of a middle-class life,
but in doing so imposed their hell on those around them. Men, who
made up the majority of alcoholics in 1955, brutalized wives and children, burned through family savings, lost jobs, broke promises, missed
dinners and events, and humiliated themselves and their families. One
desperately sad wife, writing an open letter to her alcoholic husband,
noted that a home movie of one of his binges would show his "slurred
speech, a sentence said over and over because you couldn't quite get the
next one out; the snarl at the children...your dog whimper when I demanded that you leave the table; the stumbling on the stairs; the fumbling in your hiding place for the bottle." Worst, continued the woman,
were his frantic gropings in the middle of the night, "the horrible sound
of the drinking glass shattering on the tile floor of the bathroom, and
then your mutterings as you vaguely pick up some of the fragments."[16]
The woman's well-meaning friends urged her to leave her husband:

kick him out and change the locks. "There is no hope for the alcoholic—no sure cure," they would say. The woman, not quite willing to abandon all hope, placed her trust in God.

Alcohol not only ruined lives; it undermined society. Christian temperance workers, long opposed to "demon gin" and its kin, noted new indicators of social erosion in the decade after the troops returned. Increased rates of juvenile delinquency, alcohol-related auto accidents, and divorce all seemed to suggest that alcohol was working its evil with greater vigilance against the American home and town. Although states taxed alcohol heavily, growing evidence suggested that the social costs of alcohol treatment, absenteeism, violence, and accidents far outstripped the revenues raised through its sale. Christian writer Charles Crowe indicted potables as the "major social evil in the country today." He wrote, "Alcohol leaves a sordid trail of misery, death, personal and social degradation."[17] Luther Youngdahl, a federal judge in Washington, D.C., considered liquor "one of the most devastating factors contributing to juvenile delinquency and the breakdown of the home."[18] Various police chiefs estimated that alcohol was the cause of 40 to 60 percent of all highway deaths.[19] Robert Seliger, a psychiatrist with the Neuropsychiatric Institute of Baltimore, summed up his observations: "This behavior illness . . . causes ravages worse and more varied than those of any other specific known medical and psychiatric illness." The toll it took each year in ruined lives, careers, property, marriages, children, and friendships was "greater than we can calculate."[20]

Although the costs of alcohol abuse seemed immeasurable, in part they could be counted. In 1950, George Thompson, a psychiatric researcher, estimated total monetary losses annually in the United States due to alcohol abuse to be $765 million, including $432 million in lost wages, $188 million in crime, $120 million in accidents and medical treatment, and $25 million in jail costs. As far back as 1947, Elvin Jellinek, the director of alcohol studies at Yale University, calculated that each year inebriation accounted for 1,500 fatal workplace accidents and

2,850 fatal accidents at home and on the road, in addition to 390,000 nonfatal accidents. The accident rate for alcoholics was twice that for nonalcoholics.[21] Among male alcoholics who had been married, 16 percent were divorced, and 25 percent were separated—rates far above those for the general population.[22] On average, alcoholics were losing twenty-two days of work per year, and those workers were the ones who still functioned ably enough to hold a job. They also lived twelve years fewer than nondrinkers.

What caused alcoholism? Long seen as a vice or a flaw in one's character, alcoholism was becoming more of a behavioral disease in the minds of many researchers by 1955. Certain people had a predisposition toward abusing alcohol, an inability to enjoy it the way most people could. Sidney Vogel, a psychiatrist in New York City, described alcohol abuse as an addiction, a "dreadful, unbreakable, uncontrollable, self-destructive, antisocial craving."[23] Vogel noted that alcoholics were people who drank in a "very special way...to excess, compulsively, without control, and self-destructively."[24] The alcoholic "required" alcohol, in the way that the heavy social drinker did not. He was the victim of a "need," an "uncontrollable drive," which overcame his powers of reason and drove him to "slow suicide."[25] He was sick.

Although this inability to control one's urges had long been viewed as emblematic of spiritual weakness, wartime experiences with mental illness had convinced many psychiatric researchers, and many Americans generally, that the boundary between a character flaw and mental illness was shaky. Thousands of men who had previously lived exemplary lives broke under the strain of combat, and the old saws of cowardice and lack of moral fiber were unsatisfying explanations. Moreover, many of these broken men had been able to recover, given appropriate rest, psychiatric care, and rehabilitative support, suggesting that what might have been viewed as a character flaw was in fact a form of illness—illness from which recovery was possible. Was alcoholism simply a variant on this illness?

The growing consensus of the mental health professions was yes. George Thompson pithily stated that "to the psychiatrist, the alcoholic individual is emotionally sick." The disease was not simply the aggregate of a lifetime of bad habits. Rather, it was the "result of personality illness...the symptom of a disease."[26] Alcoholics were "sick people," opined Robert Seliger, and could no longer be classified by enlightened individuals as "bums and drunks."[27] They suffered from an inner compulsion which, once turned on by exposure to alcohol, relentlessly drove the sufferer to endlessly drink more. One frank alcoholic confessed in an open letter, "It has to do with certain tensions, like some awful disease, and these tensions come and say—'The hell with life. The hell with hope. The hell with all meaning.' "[28]

Alcoholics were weak people, but their weakness was unusual and pathological. Whether inherited or acquired, the weakness prevented them from engaging fully in life. Faced with the onset of adult responsibilities and concerns, alcoholics engaged in a lifetime of denial, made tolerable and workable only through the agency of alcohol. They resembled "the psychopath," in the words of the psychiatrist George Thompson, in their ability to alter or deny reality, but differed from the true psychopath in their willingness to use alcohol to make tolerable the alternate reality.[29] One researcher, Charlotte Buhler, noted that in the majority of cases, alcohol abuse began in late adolescence and early adulthood, just as society began to foist adult responsibilities upon the individual, "when the alcoholic begins to fail, and at which point he begins to escape into the oblivion he needs."[30]

Not all Americans accepted this explanation of alcohol abuse. In 1948, for example, when professionals were already converging on a medical model of alcoholism, 58 percent of Americans who had been surveyed made no distinction between an "alcoholic" and a "person who gets drunk frequently"; 50 percent felt that alcoholics could stop drinking if they wished; and only 20 percent regarded an alcoholic as "sick."[31] Alcoholism, by its very commonness, seemed to many to be merely another vice, like gluttony or philandering. The world was filled with weak and failed people, and alcoholism was simply one more symptom of flawed inner character. The very inability of the medical profession to clearly demarcate who, exactly, was an alcoholic, or whose heavy drinking would progress to full-blown alcoholism, reinforced this view, for if alcoholism was a sickness, then it ought to be consistently diagnosable. Ruth Fox and Peter Lyon, writing in a major treatise on alcoholism in 1956, admitted the limits of the medical model: "It may be safely said, at this writing, that none can tell whether John Jones will become an alcoholic; that, if he already is, none can for a certainty, tell why; that none can with assurance state that John Jones will recover from his alcoholism, or if he does, for how long; and that if he does recover for good, none will be able to say why, what aspect of his treatment did the trick."[32]

But even as psychiatrists and the public battled over the disease explanation of alcohol abuse, some professionals and laymen looked to a middle ground. Perhaps alcoholism was not exactly a disease in the traditional pathogenic model, but a rather extreme form of maladaptive behavior. Many Americans used alcohol regularly to dull the stress of ordinary life or to facilitate social interactions, yet most did not become alcoholic. According to this explanation, alcohol abuse was not so much a sickness as a fairly pedestrian coping tool gone out of control. The question was not so much how to "cure" the disease, but rather why some people seemed capable of using this tool safely, in limited quantities, while others lost all self-mastery when exposed to its powers. Sidney Vogel, an alcohol researcher, wrote that for alcoholics, drinking "fulfills wishes, banishes care, and makes great obstacles seem Lilliputian."[33] Roger Williams, of the University of Texas, summed up the quandary of alcohol researchers when he said in 1948, "Instead of centering attention on Mr. Average Man, we must learn more about how and why different individuals differ so greatly in their response to alcohol."[34] And W. W. Bauer, director of the Bureau of Health Education of

the American Medical Association, eschewed "disease" verbiage entirely
in commenting on the state of knowledge on alcohol in 1955, noting
simply that "sensible persons in growing numbers have abandoned the
holier-than-thou attitude of repulsion toward the alcoholic and replaced
it with one of greater sympathy and intelligent helpfulness."[35]

One of the reasons alcoholism was so resistant to classification was
because it was so resistant to treatment. Some alcoholics did seem to get
better with treatment, but of psychological counseling, medical intervention, and Christian sermonizing, none predictably did the trick. All
of these approaches seemed to help sometimes, but just as frequently accomplished little. Not surprisingly, many healers espoused their own
brand of treatment, with social workers recommending social counseling on "practical everyday problems of living," physicians prescribing
bed rest, sedatives, and vitamins, and preachers prescribing spiritual
epiphany and the sustenance of a religious community.[36] All of these
healers could point to past successes, yet most could also point to even
more examples of failure. The spiritual approach seemed the most naïve,
ignoring, as it did, the plethora of psychosocial variables contributing
to the alcoholic's plight. One recovering alcoholic wrote, "A Bowery
bum knows better than a good many preachers how complicated is the
man to whom the gospel is directed, how miscalculated is much Christian counsel, how irrelevant are the little recitals of rules and the little
pep talks that pass for sermons....What do you do when you know
all the historic oughts and couldn't care less? Or, even if you care, don't
do anything about them? You don't answer a question by asking it
louder."[37]

Alcoholics Anonymous

The answer came in the form of Alcoholics Anonymous (AA), an amorphous group of 150,000 members organized into some 4,000 chapters

across the country by 1955. AA was barely an organization, though.[38] With no membership application, no fees, little formal bureaucracy, and no last names, it existed only to serve alcoholics who genuinely desired to get better—"to help the sick alcoholic recover, if he wishes."[39] And recover they did. By 1955 some 90,000 alcoholics were living sober lives due almost entirely to the work of the organization. Fifty percent of those who joined dried out immediately, and another 25 percent were able to withdraw from drinking at least for a time, before regressing and rejoining AA. Jack Alexander, who brought the organization to national renown in an article he penned for the *Saturday Evening Post* in 1941, noted that its achievements stood out "as one of the few encouraging developments of a rather grim and destructive half century."[40]

Those who joined AA did not just get cured, they stayed cured. The organization demanded of them that they admit their powerlessness against alcohol, admit wrongdoing, apologize to those they hurt, accept God, and generally surrender the fantasies which they had used to rationalize their destructive and irresponsible behavior throughout their lives. Those committed to the program found that they could not simply dry out and return to life as they had known it. Rather, a complete recentering was required, which included trading in old friends for new, old habits for new, old recreations for new, and sometimes even old relatives for new. All that had enabled the alcoholic to persevere in the drinking life needed to now be forever avoided. Leslie Farber, a psychiatrist interested in alcohol research, summed up the organization: "Where other methods tend to say, 'Now you are cured; go back to your life,' this voluntary association … is unique in offering not a 'cure' so much as a 'life.' "[41]

AA had been started in 1935 by Bill Wilson, a New York stockbroker and investor, and Robert Smith, a surgeon from Akron, Ohio. Wilson had, like virtually all alcoholics, initially denied his problem, telling his wife, "Men of genius conceive their best projects when drunk."[42] Even after he had lost his money, his job, and nearly his marriage, and realized that alcohol was destroying him, he still could not stop drinking. A reprieve came in 1934 when he was introduced to the Oxford Movement, a Christian brotherhood founded by Frank Buchman, a Protestant evangelist. Members were required to admit their sins and surrender to God before the local group. The movement offered epiphany in place of self-reliance, and oddly had been helpful to a number of alcoholics. Wilson was drawn to join the group by an associate who had stopped drinking, and found that he too was for the first time able to resist the lures of alcohol.

By May 1935, however, Wilson was dangerously close to regressing to drink. Finding himself in Akron, Ohio, one night on a business trip, and desperate for a drink, he called a local pastor to see if there was perhaps another alcoholic in the community whom he could speak with. The pastor introduced him to Robert Smith, himself at an advanced stage of alcoholism. The two men quickly established a close relationship (by odd coincidence they were both Vermont natives), and Wilson found that by helping Smith to resist drinking, he was also helping himself. It seemed that the act of converting another was the final, necessary step in the recipe. The two men stayed together in Akron for several months as they increased the size of their circle of mutually comforting alcoholics first to three, then to fifteen. By 1939 the movement had 100 adherents in 3 cities (Akron, New York City, and Cleveland), but in the wake of Alexander's 1941 *Saturday Evening Post* article the movement grew explosively. By 1957 it had 200,000 members in 7,000 groups in 70 countries.[43]

How did AA work? The organization was structured around local meetings which ran themselves. Upon first attending a meeting, an alcoholic was encouraged to pledge himself to the twelve-step program, which included admitting he was "powerless over alcohol," accepting a greater power, making a commitment to that power, admitting the wrongs he had committed and pledging to make amends for them, and last, as Wilson had discovered in seeking out Smith, carrying this message to other alcoholics. AA recognized that virtually no alcoholic could swear off drink for life, so they urged each new member to simply make a commitment to refrain from drinking for twenty-four hours, which most could do. At the end of twenty-four hours, the drinker would renew his pledge for an additional twenty-four hours, and so on. Initially, the new member was encouraged to attend meetings daily to help fortify him in keeping his pledges.

The meetings themselves were a curious mixture of socializing, bonding, self-admission sessions, mutual encouragement, and coaching. Members who were further along in their sobriety helped the new members to understand which of their habits were enabling their drinking, and gradually helped the rookies restructure their lives so as to avoid those situations and people. Successful members understood that they could never drink again—that "one drink was too much, and a thousand was never enough." They would never actually be "cured," but rather would spend the rest of their lives, one day at a time, working to stay off liquor.

The program worked for a number of reasons. First, it demanded profound humility from its adherents—the precise quality which most had lacked throughout their lives. Members had to admit that no one in the group was better than another, and that none of them had had the stamina, discipline, or fortitude to control their lives and live without drink. All AA members went by first name only, and introduced themselves in meetings as simply "an alcoholic," as a way of recognizing that whatever worldly accomplishments they could claim, they were all ultimately overshadowed by their central weakness. Wilson summed it up, "The difference between the high-bottom drunk and low-bottom drunk is that both are lying in the gutter but the high-bottom drunk has his head on the curb. We are all drunks."[44] One longtime AA member pointed out, "When anybody stops *boasting* about how much he had to drink the night before and starts *lying* about it, there's maybe just a little bit of a chance the he's getting to be one of us."[45] Joseph Hirsh described the phenomenon as the "immaturity inherent in his effort to escape from problems and responsibility."[46] AA demanded, more than anything else, that an alcoholic begin to live life as an adult.

Second was the spiritual element. The forced acceptance of a higher power was perhaps the biggest barrier to many potential members, yet virtually all successful AA members came to admit that such acceptance was crucial, an extension of the humility demanded of them, the utterly honest confrontation with their own limits, faults, and mortality. "We think that finally all of these forces can be stated in terms of a power greater than the self, which many of us call God. Call it what you will, but there is this power; it affects you; and you have to learn how to manipulate it," one AA member related.[47] AA members did not all call the power God; some referred to it as a spiritual essence or simply the force of nature, but all came to understand that there was a force in the universe greater and more important than themselves, which ordered the world in a sane manner and which they had been opposing through their lives.

The third reason AA worked was that the alcoholic was being confronted by other alcoholics. His new colleagues were experts in denial, lying, rationalizing, and all other manipulative dodges and feints that the alcoholic had spent his life exploiting. The recovered alcoholic "may not know much about Oedipus complexes," one AA member explained, "but he does know about drunks and butterflies trampling around in your stomach and all that."[48] Moreover, to a new AA member, the recovering alcoholics looked and spoke like himself. No diploma or business suit separated the two; no status differential reinforced the alcoholic's essential insecurity and self-loathing. One AA member explained, "[The psychiatrist] is well dressed, professional, of tremendously high status, and authoritative, and the alcoholic is very often scared to death of authority."[49]

Last, and perhaps most important, AA members pledged to help each other anywhere, at any time. The pledge, known as "nickel therapy," meant that any time an AA member craved a drink, he could drop a nickel into a pay phone and call another member, who would make every possible effort to talk him through the urging. Both the knowledge that others had made this commitment to him, and the knowledge that he, in turn, had made the same commitment to others, bound the alcoholic into a structured intimacy and accountability that had been missing his entire life. He was simply never alone, never left to fight his demons in isolation. One AA member spoke of the pledge: "When a man joins the AA without any strings attached, something happens to him. He belongs to the AA soul and body. He'd get up in the middle of the coldest night and cross the country in a blizzard to sit with another AA who felt the thirst on him and couldn't fight it alone. He'd *have* to. There wouldn't be any question about it, any more than about reaching for food if he was starving."[50] The pledge was quasi-religious, but even more so. "It means a million times more than getting religion seems to mean to most people," related one member.[51]

This last point, the pledge, emanated directly from the tight "groupness" of the AA structure. Organized as highly independent and discrete meetings, AA built its strength on the same principles as army platoons. By forcing a mutual dependency upon one another, members of the group produced something stronger than their sum as individuals. The AA group took on a life of its own, forcing a new social dimension upon the lives of its participants, changing the rules of their engagements, and reshaping their understanding of social mores. AA members counted on one another in crisis, certainly, but also turned to one another for fun, and often found that they could have more fun together, without alcohol, than they had had with their old friends, with alcohol. The alcoholic had become part of a group that had found a way out of hell, and thus as the group was saved, so was he.[52]

The extraordinary power of the group upon those battling alcoholism who had seemed nearly impervious to treatment suggested that a similar model could work for others battling with antisocial psychopathic tendencies. Just as AA members could bond in a group around their common battle with alcohol, could not others bond over depression, anxiety, personality disorders, and the like? And if so, could these other groups also offer hope for those who had proven difficult to cure? A number of psychologists thought so and began to experiment with delivering psychotherapy to patients in a group setting in the 1950s.

Group Therapy

Group therapy did not start in the fifties. Human beings, no doubt, had been meeting in groups to discuss their troubles and share their lives since the dawn of the species, but the first organized effort at group therapy was probably instigated by John Hersey Pratt, a physician in Boston, who used psychotherapy to counsel tuberculosis patients in group settings in 1905. A number of other early physicians, psychiatrists, and psychologists counseled groups in the early decades of the twentieth century, including Edward Lazell at St. Elizabeth's Hospital in Washington, D.C., Abraham Low at Illinois Psychiatric Hospital, L. Cody Marsh, and Jacob Moreno.[53] Moreno published a substantial book on group therapy in 1922, and later tended to claim disproportionate credit for early group therapy efforts, but he was most likely building on the work of Trigant Burrow, an underappreciated early giant in the field.[54]

Burrow was trained as both a physician and a psychologist. In 1910 he traveled to Switzerland to study with Carl Jung, and upon his return he began to focus his psychoanalytic practice on group analysis, which he later named phyloanalysis. Like Jung, he viewed mental health as a product of both individual history and cultural context; human beings, in his theory, were formed by the society around them, and by their role in that society. In 1923 Burrow established an adult summer camp in the Adirondack Mountains of upstate New York, where he and his followers studied the dynamics and biology of their group. Although his work probably strongly influenced Harry Stack Sullivan, he was denied credit for many of his observations and innovations, and was actually ostracized by the American Psychoanalytic Association after 1933 for disavowing many of Freud's theories. By the 1940s, a variety of therapists were practicing group therapy, among them Carl Rogers and Kurt Lewin, an émigré psychoanalyst. Although the movement was heavily staffed by ex-Europeans, it remained nearly an exclusively American approach to psychotherapy until the 1960s. At least one historian of the movement has called it "uniquely American...a consequence of the pragmatism of American psychiatry."[55]

Group therapy grew in the United States partially in response to the great shortage of mental health professionals after World War II (one therapist could treat many more patients in a group milieu than in one-on-one therapy) and partially in response to a series of industrial dynamic studies conducted in the 1920s and 1930s. These studies, made famous by Frank Gilbreth of *Cheaper by the Dozen* fame, are now known mostly by old black-and-white images of industrial engineers, armed with stopwatches, timing assembly line workers going through their paces. But some of these studies focused on the psychological dynamics of groups in the workplace, and discovered that the nature of workplace relationships could have a substantial impact on the productivity of the workers. One study in particular, conducted by sociologists at the University of Chicago of the Western Electric plant in Hawthorne, Illinois, found that workplace productivity was almost directly related to the health and vitality of the relationships between workers on the factory floor.[56]

Productive workplace relationships did not simply rely on kindness and decency. Elton Mayo, the lead investigator of the Hawthorne study, found that instead workers needed a leader who could establish ties of mutual respect between himself and the men, as well as set reasonable standards and protocols of work activity. Workers did not mind working hard, it seemed, so long as they felt that they were being treated fairly and being recognized within the group and by their superiors for their efforts. Edward Sapir, an anthropologist at the University of Chicago who took an interest in these studies, noted that in the absence of such leadership, a group could quickly disintegrate into an array of uncoordinated individuals working at odds with one another. He wrote of the United States Senate as a group of workers that ordinarily functioned under tightly bound rules of procedure, protocol, and leadership. But during a time of siege or political crisis, the Senate could easily disintegrate into near anarchy, becoming far more amenable to taking cues from the executive branch of government.[57]

By 1956, group therapy was a somewhat marginal but accepted approach to psychotherapy. Some 1,000 therapists across the country counted themselves among its practitioners, and a variety of social work and psychology programs had begun to mentor students in the practice. The approach seemed to work as well as many other therapeutic approaches, which is to say that it worked for some people some of the time, and that people generally improved faster while participating in group sessions than they would have had they done nothing. The approach heavily borrowed from (or contributed to) interpersonal theories of psychiatry, most notably those advocated by Harry Stack Sullivan. According to Sullivan, groups worked because for many people a component of their mental illness or unhappiness was rooted in the inability to form healthy and vibrant bonds with others, which in turn contributed to unrealistic and narcissistic images of the self. Jerome Frank, a noted professor of psychiatry at Johns Hopkins University, explained the value of the group in compensating for the attenuated ties that were common to a nation in which members of a rootless population frequently sacrificed family and community in pursuit of professional goals and business opportunities. He wrote, "The shallow and shifting sociability of the residential development, the office, the committee, and the club is not an adequate substitute because it is tainted with an undercover competition for popularity and prestige."[58]

Although most people approached therapy groups fretfully, under the guidance of a therapist they were asked to shed their pride and self-consciousness and relate to one another in a frank and honest manner, accepting one another as emotional peers without the overlay of worldly status and success. Group therapy addressed a variety of issues: workplace stresses; family tensions; sexual frustrations; fantasies; professional and personal failures; periods of joy; feelings of revulsion, shame, or excitement; sexual dalliance; dreams; compulsions; and fears.[59] Each member took turns speaking and responding and all were asked to speak to each other with respect, insight, and sensitivity. As in AA, the members of the group found sustenance and release both in honestly relating and confronting the reality of their own lives and in aiding their fellow sufferers. Frank described the healing phenomenon poignantly: "Perhaps the most potent way in which therapy groups strengthen members' self-esteem is by giving them an incentive and an opportunity to help each other. Altruism combats morbid self-centeredness, enhances the individual's feelings of kinship with others, and strengthens his sense of personal worth and power."[60]

Although each group was unique, therapists found that so long as they were put together with some attention to excluding psychotic patients, they tended to create similar bonds of intimacy, trust, and kindness among members. In a psychoanalytic sense, the members created a complex web of transferences, in which they lived out their feelings and fears by sharing their perceptions with one another. Jacob Moreno, who was best known for his use of psychodrama—a specialized form of group therapy in which members acted out roles in front of one another—believed it was important to expose the "invisible interactions" between the members of the groups to help them understand the nature of healthy adult relationships.[61] Patients soon discovered that if they insisted on remaining aloof and emotionally removed from the demands of members of the group, they would make little progress themselves. Hugh Mullan and Max Rosenbaum, two noted group therapists practicing in the 1950s, observed that as members of the group strengthened their commitment to one another, they welcomed increasingly physical, private, and embarrassing aspects of one another's life to be shared. They wrote, "We [the group] tell the patient that we do want him with us. Some individuals report that they cannot come because they have stomach pains or diarrhea. We tell them, 'Come and use our bathroom. Have your diarrhea with us. Bring your physical symptoms and feelings.' "[62]

Group therapy derived from the understanding that man, as an essentially social animal, could not separate his psyche and mental health from his social context. Thus, a powerful approach to mental illness involved trying to repair the broken bonds between patients and society, or at a more elementary level, to teach the patient how to create those bonds in the first place. Carl Jung, an important thinker followed by several of the early group therapists, recognized the central role of social interactions in the emotional lives of individuals, while at the same time understanding the largely dysfunctional nature of so many groups and organizations that the modern world had produced. In a letter written in 1955 he asserted that the three most demoralized organizations in the world were Standard Oil, the Catholic Church, and the German army, each of which demanded that all participants abnegate their individuality and honesty for the sake of group harmony. He wrote, "When a hundred clever heads join in a group, one big nincompoop is the result, because every individual is trammeled by the otherness of the others."[63] The fact that large numbers of inhabitants of the modern world had been socialized by such demeaning and dehumanizing behemoths (including communist and fascist parties in Europe and China) meant that many had lost the ability to create truly human and vital bonds, predicated on honesty, kindness, and humility.

Group therapy was not for everybody. Severe depressives, compulsives, schizophrenics, and sufferers of manic-depressive illness were probably not stable enough or didn't have a firm enough grasp on reality to be able to participate constructively in the group dynamic. Moreover, positive benefits of the group did not preclude the use of antidepressant drugs or even individual psychotherapy alongside the group therapy. But as was true in AA, the power of the group could impel a resistant patient to confront unpleasant truths about himself, and force him into honest and intimate relationships for the first time in his life. From these core relationships, the patient could take his newfound skills and self-knowledge to the wider world, where he could begin the work of creating anew his social milieu.

Alcoholics Anonymous was probably the single most successful approach to rehabilitating alcoholics by the mid-1950s, but it was hardly the only one. Psychotherapists continued to counsel private patients, usually using a psychodynamic approach, in the hope that self-knowledge and insight into one's anxiety and inner turmoil might help one to better resist alcohol. Therapists also enrolled alcoholics in more conventional group therapy, either in lieu of AA or in addition to it.[64] Physicians worked alongside therapists on overcoming the physical side of the addiction, injecting alcoholics with insulin (to help metabolize the remaining ethanol in the blood), vitamins, and general nutrients, under the theory that most severe alcoholics were actually suffering from malnutrition, having skipped multiple meals while bingeing on alcohol.[65] And some physicians advocated hospitalizing severe alcoholics in an effort to better tend to their needs while they were being weaned from drinking.

By far the most successful of the non-AA approaches was the behavior-based therapy known as aversion therapy. The patient was given a powerful emetic such as emertine and then encouraged to drink alcohol. Immediately the patient would be hit by powerful waves of nausea and throw up repeatedly. He was given repeated drinks, which induced further vomiting, until, exhausted, he was excused. The procedure was

repeated daily for a week or more, until the patient developed a powerful aversion to any hint of alcohol. He returned for follow-up reinforcement several times over the following months; the treatment produced
generally good results.[66]

A similar treatment used a drug known as Antabuse, which produced
not only nausea but sweats, a racing heartbeat, shortness of breath, and
terrible headaches. Developed first in Denmark, the drug was approved
in the United States only after some consideration for fear that the effects of the treatment could permanently injure the patient. A reporter
writing graphically about the effects of the drug described the scene:
"One drink, and they were almost knocked down. They couldn't breathe.
Their eyeballs popped. Their heartbeats jumped to 140, their heads
seemed to be splitting open, and then they were very sick."[67] Not surprisingly, several days of aversion treatment with Antabuse brought
marked results, so much so that some of the more conventional therapists treating alcoholics recommended Antabuse therapy in conjunction
with the traditional therapy they were offering.[68]

By 1960, mental health professionals were clustering around a
middle-ground theory of alcoholism. It was more than a bad habit, but
something less than an out-and-out mental illness. Advocates who believed it was an illness attempted to appropriate the name of Elvin Jellinek, the Yale alcohol researcher, calling the condition Jellinek's disease,
but the idea was not received well in the broader population. Alcoholism fit into the model of other mental illnesses and conditions insofar as
it was susceptible to treatment in a therapeutic milieu, but it seemed to
be most susceptible to the unique milieu of AA, which called for spirituality, moral reckoning, and apology—all somewhat foreign ideas to
most psychotherapists. True, aspects of AA replicated some of the socializing and humbling dynamics of more traditional group therapy, but AA
seemed as much a church or cult as it did a group counseling movement. Yet somehow, hybrid that it was, it worked.

Aversion therapy, an obvious form of behavior therapy, worked as well, and thus again pointed to alcoholism being as much disease or mental syndrome as it was vice or habit. Yet again the condition did not quite fit tidily alongside the traditional phobias and fetishes that behavior conditioning had been most effective on. Moreover, certain groups seemed far more susceptible to alcoholism, as did members of certain families, suggesting that alcoholism was either a learned cultural behavior or a genetic addiction.

Alcoholism, it seemed, was sui generis. Part inherited predisposition, part learned behavioral norm, part symptom of underlying psychodynamic stress, and part biological drug addiction, it required treatment using a multipronged approach. But it *was* treatable. That much seemed certain as the new decade dawned. The treatment was not easy. It required either intense physical discomfort bordering on torture or a profound remaking of one's entire life. Recovering alcoholics jettisoned friends, relatives, jobs, homes, and churches in an effort to create new environments for themselves that were congenial to an alcohol-free life. Senior AA counselors understood that for all its miraculous success, AA could not possibly work unless an alcoholic managed to walk in the door on his own volition, and of course far too many alcoholics lacked the drive to do just that. Cure existed, but for neither the ambivalent nor the faint of heart.

CHAPTER 6

Psychological Society

A s the United States entered the decade of the 1960s, psychotherapy penetrated the nation's zeitgeist to a surprising degree. Advice columnists, journalists, and popular authors all referred to mental health and psychotherapy in a manner suggesting that these subjects had become part of the popular ferment. Schools across the country began to employ school psychologists; universities opened mental health clinics; cities hired psychological social workers into their community health clinics; and hospital administrators integrated psychiatric social workers into their outplacement services.[1] The United States had more clinical psychologists, psychiatrists, and psychiatric social workers in practice than the rest of the world combined. *Life* magazine, perhaps the unofficial logbook for middle-class life in the United States, published an article in 1957 noting that it was the "age of psychology and psychoanalysis," as well as of "chemistry and the atom bomb."[2] Arnold Rogow, a noted social critic, grandiosely proclaimed that "where the public once turned to the minister or the captain of industry, or the historian, or the scientist, it is now turning more and more to the psychiatrist."[3]

Psychological literature was ubiquitous. Many American newspapers carried a daily advice column which was progressively turning from household hints to emotional guidance. Three columns, "Child Behavior," "The Worry Clinic," and "Let's Explore Your Mind," each had daily readerships approaching 20 million. Dime stores and pharmacies carried 15-cent pamphlets with such titles as *How to Find Your Happiness Cycle, Facing the Facts of Married Life,* and *How to Manage Your Feelings and Emotions.* Norman Vincent Peale's *The Power of Positive Thinking* and Harry Overstreet's *The Mature Mind* sold millions of copies. Even the arcane works of Sigmund Freud, republished in an affordable hardcover edition by the Modern Library, sold more than a quarter million copies.[4]

Modern life, it seemed, was preying on the emotional health of Americans. Assaulted by demands of complex workplaces, scientific and technological advancements, and a changing perception of the roles of family and church, Americans had become psychological chameleons at the expense of their mental health. Ernest Havemann, a psychological reporter, described brilliantly the multiple roles a middle-class corporation man had to play as he moved through his career:

He takes a job where he must show a modest eagerness and deference to the boss, then is made foreman of a bunch of workmen who will respect him only if he acts tough, then moves along to a higher executive position where the slightest raising of the voice may be considered gauche. In addition he is closely involved emotionally with a wife who knows nothing of his business world and children whom he can never decide whether to indulge or to discipline. He also has to get along in such varied roles as a member of the board of governors of his country club (where he is not too well thought of because he can't break a hundred), a Boy Scout leader (where his stamina on a weekend camping trip is suspect) and a deacon of the church (where piety is the most admired trait). If he sometimes feels as if he is flying into small pieces—not an uncommon neurotic complaint—who can blame him?[5]

Americans had taken to therapy, though perhaps not in the numbers which their interest in psychology seemed to indicate. At the same time, some psychologists and psychiatrists, along with general social critics, began to ponder the overall mental health of American society. Perhaps it was not the people who were sick but society itself, which was in turn corrupting the emotional integrity of its inhabitants. Freud had famously made clear that parents visited their own neuroses and dysfunctionalities upon their children, but Judd Marmor, a psychiatrist in Washington, D.C., suspected that the parents were themselves victims of "a larger system whose values and imperatives they consciously or unconsciously purvey to their children."[6] Marmor wrote, "Man shapes his institutions, but he is also shaped by them," and such institutions as capitalism or prejudice, when malformed, could trap "generation after generation" and become the source of "delinquency, crime, violence, mental disorder, and social unrest."[7]

The idea that society itself was possibly sick gained currency in the late 1950s and early 1960s. Cold War pressures, mounting nuclear arsenals capable of annihilating hundreds of millions of people, persistent poverty in the midst of plenty, and a stubborn legacy of racism indicated to many progressive society watchers that the world of the present was not conducive to mental health. R. D. Laing, an iconoclastic psychiatrist in London, suggested that the "perfectly adjusted bomber pilot may be a greater threat to species survival than the hospitalized schizophrenic deluded that the bomb is inside him."[8] K. T. Erickson and H. S. Mechanic, noted sociologists, postulated that deviance was a "natural concomitant" of life amid such distorted values,[9] and James Halliday, a psychiatrist and author, found a broad audience for his study *Psychosocial Medicine: A Study of the Sick Society*.[10] William Whyte, a widely read sociologist, vividly described the idea of a mass society that had taken hold, overlaying the Marxist vision of alienated workers on a white-collar virtual prison of "organization men."[11] Pressures to conform to corporate culture, regressive postwar social mores, a crushing work ethic, and the constant impulsion to upward mobility could unbalance even the healthiest soul. Thomas Scheff, a liberal sociologist and social critic, attacked the madness of the nation's strategy toward the Soviet Union of "mutually assured destruction" and questioned the sanity of government leaders such as Senator Richard Russell of Georgia, who famously proclaimed, "If we have to start over again with another Adam and Eve, I want them to be Americans; and I want them on this continent and not in Europe."[12] Scheff did not actually accuse Russell of insanity, but merely pointed out that his "contemporary vision of sanity and reason" was "arbitrary and distorted."[13]

Poverty and racial inequity were constant irritants to a society struggling to emerge from two decades of economic depression and war. Blacks in both the South and the North seemed condemned to eternal second-class status: in the South legally, and in the North by virtue of social and labor restrictions.[14] The health and condition of the nation's poor whites, living on the margins of society in Appalachia and the rural South, had scarcely improved since the World War II draft, when shocked army physicians had noted the rickety bones, missing teeth, festering abscesses, and untreated mental illnesses of rural draftees. The Group for the Advancement of Psychiatry (GAP), a politically and socially minded gathering of psychiatrists, noted the high rates of mental illness among blacks, poor whites, and uneducated Americans of all types. Blacks were admitted to state psychiatric hospitals at rates "consistently and overwhelmingly higher" than were whites, and had been since the 1930s.[15] Few reputable psychiatrists attributed the disparity in admission rates to genes, but rather blamed gross social inequities and racist pressures. "We are bound to say that severe social deprivation of the type so widely experienced among Negroes is of fundamental causal significance for psychological impairment," GAP concluded.[16] The paucity of black psychiatrists (there were only 400 in the country) exacerbated the situation.[17]

Moreover, deprivation for whites produced no better outcomes, with

admissions at state hospitals disproportionately high for poor and uneducated whites, as well as for offspring of broken and migrant white
families. Divorce, it seemed, was particularly malignant, with hospitalization rates three to five times higher for divorced adults than for married ones.[18] Lack of access to psychiatrists, psychologists, mental health
clinics, and inpatient psychiatric wards exacerbated the plight of the
poor, who tended to live their lives insulated from the growing psychological ethos that pervaded middle-class society. In the 1960s, mental
health professionals undertook experimental projects in rural areas of
the country, where they discovered ignorance of mental health concepts
and regressive views on sex and child-rearing. Taking a cue from Carl
Rogers's humanistic school of therapy, one experimenter began using
untrained but well-intentioned college students to treat children and
adolescents in rural Vermont whose emotional and social maladjust-
ments seemed to stem as much from lack of intimate interactions as
anything else. This early effort at the type of "big brother" program that
would become popular two decades later was rooted as much in relationship therapy as it was in role modeling.[19]

The image of a sick society caused some psychiatrists and psychologists to join their social worker colleagues in viewing their appropriate
role as beyond merely medical or therapeutic. If mental illness was the
product of dysfunctional social norms, then the committed healer must
treat more than the patient; he must treat society itself. Some therapists
who had long espoused liberal politics began to see their professional
work as an extension of their politics, viewing the patient as merely as
extension of the sick society in which he lived. Psychiatrists in the
armed forces were perhaps the first to become aware of these forces,
since society for their patients was the aberrant milieu of warfare and
battle, but many politically active psychiatrists began to see themselves
in a similar mold by the mid-1960s.[20] James Comer, a child psychiatrist
who worked with poor children in the New Haven public schools, felt
that a psychiatrist had "a very special role which goes beyond that of a

concerned citizen."[21] Others felt that psychiatrists had a moral obligation to speak up about abuses in the state psychiatric system, juvenile detention centers, juvenile courts, and the public schools. Robert Seidenberg, a professor at Upstate Medical Center in Syracuse, New York, spoke of the mental hospitals run like detention camps that the profession tolerated. "We have not been outraged enough by it, their dehumanization," he urged a panel of his colleagues.[22] His colleague Arnold Moore, in Brooklyn, New York, claimed that psychiatrists bore the duty of fixing society and educating political leaders because their "psychiatric knowledge" gave them a privileged vantage point on social problems.[23] And Richard Schwartz, a psychiatrist in Cleveland, urged his colleagues to work toward "broader social action" in rectifying the roots of poverty, rather than simply treating psychiatric problems in a clinical vacuum.[24]

The Group for the Advancement of Psychiatry endorsed activism. Through the 1960s its subcommittee on social issues preached a more holistic view of the relationship between society and mental health, and demanded that organized psychiatry make an "explicit commitment on the social responsibility of psychiatry."[25] In this vision of mental illness, individuals faced a lifelong struggle with monolithic and oppressive social institutions, which invariably resulted in the sorts of phobias, anxieties, and depressive bouts that drove them to seek psychiatric consultation.[26] A profession grounded in ethical precepts therefore had a responsibility to work actively to rectify the ills and maladaptive structures of society.

Taken to the extreme, this sort of psychiatric activism dictated an entire plank of political beliefs. Engaged psychiatrists should fight for legalized abortion, fight against overly severe penal codes, and work to redraft welfare laws. Psychiatrists should actively lobby for more expansive social welfare legislation. In 1965, Robert Blank, a politically active member of GAP, urged George Gardner of the Judge Baker Guidance Center in Boston to have all psychiatrists take "direct action on the political and community education fronts."[27] GAP took an aggressive stance in school integration debates, sponsoring a pamphlet titled *Psychiatric Aspects of School Integration*.[28] Psychiatric activists viewed racism itself as a mental disease; the GAP report stated that "maladjusted, seriously insecure or anxiety-ridden people, more in the grip of the prejudices than the average person, need psychotherapy."[29] Military psychiatrists questioned their ethical standing as they sought to heal servicemen who had been psychologically injured in the course of carrying out their military duties. One, Daniel Switkes, requested release from his military obligations in Vietnam under the rationale that he could not ethically practice psychiatry under such coerced circumstances. Robert Jay Lifton, a Yale psychiatry professor who had served as a psychiatrist with the air force, suggested that military psychiatry was fundamentally problematic insofar as the psychiatrist had a conflict of interest between his allegiance to his patient and his allegiance to the army.[30]

Challenges

In spite of the liberal rhetoric of the GAP doctors in 1965, the country was still terribly underserved by trained clinicians. The situation had improved since *Newsweek* magazine had declared that the American psychiatrist must feel like the "Dutch boy who put his finger in the dike to keep the sea out," but the gap between supply and demand of mental health services was still huge.[31] The percentage of all American physicians who were psychiatrists had grown from 4.5 percent to 7.0 percent, but this number was unevenly distributed, with the majority practicing in among psychiatrist-rich states such as California, New York, Maryland (because of generous federal health plans), and Kansas (which was singularly served by the Menninger Clinic). In many states fewer than 5 percent of M.D.s had undergone psychiatric training, and in Mississippi,

Alabama, West Virginia, and Wyoming, the portion hardly exceeded 2 percent.[32] Most of the country's millions of neurotics and psychotics were prevented by geographical, financial, and logistical barriers from seeking help. Gerald Klerman, a psychiatrist with the National Institutes of Mental Health, thought that a quarter of the nation's citizens were living with unnecessary anxiety and stress, and that one-eighth suffered from a diagnosable mental illness.[33] Even this may have understated the shortage. Klerman asked, "Who among us has not wished to be more productive or more sexually attractive, to have a better memory, play better tennis, lose weight, or delay the onset of aging? The promise of psychotherapy is that it will do all of these things without any adverse side effects."[34]

Still, the situation had improved since the immediate postwar years. The absolute number of both psychologists and psychiatrists was up, as was the number of all medical doctors who undertook psychiatric training. Better psychiatric drugs and improved patient care for the discharged had greatly reduced the number of inpatient psychiatric patients, from a high of 559,000 in 1955 to just over 350,000 in 1965, with promise of greater decline in the near future. The average length of a hospital stay for psychiatric inpatients had also declined considerably, and would continue to decrease in the coming decade. In 1971 the average length of stay for an inpatient in an Oklahoma mental hospital had declined to just twenty-eight days, and the total state inpatient population was a third of what it had been in 1955.[35]

But these declines in inpatient services were more than offset by sharp increases in demands for outpatient services. Indeed, the better psychiatric care got, the more insatiable seemed the public's demand. From 1955 to 1970, demand for outpatient services nationwide quadrupled, and the portion of all psychiatric services being provided on an outpatient basis more than doubled, to 45 percent. Community mental health centers, which essentially had not existed in 1955, accounted for 10 percent of all mental health visits in the 1970s, and that number was continuing to climb.[36] Estimates for annual costs related to mental disorders were also rising, from $2.4 billion in 1950 to more than $21 billion by 1968.[37]

Despite successes posted by Alcoholics Anonymous and aversion treatment, alcoholism rates had barely budged, and by at least some estimates were actually up slightly. Narcotics use was up, as was use of prescription barbiturates and tranquilizers, all of which indicated that increasing numbers of Americans were feeling unhappy, displaced, and insecure. The nation was growing increasingly aware of the power of psychotherapy to cure and enrich, but always the demand for psychiatric services exceeded the available supply. The time seemed ripe for a major government initiative to improve the mental health of the country.

Community Mental Health

State psychiatric hospitals in the United States, long overcrowded, reached their apex of congestion in 1957 with a total inpatient population of 559,000. At the same time, horrific investigative books, such as *The Shame of the States* by Albert Deutsch and various "Shame" articles in newspapers around the country, as well as the movie *The Snake Pit* with Olivia de Havilland, exposed the ugly reality of life in most state mental hospitals. With wards crowded to twice their intended capacity, staff stretched far beyond their ability to treat and serve, active therapy nearly nonexistent, and lengths of stay approaching ten years, mental hospitals of the 1950s resembled nothing so much as prison camps, complete with their own work crews, farms, laundries, and gates. Reports of violence among the patients were commonplace, and filth and disorder were accepted as unavoidable.

But in the late 1950s a confluence of events drove both psychiatrists and policy makers to demand change. The new tranquilizing drugs held

promise of a more malleable psychotic population, which could conceivably be placed into psychotherapy. Socially minded mental health
professionals envisioned a larger role for themselves not only in treating
society's mentally ill, but in helping all people reach their potential. The
president of the American Psychiatric Association, addressing his colleagues in 1963, told them that they were being given an opportunity
they could not afford to waste, and that they need only "inherit the
earth." "Never was chaos so great; never was Paradise so near the reach
of common folk," he told his audience.[38] That same year, President
John F. Kennedy, who had a strong interest in helping those afflicted
with mental illness, declared to Congress that with the application of
national will and resources, "all but a small portion of the mentally ill
can eventually achieve a wholesome and constructive social adjustment."[39] David Musto, a historian of psychiatry, notes that there was a
peculiarly American quality to such optimism, the "faith in the power
of social environment and in mental health experts as manipulators of
that environment."[40]

In 1961, the optimism was given direction by a report of the Joint
Commission on Mental Illness and Health, established by Congress several years earlier to "make recommendations for combating mental illness in the United States."[41] The final report, entitled *Action for Mental
Health*, recommended an ambitious agenda of government-funded research, new training grants, better use of nonphysician mental health
clinicians, and most striking, the creation of federal funding pools to fi-
nance and staff a series of community mental health centers (CMHCs)
to cover the United States in a series of "catch basins" of 50,000 persons. The CMHCs would provide a complete array of mental health
services, including psychotherapy, day hospitals, education, drug treatment, and emergency intervention. At the same time, the report strongly
recommended that no further state psychiatric hospitals be built, and
that no further patients be added to their inpatient rosters.[42] "In short,
we have new hope," the report's authors wrote.[43]

The recommendations of *Action* were realized in the 1963 Community Mental Health Centers Act, which provided initial funding to construct the CMHCs nationwide. Over the next several years, the 1963 law was augmented by further legislation to provide funding for staff and more construction of the centers. By 1971 there were 452 CMHCs spread throughout the country, equally divided between large cities, small cities, and towns.[44] The CMHCs were both freestanding and part of existing general and psychiatric hospitals. Some were sponsored by a single health-care or civic institution; many were sponsored by more than one. All received at least part of their funding through state agencies, and in turn each state tended to funnel money to the centers through the newly established Medicaid programs. Nearly 700,000 people were being treated in the centers each year, and more than 40 percent of the patients were coming from families with low or modest incomes.[45]

In some ways, the centers functioned as planned. Combining a clinical workforce of nearly equal numbers of psychiatrists, psychologists, and social workers, the centers provided psychotherapy, group therapy, narcotic and alcohol counseling, short-term crisis intervention, drug prescriptions, and programming.[46] While every center was different, at least some were taking care of the poor and severely ill; a social worker at one center in Atlanta estimated that 99 percent of the clientele were "alcoholic, schizophrenic, or former mental hospital patients."[47] Elsewhere, the centers were inundated with alcoholics and drug addicts, many from reasonably wealthy families who had been drawn to the rising drug culture of the time. At the same time, inpatient psychiatric p pulations were plummeting; by 1973 the nation's psychiatric hospitals were housing fewer than half the resident patients that they had been in 1957. It seemed that the combination of new drugs and community mental health was bringing the CMHC plan to fruition.

But all was not well. While it was true that state psychiatric hospitals were emptying, and while it was also true that raw numbers of Americans receiving psychotherapy through the CMHCs was rising, it was not at all clear that the two patient populations were the same. The central assumption of the program, that very sick inpatients could be given drugs and thus be made functional enough to live on their own with outpatient support, was proving to be incorrect. The patients coming into the CMHCs were often middle-class and poor people, emotionally troubled yet functional, who had hitherto been unable to use psychotherapy due to either high costs or lack of geographic access. But many of the sickest of the discharged patients, rather than being treated in their communities, were either living on the streets or living in nursing homes in conditions little improved from the overcrowded state hospitals they had recently departed. The tenets of the federal program had turned out to be "seriously at odds with reality," *Science* magazine reported.[48] Mark Vonnegut, a politically active medical student in Massachusetts who worked with the mentally ill during his student years, summed up his findings: "There is little evidence to indicate that major psychiatric problems were once minor ones that could have been headed off with a little sympathy and understanding. There is quite a bit of evidence to the contrary."[49]

A large portion of the discharged patients became part of a "revolving door" syndrome. Temporarily stabilized on medication, they were discharged with little more than a "friendly pat on the back" and left to fend for themselves.[50] Not surprisingly, they rapidly disintegrated, went off medication, reexperienced psychoses, and were soon returned to the state hospitals by either family or police to be stabilized and released again. Vonnegut wrote, "For all the therapeutic interaction going on between them and the community, they might just as well be back in the hospital, where their meals came regularly, routine health problems were checked, and every once in a while someone would see how they were doing."[51] Notably, most patients from wealthier families, usually in private rather than state hospitals, did not leave the hospitals after the laws were passed. Their families recognized the limits of outpatient treatment and community mental health and relied on the more intensive treatment modalities available only in a hospital to care for their kin.

For similar reasons, even the movement of certain patients to psychiatric wards of general hospitals was suspect. General hospitals were designed to provide acute, medically intensive care which would allow them to discharge patients rapidly. While psychiatric wards tended to hold patients longer than acute-care wards, they were designed and operated along a similar framework. They were effective in stabilizing a patient in crisis, but were ill-designed to house a patient who needed chronic oversight. Walter Barton, president of the American Psychiatric Association in the early 1960s, questioned the wisdom of the transition. "Is it to be assumed that the general hospital will also provide care for the brain damaged, the chronic alcoholic patient, the sexual deviate, the chronic neurological patient...?"[52] The expectation was quixotic, and most psychiatrists knew it soon after deinstitutionalization began. The drugs calmed the wards, quelled the demons, and modestly brightened prospects for fuller lives. But they could not work the miracles being demanded of them.

States were caught in a difficult position. Public outcry over custodial treatment in the state hospitals had led to reform and community-based treatment in outpatient centers, yet outpatient psychotherapy was proving more limited than many activists had hoped. One psychiatrist reflected, "The concept is great, the reality a disaster."[53] Freed from the highly structured environment of a mental hospital, patients rapidly disintegrated, often to a debased or even dangerous state. While some patients did benefit from treatment received from a CMHC, it was often little more than a "way station for human misery," in the words of Steven Sharfstein, a mental health policy scholar at the NIMH.[54] Most patients who lacked close family ties ended up on the streets or in welfare hotels if they could not be placed into a nursing home. An investigative report by the Long Island *Newsday* newspaper found that many discharged New Yorkers had "been jammed into tiny rooms, basements, and garages and fed a semi-starvation diet of rice and chicken necks."[55] Some became hazardous to themselves or to those around them. In an infamous case in California, Edmund Kemper, a discharged patient from a hospital for the criminally insane, killed his mother and six college students.[56]

Deinstitutionalization was psychotherapy's first public failure. Emerging from the 1950s with substantial public support and interest, and besotted by its own new discoveries and techniques, the profession had promised more than it could deliver. Through the vehicle of government-funded CMHCs, psychotherapy would not only assuage the neurotic, it would treat the very sick while enlivening the well. Robert Felix, director of the NIMH at the time of the initial CMHC legislation, declared his belief that the centers would not only reduce mental illness, they would provide a "climate in which each citizen has optimum opportunities for sustained creative and responsible participation in the life of the community, and for the development of his particular potentialities as human being."[57] But while the centers did deliver psychotherapy to hundreds of thousands of Americans who had previously not had access to it, they did not fill the gap left by the shrinking state hospitals.[58]

Financing

Community mental health centers gave the middle class access to psychotherapy, but so too did private health insurance. The health insurance model was still relatively new, with the oldest Blue Shield plans, which were nonprofit, dating to the 1930s, and most for-profit private plans going back no farther than 1950. By 1968 90 percent of the U.S. population had some sort of health insurance through either a private insurance company, the federal government, state governments, or some sort of corporate cooperative. The plans were skewed toward procedures, with prophylactic care and prescription drugs falling frequently beyond their purview. The plans initially did not cover mental health care, but by 1968 this was changing.

The country had experienced extraordinary growth in the number of psychiatrists in private practice. While in 1938 there had been only 1,500 psychiatrists whose practice was predominantly private, by 1948 that number had grown to 8,000, and by 1959 it was up to 11,000.[59] The number of private practitioners was growing, and so was the amount being spent on private practice. By 1969, approximately 7 percent of all U. S. health-care expenditures were going to mental health care: double that of two decades prior. While the federal and state government still paid for the preponderance of this total (68 percent), the portion paid out of pocket by the mentally ill and their families was steadily rising. In particular, patients who sought lengthy psychotherapy treatments paid a substantial portion of their fees from their own funds. While outpatient therapy in a clinic with a social worker might cost as little as $6 per session, analysis with a trained psychoanalyst could easily cost $35 per session, for a total of $460 per month at the recommended frequency of four sessions weekly. Total costs of $15,000 to $20,000 for a four- or five-year analysis were not unheard of.[60]

Private insurance companies began to respond to the growing demand for reimbursement for mental health services. By 1968, a typical plan covered 50 percent of all outpatient charges with no annual limit. Medicaid was paying for a greater and greater portion of inpatient charges, partially to compensate for the state funds no longer being spent on state psychiatric hospital patients. The army and VA systems were both spending substantial portions of their health-care budgets on mental health service. And even Medicare was purchasing outpatient therapy for its beneficiaries.[61] Insured patients took advantage of the plans, demanding greater psychotherapeutic services as their benefits rose. The most heavily insured areas of the country—Washington, D.C.; suburban Connecticut; New Jersey; San Francisco; and Los Angeles—

became magnets for ambitious young psychiatrists and psychologists, who sought to capitalize on the generous insurance reimbursements.

Fifty percent reimbursement was an enormous improvement, but still hardly adequate to bring the lowest income patients into the psychotherapeutic fold. In response, Group Health Insurance of New York (GHI) initiated a program in 1958 that allowed patients to pay only $5 per session for psychotherapy with an approved provider. Although many beneficiaries initially declined to take advantage of the benefit, an aggressive advertising program over subsequent years increased usage. Pamphlets related how "grumpy grandpas," anxiety-besieged fathers, volatile menopausal wives, alcoholic mothers, and drug-addicted teenagers had all found relief through the "science called psychiatry." One pamphlet related how a "lovable man" had become a "meddling, cantankerous old crab." Upon seeing the GHI psychiatrist, he was cured with antidepressant medication. Another told of a woman paralyzed with anxiety over world problems. Twelve sessions of psychotherapy allowed her to realize that she was not responsible for solving the problems of "Russians or A-bombs." The woman faced her previously masked fears. "Brought into the open, the fears disappeared. She's a happy woman now. So is her husband. Her children, too. Even the new baby."[62]

Psychiatric benefits created a moral hazard, even more so than did regular health benefits. Difficulty in measuring outcomes opened the plans to misuse and abuse. For every correctly diagnosed depressive who received an appropriate and effective regimen of shock treatment, many more functioning neurotics exploited the system for innumerable sessions of psychotherapy or psychoanalysis, often to little measurable benefit. While all health insurance induced demand for health services, mental health insurance did so even more. The number of practicing psychotherapists increased substantially wherever the plans were introduced, and many of the health insurance companies ultimately had to reduce mental health benefits or demand oversight by a third party. In the early 1970s the American Psychiatric Association conducted a study of mental health insurance plans and found that funding the extraordinarily high cost of strict analysis would be an "unwise use" of policy dollars, "especially when the person receiving analysis is not disabled and is pursuing his usual activities."[63]

Ossifying Orthodoxy

At the same time that psychotherapy was gaining exposure and influence in mainstream society, psychoanalysis was solidifying its leadership role in the therapeutic professions. In the two decades after World War II psychoanalysis had grown both in the number of practitioners and in influence. By the mid-1950s young psychiatrists were clamoring for analytic training. Institutes were inundated with applicants, and training analyses were filled with graduates of the nation's premier medical schools and psychiatric residency programs. One survey showed that of the 888 analysts in training in 1960, 18 percent had come from Ivy League medical schools (fifty from Harvard alone), and another 11 percent had graduated from the top tier of public research universities such as Illinois, Wisconsin, and Michigan.[64] Chairmen of many of the nation's premier departments of psychiatry were trained psychoanalysts, as were the recipients of much of the newly released NIMH research funding. Nathan Hale, a historian of psychiatry, writes that forgoing psychoanalytic training in these years relegated a psychiatrist to "second-class" citizen.[65]

The profession both spent and produced wealth. NIMH training grants for psychiatry increased from $1.1 million in 1948 to $38.8 million in 1962, with a preponderance of these funds going to analytically oriented residency programs. (The Yale and UCLA psychiatry departments, both bastions of psychoanalytic orthodoxy, were the two leading recipients of these funds.)[66] At the same time, newly graduated analysts found a strong market for their services, in which they could charge $40 to $50 per analytic hour, producing an annual income substantially greater than that afforded their nonanalyst colleagues. During the heyday of New York analysis in the late 1950s, many analysts grew rich while their social cachet increased. Historian Douglas Kirsner writes, "Psychoanalysis and its premier institute [the New York Psychoanalytic Institute] were so prestigious, the rewards of becoming an analyst so bountiful, and the intimidation and control of the inner group so effective that there was no challenge to those in power."[67]

Those training in psychoanalysis came not only from elite academic backgrounds, but from unusual social backgrounds as well. Jews, who constituted less than 3 percent of the U.S. population, made up a third of newly trained analysts, while Catholics, at 25 percent of the population, made up only 8 percent of the analysts. The analysts in training were almost entirely of professional or managerial parentage, and 13 percent had parents who were physicians. Fewer than 15 percent had been raised in single-parent or divorced households, and in a telling statistic, only 2 percent had lived in families that earned less than $2,000 per year in the 1930s, a time when 80 percent of the population had earned that amount or less.[68]

The cost of analytic training was high. Most trainees were simultaneously completing psychiatric residencies in which they earned a median of $3,000 per year. The cost of the training analysis sessions was $15 to $20 per hour, for an annual cost of $4,000 per year, in addition to the $900 cost of tuition at the institute. Many trainees moonlighted in the evenings, taking private patients or being on call at local emergency rooms, to supplement their meager salaries. With the added obligations of spouses and, frequently, young children, it was not surprising that psychoanalysts had often accrued thousands of dollars of debt by the end of their training.

Fortunately, the training was usually deemed worth the sacrifice. The imprimatur of a training institute opened up unparalleled opportunities in psychiatry: academic appointments, hospital chairmanships, editorial assignments, and of course the potential to create a lucrative private practice. Although only one of seven American psychiatrists was an analyst, these select few increasingly dominated the key leadership positions in the profession through the 1960s, dictating residency assignments, overseeing NIMH grants, formulating training curricula, and making admissions decisions on aspiring applicants to residency programs. The analysts constituted an elite cadre among the psychiatrists, who in turn set standards for the entire psychotherapeutic enterprise. The spoils of the analytic "gold rush" accrued disproportionately to those select few who had inherited the mantle of Freud. Ives Hendrick, a prominent psychoanalyst, called psychoanalysis "the brand that dominates the market."[69] Alfred Kazin, the noted social and literary critic, described it as a "very smooth" business, a perfect fit with America's growing obsession with psychology, mental health, and self-fulfillment. It was, in the apt description of the social observer Edith Kurzweil, a "psychoboom."[70]

One mark of the unchallenged authority of the profession was the growing length of analyses. Whereas Sigmund Freud had initially envisioned the psychoanalytic process taking nine months, and whereas a typical analysis in the immediate postwar years took six hundred hours (roughly thirty months at a rate of five sessions per week), by 1968 the typical analysis had lengthened to nine hundred hours, and five years later it was over a thousand. Martin Gross, writing the following decade, suggested that analysis might eventually become "a lifelong activity for the devoted."[71] Even "short-term" interventions got longer; one university counseling center found that the average number of counseling sessions for troubled students had increased from six in 1949 to thirty-one in 1954.[72] The trend, seemingly benign, undermined the integrity of the enterprise, for if analysts could whimsically lengthen the process, then there could be no objective measure of a successful outcome. Franz Alexander, professor of psychiatry at the University of Chicago, condemned the trend as evidence of "overtreatment," noting that there was no evidence to establish a relationship between length and efficacy of analysis. To the contrary, at least some psychiatrists observed that some of the most effective treatment occurred early in an analysis, and a few had even experimented with purposefully designed "brief" forms of therapy. Alexander noted sardonically, "During temporary interruptions patients often discover that they can live without their analyst."[73]

Another prerogative of the elite profession was claim on choice geographic turf. While physicians had always tended to locate their practices disproportionately in wealthy areas or near the best hospital facilities, psychoanalysts extended this trend. The two centers of analytic activity were New York City and Los Angeles, although vibrant analytic schools existed in Washington, San Francisco, Chicago, Detroit, and Boston. Of the roughly 3,500 practicing analysts in the United States in the mid-1960s, nearly 150 practiced in Washington, D.C., 60 in Beverly Hills, and hundreds along Central Park West and Park Avenue in Manhattan. One observer of the psychoanalytic scene calculated that the wealthy Long Island suburb of Great Neck had as many analysts "as the entire state of Florida," while two buildings on the single corner of Ninety-sixth Street and Fifth Avenue in Manhattan had as many analysts as "Minnesota, Oregon, Delaware, Oklahoma, Vermont, Wisconsin, and Tennessee, *combined.*"[74]

Such privilege and prestige led to professional arrogance. Psychoanalysts began to view their role in the mental health professions as almost uniquely insightful, über-scientists among a world of lesser achievers.[75] Despite the absence of most formal prerequisites to scientific inquiry— hypotheses, verifiable data collection, explicit methodology, and defined testing standards—psychoanalysts claimed to be not merely scientific, but *purely* so. One group complained that general psychiatry, a mongrel and "heterogeneous collection" of sciences, was actually diluting the rigor of psychoanalysis, a "basic science," and robbing it of its "purity and integrity."[76] Another group emphasized the advanced and complex nature of psychoanalytic science, which, like all sciences, drew upon its own specialized vocabulary. While outside observers wondered if psychoanalysts, in an effort to intimidate, did not make themselves purposefully opaque, the analysts themselves defended their arcane language as scientifically necessary. "If the terminology we use is so illusory for you, or too transient, it's only because it has to be that way," John Briggs, spokesman for the American Academy of Psychoanalysis, explained to a group of journalists.[77]

The arrogance bled over into practice. Many analysts, accustomed to practicing the most passive sort of therapy, seemed to withdraw even more amid the rising orthodoxy of the 1960s. Analyses lasting for years were punctuated by the most laconic of interpretations. Frieda Fromm-Reichmann, a famously orthodox analyst at the Chestnut Lodge in Rockville, Maryland, urged reserve in her trainees, and taught them that the ideal analyst showed "no signs whatsoever of reacting to, or participating in, the patient's communications."[78] (Fromm-Reichmann did offer that at times it might be "indicated and wise to shake hands with a patient," though one should take care not to exceed a necessary "thrift" in physical contact.)[79] Martin Gross, writing a decade later, went even further, condemning any sort of reassurance, humanism, or empathy as antithetical to the analytical relationship. He wrote, "Almost all analysts refuse to answer the common plea: 'What do you think I should do about...?'" or "For God's sake, tell me what to do." Gross cited a Brooklyn analyst's response to such pleas: "We can't help them that way. That's the job of psychotherapy, not psychoanalysis."[80]

Perhaps the greatest excesses of orthodoxy took place in the realm of the sickest psychotics. Frieda Fromm-Reichmann, for example, had strenuously argued that schizophrenia was not an organic illness, but rather resulted from a cold and emotionally withholding mother. Fromm-Reichmann drew attention within the profession by condemning the mothers of schizophrenics in the most derogatory way as *schizophrenogenic*—mothers who actually produced the disease in their children. Schizophrenics, Fromm-Reichmann argued, needed to be "cured of the wounds and frustrations of life," and needed to see the analyst as a human being who "did not turn away in estrangement or disgust."[81] In so condemning the mothers, Fromm-Reichmann drew upon the decade-old work of Trude Tietze, who dismissed the concerns of the mothers of her schizophrenic patients as efforts to manipulate the psychiatrist and thus deflect responsibility for their sick children. "It was impossible to obtain accurate data in regard to onset and completion of toilet training of their children," Tietze had complained, nor had the mothers been willing to frankly discuss their sex lives.[82] Ted Lidz, a psychiatrist with the Yale Psychiatric Institute in New Haven studying youthful schizophrenic patients a few years later, concluded that "the [schizophrenic] patient's family of origin is always severely disturbed."[83] When asked about comparative observations of families with nonschizophrenic children, Lidz responded, "There was no sense in having normal controls because it was obvious that these were such aberrant families."[84]

The analysts, however, had gone too far. With rising competition from humanistic therapists, rational-emotive therapists, cognitive-behavioral therapists, and the two nonmedical and nonpsychoanalytic professions of psychology and social work, orthodox psychoanalysis began to slip. Young psychiatrists began to perceive the cultlike rigidity of the profession, the disconnect from scientific progress. Martin Grotjahn, an iconoclastic analyst who became increasingly critical of his profession through the 1960s, remarked on the fact that too many young psychiatrists entered their training analyses "already thoroughly indoctrinated," which hardly served to encourage the inquiring mind.[85] Starting in the mid-1960s, applications to psychoanalytic institutes began to fall, even as applications to doctoral programs in clinical psychology surged. Fewer new psychoanalytic institutes were being created or were seeking affiliation with the American Psychoanalytic Association, and patient loads fell at the same time. The president of the American Psychoanalytic Association, Leo Rangell, reported a "change in the hospitality, ranging up

to sharp hostility, in the scientific and intellectual community, in medicine and in the press," toward psychoanalysis.[86] A survey of senior analysts in 1972 reported that most felt that the field had hardly advanced
since Freud's death in 1939, while a series of interviews conducted with
analysts around the same time found few who felt positively about progress in the science or in the profession.[87]

Declining interest in analytic training to some degree followed increasingly public acknowledgments of the limits of the profession. The
1970s brought a sharp reduction in claims and presumptions of psychoanalysts. They no longer claimed an ability to cure psychotics, and they
even suggested that many neurotics might be "poor candidates" for psychoanalytic treatment.[88] The goal of analysis was "educational rather
than medical."[89] Growing evidence called into question the value of
lengthy, intensive bouts of analysis, and indeed as many analysts reduced
the frequency of their contact with their analytic patients from five days
per week to four, or even three, they observed little difference in outcomes or progress. Jerome Frank, a near legendary figure in the Johns
Hopkins department of psychiatry, observed that "in actual duration of
treatment, in terms of months or years, the patient going five times a
week takes about as long to be cured as the patient going three times."[90]
Intensiveness of treatment seemed to make little difference to either
outpatient neurotics or inpatient psychotics, and all seemed to heal at
approximately the same rate.[91]

The aggregate weight of evidence was beginning to undermine psychoanalysis's credibility, even among its most passionate adherents. Their
response was to redefine psychoanalysis as more "art" than science, suggesting that its greatest use was as a path to self-knowledge, rather than as
a form of clinical intervention. Joseph Jaffe, a psychoanalyst writing in
the early 1970s about progress in psychoanalytic research, suggested that
not only was psychoanalysis better conceived of as an art, but that efforts
to make subjective judgments of its success were a "naïve form of reduc-
tionism."[92] The sorts of research results produced by rigorous studies of

outcomes of psychoanalysis had "never been compelling to the working therapist," Jaffe claimed.[93] K. M. Colby, writing in 1962, had earlier hinted at the shift: "Psychotherapy is…a practical art, a craft like agriculture or medicine or wine-making in which an artisan relies on an incomplete, fragmentary body of knowledge and empirically established rules traditionally passed on from master to apprentice."[94]

By 1972 psychoanalysis had become, paradoxically, both more rigorously orthodox and more accommodating. Faced with declining interest from both future adherents and potential clients, analysts responded in dichotomous ways, some moving to the left and some to the right. Those who renewed their commitment to Freudian precepts insisted on increased adherence to institute training, longer analyses, increasingly rigid psychodynamic interpretations of behavior, and general insularity to outside influences. Most analysts, however, understood that their era was beginning to wane. Increasingly effective drugs, shorter-term (and possibly more effective) therapy, and innovative insights into the biochemistry and physiology of the brain all convinced them that while they might continue to find wisdom in the writings of Freud and his acolytes, prudence demanded a more pragmatic and eclectic approach to treatment. Their hearts may have drawn them toward orthodoxy, but their brains, and pocketbooks, led them to heterodoxy.

Religion and Psychotherapy

One of the odder aspects of Freudian orthodoxy was its neoreligiosity. Freud had not been merely an atheist but an überatheist—his theories personified the enlightenment ideal of dispassionate reason in a godless universe. Over the decades his teachings had come to represent, for many theists, the epitome of amoral rationalism: not exactly a path to evil, but so far beyond the moral teachings of the church as to constitute a threat. Freudianism claimed to be a path to knowledge, but in so claiming ran directly counter to the long established Christian path to wisdom, which required genuflection and transcendental humility. Indeed, in the eyes of many Christians, the audacity of the Freudian claim was that knowledge could come without God, whereas in the Christian idiom divine grace was a necessary prerequisite to wisdom.

As psychoanalysis gained currency in the 1940s and 1950s, conservative clergymen rejected it. They feared the quasi-clerical role of the analyst, the presumptuousness of self-searching without soul-searching, and the oddly indulgent quality of exploring sexuality devoid of the underpinnings of sin. The process was based on "materialism, hedonism, infantilism, and eroticism," Monsignor Fulton Sheen told gathered parishioners at St. Patrick's Cathedral in New York City in 1947.[95] In his provocative book *Peace of the Soul*, which he wrote in 1949, Sheen sardonically rewrote the parable of the Pharisee in a psychoanalytic idiom:

> I thank Thee, O Lord, that my Freudian adviser has told me there is no such thing as guilt, that sin is a myth, and that Thou, O Father, art only a projection of my father complex.... Oh, I thank Thee that I am not like the rest of men, those nasty people, such as the Christian there in the back of the temple, who thinks that he is a sinner, that his soul stands in need of grace.... I may have an Oedipus complex, but I have no sin.[96]

Sex, in the psychoanalytic system, was detached from mature love, devoid of meaning beyond the function of procreating. The theologian Fritz Kunkel, writing of "the great pagan Freud," preached that sex should not be seen as sublimated into cultural achievements, as Freud had conjectured, but rather should be viewed as a precursor to "higher love." He wrote, "The acorn is not 'sublimated' into an oak tree and a child is not 'sublimated' into a man."[97] While psychoanalysis might not have initially rejected God, its mature form in postwar America most certainly did. Modern psychoanalysts understood that for Freud, God was "derivative": little more than the projection of an infantile need for a father.[98]

Most clergy, and many psychotherapists, were more balanced. Neither analysis nor therapy necessarily precluded faith. The two could be seen as complementary rather than competitive. Proponents of this view held that psychotherapy worked on the unconscious components of the psyche, whereas religion, particularly of the Judeo-Christian sort, worked on the conscious. Several prominent clerics, among them Paul Tillich and William Roberts, urged both sides to recognize the potential symbiosis of divergent paths to spiritual peace. Tillich wrote that "the patient comes to the therapist principally because he cannot accept himself," while Roberts urged the minister and the therapist to both "speak with confidence of their own victories won over doubt and weakness."[99] The message of these more enlightened clerics was one of acceptance; a man immersed in misery might require therapeutic intervention before he could accept God in a meaningful way, but in the same way a well-analyzed man probably needed God to achieve true psychic peace. Karl Stern, a psychiatrist and convert to Catholicism, warned his colleagues of denying their patients the comfort of God. He wrote, "If the analyst succeeds in *reducing* the religious content to primary psychological substrata, he would deprive the patient of his most precious gift." One should neither propagate the "fallacy of angelism" nor undermine the glory of God.[100]

The debate hinged over two misunderstood concepts: the role of guilt, and the necessary dichotomy of conscious and unconscious. Christian moral teaching required guilt, for it was through remorse over primordial guilt that a Christian turned to Christ for intervention and redemption. Psychoanalysis and psychotherapy also focused their energies on guilt, but worked to rid individuals of the emotion, rather than leverage it for spiritual advancement. The two seemed irreconcilable, but a number of therapists and clergy argued that this was only so if one failed to recognize that guilt could be both conscious and unconscious, and that psychoanalysis worked to dismiss only the unconscious type. Gregory Zilboorg, a prominent pychoanalyst in New York City in the 1940s and 50s, wrote in 1949 that psychoanalysts "relieve their patients from feeling guilty about things of which they really are not guilty, and leave them with the sense of guilt about things of which they really are guilty."[101]

If guilt could be divided neatly into two, the unconscious guilt of the suffering ego and the conscious guilt of the tortured soul, then the roles of analyst and cleric were independent and not necessarily in conflict. The first type of guilt was not so much immoral as amoral—guilt without sin—and required a psychic purging. The second, by contrast, required a conscious act of contrition to resolve.[102] Confusion of the two spheres was partly a result of divergent cultures. The Catholic clergy, who repeatedly took the strongest anti-Freudian stands, served a congregation that had largely resisted psychotherapy, whereas Protestant and Jewish clergy, both somewhat more reconciled to the therapy, preached to parishioners who were generally more psychologically sophisticated. Harry McNeil, a theologian writing in the late 1940s, pondered Catholic discomfort with Freudian models. Perhaps, he posited, Catholics actually viewed sex as *more* significant than did Freud. "That may explain why they hesitate even to talk about it and resent Freudian outspokenness."[103]

Whether by design or happenstance, though, clergy began to move toward delivering therapy during the 1950s. In part it was pragmatic; a growing awareness of the high prevalence of mental illness coupled with perpetual shortages of trained professionals meant that the task of delivering therapy would devolve on whoever was available and present, such as internists, teachers, coaches, and clergy. The National Association for Mental Health began in 1954 to distribute a pamphlet entitled *Clergy and Mental Health*, and the Institutes of Religion and Health was established in 1953 expressly to offer clergy advanced training in therapy.[104] Various seminaries began to offer pastoral counseling courses in an effort to better prepare their students for the complex emotional scenarios into which they might be drawn. Nearly a third decided, upon exposure to therapeutic concepts, that they might benefit from psychotherapy themselves, and almost all appreciated the expanded understanding gained through even modest training in psychotherapy.[105] "I found in what [Congregational minister Anton] Boisen called 'the wilderness of the lost' you discovered the needs of people at the ground level, naked both emotionally and physically," the resident minister at St. Elizabeth's Hospital in Washington, D.C., offered.[106]

A certain group of clergy resisted the training. For these more traditional, and disproportionately Catholic, clergy, the very process of psychotherapy undermined the moral authority of the Church. In the minds of these pastors, alleviating guilt was precisely what the Church ought *not* to do, for even if the guilt had been produced without sin, it was helpful in driving a parishioner to confession and repentance. In this understanding, psychotherapy could not be a complement to confession and prayer, for it must inevitably distract the penitent from his true calling. George Scarlett, a theologian and psychologist, explained the clergy's fear of therapy as stemming from the belief that the sorts of feelings and fears that therapists tried to alleviate ought to be resolvable through prayer and the acceptance of Christ.[107] While therapists sought to help their patients reach their own potential, Christianity (and, to a lesser extent, Judaism and Islam) taught that the path to fulfillment lay through fulfilling the demands of a jealous God. The German theologian Jurgen Moltmann, grappling with these issues, ultimately rejected the claims of therapy, because its aims of helping people discover their authentic selves ran counter to Christian ideals of fealty to one's devotion. He wrote, "It is to this, and not to himself, that he seeks to live."[108]

Clergy who were suspicious of psychiatrists and psychologists were responding in part to the social and cultural differences that divided the professions. Therapists were more rootless, skeptical, and liberal than were members of the clergy. Fewer than 50 percent of clinical psychologists believed in God, while the vast majority of clergymen did. Therapists maintained views on premarital sex, divorce, and abortion that were radically at odds with both the clergy and the general population. Carl Rogers, founder of humanistic psychology, admitted in a study conducted in 1972 that psychotherapy was "subversive" and "promoted a new model of man contrary to that which had been traditionally acceptable."[109] In the late 1970s, Robert Hogan, a clinical psychologist and researcher, admitted that a psychologist who spoke seriously about religion would be "branded a meathead; a mystic; an intuitive, touchy-feely sort of moron."[110] In short, psychotherapists of all stripes felt that the individual was the supreme being, whereas deists felt that God held that title.

Ultimately, most pastors and therapists recognized the need for both. Humans were multidimensional creatures, with separate spiritual and psychological sides. Many people sought the counsel of their pastor to guide them spiritually and their therapist to untangle the roots of anxiety, fear, depression, and angst. Tillich, the notably humane theologian, spoke for many when he proclaimed that "having to live and die alone creates enough anxiety for man, and the problem should not be compounded with neurotic problems induced by condemnatory religion."[111] And an anonymous psychiatrist, writing two lengthy articles in the *Atlantic Monthly* in 1954, urged the two sides to learn from each other and to employ combinations of their differing approaches to provide spiritual peace to the many who sought it.[112]

Even the most orthodox psychoanalysts could understand the role of religion in life. Jung famously accommodated religion in his own personal brand of psychoanalysis, and grounded his vision of mental health in communitarian faith. In 1932 he declared that of the many hundreds of patients he had treated above age forty, there had not been one "whose problem in the last resort was not that of finding a religious outlook on life." They had all fallen ill after losing faith in whatever creed they had been raised in, and "none of them had been really healed who did not regain his religious outlook."[113] But more surprising was the observation of Edith Weigert, grande dame of Washington psychoanalytic circles and analyst to legions of analysands in training. In an interview in 1955, she stated her belief that one simply could not dismiss God from the psyche:

> If we call religion the need for absolute dependence, then I have never in my life met a genuinely irreligious person. Whenever we are able to investigate the repressed unconscious thoroughly enough, we discover in every person a deep need for security. The neurotic as well as the "adjusted" individual, the believer as well as the agnostic, all of them are only too eager to be "saved," to be accepted by a God who comforts them and their friends and destroys their foes.[114]

Social Work

In contrast to psychoanalysts, social workers struggled to define themselves professionally in the 1950s and 1960s. Their efforts had been largely ineffective, however, and social workers were best known for fostering communication, facilitating the exchange of ideas and thoughts, and validating experiences and feelings, rather than for their high professional standards. Marion Sanders, a leader in the profession in the 1950s, described a hypothetical scenario: "The day after the bomb fell, the doctor was out binding up radiation burns. The minister prayed and set up a soup kitchen in the ruined chapel. The policeman herded stray children to the rubble heap where the teacher had improvised a classroom. And the social worker wrote a report; since two had survived, they held a conference on Interpersonal Relationships in a Time of Intensified Anxiety States."[115] This dark humor communicated the main problems of the trade: vagueness of purpose and general inconsistency in training and technique.

The profession faced problems of its own making. Rooted, as they were, in interpersonal relationships, clinical social workers tended to be more affirming than insightful, and thus faced difficulty in adopting professional standards. George Pikser, the executive director of the Jewish Social Service Agency of New York, called it the "sick man of the professions."[116] Long attuned to welcoming the stranger, calming the disaffected, and binding the social wounds that divided people, the craft seemed incapable of making the necessary exclusions implicit to professional standards. Social work schools had few prerequisites or entrance requirements; social work societies and associations had no membership criteria; and the workers themselves were neither licensed nor certified. While graduates of a few select schools of social work did accrue some professional cachet from their academic backgrounds, most social agencies were lax in demanding proof of particular curricular items or standards. A report on professional issues in social work issued in 1963 concluded that the stereotype of the social worker who "disdains facts in favor of feelings" was frequently "all too true."[117] Social workers who desired more rigorous and advanced training in their field often needed to pursue it in non–social work disciplines such as sociology, psychology, or medicine.

Private practice, however, emerged in the 1950s and 1960s as the route to professionalization. Social workers had engaged in psychotherapeutic-like activities practically since the inception of the field, but many had hesitated to pursue the trade vigorously.[118] While the issues that social workers confronted with their clients in agency settings often overlapped with the kinds of conflicts that psychiatrists and clinical psychologists counseled their patients on, private practice per se seemed at odds with the ethos of the profession.

But for social workers compelled to make a living, the lure of private practice was difficult to resist. The number of clinical social workers in private practice rose from just 30 in 1935 to more than 1,500 by 1962. Those who migrated to private practice defended their decision on

professional grounds and pleaded with their colleagues for ethical in-
dulgence. Daniel Jennings asked his colleagues, "Is there anything inher-
ently evil, immoral or unethical in practicing social work outside the
aegis of a duly incorporated private agency or government agency?" He
answered his own question, "We must consider that all so-called self-
seeking is not bad." Indeed, it was probably "indispensable."[119] Other social workers were less tortured by the move, claiming it was merely a
natural evolution of a "dynamic and creative profession to changing
needs," or that it was serving an ever-growing population of unhappy
individuals and families who could find no succor in the traditional
therapeutic professions.[120]

Social workers who moved to private practice maintained that the
high standards in their work were "bound and controlled by social work
values and ethics" and filled a gap left by psychotherapists of other persuasions who focused almost exclusively on individual growth at the
expense of family and society.[121] Social workers in private practice spoke
of "restoring family equilibrium," repairing damaged marriages, helping
children with issues of adjustment, and helping individuals function in
demanding circumstances.[122] While their world drew on the principles
of the interpersonal and humanistic psychotherapies of Sullivan and
Rogers, they claimed that their styles were grounded in a perspective
and orientation unique to social work. And while no sharp border
divided social work from psychology or psychiatry, social workers generally spent less time with clients exploring issues surrounding the formation of the ego and self, and more time exploring the practical
barriers that prevented their clients from creating satisfying adult relationships. The practice combined the pragmatism of Ellis's rational-
emotive therapy with the interpersonal focus of Sullivan and Horney.

The profession owed its malaise and ambivalence at least in part to
its marked gender imbalance. From its earliest days it had been populated almost entirely by female workers, and the patterns of its practice
tended to track the needs of women. Employment in agencies, rather

than in private practice, allowed women to work limited hours, take extensive vacations that dovetailed with school calendars, and work part-time. Many social workers withdrew from the field during the years in which they were raising young children, returned part-time during their children's adolescence, and then to full-time work later in life. One exasperated male social worker, desperate to increase his earnings, asserted that the profession's troubles were largely due to the predominance of women in its ranks, "and that the women actually would like the situation to remain very much as it is, with all of its misfortunes, because being a relatively less attractive occupation, it is protected from the intrusion of crude masculine aggressiveness."[123] The same man pointed out that social work, for most of its practitioners, constituted either a supplementary source of family income, or else the sole source of income for single, childless women. He wrote, "Rarely does she have the same financial goal as does a man to really strive, by any means possible, towards a higher rate of compensation."[124]

Social workers in private practice faced competition from the very agencies many of them had emerged from. Nonprofit social service agencies tended to provide similar counseling services to community members at reduced rates, subsidized by philanthropic or government funds. While these subsidized sessions were aimed at the poor, few agencies barred middle-class clients from using their services. Thus, private practitioners found their rates artificially depressed, their natural market being with upper-middle-class and well-to-do clients who tended to shun agency settings. More entrepreneurial social workers located their offices in wealthy suburbs to better serve their clients, or opened specialty practices in marriage counseling or adolescent development, all aimed primarily at clients with time and resources to pursue such self-improvement. No other service-oriented profession faced quite the same competition from the public and nonprofit sphere, as lawyers and physicians who provided pro bono services generally imposed a means test on their clients and patients who sought charity services. Reduced fees, of course, tended to diminish the status and attractiveness of the profession.

As certain social workers began to pursue private clients more aggressively, they inevitably clashed with psychiatrists and, to a lesser extent, psychologists. Psychiatrists denigrated the "discount" therapists, but feared the incursion on their professional niche.[125] Social workers tried to appease their colleagues in psychotherapy by claiming that they were "nonmedical" in approach and had a different orientation, but the similarities in activities and practices of the two professions were apparent. Psychiatrists could administer drugs and electroshock and admit patients to a hospital, but for the most psychodynamic among them, these were unattractive modalities of treatment. Psychoanalysts and dynamic psychotherapists prided themselves on using the same tools as social workers to evince personal truths, reorder their patients' psyches, and improve mental health. Talk therapy was central to the work of both professions, and the fact that psychiatrists arrived at their work with much broader and deeper knowledge of neurophysiology, endocrinology, and pharmacology did not seem relevant in distinguishing professional purviews. The Group for the Advancement of Psychiatry grappled with the issue shortly after World War II, and feebly concluded only that doctors approached psychotherapy from a perspective of sickness ("How sick is the patient?") whereas social workers approached it from that of wellness ("How well is the patient?").[126] The distinction was not compelling and did not augur for peaceful professional relations in coming years.

By 1955, many social workers were rallying around licensure as the most promising path to increased professional status and compensation. Incapable of internally regulating itself, the profession turned to state regulatory bodies to create laws defining who could call themselves social workers and who could practice. A social worker in Ohio admitted, "We have the knowledge but we do not have the status to put our knowledge to practical use," and urged passage of licensing legislation.[127] In New York, Ohio, Wisconsin, and California, chapters of both the

American Association of Social Workers and the National Association of Social Workers lobbied state legislatures to pass laws defining a social worker as one who had graduated from an accredited two-year social work program, had been supervised in clinical practice for a set period of time, and had possibly passed a licensing exam. While there was some debate over the wisdom of the measures, most social workers agreed that the heightened standards, prestige, professional respect, and compensation that stood to be gained outweighed the costs. Current social workers could be grandfathered into the profession, while future social workers would understand the professional hurdles that lay before them at the outset of their training. An apocryphal story was told of a wily governor facing a group of assembled social workers lobbying for such a bill. "Gentlemen, are you concerned with advancing the health, safety and welfare of the people under the police powers of this state, or are you primarily interested in creating a monopoly situation to eliminate competition and raise prices?" the governor asked. The group's spokesman replied, "Governor, we're interested in a little of each."[128]

Psychotherapy in the 1960s continued to evolve. Buffeted by conflicting forces of political activism, psychoanalytic orthodoxy, pastoral ambivalence, and growing social work professionalism, the craft grew but continued to splinter. Increasing numbers of Americans were gaining access to psychotherapy, both because of greater absolute numbers of therapists and because of new government support for the practice, but they faced a balkanized profession that could not seem to agree on practice standards or benchmarks for success. Americans liked therapy and were willing to experiment with it both to cure mental illness and to merely improve their relationships and general happiness. But the therapists themselves could not seem to agree on their goals or even on what, exactly, constituted therapy.

CHAPTER 7

Narcissism

In the 1970s a "culture of narcissism" descended upon the country, in the words of cultural historian Christopher Lasch.[1] Social structures and mores, weakened by the intergenerational rifts of the previous decade, gave way to alien forms of social discourse and organization. The journalist Tom Wolfe remarked on the "third great awakening" unfolding before him, while social critic Jim Hougan witnessed the rise of millenarian sects—cultlike groups of people who looked forward to a new messianic age to dawn with the coming of the third millennium.[2] Many Americans, particularly the youthful baby boomers, jettisoned their place in the historical ferment and turned to self-gratification as a new faith. Lasch wrote that the narcissistic individual of the time gave "no thought to anything beyond [his] individual needs,"[3] while Perry London, a California psychologist, described how the mantra of "do your own thing" had become a "hallmark of optimal adjustment."[4] Heinz Kohut, professor at the University of Chicago and the dean of academic psychoanalysis, traced the profound shift from the Oedipal to the narcissistic in his 1971 book, *The Analysis of Self*, in which he called narcissism the "paradigmatic" complaint of the era.[5]

Narcissistic culture was a perverse outgrowth of the societal soul-searching of the previous decade. But whereas the idealism of the sixties had impelled many social critics to seek ways to heal society, the self-absorption of the seventies led many of these same social malcontents to seek ways to heal their own damaged selves. The "sick society" that had been blamed for poverty, violence, and social inequity was now blamed for angst, alienation, and psychic turmoil. Herbert Fensterheim, professor of psychology at Cornell, wrote that while human beings sought a life of "dignity and self-fulfillment," modern society imposed life patterns that were "incompatible with these aims."[6] Psychologists examined the nature of happiness—a state which the original Freudians had tended to dismiss as infantile and unachievable—and found present life patterns to be incompatible with the ideal. One survey sought to rank sources of unhappiness and found that beyond economic and material want its major causes were "job," "community, national and world problems," and "personal characteristics."[7] By contrast, the primary sources of happiness were found to be children and marriage—supporting the notion that those with more traditional life trajectories were generally better off amid the dislocation of modernity.[8]

Society was changing. Americans were breaking economic, gender, and racial bonds, which, while liberating for millions, was also undermining the solidity and grounding of the culture. Many Americans fled from churches, fraternal organizations, civic associations, extended families, and communal ties. Unprecedented numbers relocated to attend university and then failed to return home. Large numbers continued to migrate south and west, devastating the old "rust belt" cities of the Great Lakes and northern Midwest, while at the same time the white flight from older urban cores continued into the suburbs and beyond. Gerald Klerman, a psychiatrist, wrote of how the "secular orientation and geographic mobility" of the time meant that "fewer friends and family were called upon for support when individuals [found] themselves lonely, disabled, or distressed."[9] Attenuated bonds of kin and community drove people to more impersonal and structured forms of support such as the welfare and health-care systems and, increasingly, therapy.

In the 1950s and 1960s Americans had grudgingly accepted psychotherapy as a periodic necessity, but in the 1970s they embraced it whole-
heartedly. Mainline publications listed the symptoms of "maladaption"
and "discontentedness," and explained to their readers when and how
to pursue therapy and the optimal type of therapy for each complaint.
The venerable *Saturday Evening Post* enumerated eleven categories of
mental fitness ranging from the pristine "no symptoms, superior functioning in a wide range of activities, life's problems never seem to get
out of hand," to the mediocre "moderate symptoms or generally functioning with some difficulty (e.g., few friends and flat affect, depressed
mood and pathological self-doubt)," to the pathetic "needs constant supervision for several days to prevent hurting self or others, makes no attempt to maintain minimal personal hygiene."[10] Alcoholics Anonymous
continued to grow, but was now joined by a plethora of new support
groups based at YMCAs and Salvation Army stations, such as Parents
without Partners, Weight Watchers, and Planned Parenthood.[11] Christopher Lasch describes the phenomenon of "psychological man" of the
late twentieth century:

> Therapists, not priests or popular preachers or self-help gurus or
> models of success like the captains of industry, become his principal
> allies in the struggle for composure; he turns to them in the hope of
> achieving the modern equivalent of salvation, "mental health." Ther-
> apy has established itself as the successor both to rugged individual-
> ism and to religion; but this does not mean that the "triumph of the
> therapeutic" has become a new religion in its own right. Therapy
> constitutes an antireligion, not always to be sure because it adheres
> to rational explanation or scientific methods of healing, as its practi-
> tioners would have us believe, but because modern society "has no
> future" and therefore gives no thought to anything beyond its im-
> mediate needs.[12]

Narcissistic culture challenged prevailing stereotypes, including those of mental health. The thirty-year-old trinity of psychotherapy—psychodynamic; humanistic and interpersonal; and cognitive and rational-emotive—now splintered into countless sects and fragments as wandering souls sought gurus and shamans to heal their psychic wounds. While few therapists dispensed entirely with the traditional Freudian pillars of angst, repression, and catharsis, many twisted these tenets into new and almost unrecognizable forms. Jerry Rubin, the Yippie leader and political muckraker, wrote of his own psychological odyssey: "In five years, from 1971 to 1975, I directly experienced est, gestalt therapy, bioenergetics, rolfing, massage, jogging, health foods, tai chi, Esalen, hypnotism, modern dance, meditation, Silva Mind Control, Arica, acupuncture, sex therapy, Reichian therapy, and More House—a smorgasbord course in New Consciousness."[13] Other Americans took the less innovative route of chemical therapy, doubling consumption of psychotropic medication in a decade and turning to "mind drugs" (antidepressants, tranquilizers, antipsychotic medications) for 20 percent of all prescription pharmaceuticals in 1971.[14]

Even corporate America, the conservative bastion of social mores, turned toward psychotherapy. Growing awareness of the toll taken on the workplace by depression, anxiety, alcoholism, and, to a lesser extent, narcotics abuse induced many large corporations to establish therapy programs where workers could be counseled through their troubles. An NIMH study showed that as much as 70 percent of all workplace absences and medical leaves had a psychological component.[15] Many companies responded by bringing psychologists directly to the workplace, establishing counseling offices in businesses and factories, or else contracting with outside providers to work exclusively with their employees. Other companies encouraged employees to take "mental health days" off or forced employees to use granted vacation leave, in the hopes of avoiding professional exhaustion and "corporate burnout."

The search for happiness led to bizarre abuses at times. Many of the founders of the newer innovative therapies were scoundrels and charlatans, hawking their psychic wares no less shamelessly than their nineteenth-century predecessors had plied nostrums and snake oils. Some were ultimately investigated and defrocked; others fled before science could unveil their frauds. L. Ron Hubbard, the founder of Dianetics and the Church of Scientology, was barred from both France and England and investigated in the United States by the Internal Revenue Service. Werner Erhard, the founder of Erhard Seminars Training (est), fled the country in 1991 after former adherents accused him of sexual abuse and fraud. Others simply closed up their shops after community opinion turned against them, or renamed and relocated their enterprises.

Drug companies were more careful but sometimes equally excessive. Starting in the late 1960s they began to aggressively market psychotropic drugs to psychiatrists (and later general internists) while redefining the range of diagnosable mental illness. One drug company advertisement aimed at psychiatrists showed a woman "imprisoned" behind mops and brooms with the caption "You can't set her free but you can help her feel less anxious."[16] Another, portraying a man distraught at his wife's emotional vacillations, told psychiatrists, "In premenstrual tension, your prescription of Equanil can help ease his wife's anxiety, thus reducing her irritability and nervousness."[17] And another, still harping on the dysphoria caused to men by their bothersome wives, went, "She has insomnia...so he's awake. Restless and irritable, she growls at her husband. How can this shrew be tamed?"[18]

Attenuated social bonds and broken social conventions in the 1970s created a psychic vacuum, and psychotherapy largely filled it. An article in the popular *St. Louisan Magazine* noted, "Once the only people who saw 'headshrinkers' were the very sick, the very famous, or the very crazy. Today, however, people from all walks of life are seeking psychotherapeutic help or thinking about it."[19] Decades later, in a cultural backlash, Americans would reestablish many of the cast-off conventions. Americans would again fill their churches, marry young, and reinvigorate political and civic groups, bringing American church attendance and birthrates to the forefront of the industrialized world. But for the moment, a frenzied iconoclastic generation turned instead to a dizzying array of therapeutic sects, cults, and isms in their efforts to achieve the happiness and self-satisfaction that had suddenly become so important in their lives.

Gestalt

The narcissism of the 1970s pushed humanistic psychotherapy to the forefront. Humanistic therapy had constituted a minority approach in the therapeutic community through the 1950s and 1960s, never becoming one of the dominant modes of psychotherapy. In part this was due to the its lack of clear boundaries or even a cogent definition. Humanists marketed themselves as holistic healers who approached their patients with empathy, drawing from both interpersonal and analytic schools, but seemed incapable of distinguishing themselves clearly from their more dynamic colleagues. Their attempts at self-definition were so broad as to be useless, with one humanistic psychologist, James Bugental, offering no better explanation than that humanistic psychology's goal was the "preparation of a complete description of what it means to be alive as a human being."[20] Drawing from Carl Rogers's "client-centered" approach of the 1950s, humanism insisted that "meaning [was] more important than method," and that humanistic therapy sought to "expand or enrich man's experience."[21]

Despite such amorphous and grandiose claims, humanism was a legitimate school of psychology and clinical therapy. At heart it was empathetic, holistic, and deeply practical. It accepted unhappiness as a common component of the human condition, sought to guide its clients toward happiness, and understood interpersonal relationships to be the essential and perhaps only path to human vitality. Rooted in the psychology of the interpersonal, it dismissed Freudian claims of the unique relationship between patient and therapist. In the humanistic world, the therapist was simply another person with whom the patient could bond, albeit one who made himself especially available. The therapist was really nothing more than a "good parent" and a "decent human being," in the judgment of Hans Strupp, a prominent humanistic therapist of the time.[22] Strupp denied the uniqueness of the "formal psychotherapeutic setting" and felt that "any good human relationship" could be the basis of a positive therapeutic relationship.

Humanism, like psychoanalysis, placed high demands on the patient, for only willing patients could invest in the therapeutic relationship and benefit from the bonds created therein. Humanists wrote of the "good client" who was capable of the "psychotherapeutic change" that transpired when the therapist helped him to rearrange his thought patterns.[23] Clients engaged in humanistic therapy learned to trust another person, benefit from his or her advice, and perceive the nuanced tensions and dangers in the world about them while staying aware of the good. They learned to dismiss their own unconstructive and visceral reactions to people, and to invest in relationships that could potentially bring fullness to their lives. Humanism, like cognitive therapies, was predicated on *learning*, but it was particularly focused on learning how to bond with people. Strupp viewed humanism as a therapy based on learning and accepting "corrective emotional experiences."[24]

And humanism was, above all, pragmatic. Its broad goals were learning, growth, happiness, and human bonding. Most humanists considered themselves "eclectics," meaning simply that they were pledged to no particular type of therapeutic technique. Such eclecticism was really Sullivanian pragmatism writ large, and it seeped into the practice patterns of many psychiatrists and psychologists in the 1970s, who found themselves using whatever approaches and techniques seemed to work best. Even the most orthodox Freudians were known to depart from the master's teachings when the need called for it; Marvin Goldfried noted pithily that most analysts "dilute the pure gold of psychoanalysis with whatever nonanalytic copper is indicated by the case at hand."[25] It was a softer, gentler approach to mental health, one that understood that humans were fallible and often weak, and that simple happiness, rather than more austere self-knowledge, was an elusive but worthy goal.

Humanism, moreover, was probably the first truly holistic psychotherapy. The term "holistic" was as prone to abuse as "humanistic," but it connoted an assumption that balance lay at the core of mental health. For humanists, imbalance, lack of perspective, and lack of proportion could all contribute to a sense of alienation—of not living life entirely as it was intended to be lived. Humans compensated for imbalance in their lives through hard work, suppression of urges, repression of negative feelings, fantasy, and self-deception, yet all such coping mechanisms carried with then the promise of deep unhappiness. Taking their cue from Kurt Goldstein's 1939 work, *The Organism,* humanists understood that a happy life was a life lived "in the moment," respectful of nature's guiding forces, divine intentions, and natural predilections.[26] A life lived out of balance was a path either to unhappiness or, more likely, to false happiness: a happiness predicated on self-deception and on artificial goals. True happiness could be achieved only through investment in relationships, sensitivity to one's true needs on all levels, and a willingness to accept the person one was intended to be.

Humanism in the 1970s expressed itself most visibly in the perverted format of Gestalt therapy. A creation of the German psychoanalyst Fritz Perls, and to a lesser extent his colleagues Ralph Hefferline and Paul Goodman (as well as Fritz's wife, Laura), Gestalt therapy grew out of Goldstein's holistic concept of the *Gestalten* (German for "shape" or "form"), in which mental health and philosophical goodness were predicated on allowing a being to take its natural shape. First laid out formally in 1951 in *Gestalt Therapy* by Perls, Hefferline, and Goodman, the philosophy demanded that its adherents strive toward their "actuality." "Can you genuinely *feel* it? Can you feel that it is *yours*?" the authors asked.[27] People who had become separated from their actuality were anxious, bored, and depressed, and strove in vain to achieve a "full experience" despite the impossibility of doing so.[28] Living an artificial life, many people pursued a vision of what life "should be" rather than make efforts to "actualize" themselves.[29] Perls told his students, "You do not allow yourself—or you are not allowed—to be totally yourselves, so your ego boundary shrinks more and more. Your power, your energy, becomes smaller and smaller."[30]

Gestalt therapy combined the holistic base of humanism with a more bullying insistence on experiencing life in the here and now.[31] Perls's therapy was often delivered to acolytes gathered en masse at his institute in California (later moved to Vancouver Island), where which he implored them to seek lives of brutal self-honesty and legitimacy. Drawing on a Freudian sort of epiphany moment, Gestalt therapy pushed its adherents to focus with Zenlike concentration on an object, moment, or feeling in an effort to perceive the essence of the object, stripped of artifice. The approach emphasized "leaps" of insight during which the patient, client, or acolyte would pierce through the veil of subterfuge imposed upon him by modernity and social expectation and become that which he was meant to be.[32] A student of Perls described one such leap so:

It was an unusual experience. The word "now" is very successful in bringing about the feeling of the immediateness of being. This gave me a sense of fear that I can describe only as breathing very deeply while feeling a constriction in the chest. On the other hand, an instant's experience was much richer than ever before, and I could actually see things in the environment at which I had only *looked* before. I was in my room, and as I went through the experiment I felt a drive to straighten out and put in order whatever was amiss. It was like seeing the things in it for the first time or after a long absence. The objects had an identity of their own, stood around me, but were in no way continuous with me.[33]

Perls described his own observations of these Gestalt "shifts." He told of patients who, upon achieving the insight, cried out, "Suddenly I feel like jumping into the air!...I'm walking, really walking!...I feel so peculiar—the world is there, *really there!* And I have eyes, *real eyes!*"[34]

Gestalt philosophy correctly deduced that many Americans, perhaps most Americans, felt that their lives were not unfolding as they should. Assaulted by withering community ties, declining familial loyalties, and shifting roles, Americans felt adrift, dislocated, and ersatz. Their daily activities felt contrived and pointless, and their efforts to imbue these activities with meaning were unsuccessful. Perls's argument to live more vital, genuine lives fell on willing ears, and in his time he was perceived as a guru who had accomplished breakthroughs in overcoming the alienation of modernity.

But Perls was also an extraordinary narcissist who reestablished and reinvented himself throughout his life, and implored his followers to dedicate their own lives to self-gratification. For Perls, cultural mores, religious dicta, and philosophical ideals of goodness and truth were mere barriers to the pursuit of the good gestalt. An atheist in the most profound sense, Perls, and his followers, found no belief system to be impelling beyond that of self. His Gestalt "prayer," meant to offer hope but in its own way nihilistic, went as follows:

> *I do my thing, and you do your thing*
> *I am not in this world to live up to your expectations*
> *And you are not in this world to live up to mine*
> *You are you and I am I*
> *And if by chance we find each other, it's beautiful*
> *If not, it can't be helped*[35]

Rarely have more depressing and hopeless lines been penned in the service of human aspirations.

Multiplying Therapies

As the 1970s progressed, American psychotherapy became increasingly balkanized. The dominant triad of psychodynamic, cognitive, and humanistic therapies splintered repeatedly into relaxation, encounter, shock, deep massage, Zen, primal scream, rebirthing, meditation, recovered memories, and more. Poorly trained or self-trained therapists reinvented themselves as progenitors of new schools and techniques of therapy, and opened practices with little regulatory hindrance. Many aggressively promoted themselves with pamphlets, quasi-academic articles, books, training seminars, retreats, ashrams, and psychoactive communes. In the rootless and migratory zeitgeist of the time, an unusual number achieved modest success, and some became wealthy and influential. All claimed innovative techniques, breakthrough understanding, and supersession of the psychological and psychotherapeutic creators who had come before. Professional modesty was in short supply. One wag observed that the old army rule, "If it works, it's obsolete," held true for the psychotherapy of the time.[36]

The most benign of these new therapies could be loosely grouped into a "relaxation" approach. Based in Buddhist (particularly Zen) teachings of mastery of one's own mental state, and to a lesser degree in the therapeutic relaxation techniques pioneered in psychology laboratories in the 1950s, the approaches gained currency through the 1960s as young people traveled to South and East Asia to absorb cultural and religious teachings that deemphasized material pursuits.[37] The ancient practice of Yoga gained new adherents in the West, and a new adaptive Zen technique known as transcendental meditation (TM) gained inroads, particularly on the West Coast of the United States. At the same

time Naotake Shinfuku, a Japanese psychiatrist, began to promote
Morita therapy as a path to anxiety control, and Anna Rolf promoted
her deep-massage "Rolfing" therapy.[38]

Transcendental meditation, a creation of the Indian spiritual leader
Maharishi Mahesh Yogi, was probably the most influential of the newer
relaxation techniques, claiming 600,000 adherents worldwide by 1976.[39]
TM required adherents to meditate in solitude upon a word or phrase
for twenty minutes per day while breathing in a deep and controlled
manner and attempting to cleanse their minds of intrusive or even practical thoughts. Clinical scientists who measured metabolic and physiological responses to the meditation found that practitioners were able to
slow their hearts, cease producing sweat, and consume less oxygen.[40]
The brains of those immersed in meditation produced significantly
more alpha waves (associated with relaxed states), while their bodies
produced less testosterone, epinephrine, and lactate—all associated with
anxiety, fear, or aggression. Diminished oxygen use was particularly significant, for it indicated a slowing of metabolic processes generally. Herbert Benson, a psychology researcher at Harvard, noted, "You can fudge
breathing, but you can't do a thing about oxygen consumption because
your body needs it."[41] Studies showed that the meditators consumed
oxygen at the same rate as did most people after sleeping deeply for several hours.

A second grouping of new therapies were based on the group approaches of Jacob Levy Moreno and Alcoholics Anonymous and
grounded loosely in the interpersonal psychology of Harry Stack Sullivan. In a new tack, however, these "encounter" therapies tended to be
far more aggressive, and at times even brutal. Ranging from the "assertion therapy" of Herbert Fensterheim to the Erhard Seminars Training
(est) of Werner Erhard, these systems bullied their clients into confronting difficult truths, memories, and frailties in public contexts in an effort
to negate social artifice, false pride, and pretense.[42] In est and other
"marathon" encounters, clients were required to spend hours or days

with others group members in situations of enforced intimacy and emotional honesty. These "encounters" were thought to accelerate the sorts of psychological breakthroughs that more conventional group therapies could accomplish only in much longer periods.[43]

Price Cobbs and Judith Klein developed an odd offshoot of the encounter groups in the 1970s which they described as ethnotherapy. Combining encounter group confrontation techniques with the ethnic identity politics of the time, ethnotherapy used ethnically homogenous therapy groups to explore issues of identity, stereotypes, self-loathing, and group pride. African-Americans found the approach particularly helpful, given the unique challenges they faced in creating positive identities while confronting both racism and poor group accomplishment, but Jews and Italians-Americans joined the groups also. Religious ritual, unconstructive gender roles within the ethnic group, sexual tensions, in-marriages and out-marriages, and the allure of the "other" were all rich topics for ethnotherapy discussion. One therapist, Joseph Giordano, brought together a group of Italian men married exclusively to non-Italian wives, while Klein specialized in the odd sexual dynamics of Jewish men and women, who seemed to continually disappoint each other. Her colleague, Irving Levine, noted, "The intensity of the sexual warfare surprised us."[44]

Weirder than the encounter groups and the relaxation therapies were those therapies that could be generally defined as "recapture" therapies. Derivative of L. Ron Hubbard's Dianetics, which grew in popularity through the 1950s and 1960s, these therapies included primal scream, Z-therapy, past-lives therapy, and rebirthing therapy. All aimed to help clients and patients recapture lost memories, relive past traumas, face repressed memories, and admit to base truths of their own histories. The aggressiveness of their approaches, however, coupled with therapeutic rigidity and often poorly trained and unempathetic practitioners, could lead to bizarre and even tragic outcomes.

Hubbard's Dianetics grew out of his own science-fiction interests and was initially dubbed the "poor man's psychoanalysis."[45] The therapy proposed the existence of "engrams" (stored impressions in the mind), which could be recalled through lengthy "auditing" procedures that practitioners claimed could help a patient recall or relive traumatic events from childhood, infancy, or even from within the womb.[46] One woman who had completed a successful audit with her husband described the experience thus: "My husband took me back to what I believe was the prenatal period of my life. I began to feel as if I were drowning. I brought up phlegm...and my eyes were running. I almost choked and began gasping for breath. Apparently my head was twisted to one side in my mother's womb. The pain was intense."[47] The woman, who had been plagued with illness throughout her adult life, was confident that she was now cured. "I believe it with all my heart," she said.

Dianetics gave rise to Arthur Janov's primal scream therapy of the 1970s, which used Dianetic-like audits combined with screaming to return patients to traumatic infantile events and help rid them of repressed psychic demons. A fringe movement confined almost exclusively to wealthy people in coastal California, primal scream gained some notoriety when ex-Beatle John Lennon and his wife Yoko endorsed the technique and sang about it on their album *Plastic Ono Band*. Elevating the "crybaby" to a new sort of cultural icon, primal scream was truly bizarre. The therapy encouraged patients to wear diapers, suck their thumbs, and generally embrace not just their "inner child" but their inner infant. One reporter described a grown woman sucking her thumb, crying, and looking at an infant photo of herself while saying, "Daddy, don't hurt me. Daddy, please love me."[48]

Stranger still was Robert Zaslow's Z-therapy, which combined primal scream with a laying on of hands and sharp quasi-abusive pokes and tickles from the therapist, who insistently demanded brute honesty and emotional epiphany from the patient. Called by an observer one of the most "bizarre and highly controversial methods of dealing with mental problems since the use of branding irons to exorcize evil spirits in medieval times," the technique claimed success in as little as two sessions. Zaslow, as was typical of many therapeutic progenitors and gurus of the 1970s, claimed the significance of his discovery rivaled "Darwin's theory of evolution."[49] Like many of the short-term recapture therapies, treatment was expensive; Zaslow charged thousands of dollars for a course of treatment of as little as two or three sessions.

All of the recapture therapies were built upon the most basic psychoanalytic notions of psychic trauma and repression, which Freud had promulgated nearly three-quarters of a century previously. All promised quicker paths to self-discovery and awareness of one's own unconscious than did traditional psychoanalysis—sometimes much quicker. Despite the taint of fraud and quackery that hovered over the new therapies, all were significantly cheaper than a comparable course of psychoanalysis, and many produced satisfied clients.

The danger of all such therapies, however, was the possibility of creating false memories. Unlike the slow approach of most traditional therapies, during which the therapist remained either utterly passive or at best empathetic and benign, the recovery therapies relied on far more aggressive intervention and encouragement from therapists who, in their enthusiasm, could push naïve clients to "remember" events that had simply never transpired. The whole idea of a "recovered" memory, in fact, was problematic, and many therapists and psychologists doubted the veracity of vivid memories of sensations and emotions that dated to infancy or before. David Holmes, a psychologist and skeptic of the therapies, felt that all such therapies should come with "protective product warnings" that indicated that the "concept of repression has not been validated with experimental research."[50]

The most controversial of recovered memories involved childhood experiences of rape or incest. Patients remembered fathers, uncles, and brothers forcing fellatio upon them, or raping, strangling, and physically pummeling them. One woman described her experience in a support group: "Today I had a physical flashback—which means I physically re-experienced my father's hands on my breasts and I choked and gagged because it felt like his penis was in my mouth again."[51] While many such memories were accurate and allowed patients to resolve terrible emotional traumas and move ahead with their lives, at least some of the memories were false. Family members defended themselves vociferously as siblings and parents accused therapists of sowing hostility and imposing false images upon their relatives. Undoubtedly some of the therapists were guilty of excesses. One therapist included on her list of symptoms indicating repressed experiences of incest such banal responses as fear of the dark, gastrointestinal problems, eating disorders, drug abuse, nervousness, ambivalence about intimate relationships, and "feeling crazy."[52] If such symptoms were truly markers for incest survival, then virtually the entire American population could be counted in the group.

The laying on of hands, physical touching, and blurring of traditional boundaries between therapist and patient facilitated sexual indiscretion on the part of some therapists, and in the late 1970s reports emerged of therapists having sex with patients either outside the confines of therapeutic relationships or as an actual component of the therapy. Although the vast majority of legitimate psychologists, psychiatrists, and social workers denounced these "Don Juan therapists," a study conducted by the California State Psychological Association found that 5.5 percent of male Ph.D. psychologists had had sex with female patients, and that an additional 2.6 percent had had sex with patients within three months of the end of therapy (percentages for female psychologists, while not negligible, were significantly lower).[53] Some scurrilous therapists claimed that sexual intercourse was a legitimate therapeutic technique for treating patients who resisted physical and sexual intimacy, citing the well-known work of William Masters and Virginia Johnson in St. Louis as proof. But the Masters and Johnson sex therapy work had never involved sex between clients and therapists, and in fact it had rarely involved public sex at all. Rather, their work focused on couples whose sexual difficulties were emblematic of or perhaps central to deeper problems in the relationship, and required the couples to experiment with sexual techniques only in the privacy of their hotel rooms or at home after their sessions were completed.

Still, a heightened focus on sex was part of the therapeutic milieu of the narcissistic era, when all barriers to satisfaction and gratification were seen as legitimate targets for therapeutic inquiry. Thomas Szasz, a psychiatrist famous for his iconoclastic and sometimes hostile views of traditional psychiatry, quipped, "In the past, people in the Christian West believed that women should have as many children and as few orgasms as possible. Now they believe just the opposite."[54] Couples complained of "sexual anorexia" (a lack of desire for sex) or poor technique or simply the inability to experience orgasms, and sought the expert advice of Masters and Johnson and colleagues. And protestations aside, some therapists admitted to using sexual "surrogates" to have sex with patients who required practice time for their newly acquired techniques. Such activity technically constituted prostitution, but the medical nature of the work sufficiently protected the surrogates from vice squads.

The oddest component of the many "kooky therapies" that proliferated in the 1970s was the striking level of efficacy reported by patients. Although Jerome Frank of the Johns Hopkins department of psychiatry railed against the "charlatans" who "preyed on the gullible and the self-deluded," the fact was that many of the patients and clients of these fringe leaders claimed to be cured, happy, and satisfied.[55] America had always hosted more than its share of quacks and medical cults; Morris Fishbein, who edited the *Journal of the American Medical Association* for more than a quarter century, noted jocularly that "a new one like Dianetics simply adds to the fun and the fury."[56] Yet much medicine, particularly in mental health care, operated in the realm of the placebo, and certainly trust in a healer and belief in his technique could often make up for unsound physiology and biochemistry. Leon Eisenberg of the Harvard department of psychiatry commented on the kooky therapies:

"If you want to believe enough, almost any therapy will work with some people. A certain number will get better with [prominent evangelical preacher] Oral Roberts, a certain number with Robert Zaslow, and a certain number at the shrine at Lourdes."[57]

At the same time, even the most mainstream of therapists were changing their approaches. Whereas in the mid-1950s nearly half of all professional psychotherapists described themselves as either orthodox or modified Freudians, by 1976 this percentage had dropped to 10 percent. Meanwhile 55 percent described themselves as "eclectics," meaning that they were willing to try whatever worked.[58] Mental health practitioners were being called upon not simply to treat illness, but to "remove distress," in the words of Gerald Klerman of the National Institute of Mental Health. Psychiatrists and psychologists not only healed but eased "emotional discomfort" and helped patients to "cope with life's vicissitudes and social change."[59] The flowering of alternative therapies was in part a response to these new, vaguer demands being placed on mental health professionals.

Anti-Psychiatry

While some Americans embraced the flowering of new psychotherapies enthusiastically, others dismissed psychotherapy entirely. Psychiatry, and to a lesser degree clinical psychology and social work, had always had its critics; religious orders had long expressed skepticism of the healing power of so godless an enterprise. But in the late 1960s and through the 1970s a new order of critics attacked psychotherapy by claiming that racism, sexism, and autocracy lay embedded in its work.

Critics attacked psychiatry on multiple grounds. Some worried that the U.S. government could use psychiatry to control its citizens' behavior, with a former head of the Soviet secret police describing how psychiatrists in his homeland were used as unwitting agents of the Communist Party, through which the government could "achieve dominion over the minds and bodies of the nation."[60] Others noted the consistent antiwoman bias in the mental health professions. Phyllis Chesler, a feminist scholar at the City University of New York, described in her book *Women and Madness* how psychiatry routinely oppressed women by overdiagnosing them with madness, while Natalie Shainess, a psychoanalyst in New York, agreed that many psychiatrists were "contemptuous of women."[61] Other critics viewed psychiatry as a vehicle for continually suppressing African-Americans, disparaging even those few trained black psychiatrists as "institutionalized" into white psychiatry and becoming "honorary whites."[62]

More pernicious were the radical attacks on psychiatry, emanating from British psychiatrist Ronald (R. D.) Laing, his colleague David Cooper, and later, American psychiatrist Thomas Szasz. Laing delivered his critique of psychiatry in two well-received books he wrote in the 1960s titled *The Divided Self* and *The Politics of Experience*. With his break from the psychiatric establishment, the classically trained Laing expressed doubts about the integrity of many psychiatric diagnoses, particularly schizophrenia. Laing was concerned that psychiatrists were imposing a medical diagnosis upon a series of symptoms and syndromes that might simply be the uninhibited expression of honest feelings and thoughts, and he questioned the sanity of anybody attempting to live amid the contradictory forces of modern society. What psychiatrists called a nervous breakdown might be little more than the removal of the "veil of the false self" that had served to maintain the façade of normalcy.[63] Psychiatrists, in Laing's view, continually suppressed honest expression of emotions to maintain social order for a demanding state. In this view, madness could just as well be seen as a form of social revolt as a form of mental illness.[64]

Cooper echoed Laing's critique, but focused on the breakdown of the family in postwar Europe and the United States. Attacking the "violence of psychiatry," Cooper demanded that all functionaries within the mental health systems—psychiatrists, psychologists, and nurses—explore the madness they harbored in themselves.[65] He demanded a "Madness Revolution" to "counteract the violence of Western society" and attack not just psychiatry but capitalism, consumerism, and even wage labor.[66]

Thomas Szasz, a radical American psychiatrist, further extended Laing and Cooper's antiauthoritarian view of psychiatry. Claiming that mental illness simply did not exist, he understood the medical description of mental illness to be simply a "socially validated verbal construct."[67] Like Laing, he doubted the existence of even so obvious a mental syndrome as schizophrenia, but unlike Laing he refused to consider an organic basis to any mental illness—particularly schizophrenia. Schizophrenia was, in his view, simply a "discrediting function," trumped up by psychiatrists to avoid having to take patients' complaints at face value.[68] Szasz denied the validity of therapy, considering it nothing more than a coercive conversation, and he viewed the entire Freudian idea of the unconscious as specious. He wrote of the unconscious, "I believe it is cognitively more accurate, and morally more dignified, to regard it as a lie rather than a mistake."[69]

At heart, Szasz was an extreme libertarian who hated all forms of governmental and institutional coercion, including involuntary psychiatric treatment and hospitalization. Indeed, his fear of all forms of authority led him to deride Alcoholics Anonymous, narcotics prohibition, alcohol treatment generally, and any sort of coerced attendance at therapy sessions as forms of government control. He repeatedly pointed out that the only two ways you legally could lose your freedom in the United States were through criminal imprisonment or "breaking the mental hygiene law."[70] Schizophrenia, in his view, had become the "Christ on the cross that psychiatrists worship" precisely because it was the diagnosis that gave them the greatest authority over their patients.[71] In the world of Szasz, schizophrenia was not an illness, it was an "epithet and an injunction."[72]

Szasz was a paranoid kook who was sloppy with his facts. Contrary to his arguments, the vast majority of Americans who sought psychiatric or psychological counseling did so voluntarily, facing neither government coercion nor social pressure. In fact, social pressure generally worked *against* psychiatric consultation, rather than for it. By 1965, when Szasz was penning his opus of screeds, the sciences of neurochemistry and physiology were beginning to elicit understanding of the biological and organic bases of many mental illnesses, particularly schizophrenia. Many mental illnesses also responded well to medications and shock, further validating an organic understanding of mental illness. Szasz's worldview, predicated on the assumption that mental illness simply did not exist, could not stand up to clinical and laboratory inquiry.

Szasz's work was further extended by Peter Breggin, an American psychiatrist who continued the antipsychiatric jeremiad into the 1980s. Breggin agreed with most of Szasz's conjectures, but reserved particular vituperation for the drug companies that aggressively purveyed their wares to America's unhappy denizens through their network of corrupt sales representatives and compromised physicians. Attacking the "psychopharmaceutical complex" in his book *Toxic Psychiatry*, Breggin derided the "faddish diagnosis" of panic disorder that he accused the Upjohn pharmaceutical company of fabricating for the sake of hawking their best-selling tranquilizer, Xanax.[73] Like Laing, he considered society to be sicker than the diagnosed mental patients, and like Szasz he questioned the biochemical basis of modern psychiatry as well as the policing powers of the profession. He wrote, "He or she [the psychiatrist] can prescribe drugs or shock, lock you up against your will, talk behind your back with your husband, wife or parents, and make plans for your future without consulting you."[74] In the drug-oriented treatment milieu of the 1980s, he warned that "innumerable adults" would wind up "taking drugs, getting shock treatment, or being locked up in a mental hospital—or all three."[75]

Despite their rhetorical excesses, Laing, Cooper, Szasz, and Breggin made some legitimate points. Mental illness was different from physical illness, and attempts to force mental problems into existing disease models were fraught with difficulties. Alcoholism was not really a disease—certainly not on the order of a pathogen-based syndrome like tuberculosis or malaria—and much depression could easily be viewed as part of a normal spectrum of human moods rather than as a diagnosable and treatable illness. Psychiatrists did sometimes try to force labels on moods or behaviors in an effort to demonstrate mastery over them, and in so doing they often oversimplified a complex array of feelings. And certainly there were times when psychiatrists overprescribed or overanalyzed in an effort to elevate both their professional status as well as their incomes.

Still, to suggest that mental illness did not exist, simply because it did not neatly fit into preexisting pathogen-based disease models, was a grotesque distortion of reality. The history of postwar mental health care had been a series of small victories based on expanded access, increased training, and broader education. Almost everybody who worked with the mentally ill agreed that the United States needed more, rather than less, mental health care. Millions of American who could benefit from psychotherapy, antidepressant medication, or even shock therapy were living compromised lives for want of information or proximity to healers or mental health facilities. Flawed though the mental health professions might be—and certainly some accusations of arrogance, hyperscientism, and even narcissism were true—such flaws should not blind observers to the great good already accomplished by psychiatrists, psychologists, and psychiatric social workers, and the potential for more good in the future.[76]

Moreover, if alcoholism, narcotics abuse, depression, and even schizophrenia did not fit easily into a traditional disease mold, the solution was to create a more nuanced description of these syndromes rather than to dismiss them entirely. Alcoholism clearly existed, as millions of spouses and children of alcoholics could attest, and it was a dreadful problem that ruined millions of lives and cost countless dollars in lost productivity. Many, if not most, alcoholics recognized that they had a problem which was destroying their lives and defying their mastery. Disease or not, it was *something*, and something dreadful. And if "disease" was not precisely the correct medical moniker, then the solution was to create a new one, not to deny its existence. The hundreds of thousands of Americans who by 1965 had successfully overcome their alcoholism with the help of Alcoholics Anonymous and other psychological support mechanisms would take offense at the accusation of the antipsychiatrists that they had simply stopped drinking because they no longer felt like drinking. In their minds, they had conquered a dreadful disease, perhaps the worst that a human could ever suffer.

Outcomes

An unambiguous record of successful treatment and therapy since the expansion of mental health services after World War II would have been the best retort to antipsychiatrists, but this was not to be. While psychotherapy could point to a good many accomplishments, its record was far from clear, and in fact the multiple outcomes studies of the 1960s failed to establish clear hierarchies of diagnoses, therapeutic efficacy, techniques, and training. If anything, the picture was more muddied by 1976 than it had been a decade before.

Psychoanalysis fared the worst under the focused gaze of outcomes research. An eighteen-year study by the Menninger Foundation revealed the startling conclusion that of forty-two patients in psychoanalysis or psychoanalytically oriented therapy, six had gotten worse over the course of the therapy, eleven emerged unchanged, seven improved only slightly, and eighteen (43 percent) showed moderate or significant improvement.[77] The results could not be viewed as very encouraging.[78] Moreover, the Menninger Foundation undermined its own credibility by burying the results amid lengthy statistical verbiage and jargon. Sol Garfield, a distinguished and highly experienced psychotherapy researcher at Washington University in St. Louis, admitted that even after numerous perusals of the document he "did not really know what the findings on outcome were." He wrote, "In terms of not reporting data on outcome, the report is a masterpiece."[79]

But while psychoanalysis could not stand up to rigorous observation, most psychotherapies could. As the federal government became the dominant purchaser of psychotherapy services through its Medicare and veterans health programs as well as through the many private insurers it contracted on behalf of its civilian employees, government purchasing officials questioned the value of the services. In 1978, both the White House and Congress launched investigations into the efficacy of psychotherapy, and both concluded that at least two-thirds of people who used psychotherapy demonstrably improved within a relatively short period (versus only 40 percent of mental sufferers who improved without professional help). "One can almost hear an audible sigh of relief among research investigators as it begins to appear that the effectiveness of the psychosocial therapies can be detected scientifically," the authors of the White House report wrote.[80] Both government groups, as well as university-based researchers, produced the two-thirds number repeatedly, regardless of the disparities in diagnoses, patient demographics, "schools" of psychotherapy, and professional background of the therapists. There appeared to be little difference in success rates posted by psychiatrists, psychologists, and social workers. Humanists did as well as rationalists who did as well as eclectics, and even the more modified psychodynamic therapists could produce respectable results provided they were empathetic and flexible.[81] The only serious requirements were that the therapist be empathetic; that the patient feel comfortable with the therapist; and that the patient desire to make a reasonable effort at the therapy. This last precondition suggested that mental hygiene education was probably as important as the orientation of the therapist in determining a successful outcome.

When psychotherapy worked, its results were practically beyond value. One happy patient, when asked what had changed, responded, "Heavens above! I could write a book! My whole life has changed and I now live comfortably with myself and my family.... I am now at peace with myself. I no longer feel such a failure inside.... I have discovered I'm more capable than I thought myself.... I can pretty much take each day as it comes now and even derive much satisfaction from little things."[82] But just as frequently, the outcomes were more qualified or were perceived as incomplete. One woman admitted to a great deal of intellectual insight, but noted that "little change (i.e., emotional) actually took place."[83] Others felt that the therapy had been of little help, and possibly a waste of time and money.

Part of the problem in measuring outcomes was the shifting definition of success. Whereas thirty years before, success might have been defined as restraining a suicidal depressive or helping a compulsive phobic to venture outside, success was now frequently defined as achieving one's life potential, or becoming "self-actualized," in the words of Abraham Maslow. Authors of the White House task force report had noted that "positive mental health" was the "new cry," and that even so lofty a goal as "spiritual oneness with the universe" was hardly beyond the sights of some psychotherapy patients.[84] In this rescaled definition of success, patients sought not merely competence in their therapists, but "empathy, warmth, and genuineness," in the words of Jerome Frank.[85] The new therapeutic relationship was not supposed to be merely normal but supernormal, a vital human bond of unusual intensity. Such a relationship was in marked contrast with the aloof and dispassionate analyst of the original Freudian vision.

A second problem with measuring success was in the measurement itself. Psychological researchers had always had difficulty quantifying the clients' progress in therapy, but now they found that the closer they looked, the more distorted a picture they acquired. The observation itself distorted the picture, for researchers discovered that in observing the patients, they intervened in the therapeutic process. On the other hand, relying on the therapist for outcomes judgment violated every norm of "blind" scientific observation, insofar that the observer in this case had a vested interest in reporting a particular outcome. Charles Krauthammer, a psychiatrist and director of the division of sciences at the federal government's Alcohol, Drug Abuse, and Mental Health Administration, noted that observing therapy created a sort of "therapeutic Heisenberg uncertainty principal" in which the act of observing prevented objective observation.[86] Problematic also was the effort to standardize outcomes from two entirely different therapeutic modalities, each with a different set of goals and different targeted patient population. Jerome Frank pithily summed up the insurmountable challenge: "To try to determine by scientific analysis how much better or worse let us say, gestalt therapy is than transactional analysis is in many ways equivalent to attempting to determine by the same means the relative merits of Cole Porter and Richard Rodgers. To ask the question is to reveal its absurdity."[87]

Many therapists agreed with Frank's assessment. Patients entered therapy for a wide variety of reasons, with many very different goals. While one patient might hope to simply be able to establish more intimate relationships with women, another might hope to be able to leave his house, while another might hope to overcome her crippling bipolar disorder, and another still might hope to remain discharged from a mental hospital while being stabilized on Thorazine. The array of mental complaints was so vast that grouping all therapies and all patients under one scale of "success" seemed overly simplistic. "It's a stupid question," Gary VandenBos of the American Psychological Association retorted. "It's like asking, 'Does surgery work?' "[88] Still another psychotherapeutic researcher, dismayed at the lack of clarity resulting from the reams of studies conducted between 1950 and 1975, said, "The best I can say after years of sniffing about in the morass of outcome literature is that in my optimistic moods I am confident that there's a pony in there somewhere."[89]

In part, though, therapists' resistance to measurement and judgment was a defensive ploy. For all the variety of mental illness complaints, they paled next to the near infinite variety of physical complaints treated by the mental health practitioners' medical and surgical colleagues. Yet physicians and surgeons measured their own success with brutal honesty and transparency. Peer-reviewed clinical journals published tens of thousands of papers yearly that purported to precisely measure hospital discharge rates, lengths of stay, remission rates, five- and ten-year survival rates, cure and partial cure rates, and rates of improvement for many hundreds of diagnoses treated with many thousands of surgical procedures and medical and pharmaceutical interventions. The more honest response to measurement difficulty in mental illness was to measure more, not to measure less. If comparing schizophrenics and agoraphobics was like comparing apples to oranges, then researchers had merely to create different categories in which to place outcomes measurements. The question of outcomes success was challenging and troublesome, but certainly not "absurd."

Then, too, therapists in the 1970s were becoming increasingly leery of the stunning successes posted by psychopharmacologists. For all of the messiness of psychoactive drugs—and pharmaceutical researchers were still a decade away from the first "clean" antidepressants—they were proving to be panaceas to many thousands of previously untreatable depressives, psychotics, and obsessives. Many psychiatrists, trained in the most orthodox analytic milieus, were slowly surrendering their orthodoxy to the promise of drugs. Robert Gibson, medical director of Sheppard Pratt Hospital, stated in 1976 that the recent advances in psychopharmacology had been "too important to ignore."[90] Lithium, the newest wonder drug in the psychopharmaceutical armament, was allowing many sufferers of bipolar disorder to attain emotional peace for the first time in their lives, while second- and third-generation tricyclic antidepressants were significantly more effective and cleaner than previous drugs had been. Indeed, even as the 1970s brought forth a cornucopia of new psychotherapies, many of the most knowing mental health experts understood that the greatest promise likely lay in further neurochemical and neurophysiological research. Nathan Kline, a biologically oriented New York psychiatrist, claimed a 90 percent success rate with his patients. He told his patients, "You can't fight the medication. It will work whether you 'believe in it' or not."[91]

Ultimately, the flowering of therapies in the 1970s would be a grand conclusion to a passing era rather than an overture to a new one. Even as more Americans than ever before sought out psychotherapy in its many guises, better drugs were finally beginning to demonstrate the enormous potential of psychopharmacology. Short-term therapies were conclusively proving to be as effective as lengthier ones, meaning that Americans who were serious about improving their mental health need not make the multi-year commitment of yesteryear. And nascent comparative research in psychotherapy was beginning to demonstrate that some therapies were indeed simply better at curing certain mental disorders than others. That research, however, was still undeveloped and, to many psychotherapists and their patients, unpersuasive. It would take a decade or more before a true turnabout would come in psychotherapy.

CHAPTER 8

Narcotics

From the middle of the 1960s many young Americans increasingly began experimenting with drugs. What had been only a marginal practice in 1940 rapidly became mainstream, almost commonplace. While in 1960 the numbers of marijuana smokers in the country had been negligible, by 1970 nearly 20 percent of American high schoolers had used the drug, and more than 40 percent of college students had.[1] By 1981 the number of young marijuana smokers had surpassed young cigarette smokers.[2] The age of first use of marijuana declined substantially as well, from roughly twenty-two years in 1965 to fourteen in 1970, and the potency of most of the drug sold on the street was also rising.[3]

The increasing use of marijuana disturbed physicians and public health officials not only because it suggested an antiauthoritarian and nihilistic attitude among young people, but also because it foreshadowed use of more toxic drugs later. While marijuana was not physically addictive, it could become psychologically addictive and led often to experimentation with and addiction to opiates. Ninety percent of all youthful marijuana smokers used the drug fewer than a dozen times and then desisted, but 10 percent took to using it habitually, often immersing themselves in a drug culture that could lead frequently to morphine and heroin use, as well as experimentation with methamphetamine ("speed"), LSD, and cocaine. John Ingersoll, the director of the Federal Bureau of Narcotics, worked to curb the common misconception that marijuana was safe. The chronic user or "pothead" often socialized exclusively with other heavy drug users, who goaded one another to try more addictive drugs that could produce more intense highs. Ingersoll warned, "If you associate with a group whose orientation is drug-seeking and you accept this style of life, you are likely to look for bigger and bigger kicks."[4] In fact, two-thirds of all regular drug users in 1969 admitted to using more than one drug regularly.

Even when marijuana did not lead to harder drugs, it was dangerous enough on its own. Robert DuPont, a psychiatrist and the director of the National Institute of Drug Abuse in the 1970s, tirelessly spoke with parents and students about the dangers of even modest marijuana use. Marijuana's active ingredient, delta-9-tetrahydrocannabinol (THC), was fat-soluble and hydrophobic, meaning that with one use it was quickly absorbed into the body's fatty tissues (including the brain), but it leached into the blood and urine quite slowly and could remain in the system a long time after. THC from one marijuana cigarette could be detected in the smoker's urine a week later. The modest "high" that smokers experienced was the result of diminished brain functioning that blocked memory formations and distorted perceptions of time and space. DuPont told parents that the experiences of "dreamy relaxation, heightened sensation, and stretched-out time" were "direct results of brain poisoning."[5] Some researchers detected diminished brain functioning in heavy marijuana users months after they had ceased using the drug. The drug also decreased sperm production and distorted ovulation cycles, and it impaired judgment, affecting everything from driving skills to sexual activities.

Heavy marijuana use distorted other behaviors as well. Those who embraced the drug culture often lost interest in school and work and rationalized their diminished ambition and drive with an antiestablishment philosophy. DuPont testified that these heavy users tended to become alienated from their parents and their parents' value systems, lost interest in social, athletic, and cultural activities, made new sets of friends who were frequently also enamored with drugs, and dropped out of school at disproportionately high rates. There was some evidence, too, that marijuana use spurred alcohol use and addiction, and the attendant long-term problems that came with them.[6]

Heroin use increased as well. More than 500,000 Americans were addicted to heroin in 1975, up from a low of 20,000 in 1940.[7] Of that number, more than half had become addicts since 1965, and nearly two-thirds had become so since 1963.[8] Moreover, in the words of Edward Bunker, a reporter and ex-addict, this "wildfire growth" had come amid "relentless attack and draconian sentences."[9] Heroin users seldom managed to quit or control their use of the drug, and their lives thus tended toward decline. Inevitably they alienated themselves from their family and friends, lost possessions and jobs, and, racked with the compulsion to continue their habit, turned to theft.

The raw ingredient for heroin, the opium poppy, was easy to grow in certain parts of the world, which led to copious quantities of cheap raw opium—a sort of gummy paste—being produced. But in the transformation to heroin, $30 of opium would go through so many markups, bribes, payoffs, and refinements that the finished product retailed for $300,000.[10] Such exorbitant street prices drove the cost of a typical heroin addiction to $35 per day by 1972, most of which was raised by burglary, assault, or prostitution. And since the cost of fencing stolen goods robbed them of about 80 percent of their value, the typical heroin addict needed to steal $64,000 of property annually to support the habit.[11] In a speech before Congress that year, Senator George McGovern estimated that total national crime-related costs of heroin addiction were $4.4 billion.[12] The *Los Angeles Times* reported that one heroin addict had admitted to 250 burglaries over fifteen months to support his habit, not to "live regally," but to avoid the "sweating, stomach cramps, vomiting, diarrhea, and worse" that came with heroin withdrawal.[13]

Drug use in the United States had waxed and waned in the past. In 1900, for example, about a quarter of 1 percent of the population was addicted to narcotics; but by 1940 the rate had fallen sevenfold.[14] Shakier estimates put the rate of adult opiate use in the United States in the mid-nineteenth century at 4 percent or even higher, but this was driven in part by ubiquitous opiate-laced cough suppressants and elixirs.[15] Beginning in 1914, a series of narcotics restriction acts were passed that substantially reduced addiction among Americans, but by 1951 the number of addicts began climbing again.[16] In that year, a reported 60,000 Americans were regularly using either morphine, opium, or heroin, although the Federal Bureau of Narcotics quietly admitted that the true number might be as high as 1 million.[17] It was likely that this higher number included those using modest amounts of dilute opium or codeine, which they obtained through prescription.

Drug addiction was dreadful. Like alcoholism, it robbed its victims of normal human pathos and empathy, driving them to sacrifice virtually all they valued in favor of feeding their cravings. Writing in 1956, Marie Nyswander described addiction as a medical entity that "ravages the patient, destroys the entire fabric of his life, and adversely affects the lives of his family and others close to him."[18] Herbert Brown, profiling the life of a typical addict in *Life* magazine in 1951, described it thus:

He needs a shot when he first wakes up.... He needs at least two more during the day and if he can afford them, takes five. If he doesn't get them every organ and nerve from his soles to his scalp begins torturing him. His body "falls apart." He vomits. He sweats. Hideous cramps grip his stomach: he has diarrhea; his members jerk and twitch, even his nose runs continuously. Morbid fears assail his mind. He cannot voluntarily stand this; no human can. He will do anything—no matter how degrading or dishonest—to get dope. If he is lucky enough to be arrested now he will tearfully admit he didn't know it could get to be like this; if he had, he never would have started.[19]

Nobody had any idea how to solve the problem. Drug enforcers tended to divide into "supply" and "demand" camps, with the supply-side proponents advocating "wars" on narcotics producers and the demand-siders advocating education and treatment. Supply-side approaches were unrealistic. Opium was grown in lawless zones in South and Central Asia, well beyond the reach of America's narcotics agents, while marijuana was commonly grown in small, essentially undetectable patches. The drugs in both their raw and processed forms were smuggled into the United States on hundreds of small boats and planes that could easily evade Coast Guard and border patrols, or else they were hidden in secret compartments in automobiles and luggage. The extraordinary value of refined narcotics induced smugglers and dealers to take extreme risks to secure their shipments. Smugglers secured heroin in condoms given to human "mules" who either swallowed them or secreted them in their rectums. Clandestine shipments were fed to snakes and sometimes sewn into live animals. Narcotics officers could hope to stop only a small portion of the flow.

But demand-siders had little more to offer. Effective treatment for narcotics addiction simply did not exist in 1970. Conventional psychotherapy appeared to be useless, as did most chemical and behavioral treatments. Group therapists had yet to develop the appropriate tools to reach these difficult clients, and few of the newer humanistic or cognitive therapists even attempted to treat them. The most successful drug "treatment" in 1970 was probably prison, which enforced abstinence and allowed the user at least temporarily to wean himself physically from his addiction. Most users, however, quickly returned to drugs upon release, and few were able to command the communal supports and personal discipline necessary to chart new paths. Art Linkletter, one of

America's best-known television personalities, whose daughter died of an overdose of LSD in 1969, told a group of assembled delegates at the United Nations in 1971, "The American people have been forced to acknowledge the bitter irony of our times. We walk on the moon, yet at least 250,000 of us are heroin addicts. We probe the secrets of the living cell, yet our hospitals are crowded with men and women who cannot throw off alcohol or other drugs."[20]

Drug Culture

Increase in drug use both emanated from and contributed to a thriving drug subculture in the 1960s. Born in political protests, the drug culture was youth-oriented, antiauthoritarian, and arrogant—a true "counter-culture" in opposition to prevailing cultural norms. One narcotics counselor described the drug culture as "an alternative to the culture of the larger society in which it exists," a way of disengaging from mainstream society through social ties and chemical enablers.[21] Drug use bound the adherents together in a shared experience, yet at the same time it trapped them in a social structure as confining as any mainstream social structure, which insidiously encouraged progressively greater drug use.

The drug culture differed from the long-established drinking culture insofar as drug users—particularly those who used hallucinogens such as marijuana and LSD—often came to glorify drug use as a means to existential insight. Samuel McCracken, a professor of English at Reed College in Oregon and a close observer of the youth drug scene, described how drug users, in marked contrast to alcoholics, often became "true believers," convinced that drug use allowed them to attain a higher plane of living. The fact that heavy marijuana users called themselves "heads" or "potheads," and referred to inebriation as "turning on," glorified drug-induced hallucinations not merely as a path to euphoria but as a path to self-knowledge and heightened creativity. The "atmosphere" of the drug culture, McCracken wrote, was "redolent with the heavy claim that marijuana and LSD [were] good for the consciousness."[22] Unlike alcohol, which was used as an aid to "turning off" and dulling the senses, marijuana promised its users a more "adequate emotional response," helping them to achieve (so they claimed) "superhuman" insight, to "see what is not there."[23] McCracken cited Aldous Huxley, who, enamored with mescaline, wrote, "This is how one ought to see, how things really are."[24]

Just as alcoholics rationalized their drinking in part by associating exclusively with other drinkers, drug users buttressed their worldview by cavorting nearly exclusively with other drug users. An antiauthoritarian belief system often drew young users to the culture, but once immersed in it, they found few outlets beyond increasing drug use. For the heaviest users, particularly those who had graduated to the highly addictive opiates, drug use became all-consuming: the central activity of their being. Mac Proctor, a narcotics counselor, described the addict's life as a "ritual drama centered around the feeding of his habit." For most, seeking the daily fix was "so preoccupying that it is the only life they know."[25]

The allure of the drug culture was further strengthened by entertainers and cultural icons, particularly those attractive to the young, who tended to heavily use drugs. Reports of rock stars overdosing or performing while high created an impression among the young that the most attractive and successful of the nation's creative individuals not only sanctioned drug use, but actively encouraged it. Heroin use among jazz musicians was commonplace, and marijuana was pervasive at rock concerts and other youth-oriented events. Elvis Presley, the great musical star of the 1950s, used massive amounts of drugs, "from the time he woke up in the morning until the time he went to sleep at night," his physician reported.[26] Art Linkletter testified that his daughter was, in part, a "victim of the reckless urge to experiment with hallucinogenic chemicals that became the fashionable thing to do." An "insane desire to take pills, marijuana and LSD" had pervaded the entertainment industry.[27]

The drug culture rose as ties of church and family declined, though the precise mechanism of causality was ambiguous. Certainly drug abuse was toxic to family life. One Gallup poll indicated that Americans considered drug and alcohol use the single most important cause of divorce, the "most harmful" to family life.[28] But drug abuse also shadowed declining church attendance through the 1960s. The correlation made sense, for the ideals most respected by heavy drug users—rejection of societal mores, skepticism of established hierarchies, dismissal of conventional spirituality—were precisely those enshrined in conventional religious practice. Most of the world's major religions, and particularly the Judeo-Christian faiths that dominated the American landscape, were built upon ideals of self-abnegation. The drug culture, which placed pursuit of a more vital personal reality as its greatest goal, lay in direct conflict with the church's credo of self-denial. The great Jewish philosopher Martin Buber had expressly criticized drug use for the reason that it drew its adherents away from communal life and norms. He wrote, "The waking have one world in common, whereas each sleeper turns away to a private world of his own."[29]

Pastors had unusual insight into the drug problem, perceiving a connection between increasing addiction and a spiritually depleted people. Just as the church had long been a path to salvation for the alcoholic, so, pastors believed, could spiritual succor offer a viable alternative to drugs. They believed that a loving God could conceivably offer a path away from addiction. Donald Thorman, a Catholic writer and theologian, had expressed his belief some years before that the "real cure must take place in the mind of the addict, a complete reorientation of his entire moral and mental outlook."[30] But as the church declined in importance for an entire generation of young Americans, this path to salvation and relief was increasingly blocked.

A separate path to drug use lay not through the counterculture but rather through the forests of Vietnam. Troops serving in Southeast Asia turned increasingly to heroin as a way of coping with the terror and boredom of combat. By 1971 between 10 and 15 percent of U.S. troops in Vietnam were addicted to a drug (usually heroin), meaning that upon their discharge an additional 40,000 addicts joined ranks with America's domestic drug users.[31] United States representative Robert Hampton Steele, who had investigated the extent of the army's drug problem in Asia, wrote of the "white plague of heroin [that] blanketed the U.S. military command in Indo-China."[32]

The army's drug problem differed significantly from the situation at home. While domestic drug use emanated from angry, disaffected youths seeking alternatives to mainstream society, military drug use grew from the unique mixture of terror and boredom specific to jungle combat. One soldier described the environment in Vietnam that drove American kids to heroin despite no previous history of drug use: "There is nothing to do, I mean nothing at all. All you do is stand there and watch for people trying to attack, and there's nobody trying to attack. You can't read, you can't listen to the radio. It drives you crazy."[33] Heroin, easily available for as little as two dollars per dose, was a frequent answer, and officials and medical authorities had few tools with which to combat its use.

Marijuana could also lead to heroin use, but more frequently it led to experimentation with LSD, barbiturates, and alcohol. By 1971, barbiturates and LSD had surpassed heroin as favored drugs, and the trend was continuing. One in seven college students admitted to having tried LSD, and an increasing number of high schoolers were turning to barbiturates ("downers") to achieve a relaxed, blissful state that left neither telltale odor nor hangover.[34] Sidney Cohen, a drug researcher at UCLA, pointed out that barbiturates offered "escape for the price of one's lunch money."[35] At the same time, teenage alcohol use doubled from 1969 to

1973, accompanied by a rise in teenage arrests.[36] Auguring worse problems to come, use of "pop" (highly sweetened) wine, popular with teenagers and even middle-schoolers, rose elevenfold over the same period. And there was evidence that many young people were mixing alcohol with marijuana or barbiturates to gain a "double high."[37]

By 1978, the National Institute of Alcohol Abuse and Alcoholism reported that 3.3 million teenagers, nearly one in five, had a drinking problem.[38] Rates of youthful drug and alcohol use were peaking; marijuana was ubiquitous in high schools and colleges; and wealthier students were turning to newly fashionable cocaine for recreation. Supply-side efforts to eradicate opium poppies, LSD laboratories, marijuana crops, and illegal barbiturate and amphetamine distribution networks had largely failed. Equally dismaying, efforts by the mental health community to "treat" young addicts and alcoholics had been only minimally successful. The nation's substance abuse challenge was looming as one of the gravest threats to its mental health, yet the mental health professions had few ideas on how to proceed.

White-Collar Use

Drug use rose in adults as well as in youth. Through the late 1960s and early 1970s employers watched with concern as absenteeism, petty theft, dereliction of duty, and attrition all rose due to increasing drug use in the labor force. In 1967, 7 percent of employers answered yes to the question "Do you have a drug problem in your company?" By 1970, 41 percent answered so.[39] In New York, a 1972 study found 34,000 heroin users in "conventional" jobs, while General Motors found that 13 percent of applicants for jobs in a diesel division tested positive for heroin.[40] By 1983 the problem had spread throughout the economy, with drug use accounting for $26 billion in lost productivity and increased criminal activity per year, as well as countless workplace errors, lies, and unreported thefts.[41] Even the highly respected professions of law, medicine, and accounting were affected, with medicine hit particularly hard due to easy workplace access to synthetic opiates. A 1983 study estimated that 4 percent of doctors and nurses were narcotics addicts.[42]

Workplace drinking had risen as well. Whether because of increased stress, frequent relocations, rising divorce rates, the general influence of the pervading drug culture, or "generous expense account entertaining," as suggested by one researcher, executives indulged ever more frequently and their productivity suffered accordingly.[43] Professional stature gave executives some protection from outside scrutiny, as did a generally permissive attitude toward alcohol use as a component of sales, team-building, deal-making, and stress release. One alcoholic advertising executive admitted that his problem had started with the classic "three-martini" business lunch, which progressed to the three-martini stress reducer after work. Before long he was drinking ten to twelve drinks per day, starting ever earlier. He wrote about his self-destruction:

> About the time we began losing accounts, I had decided there was no reason I shouldn't have a few drinks before getting to the office in the morning. I found a convenient bar that was pleasant and, I thought, up to the executive level. I would have at least one and sometimes three double vodkas on the rocks. This was preceded by at least a couple of drinks before I left the house, because it finally got to the point where I had to have something to drink to get me going in the morning.... On the job, I was able to convince myself that, far from losing any ability, I was probably better than ever. I had been wronged by people taking business away from me. I was the head of a fine company, with fine people; it was just the times that were against me.[44]

Drug and alcohol use in the workplace was both a separate phenomenon from the broader youth drug culture and an extension of it. Drug use by workers was rarely political in the way that drug use by juveniles was, and it was usually hidden rather than proudly paraded as a badge of identity and autonomy. But underlying both trends were fissures in the basic structures of town, church, and family. Drug and alcohol use by workers reflected a sense of personal alienation, whether due to professional pressure, family breakdown, or dissatisfaction with a job. Long a social lubricant, alcohol (along with barbiturates) was increasingly becoming a professional one, allowing bored blue-collar workers, tense executives, and exhausted professionals to better cope with the artificial quality of life in modern companies and organizations. Use of drugs and alcohol by adults was similar to use among the young, in that it allowed users to separate themselves from the distasteful reality of the world in which they were living.

Advances in Treatment

Neither psychiatry nor clinical psychology had achieved any success in treating drug addiction over the previous half century. Psychiatry generally treated drug addicts with enforced hospitalization, frequently in the United States Public Health Hospital in Lexington, Kentucky, where 1,500 addicts "dried out" for four to six months. This treatment was highly ineffective, however. Officially, 40 percent of the discharged patients relapsed during the 1950s and 1960s, but unofficially most hospit l administrators placed the rate much higher.[45] When a study was conducted in 1972, officials at the hospital discovered that only 3 percent of a group of tracked patients had been able to resist heroin for the nine months after discharge. The head researcher, George Vaillant, admitted that it was "dramatically clear" that hospitalization and imprisonment were "virtually useless in producing abstinence."[46]

In the 1970s, psychiatrists and psychologists came to understand that effective drug treatment must fundamentally alter every aspect of the lives of the users, from their networks of friends to their personal philosophies to their thinking patterns. No one tool could promise redemption, but perhaps a combined attack using conventional psychotherapy, group therapy, behavioral therapy, self-help structures, and punitive imprisonment could be used to begin to battle addiction. Robert Felix, the director of the National Institute of Mental Health, wrote in 1963 of the "futility of attempting to rehabilitate the patient without effecting changes in his family environment," and of the importance of "long-term community programs and services to provide step-by-step support" for the returning addict.[47] Other psychiatrists recognized the need for "social integration" of recovering addicts, suggesting the need to remake the addict's entire world rather than simply reforming his drug habit.[48]

Conventional psychotherapy had proven to be nearly useless in combating drug use. Neither psychoanalysis nor the humanistic and cognitive psychotherapies seemed at all effective in countering it, and the general sources of angst and discomfort that most therapists focused on in therapy—childhood loss, feelings of betrayal and rejection—seemed irrelevant. One father, desperately seeking help for his heroin-addicted teenage son, described the questions a psychiatrist asked during a joint family session: "Did [Sean] resent the birth of his sister? Was he having any sex problems? Why couldn't he get along with his parents?" When the psychiatrist asked why Sean's mother was in tears, adding, "That kind of over-emotionalism isn't going to help your son," the father gave up in disgust. He wrote, "Her firstborn boy shooting heroin and he wondered why she was crying."[49]

To some degree, drug addiction forced both psychiatrists and psychologists to turn to models of mental health more heavily promoted among social workers. Drug addiction had some disease-like qualities (it was biochemical and neurochemical) and some behavioral components (compulsions, antiauthoritarian predilections), but drug addicts also reinforced their addictive lifestyles through selective social interactions. They associated almost exclusively with other addicts and took part in activities where drug use was well tolerated if not outright encouraged. One psychiatrist investigating the phenomenon of juvenile drug use noted that youthful users tended to migrate from one drug to another, suggesting the problem was not addiction to a particular drug, but addictive behavior generally, which he deemed to be a form of "social deviation."[50]

Drug addiction needed to be defined before it could be cured, and no profession in 1970 seemed to be able to do so. Recreational drug use had gone through periods of greater and lesser social acceptance over the previous century; in the nineteenth century, for example, opium dens were run legally in London, while in the United States both heroin and cocaine were routinely added to elixirs, cough suppressants, and even beverages.[51] The activity was considered either a form of social interaction, a vice, or a habit gone awry, but it was never referred to as a disease or illness. Starting in the 1920s, however, psychiatrists began to describe drug use and addiction as a response to underlying "psychoneurotic deficits." Lawrence Kolb, one of the nation's first dedicated narcotics researchers, wrote, "The psychopath, the inebriate, the psychoneurotic, and the temperamental individuals who fall easily victims to narcotics have this in common: they are struggling with a sense of inadequacy, imagined or real, or with unconscious pathological strivings."[52] That is, while drug abuse was not itself an illness, it was perhaps symptomatic of an underlying illness.

In the decades after World War II, disease theories of drug use closely mirrored those of alcohol, with explanations ranging from genetic disorders to progressive diseases to genetic tendencies toward drug use. This last was most promising, since it acknowledged that the drug abuser had at least some control over his decision to use drugs, but perhaps had been given a push toward abuse by a genetic proclivity toward compulsive behavior or depression. The disease label was problematic, since it suggested to most people a bacterial or viral cause, which was inapplicable to addiction. Yet "disease" in the sense of a progressive set of disabling symptoms did apply, since most addicts (and alcoholics) progressed through a fairly predictable set of steps en route to full-blown addiction. At the same time, geneticists and sociobiologists were concluding that most human behaviors resulted from complex interactions between an individual's genotype and his surrounding environment. For example, genetically inherited IQ was an important component of strong academic performance, but high-IQ individuals rarely reached their academic potential in the absence of a supportive and academically inclined environment. Floyd Bloom of the Salk Institute admitted in 1983, "We are not even close to understanding what goes on in the brain of an addict."[53]

Skeptics, however, rejected the disease model. While most admitted that some people were more psychologically vulnerable than others to the lure of substance abuse, calling this vulnerability a "disease" denied the user responsibility for his choices and removed the moral taint associated with drug abuse and alcoholism. These skeptical scientists argued that everybody would like the effects of heroin if they allowed themselves to try it, and that the idea of genetic predisposition was an excuse that masked the true root of addiction: absence of self-discipline and personal responsibility. Paul Verden and Daniel Shatterly, two skeptical alcohol researchers, argued in the early 1970s that calling alcoholism a disease was "about as useful as claiming that juvenile delinquency is a disease. It is in truth no more than a slogan."[54] Rather, the two researchers argued, alcoholism was really a "complicated set of impulses, feelings, thoughts, and acts," which, while problematic and therapeutically elusive, hardly comprised a disease.[55]

Research emerging in the 1970s did little to resolve the problem. American Indians, for example, long thought to be particularly susceptible to alcoholism, were found to be no different than Europeans in metabolizing ethanol.[56] On the other hand, research conducted in the 1980s at Harvard and at the National Institute of Alcohol Abuse and Alcoholism showed that many severe alcoholics lacked a particular enzyme useful in the metabolic cycle, suggesting that alcoholism contained a genetic basis, despite not falling easily into the "disease" category.[57] Summing up both the public's and the scientific community's ambivalence on the subject, one science journalist in 1983 noted that "most people now know it's [alcoholism] a disease, but they still don't believe it."[58]

Some alcohol researchers investigated the phenomenon of the "social drinker"—those individuals who drank regularly but in moderation. Did such a creature exist? Most alcohol researchers agreed that only about 10 percent of all Americans who drank had a drinking "problem," insofar as they had lost control of when and how they used alcohol. But the 10 percent figure masked a larger problem: alcoholism's progressive quality. Many, if not most, of these social drinkers were alcoholics-in-the-making, destined to gradually lose control over their drinking. The one-drink-per-day drinker in his thirties would likely become a three-martini-lunch drinker in his forties who would gradually progress to full-blown alcoholism in his sixties. Norman Desrosiers, director of an alcohol treatment center, subscribed to this view. The term "social drinker," he felt, was meaningless, insofar as it designated those people who drank *only* in social situations, and then only in extreme moderation: perhaps one or two drinks. Far more likely, he argued, the social drinkers were really masking underlying feelings of depression, inadequacy, and anxiety, and were thus really pre-alcoholics, part of the great population of people who "adjust to life with the aid of chemical means."[59]

What emerged in the 1970s from this morass of theorizing was a complex and unsatisfying theory of addiction that acknowledged the genetic, social, environmental, behavioral, and psychological roots of drug and alcohol use. Alcoholics and addicts seemed to emerge from a drug-using culture relying on drug and alcohol use to dull the pain and disappointments of work, social interactions, and life generally. At the same time, people with a proclivity toward drug use tended to seek out those parts of society that enabled or even encouraged them to use. The tendency to use was further exacerbated by residual feelings of guilt, anxiety, childhood trauma, and sadness, which pointed to a more psychodynamic model of addiction.

The one word that summed up all aspects of drug abuse was immaturity. As more research emerged, it pointed to the fundamental inability of addicts and alcoholics to take responsibility for their lives, to clearly see reality, and to shoulder the burdens of adulthood. Youthful drug addicts engaged "in a good deal of fantasizing about being cared for, catered to with food, money and sex by what is essentially a mother figure," authors of a lengthy research study wrote.[60] A five-year research project at a New York drug treatment facility pointed repeatedly to the ability of addicts to deny reality and to excuse themselves from responsibility for their life choices and failures. Young addicts, for example, frequently resisted work in all forms despite verbally endorsing its importance. When faced with failure, they tended to blame others and refused to see their failings as a natural consequence of the abrogation of their own duties. The New York research group summed up its results thus:

> The various components of the addict's personality—his extreme immaturity, narcissism, difficulty with authority, feelings of omnipotence and poor reality perception—conspired to create severe problems in placing him in employment. Most addicts had left school prematurely, lived for years waiting only for the next "shot," developed no work skills, had little work experience and poor work habits, with the result that they had little to offer in a competitive labor market. They were unprepared for the harsh reality confronting them, namely, that these deficiencies automatically limit the opportunities available to them. One young man, who had lived almost exclusively by means of illegal activities and was increasingly

frightened by the growing prospect of being jailed, protested having to start at the bottom with a smaller weekly salary than he formerly made in a day selling drugs.[61]

This theory of essential narcissism supported a pastoral understanding of drug abuse that tended to frame it in moral and theological terms. Drug use, for many pastors, reflected an underlying spiritual crisis, in which users sought a chemical proxy for God. Given that the essential tenet of all Western religions was subordination of self to the Lord, the immature narcissism of drug addicts pointed to exactly this void. Unable to submit to God, drug addicts and alcoholics pursued self-gratification to their own destruction. Alcoholics Anonymous recognized this tendency by demanding of its followers acceptance of a higher power (the infamous twelfth step), while the Salvation Army had long used this model to good effect in gleaning converts from drunkards. It was no accident that drug and alcohol abuse rose in the United States precisely as church attendance declined, nor was it mere serendipity that evangelical Christians abstained from alcohol at double the national rate. Donald Thorman, the writer and theologian, concluded his reflection on the Christian roots of drug addiction: "Narcotic addiction is by no means a theological problem alone, but whether those involved recognize it or not, many of the most serious differences of opinion are, in the words of Cardinal Manning, 'at bottom theological.' "[62]

New Cures

With the failure of narcotics treatment through conventional psychotherapy, therapists turned to groups. Initial efforts at creating a treatment parallel to Alcoholics Anonymous that addressed the needs of drug addicts had not been successful. The first of these groups, Narcotics Anonymous, founded in New York City in 1950, had attracted some following but had failed to achieve the success of its more celebrated relation.[63] Drug addicts who attended the meetings found the same supportive camaraderie as that found in Alcoholics Anonymous meetings, yet for some reason the social support of the group failed to wean the addicts from their potions. Drug addicts resembled alcoholics in their dependency on chemical mood enhancers and in their long-term self-degradation, but they seemed to be more intensely enslaved to the substances they used, and less capable of casting them off even when girded with encouragement and support.

Drug addicts succumbed to their addictions rapidly. While alcoholics might take decades to progress from initial taste to full-blown alcoholism, drug addicts could become irreversibly addicted in months or weeks. Once addicted, their brains appeared to undergo a fundamental change: Many would never live entirely happily without drugs again. While Alcoholics Anonymous had produced tens of thousands of lifelong abstainers by the mid-1950s, the various narcotics treatment programs had scarcely produced any. Through hospitalizations and treatment programs, addicts could move beyond initial withdrawal symptoms, but they quickly reverted to drug abuse upon release. "It is simple enough to withdraw a drug addict from drugs," Marie Nyswander reported of her experiences treating addicts in the 1950s. The problem was *keeping* them off drugs. Nyswander reported that the majority of patients she had treated had a "history of relapsing to the use of drugs within one to twenty-four hours upon release from an institution."[64] This was a far cry from the months and years alumni of Alcoholics Anonymous frequently posted before backsliding.

Over the next twenty years, however, various experiments with drug treatment vindicated the Narcotics Anonymous approach. As treatment programs began to post more frequent successes in the late 1960s and into the 1970s (though never as frequent as the alcohol treatment programs), they came to rely on some of the basic tenets of AA—group support, use of past addicts as role models and counselors, reeducation, and spiritual succor. For drug addicts, however, these services needed to be delivered more intensively and in a more controlled environment. Outpatient treatment seemed almost useless for the confirmed heroin addict, for example, and lengthy stays in hospitals or residential treatment centers appeared to be necessary prerequisites to successful follow-up group therapy.[65] Drug addicts did need "positive peer-group pressure," but they also needed to be taught an entirely new approach to life sans drugs.[66]

Drug addicts fundamentally differed from alcoholics in that many of them actually seemed to *believe* in drugs. Narcotics provided not merely a temporary respite from misery, but a foundation for life. Young addicts frequently created worlds and lives centered around drug use, in which they socialized only with other users and glorified their use as a badge of honor and identity. Most alcoholics understood their drinking to be degrading, even if they publicly denied it, but drug addicts often found drug use uplifting and immersed themselves in a "culture of addiction."[67] The fact that so many drug addicts were young and had never developed an identity independent of drug use exacerbated the habit. Virtually all alcoholics could remember a time in their adult lives when they had not been alcoholic, and many yearned to return to that earlier, more honest time. But few young addicts had ever lived adult lives, or even adolescent lives, drug-free. Drug use defined their very being.

The solution was necessarily radical. As with alcoholics, counselors needed to help the addicts re-create their lives in a new drug-free mold. Old drug-addicted friends and drug-centered activities needed to be traded for drug-free support networks. But different from alcoholics, many drug addicts needed to be taught an entirely new philosophy of life. They needed to be indoctrinated to a new way of living and taught not to glorify the narcotic life. Mac Proctor, a counselor at Exodus House in New York City, one of the more successful of the drug treatment programs that emerged in the early 1970s, pronounced that it was of "prime importance that the community come to view narcotic addiction and drug abuse as pathological, thus eliminating the glamour of its underworld aura."[68]

Successfully treating drug addicts, as with alcoholics, required helping the addicts to fill the void in their lives that had once been dominated by drugs. But again, different from alcoholics, the void in this case was not merely social and emotional, but philosophical. Even more so that did Alcoholics Anonymous, most successful drug treatment programs needed to emphasize the spiritual component of rehabilitation—of creating a life of meaning without the aid of chemicals. Drug addicts needed to be taught what it was to experience a healthy sense of achievement and productivity now that they no longer based their identity on taking drugs. Proctor wrote of the need for a "radical redefinition of productive relationships" and an acceptance of a "code of ethics" independent of drug use.[69] Jim Gibson, an ex-addict who ran a treatment program in Mendocino, California, stated succinctly, "The cure for drugs and drug addiction is a meaningful life."[70] Such an effort required a substantially more intensive rehabilitation approach than weekly AA meetings, and many successful drug treatment programs resembled nothing so much as army boot camps in their all-encompassing approach to reeducation. One youthful drug addict described the program which finally weaned him from heroin as "strict, almost military in structure, but warm as a womb."[71]

Not surprisingly, religion often played a major role in successful drug treatment. While Alcoholics Anonymous required acceptance of a higher power as part of its path to cure, that component of the twelve-step process had always been the most controversial, and the most difficult for many alcoholics to accept. Many recovering alcoholics endorsed the idea only tepidly, and considered God a mere coda to the more important aspects of their rehabilitation such as making amends and taking responsibility for their failings. But for many drug addicts God became an essential component of their path out of addiction. Because they had shaped their personal identities around drug use from a young age, they lacked emotional and social coping skills. In the absence of drugs their lives were often dull and meaningless, and they often had few professional or personal accomplishments that could serve as points of pride. For many, God filled the void, and church teachings provided the basis of a new drug-free credo. Richard Dunn, a Protestant cleric in Chicago who was active in Gateway House, a fundamentalist Christian drug treatment center, concluded that it was precisely the demanding and rigid quality of fundamentalism that made possible many successful treatments. He believed that puritanical abnegation was the correct response to the narcissistic and hedonistic credo of the typical drug addict. Dunn wrote, "Religion has to do with subduing the ego, the voluntary taking up of a self-denial and service to the Higher Power."[72] In this vein, many fundamentalists believed that the social progressivism and moral laxness of the mainstream Protestant denominations in the 1970s not only failed to help drug addicts—they might actually have been part of the problem.

A secondary drug treatment tool used to augment the increasingly effective treatment programs in the 1970s was methadone. A synthetic opiate closely related to morphine, methadone could be given in one daily dose that reduced much of the craving and erratic behavior experienced by heroin addicts. As with heroin, methadone often made users sleepy and ineffectual, but they seemed to experience a far less intense high while on it, and thus were better able to participate in normal daily activities.

Methadone treatment was controversial. An NIMH study conducted in 1970 was skeptical of its utility, and chided drug treatment professionals for their premature willingness to endorse its use.[73] Methadone was, if anything, more addictive than heroin, insofar as withdrawal from it was far worse and took longer. Methadone users never really got off drugs; they simply switched to a cleaner drug that could be taken orally rather than intravenously. The specter of the government handing out synthetic opiates to willing citizens drew the ire of more conservative civic groups. Some progressive advocates suggested that a better approach might be to simply hand out daily supplies of heroin, which would at least minimize the crime, filth, and violence associated with the drug trade.[74] But most knowledgeable drug abuse researchers scoffed at the idea. One researcher, Robert Newman, pointed out, "If you want to eliminate the pusher, you've got to compete with him. That means giving every addict all the heroin he wants. Are you really going to give a 14-year-old kid as much heroin as he wants? Of course not."[75]

As the drug culture reached a frenzied peak in 1979, drug counselors settled on a mixture of treatments to help their hard-to-reach charges, including residential treatment, group support, fundamentalist moralizing, and methadone. Traditional psychotherapy had failed to work, but many techniques born of psychotherapy—group therapy, talk therapy, personal education, psychic reorientation—undergirded successful treatment approaches. Drug addicts did benefit from speaking about their personal histories and working through psychic traumas, but in addition, they usually needed doses of military boot camp, methadone, personal responsibility, and a healthy fear of God.

CHAPTER 9

Psychoanalysis in Decline

Although psychoanalysts continued to hold leadership positions in departments of psychiatry well into the 1990s, as a profession psychoanalysis had been in decline since the mid-1960s. Psychoanalytic institutes reported declining enrollments in their training analysis programs, and progressively fewer psychiatric residents elected to enroll in psychoanalytic training.[1] Psychoanalysts treated fewer patients with traditional long-term psychoanalysis, and filled their schedules instead with therapy patients who came only once or twice per week. Hans Strupp reported that the profession was increasingly being described as "antiquated, passé, and even defunct,"[2] while one practitioner reported that the profession was "starved" for patients.[3] In 1980, the American Psychiatric Association signaled its disregard for the profession by removing nearly all mention of neuroses from the third edition of the *Diagnostic and Statistical Manual*—the most important reference tool for practicing mental health professionals.[4]

By 1990 the profession was hitting bottom. That year the American Psychoanalytic Association conducted a survey of its 3,000 members and found that the typical analyst saw only two analytic patients weekly.[5] The analysts as a group were old (typically near sixty) and mostly male.

Tanya Luhrmann, a sociologist studying the profession, described the experience of watching the annual meeting of the American Psychoanalytic Association as akin to "watching dinosaurs deliberate over their own extinction."[6] As a group, the members still cleaved tightly to the writing and teachings of Freud, who had died more than a half century earlier. While some prescribed antidepressant and antianxiety medications, as a group they tended to eschew pharmacological treatments and regard skeptically the growing evidence of the physiological and biochemical bases of mental illness. Robert Michels, chairman of psychiatry at Cornell, estimated that "perhaps one in ten thousand Americans" was in analysis.[7]

Analysis had priced itself out of existence. Historically both practitioners and patients had disproportionately come from the elite moneyed classes, but now declining insurance coverage made the endeavor unaffordable to all but the wealthiest Americans. Analysts in 1990 were typically charging $100 per session (clinical social workers charged $50 or less), and a typical analysis required between 450 and 600 sessions, compared to between 15 and 20 required in most forms of psychotherapy. Hans Eysenck, an influential British psychiatrist, chided the profession for providing an "elitist" treatment, for which "only the brightest, best educated, wealthiest and least ill are considered."[8]

The analysts needed to be nearly as wealthy as their patients to consider entering the profession. The typical training analysis by 1990 had stretched to seven years, which needed to be accompanied by four years of six-hour-per-week seminars and three supervised analyses. Psychiatrists generally estimated the cost of training as $40,000 per year in lost earnings, plus $20,000 in fees per year for their own training analyses for however long they took.[9] Considering that analytic training failed to add earning potential for most board-certified psychiatrists, the training was reserved for either the independently wealthy or the extraordinarily committed.

More important than cost, however, was the simple fact that studies repeatedly demonstrated that psychoanalysis did not work. The Menninger Foundation's report in 1972 had indicated such, but so had many others. The American Psychoanalytic Association's own study of psychoanalytic efficacy, conducted in the 1950s under the guidance of Harry Weinstock, produced such damning data that the effort ended with obfuscation and censorship.[10] When data were finally released the following decade, they showed that only one in six patients treated in analysis was ultimately cured, although those patients diagnosed as "neurotic" fared slightly better.[11] A second report published in 1967 showing considerably better results was attacked on methodological grounds, with Arthur Shapiro, a psychiatrist at Mt. Sinai Medical School, stating that it could "in no way be considered a serious scientific document....There were no controls, no independent evaluation of the patients." Forty-three percent of the sample had not completed treatment, and results of that 43 percent had been discarded. Shapiro decried the "fudge factor" that had been used in selecting for the study.[12]

Other studies over the years produced similar results, with most indicating a nearly 90 percent spontaneous remission rate for neurotic patients over five years, while remission rates for neurotic patients in analysis were actually somewhat lower.[13] George Engel, a psychiatric researcher, wrote in 1968 that psychoanalysts simply "haven't delivered the goods,"[14] while Hans Eysenck concluded in his 1975 study of British psychiatry that "now it is taken for granted even by leading psychoanalysts that the therapeutic value of psychoanalysis is severely limited."[15] Eysenck, in fact, was scathing in his denunciations:

> This is not to say that it may not be fun for some rich and mildly neurotic Americans to talk about their sex lives with a sympathetic and unusually intelligent and well-read psychoanalyst, or that many people who find difficulties in getting hold of a friendly listener to their tales of woe may not find it worth their while to pay an analyst

to fulfill that function. But as far as the systematic, scientific theory of neurosis is concerned, and such deductions from such a theory as might lead to improved methods of treatment, the Freudian theory is as dead as that attributing neurotic symptoms to demonological influences, and his method of therapy is following exorcism into oblivion. And with it goes the only systematic medical model of neurosis.[16]

Moreover, scientific studies of certain analytic shibboleths, such as repressed infantile memories and children's sexual urges, undermined the claims of analysis. Most studies of memory indicated that children were simply incapable of constructing memories until age three or four, meaning that memories from the earlier years had not been lost; they had never existed. A study conducted by the Social Science Research Council concluded that virtually all types of memory were "poor at the earliest level" and that they improved "by a fairly constant rate at a later period."[17] Studies of college students showed virtually no correlation between breast-feeding at infancy and adult psychological health. Possibly significant as well were Jane Goodall's anthropological chimpanzee studies in Tanzania's Gombe Reserve. Despite the fact that young male chimpanzees shared a nest nightly with their mothers for their first five years, Goodall never once observed sexual activity between them, or even efforts toward that end. If, as Goodall speculated, human infantile sexual development paralleled chimpanzee development, this observation argued against the existence of an Oedipus complex.[18]

The controversial claims from the 1950s and 1960s of psychoanalysis's efficacy in treating schizophrenia were similarly debunked. Joanne Greenberg's well-known experience at Chestnut Lodge hospital, which she described in fictionalized form in *I Never Promised You a Rose Garden*, had been frequently cited as evidence that schizophrenic symptoms could be alleviated through intense psychoanalysis. But actual studies of schizophrenics treated at Chestnut Lodge and other analytically oriented hospitals found them to fare no better than their counterparts at traditional psychiatric hospitals. Tom McGlashan, a psychiatrist at Chestnut Lodge, investigated the Greenberg case and reclassified her ailment as borderline personality disorder rather than schizophrenia.[19] Philip May, a psychiatrist at UCLA, proved conclusively in the late 1960s that medication was by far the most effective treatment for schizophrenia, while analysis and therapy accomplished little.[20]

The failure of analysis was all the more striking when contrasted with the success of cognitive and behavioral therapies, which seemed to be highly effective for certain diagnoses. A growing list of diagnoses, among them obsessions, compulsions, phobias, certain personality disorders, and behavioral tics, seemed to respond to cognitive and behavioral therapies yet resisted cure through psychodynamic approaches. Psychoanalysis, by contrast, could point to few, if any, specific syndromes for which it seemed particularly effective.[21]

Assaulted by overwhelming evidence of psychoanalysis's inefficacy, declining insurance reimbursement, growing competition from cheaper and faster therapists, and a dwindling patient pool, analysts either fled the field or else blindly recommitted themselves to their endeavor. A certain number of psychoanalysts even became more orthodox in the 1980s, refusing to acknowledge the insurmountable challenges confronting their profession. One analyst in New York underwent two training analyses—the first lasting for six years, the second for nine—and was considering a third to iron out the remaining tics in his personality.[22] Another, who had trained at Chestnut Lodge, became "convinced" that analysis could work on schizophrenia, even amid strong evidence that it did not.[23] Another successful analyst from Washington, D.C., speaking to a reporter, explained that he loved owning nice things because his mother was a "beautiful thing." He explained, "All these things [in his house] are like having her and wanting to touch her. It's her body. All these things I like are her body."[24] These men, representing the fringe of the profession, were so committed to psychoanalytic dogma as to no longer be open to persuasion.

By 1990, the remnants of the profession were surviving on faith. Rejecting statistical evidence, personal experience, multiple studies, and thousands of pages of reasoned critiques, the remaining psychoanalysts clung to their dogma in a mixture of denial, professional fear, and blind belief. Analysts continued to dismiss the claims of other therapists, or else they accepted their claims while disparaging their stated goals. Martin Gross described one analyst's derision toward briefer and non-analytic therapies: The therapies were "mere symptom relief," while psychoanalysis was the "surgery of the soul."[25] Hans Eysenck was more willing to condemn surviving analysts as outright charlatans. He noted, "Few patients are warned before undergoing analysis that not only is there no evidence that it will improve their status, but there is evidence that it may actually make them worse."[26]

The case of *Osheroff vs. Chestnut Lodge* signaled the close of the analytic era. Rafael Osheroff, a forty-two-year-old nephrologist, was admitted to Chestnut Lodge in 1979 for severe depression and anxiety. Osheroff had suffered from depression at various times during his life, and at the time of admission his depressive episodes had become increasingly worse over the previous two years. He had been taking tricyclic antidepressants, which had produced modest improvement, but he had ceased taking them and his psychiatrist in New York, Nathan Kline, had recommended hospitalization. At Chestnut Lodge he was treated with individual psychotherapy four times per week over seven months, during which time he lost forty pounds and became extremely depressed and agitated. He consulted with a Washington psychiatrist, who discussed the case with the medical staff at Chestnut Lodge. The Chestnut Lodge staff elected to continue treatment with psychotherapy and eschew antidepressant drugs.

After seven months, Osheroff's family reclaimed him from Chestnut

Lodge and had him admitted to the Silver Hill Foundation in Connect-icut, where he was treated with tricyclic drugs and phenothiazines. He improved dramatically and was discharged after three months, at which point he reentered medical practice and rejoined his family.

In 1982 Osheroff sued Chestnut Lodge for negligence, claiming that by withholding drug treatment the facility had unnecessarily prolonged his depression, damaging both his professional reputation and his rela-tionship with his family. The Maryland Healthcare Arbitration Panel found in favor of Osheroff and awarded him damages. Both sides ap-pealed the case in the Maryland court system, and they eventually set-tled out of court for an undisclosed sum.

The Osheroff case drew widespread attention from the analytic community. The arbitration process had drawn on the expertise of nu-merous eminent academic psychiatrists who testified about the lack of empirical evidence for the efficacy of psychoanalysis and psychody-namic therapy, particularly in the case of severe depression with possibly psychotic complications—Osheroff's eventual diagnosis. Physicians at Chestnut Lodge had argued that Osheroff suffered from a personality disorder, which might have called for a more psychodynamic approach, but the psychiatrist who treated Osheroff after his discharge found that the diagnosis of personality disorder was inconsistent with Osheroff's success as a physician, husband, and father. In fact, all evidence at the time of Osheroff's admission suggested that the most effective treatment would have been some combination of tricyclic antidepressants, pheno-thiazines, and electroshock therapy. In a lengthy study of the case, Ger-ald Klerman, a psychiatrist at Cornell Medical Center, pointed out that in 1979 there were "no reports of controlled trials" to support the use of intensive dynamic psychotherapy in a case such as Osheroff's.[27] There was evidence that cognitive-behavioral therapy may have been helpful in Osheroff's case, but Chestnut Lodge had long used psychoanalytically oriented therapy almost exclusively. Klerman emphasized in his analysis of the case that at issue was not "psychotherapy versus biological therapy but, rather, opinion versus evidence."[28] The day when psychiatrists could avoid scientifically grounding their work was ending.[29]

Biological psychiatry was ascending in importance and credibility in the 1980s. While psychoactive drugs had long existed, before Thorazine they had been "little more than the chemical counterpart of a hammer blow to the head," in the words of Edward Dolnick, a historian of psychiatry.[30] Thorazine and reserpine had changed the way psychiatrists treated schizophrenia, but more important, they had changed the way psychiatrists understood schizophrenia. Both drugs, part of a class of antipsychotic drugs called neuroleptics, were highly effective in reducing the symptomatic hallucinations and delusions of schizophrenia, yet had almost no effect on healthy subjects. The discrepancy in response to the drugs indicated that the brains of schizophrenics were physiologically different than those of healthy people. Schizophrenia was very much a biological condition, even if rooted partially in environmental stressors.

Various schizophrenia treatments were tested during the 1960s, and all pointed to anatomical or physiological causes. Psychotherapy rarely had any effect, and electroshock worked little better. Neuroleptics were the only proven treatment, and they were no more potent when combined with therapy. In the middle of the decade Philip May, professor of psychiatry at UCLA, treated 228 schizophrenic patents with a variety of approaches, including electroshock, drugs, therapy, and various combinations thereof. The results conclusively demonstrated the superiority of drug treatment; nothing else worked even remotely as well.[31]

In the 1970s, scientists conducted similar studies of the comparative efficacy of drugs and therapy in treating depression, bipolar disorder, and various anxiety complaints. All made use of double-blind techniques, using patients in control groups, on placebos, and on active medications including MAOIs and tricyclics (for unipolar depression) and lithium (for bipolar disorder), and all demonstrated the substantial superiority of medication over all other treatments. Unlike the schizophrenia studies, however, studies with depression and anxiety indicated that while drugs alone worked better than therapy alone, a combination of the two was superior to drugs alone.[32] In particular, a 1977 study by Rush and Beck demonstrated that treating depressive disorders with antidepressant medications in conjunction with cognitive-behavioral therapy garnered superior results.[33]

Psychiatric disorders clearly had biological causes. What was confusing was that in nearly all cases, biology alone could not wholly explain the presence or absence of psychiatric symptoms. Most sufferers of chronic depression and bipolar disorder had a genetic propensity toward their conditions, but all appeared to require environmental triggers as well. Thus, while drugs were effective for these conditions in most cases, drugs used in conjunction with certain types of therapies worked even better. A research group headed by Klerman compared the combination of drugs and therapy to a cocktail. Klerman wrote, "As with the martini, if a little gin is good, a lot of gin is better, and adding a little vermouth offers something more."[34] Even schizophrenia, that most physiological of psychiatric disorders, seemed to owe at least part of its etiology to environment. In sets of identical twins where one twin had schizophrenia, for example, the other twin had schizophrenia in 50 percent of cases. This was fifty times the prevalence of the disease in the general population, yet it did not explain why in half the cases the genetically identical twin did not get the disease.

It was most likely that an environmental agent worked in conjunction with biology to cause schizophrenia. Solomon Goldberg, a researcher at the NIMH, confirmed the existence of a biological component of the disease when he found that while schizophrenics treated with neuroleptics improved far more frequently than those left untreated, certain discharged patients appeared able to avoid relapse once drugs were discontinued, provided they commanded a great deal of social support.[35]

Neuroscientists, too, advanced understanding of the biochemistry of depression, anxiety, and bipolar disorder by explaining the actions of many of the psychoactive drugs. Most of the drugs, as well as electro-shock therapy, appeared to work by modulating the body's production or use of dopamine and norepinephrine, two of the brain's more common chemical transmitters. Whether by blocking absorption of these chemicals or inducing the body to make more, the drugs changed mood by altering the speed at which various brain cells communicated with one another. The dopamine mechanism also explained the involuntary bodily tics associated with Thorazine use, for the tics appeared to be rooted in neurochemical imbalances in parts of the brain stem that co-ordinated motion. In modulating dopamine levels in the cerebrum in an effort to control schizophrenic symptoms, psychiatrists inadvertently altered dopamine levels in the brain stem, causing twitches and tics.[36] Electroshock therapy, insulin therapy, and even light therapy, for use in seasonal depression, all appeared to mitigate symptoms by altering bio-chemical balances in the brain.[37]

Psychosurgery, too, was partially resuscitated as a treatment option for certain kinds of seizure disorders, albeit in a highly refined form in which only the smallest fiber bundles were cut, sometimes through chemical or electrical cauterization. Vernon Mark, a neurosurgeon, pref-aced an article he wrote in 1974 on newer developments in psychosur-gery with the caveat that while the case for surgery might not be as compelling as the case against it, the case for its use in limited circum-stances was "more rational, factual, and ultimately more humanitarian."[38]

New insights into the biological bases of mental illness, coupled with general disenchantment with psychoanalysis, marked the end of analysis as an important form of psychotherapy. While a few analysts would per-sist with their work, most of the major psychoanalytic hospitals and in-stitutes, including the Menninger Clinic and Chestnut Lodge, were headed for bankruptcy. A long and influential chapter in the history of psychotherapy was drawing to a close.

Advances in Cognitive Therapy

Cognitive therapy advanced as psychoanalysis declined. Rooted in Albert Ellis's rational emotive therapy (RET), cognitive therapy and its close adjunct cognitive behavioral therapy (CBT) were largely the products of Aaron Beck, a professor of psychiatry at the University of Pennsylvania. Beck, like Ellis, had been trained in classical analytic technique, but had discarded it in favor of the more rational approach of RET. Like Ellis, he viewed disjointed and biased thinking as the cause of much depression and anxiety, and sought out ways to counter patient's "automatic thoughts," maladaptive thinking patterns, consistent biases against themselves, and catastrophic ideations. Drawing also from Adler and Horney, and adding a great deal of his own systematic empirical research to the mix, he published his theory and techniques in two volumes: *Depression: Clinical, Experimental, and Theoretical Aspects* (1967) and *Cognitive Therapy and the Emotional Disorders* (1976).[39]

In both depressed and anxious patients, Beck consistently observed "dichotomous" thinking. Uncomfortable with ambiguity, patients tended to view life as either perfect or disastrous, and to view normal setbacks as catastrophic. Beck felt that this "catastrophizing" was one of the greatest impediments to healthy thinking, and sought techniques to thwart it.[40] In his 1976 book, he recounted the following example of the phenomenon:

Anxious Patient: I think I'm dying.

Therapist: What makes you think so?

Patient: My heart is beating hard. Things seem blurred. I can't catch my breath.... I am sweating all over.

Therapist: Why does this mean you are dying?

Patient: Because this is what it is like to die.

Therapist: How do you know?

Patient: [after some reflection] I guess I don't know. But I *think* these are signs of dying.[41]

One of Beck's major contributions was his discovery of techniques by which he could focus patients' attention on their own poor thinking skills and reeducate them in more constructive patterns of thinking. Rather than the deep personal insight promised by psychoanalysis or the consciousness raising of the radical therapies of the 1960s, Beck offered a stern dose of common sense. He directed patients' attention to their own poor use of statistical reasoning, their own sampling biases, and their own automatic thoughts. He noted the "astonishing contrast between the depressed person's image of himself and the objective facts," and sought to bridge this gap by repeatedly focusing his therapy sessions on the poor thinking out of which it grew.[42] Using simplicity and common sense as guides, he tended to take patients' reflections at face value rather than seek repressed meanings in them. He criticized psychodynamic therapists precisely for their unwillingness to accept patients' thoughts as valid. He wrote in 1985, "No matter how complicated a patient's problem may be, a therapist has it in his power to make it even more complicated."[43]

Beck's other major contribution to cognitive therapy was his willingness to test his techniques empirically. In a quarter century of studies, Beck compared progress for depressed and anxious patients being treated cognitively, psychodynamically, and pharmacologically, and consistently discovered that patients treated cognitively outperformed those treated psychodynamically, and often outperformed those treated pharmacologically. For certain symptoms, combinations of cognitive therapy and pharmaceuticals worked better than either one independently, and for nearly all diagnoses any therapy at all worked better than doing nothing—though placebos were surprisingly helpful in certain anxiety disorders.[44]

Not everybody agreed with Beck's sunny judgments of cognitive therapy's promise. Studies conducted by other researchers at the same time found that in certain cases, cognitive therapy performed little better than humanistic or even psychodynamic therapies, although these skeptical researchers admitted that cognitive therapy outperformed other techniques for most anxiety disorders and phobias.[45] A large meta-analysis (a retrospective study of previous studies) conducted in 1989 established conclusively that in unipolar depressive disorders, cognitive therapy was superior to other types of therapies, as well as substantially superior to placebo treatment or doing nothing.[46]

The weakness of all of the outcomes studies of the 1970 and 1980s lay in measurement and sampling size. Despite advances in diagnostic techniques, mental health professionals still differed over the precise mix of symptoms that defined one condition over another, and tended to view certain aspects of an illness as more or less significant. Two professionals might agree on a diagnosis of depression, but might disagree over the subcategories of complications, and might further disagree on the precise mix of symptom alleviation indicating that the depression had been successfully treated. Moreover, in contrast with the hundreds or thousands of patients observed in large pharmaceutical studies, samples for therapy studies included dozens of patients or fewer. Such limited sample sizes tended to distort findings.

Still, by 1985 most mental health professionals from all disciplines agreed that cognitive therapy was better, faster, more consistent, and cheaper. Many therapists mixed cognitive therapy with aspects of humanistic therapy, or retained pieces of psychodynamic therapy in their practices, but few could afford to disregard the opus produced by the cognitive specialists. The corpus of outcomes literature was too compelling to ignore, and the cures wrought were too alluring in an age of diminished insurance reimbursement. Furthermore, newer research on learning and conditioning suggested that the sorts of abstract connections made in Freudian therapy were incapable of truly moderating the maladaptive thoughts of most therapeutic patients.

However, while most therapists had moved toward cognitive therapy and away from psychodynamic therapy in the 1970s, several studies in the 1980s indicated that a sizable number of therapists adhered to no particular type of therapy at all. These *eclectic* therapists pledged allegiance to no school and used whatever therapeutic tools seemed to work. Many switched approaches for different patients, and all drew on insights and theories from a variety of sources. One 1982 study found that more than 40 percent of clinical psychologists described themselves as "eclectic," with the next most common descriptions, "psychoanalytic" and "cognitive-behavioral," being claimed by just 11 percent each. The third most frequent, at 9 percent, "person centered," was nearly as vague an indicator of therapeutic approach as was "eclectic."[47] Other studies indicated similar ambivalence about aligning with a particular school of therapy, although psychiatrists tended to be more beholden to Freud and less willing to experiment with eclecticism.[48] Even of those psychologists who aligned themselves with the division of humanistic psychology of the American Psychological Association, only 8 percent considered themselves primarily humanistic, while 30 percent defined themselves as eclectic.[49] Donald Greaves, a psychiatrist in Evanston, Illinois, explained, "The buzzword in our profession these days is 'pragmatic eclecticism.'"[50]

Besides eclecticism, psychotherapists of all persuasions agreed on shortening the length of therapy. From the 800-hour analysis of a quarter century before, typical therapy had declined to 800 minutes. Dwindling reimbursement had driven this trend, but so too had patients' unwillingness to subject themselves to years of therapy that they rightly judged to be ineffectual. Moreover, a growing body of evidence suggested that not only was therapy beyond twenty sessions useless, it might actually worsen the initial condition. Lengthy therapies did little to

boost the patient's confidence in his own abilities, and possibly exacerbated tendencies toward passivity and dependence on others. Therapists
who administered overly long therapeutic sequences created counter-
productive relationships with their patients, and risked distorting their
patient's view of the therapist's own role in the healing process. James
Mann, a psychiatrist who wrote critically of overly long therapies, noted
that the psychiatrist or psychologist who persisted in dragging out therapy convinced himself that "no patient can long survive without his
close and indefinitely prolonged attention."[51]

Therapists had been experimenting with shorter-term therapies
since the 1960s, when psychiatrists at London's Tavistock Institute attempted to shorten traditional analysis.[52] In the absence of evidence to
the contrary, however, most psychiatrists persisted on extending analysis
and analytically oriented therapy for three years or more. Growing evidence for cognitive-behavioral therapy, however, pushed most therapists
away not only from analysis but from the entire drawn-out analytic
conception of time. Cognitive therapists found that they were generally
able to achieve their best results in the first twelve sessions, and few patients continued to make progress after the twentieth session. Two psychiatrists at the Harvard Community Health Plan concluded from their
observations of many hundreds of therapeutic patients that fewer than
2 percent could benefit from long-term therapy.[53] Some therapists even
experimented with single-session therapy, and while this was obviously
extreme, evidence did suggest that in the cases of certain phobias, measurable progress could be made in as little as one hour.[54]

Technological change in part explained the shift. The invention of
the video camera had made it possible to film therapy sessions (with patients' permission) and chart progress over time. Video images revealed
that while patients did change during therapy, much of the change and
insight appeared to happen early. Analytic claims to more subtle long-
term changes were not born out by video images. The analysts most
likely believed their claims, but their closeness to the patient made it

difficult for them to accurately judge changes over time. One psychiatrist offered this explanation: "Psychotherapy has traditionally been very loose in this respect. Therapists say things like, 'Well, the patient is still impotent, but now he doesn't mind.' "[55]

Therapists also experimented with varying the length of individual sessions. Jacques Lacan, a French psychoanalyst notorious for his radical ideas and techniques, had varied sessions with different patients, sometimes cutting them off five minutes after their arrival. He liked to keep patients alert and focused, and believed that varying the session length unpredictably forced them to work more intensively. Few American therapists became outright Lacanians, but many tried shorter sessions, partially for their therapeutic value and partially to accommodate their patients' busy schedules. Some therapists turned to phone sessions as well, although most admitted that the phone was an imperfect substitute for face-to-face therapy. Too much nonverbal information was lost; too many physical cues were missed. One therapist related his attempts to treat over the phone a patient with multiple-personality disorder. "I had no idea he was crying until an alternate [personality] came on the phone and said, 'Doctor, don't you know tears are streaming down his face?' "[56]

More problematic for many therapists was the growing awareness that spontaneous remission of psychiatric symptoms was observed consistently in a third of all patients. At least a dozen investigations conducted between 1942 and 1965 had shown that a third of all patients complaining of psychoneurotic symptoms got better on their own.[57] While the rates of remission varied by complaint, the overall statistic of one-third did not. This did not suggest that psychotherapy was ineffective (patients treated with therapy recovered at double that rate), but it did suggest that many psychiatric complaints were perhaps less pathological than the therapeutic professions wished to admit. Therapists did add value with their work, but perhaps the real value was less than they claimed.

One more observation in the 1980s shook therapists' confidence in their own rectitude. A growing body of literature indicated that far more important than the school of therapy a therapist hewed to was the personal qualities of the therapist him- or herself. Patients who worked well with one therapist might fail with another, but some therapists seemed to work well with very few patients at all, suggesting that they simply lacked the skill, insight, and empathy required of a competent therapist.[58] A group of researchers at Johns Hopkins University and the University of Pennsylvania studied hundreds of patients in therapy with professionals from a variety of orientations in the 1980s and found that regardless of "school," all successful therapists shared a number of traits, including empathy, honesty, and the ability to connect quickly and intensely with a variety of people. The study, directed by the eminent psychological researcher Lester Luborsky, indicated that the traditional assertion that different people benefited best in different sorts of therapeutic milieus was probably wrong. Good therapists could help many people with many complaints, and bad therapists could help few, regardless of the particular technique each might use.[59]

Hans Krupp, a researcher at Vanderbilt, furthered the "good therapist" hypothesis. Dividing thirty patients between trained psychotherapists and well-liked but untrained humanities professors, Krupp found that the two sets of patients improved at similar rates.[60] The discovery that untrained though highly intelligent and empathetic professors, many of whom had been in therapy themselves, could effectively treat many nonpsychotic complaints meant that much of the therapeutic theory being argued over and touted was simply irrelevant. Effective psychotherapy seemed to require little more than a willing patient and an intelligent and understanding counselor who met and spoke regularly and in confidence. The mere process of connecting with another human was itself deeply therapeutic, as had been suggested by Harry Stack Sullivan and Karen Horney a half century before. Theory was not destructive, but it was perhaps less important than so many therapists would have liked to believe.

Professional Shifts

Changes in the professional landscape of therapy accompanied changes in therapeutic techniques. Psychiatry, long the leader in prestige and influence of the therapeutic professions, lost allure rapidly after 1970, while clinical psychology and clinical social work both grew. Arguments surrounding insurance reimbursement, prescription privileges, and hospital admitting privileges for non-M.D.s persisted into the 1990s, as both psychology and social work incrementally gained ground in their efforts to dethrone psychiatry. Psychiatrists, in response, retreated to the biological and medical edges of mental health care, becoming the pharmacological agents of mental health treatment who worked in conjunction with nonmedical therapists to provide multipronged treatment. The move was largely involuntary for the psychiatrists, but by 2000 it was essentially complete.

The number of psychiatrists changed little from 1960 to 1980. Training programs that had produced 800 psychiatrists per year in 1960 were producing 1,000 in 1980, despite the recognized need in the 1950s for training an additional 2,500 psychiatrists per year. American-trained psychiatrists continued to dominate private suburban practices, while foreign-trained psychiatrists filled the vacant slots in state hospitals and clinics. The profession still preferred urban areas and the coasts, with the Northeast of the country hosting one psychiatrist for each 11,000 citizens and the South hosting one per 34,000.[61] More than half of the nation's psychiatrists practiced in just five states, and no child psychiatrists at all practiced in the mountain states.

Young physicians were rarely choosing psychiatry. In 1955, at the peak of the profession's allure, 7 percent of graduating American M.D.s each year opted for psychiatric residencies; by 1990 that had declined to just over 3 percent. Salaries were part of the issue, as full-time psychiatrists continued to be among the lowest paid of the board-certified specialties in medicine and surgery. But a general sense of unease surrounding the appropriate roll of psychiatry in the medical specialties also dissuaded young doctors from seeking training in the field. Psychoanalysis, long the prestigious activity that was the sole purview of psychiatry, had fallen, and biological psychiatry was not yet promising enough, or perhaps not rigorous enough, to compensate for the absence of analysis. The most scientifically oriented young physicians found psychiatry's diagnostic vagueness frustrating, yet the analysis that had once lured the more philosophically inclined medical students to psychiatry no longer existed.

Demographics played a role as well. Asian-Americans had risen to 16 percent of the medical school classes, from 6 percent a decade previous, and they were the least likely of all students to choose psychiatry as a career.[62] Then, too, the increasing allure of clinical psychology as a field meant that the high-achieving students most interested in therapeutic careers could bypass medical school entirely and enter the therapeutic professions through psychology doctoral programs. Psychiatry was disproportionately populated by former humanities majors, women, Easterners, liberals, urban denizens, and graduates of prestigious private colleges. The medical schools of New York University, Harvard, Columbia, and the University of Illinois placed six times the average percentage of their graduating classes into psychiatry. By contrast, medical schools at Notre Dame, Louisiana State University, and the University of Tennessee placed barely any.[63] Increasingly, psychiatry attracted a very specific and unrepresentative sort of medical student who seemed to exist at only the most urbane and elite medical schools.

As psychiatry declined, both clinical psychology and social work thrived. From 1960 to 1980, both the number of doctorates awarded in clinical psychology and the number of master's degrees awarded in social work quadrupled.[64] Both professions won reimbursement from Blue Shield and other private insurance plans, and psychologists gained prescription privileges in a number of states.[65] By 1977, psychologists were licensed in every state in the country as independent practitioners, and by 1991 the American Psychological Association claimed membership of more than 100,000.[66]

Psychiatrists firmly resisted virtually all of these steps. Physicians' groups lobbied Blue Shield plans to resist direct reimbursement for psychologists (preferring that they work as adjuncts to psychiatrists and get paid through them as contracted agents), and they lobbied state legislatures to vote against prescription bills. Blue Shield of Virginia opposed reimbursing psychologists, suggesting that "every coot and crank in the nation will want to send his bills to Blue Shield," in the words of science reporter Eliot Marshall.[67] Psychologists responded by arguing that bringing psychologists (and social workers) into national reimbursement schemes was the only way to grant poorer individuals access to psychotherapy; there were simply not enough psychiatrists to do the job. Moreover, in matters of prescription privileges, psychologists argued that they were at least as qualified to prescribe psychoactive formulations as were the internists and general practitioners who were writing the majority of the nation's psychiatric prescriptions.[68]

Despite these advances, clinical psychology struggled for professional respect. Large numbers of psychologists continued to train under the supervision of psychiatrists within departments of psychiatry in medical schools and hospitals, leading one critic to describe the profession as "ancillary"—more akin to nursing and occupational therapy than a truly independent profession, rendering psychologists little more than "guests in other people's agencies and hospitals."[69] The profession's training programs were still seen as overly applied and vocational, and tended to be housed in secondary campuses of state universities or in lesser private universities. Although the Psy.D. and Ed.D. degrees were frequently replaced during these years with the Ph.D. degree, the applied Ph.D. programs tended to be housed in schools of education, social work, and allied health professions, rather than in medical schools or academic departments of psychology. Freestanding schools of applied psychology, independent of established universities, offered the degree as well, particularly in California, while virtually no top-tier research university offered a doctoral program in clinical psychology.[70]

Lack of consensus regarding standards in the profession undermined the integrity of the training process. Various schools, departments, and even individual professors continued to cleave to antiquated theories and approaches to psychological diagnosis and counseling, even in the face of countervailing evidence. Tenured professors preached long-outmoded approaches to mental health and taught obsolete techniques for therapy and treatment. Although younger researchers entering the academy made efforts to pull the profession to a more scientifically rigorous model of practice, simmering disagreements between faculty members and professional adjuncts continued to wreak havoc on naïve students seeking guidance and professional judgment. Doctoral students surveyed in the 1970s described the "ivory tower of bullshit" and "dehumanizing experiences" they had been exposed to in graduate school. Professors were "narrow" and "squabbling": "niggling men growing old in despair."[71] Most professions could find similar malcontents within their ranks, but psychology seemed particularly vulnerable to the criticism.

Social work was faced with similar problems. Like clinical psychology, it was also considered ancillary and dependent, lacking in admitting and prescription privileges and beset with low prestige and a weak research base. Although the profession grew in size, it did not grow in authority. In the 1980s, efforts failed to establish a doctoral degree in social work as the field's preferred credential (although many social work schools did offer the D.S.W. degree for social work researchers), as did efforts to raise admissions standards and licensing requirements.[72] Salaries remained low, even in private practice, and few practitioners could sustain themselves in full-time private clinical work. The profession's major asset continued to be its low prices for clients and its relative accessibility for mid-career professionals; the two-year degree, frequently completed on a part-time basis, was simply much less demanding than the five- to seven-year full-time course of study required for the Ph.D. in psychology. [73] Although social workers argued that they brought unique perspectives to therapy, in fact they were schooled in similar techniques as were clinical psychologists, albeit with more stress placed on interpersonal theory, and concomitantly less on cognitive and behavioral models.

By 1990, the landscape of mental health had changed substantially. Psychiatry, once immersed in psychoanalysis and psychoanalytic therapy, was now largely a biological and neurochemical profession. Psychologists and social workers had displaced psychiatrists as the mainstay of the therapeutic workforce. Cognitive and behavioral therapies were on the rise, although many therapists continued to reference interpersonal theories as their dominant influence. And while Freud was maligned and dismissed, his influence still had not completely disappeared. Periodic talk of repression, catharsis, transference, and complexes continued, even if such terms disappeared from psychiatric reference manuals and from academic psychiatric research.

CHAPTER 10

Biology

The Age of Biology

The age of biological psychiatry had no clear beginning, but rather emerged gradually from incremental advances from the early 1960s in neurophysiology, psychopharmacology, genetics, and molecular biology. Psychiatric and pharmaceutical researchers continued to modify the old standbys—lithium, MAOIs, tricyclics, and Thorazine derivatives—but in addition they developed new classes of tranquilizers and antidepressants and new techniques in electroshock therapy. Obsessive-compulsive disorder, once seen as nearly untreatable, responded to doses of clomipramine, while panic disorder and agoraphobia fell to more highly refined antianxiety formulations. In a trend that one medical reporter dubbed the "biostampede," some optimistic psychiatrists hoped to find chemical switches for all mental illnesses.[1]

New drugs and processes worked more effectively that the old ones, with fewer side effects. Electroshock therapy had never been wholly discarded, but it had always been used with extreme discretion due to the severe memory loss and periodic spine fractures associated with its applications. In its 1990 iteration, however, the treatment used a different sort of shock wave at a lower voltage to effect antidepressive changes without distorting the memory process. Patients who submitted to a full regimen of ten to fifteen treatments recovered rapidly from severe depression, catatonia, and even some forms of parkinsonism. One patient described his experience, "It is a nonentity, a nothing. You go to sleep, and when you wake up, it is all over. It is easier to take than going to the dentist."[2]

Psychiatrists turned PET and MRI scanners on subjects' brains to elicit new understanding of mental processes through *neuroimaging*. By observing electrical activity and brain-wave emissions from various parts of the brain during different emotional and mental states, scientists identified the loci of happiness, joy, fear, anxiety, and sadness.[3] New biological insights into the basis of memory identified the hippocampus and the prefrontal cortex as two parts of the brain critically important to memory formation, dashing the hopes of the recovered memory specialists, who insisted that memories existed before the age that either of these brain components were fully functional.[4] Continued study of the neurotransmitters dopamine, norepinephrine, acetylcholine, and serotonin brought new understanding of the nuanced and sophisticated ways in which neurons communicated with one another to create memories and evince emotions. Serotonin, in particular, appeared to be critical in modulating emotion and mood, and was implicated in illnesses as varied as depression, impulsivity, obsessiveness, and anorexia. Thomas Wehr of the NIMH noted, "Serotonin sets the tone, the thermostat of how we act. It is very promiscuous, affecting so much of our behavior."[5]

Young psychiatrists entered a profession that by 1990 was far more biological than psychological, and they celebrated their ability to effect change in their patients. Whereas psychotherapy took years to master and worked unpredictably, treating mental illness with medication was straightforward, measurable, and transparently effective. One psychiatric resident described his newly acquired knowledge: "I feel good about those skills. It's something people sort of belittle because it's kind of a cookbook, but when you see a large number of patients and it is abundantly clear that they need their medication, and you give them a medication and they come back two weeks later enormously grateful because their business is back to functioning, it's nice."[6] Although medication violated the implicit puritanism of psychology, its efficacy was undeniable. One long-suffering patient, recently introduced to one of the newer drugs that regulated serotonin levels, explained, "It was as if a light had been turned on inside my head.... I became so much more clear-headed. It's like trying to explain to a person who's colorblind what colors look like. It's not until you see them yourself that you can know what they mean."[7]

Though long in the making, the new biological age flourished with the introduction in 1987 of Prozac, the most commercially successful drug in the history of the pharmaceutical industry.[8] Prozac, a new sort of antidepressant that exclusively regulated serotonin levels in the brain (as opposed to the tricyclics, which had increased levels of both serotonin and norepinephrine), was extremely clean. James Halikas, a professor of psychiatry at the University of Minnesota, noted, "Instead of using a shotgun, you're using a bullet."[9] It induced few side effects, was broadly effective against many depressive disorders, and was easy to prescribe. Unlike tricyclic antidepressants, which needed to be carefully dosed, Prozac was dispensed in twenty-milligram capsules that seemed to suit almost everybody. Jonathan Cole, a psychiatric researcher, described the Prozac phenomenon as "one pill a day for ever."[10]

Under the influence of Prozac, many patients not only felt well for the first time in years; they often felt "better than well," in the words of Peter Kramer, a psychiatrist who popularized the image of the drug in his book *Listening to Prozac*.[11] Kramer described patients who underwent fundamental changes in temperament on the drug, raising questions about the true nature of people's personalities. Kramer wrote, "There had always been the occasional patient who seems remarkably restored by one medicine or another, but with Prozac I had patient after patient become...'better than well.' Prozac seemed to give social confidence to the habitually timid, to make the sensitive brash, to lend the introvert the social skills of a salesman.... [My patients] believed Prozac revealed what in them was biologically determined and what was merely...experiential."[12]

Prozac's actions gave rise to the phenomenon of "cosmetic psychopharmacology." So clean was the drug's action, and so few were its side effects, that psychiatrists began to prescribe it for symptoms that, in the past, would not have merited pharmacological intervention. Patients whose chief complaints included shyness, lack of enthusiasm for work, or moribund social lives sought from Prozac not just relief, but fundamental personality change. Kramer documented how more than one previously shy and unapproachable patient was now approached on the street for directions, as if somehow the drug had "stimulated the patient to display subtle cues of accessibility."[13] Couples who had previously been uncommunicative could now confront each other more directly when one or both were released from their inhibitions by Prozac. The drug cleansed the psychic palate to grant patients confidence and vitality previously denied them. Millions who had trod life's rocky paths now faced roads devoid of major psychic barriers. Prozac was the harbinger of an age.

Prozac's extraordinary efficacy, coupled with its lack of side effects, led hundreds of thousands of internists to prescribe a psychoactive drug for the first time. While previously almost all antidepressants had been prescribed by psychiatrists, who provided psychotherapy while supervising the medication, Prozac's "one pill a day for ever" regimen was simple enough (and safe enough) to induce general practitioners and internists to prescribe it without referring the patient to counseling or to a trained psychiatrist. In the decade following Prozac's introduction, the number of people soliciting mental health treatment from general practitioners doubled. Overuse was foreordained. Internists rarely took the time to carefully question a patient before prescribing, and tales of mistreatment emerged in the unregulated environment. One patient related how her physician had prescribed a year's worth of the drug after barely engaging her in a discussion regarding her mood. She had in fact seen her parents murdered in the Holocaust, and suffered repeated flashbacks of the scene. Joseph Glenmullen, writing in his book *Prozac Backlash*, chastised the medical profession for its whimsical use of the drug. "Are Holocaust memories really a 'disease,' a 'biochemical imbalance' that should be 'corrected' with a pill?" he wrote.[14] Arthur Kleinman, an anthropologist, expressed concern at the trend toward "medicalizing ordinary unhappiness."[15]

Part of the impulse toward biological psychiatry was financial. As greater numbers of nonmedical doctors provided psychotherapy, reimbursement for the service went down. Psychiatrists who decided to curb their psychotherapy efforts in favor of medicating patients preserved their incomes, or periodically saw them rise. At the same time, medicating helped to differentiate their expertise from that of the ubiquitous "clinical therapists," who were not authorized to prescribe. Where psychologists had once competed with psychiatrists for the psychotherapeutic dollar, now social workers, clinical lay therapists, and the new "professional therapists" of uncertain educational background appeared everywhere. Some of these newer providers crassly advertised their wares with glaring boasts of "Success in 10 weeks—or your money back," or "obsessions and addictions...insurance accepted."[16]

Psychiatrists, to some degree, were responding to trends in other medical specialties. Surgeons had long outearned their medical colleagues by charging for "piecework"—that is, by pegging their fees to procedures. Internists and medical specialists began moving toward this billing pattern in the 1970s and 1980s by focusing a greater part of their practices on procedures at the expense of diagnostics and analysis. In order to increase their incomes, physicians who had emerged from the medical (as opposed to surgical) disciplines such as cardiology, pulmonology, nephrology, and neurology began to perform more invasive tests and subsurgical corrective procedures, which could be billed at rates more akin to surgery than to medical diagnostics. Psychiatrists, who had no such procedures at their disposal, felt comparatively squeezed and raised their fees accordingly.

But with so many nonphysicians competing with them for psychotherapy patients, psychiatrists were limited in their ability to raise rates. Therapists with two-year credentials, many of whom practiced part-time, could substantially undercut psychiatric rates, and few insurance companies were willing to reimburse psychotherapists at the rates demanded by psychiatrists. Patients fled to the nonmedical therapists, forcing psychiatrists into psychopharmacology, even if that was not their preferred form of treatment. One aging psychiatrist ruefully described the developing landscape: "All of this is having its inevitable effects, slowly becoming more and more apparent, that those of us who will continue to do psychotherapy because it is the most exciting and challenging thing for us to do within psychiatry and within medicine, will have to gradually accommodate ourselves to a relative decline in remuneration as compared with other physicians."[17]

Psychiatrists who moved toward pharmacological practices could see three or four times as many patients per hour as could therapeutic psychiatrists, and charge nearly as much per patient. Ironically, the arrangement forced psychiatrists to collaborate more closely with psychologists and social workers. Most of the medicated patients required or sought therapy as an adjunct treatment, and psychiatrists were forced to refer them to nonmedical therapists who were now providing the preponderance of all therapy. Most of the outcomes research indicated that patients improved faster and more completely when treated with a combination of drugs and therapy, and therapy was increasingly the exclusive purview of psychologists and social workers. The various professions, long in competition, now increasingly worked in tandem.

Psychiatrists, however, continued to fear for their turf. Psychologists had lobbied for prescription privileges since the early 1980s, and were now gaining these privileges in certain states. Although the privileges

were often limited—precluding them from prescribing opiates, for example, or from prescribing anything independent of physician oversight—the trend seemed ominous. One psychiatrist resigned himself to
a declining professional role. "Let us face reality," he wrote to his colleagues. "Just as sure as God made little green apples, pears and peaches,
eventually this bill or one that will be quite similar will be passed. The
'special tool' that has been the unique property of psychiatrists will
eventually be shared with the 'aliens.' "[18] He concluded, however, that
"obstructionism" was "not the way."[19] Rather, psychiatry must continue
to lead the mental health professions through more firmly grounding
itself in biomedical sciences and clinical investigation, instead of by regulating its adversaries out of existence.

Clinical psychology, in turn, faced pressure. The profession had now
firmly abandoned its roots in laboratory science, as the Ph.D. degree in
psychology had largely given way to the doctor of psychology (Psy.D.)
and doctor of education (Ed.D.) degrees—both granted for three to
four years of clinical training with little or no expectation of original
research. Although outcomes studies had shown that a therapist's research background did not necessarily indicate clinical efficacy, in dispensing with research training the profession had lost its claim to
professional superiority over social work. A psychologist technically was
a scholar of the human mind. How, then, could a professional who had
never undertaken scholarly work claim that mantle with any more legitimacy than could a clinical social worker or a lay psychotherapist?
At the same time, as social workers and lay therapists earned their
own doctorates—in social work (the D.S.W.) or in psychotherapy (the
Ed.D.)—the title of "doctor" declined in prestige. Lee Sechrest, chairman of the department of psychology at the University of Arizona, responded to a question concerning the "thousands more psychologists"
who were produced every year by stating, "One of the fundamental
problems is that I don't think we are graduating thousands of psycholo-

gists. We are graduating thousands and thousands of practitioners who are peripherally acquainted with the discipline of psychology."[20]

Even psychology's roots in testing and evaluation were in question. The Rorschach test, for example, was still being used by psychologists decades after its legitimacy had been disproved. Multiple studies had demonstrated weak correlations between psychologists' interpretations of the test results and the long-term mental situations of the subjects. Individuals deemed by the test to be neurotic, unrealistic, resistant, delusional, obsessive, or even psychotic often functioned perfectly reasonably in reality. Through testing, psychologists interpreted their subjects' willingness or unwillingness to see the obvious; to rotate the image too early or too late; to react or fail to react to the presence of color in the inkblots; to see or fail to see sexual or violent imagery. All too frequently, their interpretations simply confirmed preexisting diagnoses, suggesting that psychological testers were heavily laden with their own biases. Robyn Dawes, an esteemed research psychologist, wrote, "The Rorschach is indeed 'projective'—for the interpreter." That is, the interpretation might indicate more about the mental state of the psychologist than the patient.[21]

Managed Care

In the late 1980s, health insurance in the United States moved away from traditional indemnity compensation in which insurance companies reimbursed beneficiaries for incurred expenses with few restrictions. Significant inflation in the health-care sector through the 1970s had caused corporations and other large purchasers of health insurance to carefully scrutinize their policies for excess and waste. Their response in many cases was managed care—a catchall term for new health insurance products that forced patients to obtain treatment from preselected physicians, and then only after obtaining permission from the insurance company for many ailments.

Managed care took many forms. Initially health maintenance organizations (HMOs) dominated the landscape, but by the middle of the 1990s HMOs had splintered into a variety of forms such as preferred provider organizations (PPOs), physician hospital organizations (PHOs), independent practice associations (IPAs), and point-of-service plans (POSs). All used the same assortment of tools—controlled access to specialists, limited rosters of physicians, and prenegotiated reimbursement rates with doctors and hospitals—to hold down costs, although different plans enforced these restrictions more or less aggressively. The most stringently "managed" organizations refused to pay for any care outside of tightly controlled lists of member physicians, and paid doctors a set fee each month to provide complete medical treatment for a patient, regardless of the patient's medical needs. The more loosely structured plans, such as the PPOs, allowed members to use any physicians, but required them to pay a steep copayment fee for using "non-preferred" providers.

Managed care was largely built around controlling health-care costs, which had risen at double the rate of inflation nearly every year since 1965. It accomplished this principally by preventing patients from seeing specialists (who charged at much higher rates than did primary care physicians); by prenegotiating reimbursement rates with hospitals; by barring patients from using expensive drugs when less expensive substitutes existed; and by selectively steering patients to physicians who had established records of parsimonious treatment. Often, patients were required to obtain permission from the managed care company before seeing a specialist, or before seeking elective consultations and procedures. "Utilization review" specialists, often nurses, garnered unusual degrees of authority within the health-care system, as they often had the power to deny payment for treatment that a patient or his primary care physician might deem desirable. They became the supreme gatekeepers in the system.

Mental health care fit poorly into the constellation of managed services. Ambiguous diagnoses and treatment regimens, combined with uncertain outcomes, left mental health care at the mercy of the gatekeepers. Most managed care organizations subcontracted with specialty managed mental health care organizations to oversee their mental health components. These specialty administrators often limited members to twenty psychotherapy sessions per year, with a limited roster of inexpensive providers. Whereas many Americans in the 1960s and 1970s had been reimbursed for an unlimited number of therapeutic sessions per annum, patients who now wished to undergo intensive and long-term therapy were forced to pay from personal funds.[22] Even patients undergoing short-term therapy needed to gain permission from the utilization review professionals for initial consultations, for the first five to ten sessions, and then for additional sessions beyond the tenth. "It's turned health care into a giant game of 'Mother, may I,'" said Stephen Hersh, a psychiatrist in Washington, D.C.[23] A psychologist in Minneapolis, Gregory Korgeski, noted that, "a better term might be 'managed abandonment.'"[24]

Managed care grossly distorted the practice of psychotherapy. Therapists, eager to extend the number of allowable sessions, inflated diagnoses or otherwise misrepresented the severity of patients' conditions. They tended to push patients to try medication first and limited psychotherapy second. Patients who were uncomfortable with a particular therapist were discouraged from switching unless they could document their lack of progress. The burden of proof for securing continued treatment past the initial ten sessions fell to the patient and his therapist, placing both in the odd position of having to prove the patient's continued illness. Paul Ling, a psychologist in Quincy, Massachusetts, described the distasteful nature of the relationship between healer and payer, in which the utilization review personnel became highly intrusive in the therapeutic relationship. Questions such as "How *many* times was your patient raped as a child? Was it really *that* bad? Couldn't your patient go to

AA instead of seeing you?" were indicative of the adversarial quality of the relationship.[25]

Managed care effectively ended the viability of psychoanalysis as a treatment option for almost all Americans. But worse, it also tended to push Americans into a more medicated model of mental health care, even though outcomes data indicated that psychotherapy was useful, particularly in conjunction with medication.[26] Some patients responded by paying their therapists from their own funds, forcing them to negotiate more carefully over hourly rates and treatment durations. Therapists, in turn, learned to market their services partially on price, meaning that those who had charged less in the past were now increasingly attractive to prospective clients. Generally, the trends further pushed psychiatrists away from providing psychotherapy, and created opportunities for social workers and lay therapists to enter the therapeutic professions. Psychotherapy was simply no longer a viable professional option for most psychiatrists, who could earn far more as diagnosticians and prescribers than they could as counselors and discussants.

Success

Medicine worked. The new selective serotonin reuptake inhibitors (SSRIs) Prozac, Zoloft, and Paxil were tremendously effective in alleviating severe depression. In addition, they were highly effective in treating obsessive-compulsive disorder (OCD)—a disease occurring in approximately 1 percent of the population which had been resistant to psychotherapy and traditional antianxiety formulations. Effective treatment of OCD required higher doses of the SSRIs (eighty milligrams of Prozac per day, rather than the usual twenty milligrams used in depression), but at the correct dosage the drug alleviated symptoms in 80 percent of sufferers. A certain percentage of patients continued to be treated with tricyclics and MOAIs, either because their depression responded better to those formulations, or because they were better able to tolerate the side effects. Although the SSRIs generally produced few side effects, they did tend to diminish sexual response and in some patients caused restlessness and insomnia.

Other psychiatric disorders responded well to medication, too. Most forms of anxiety could be treated with diazepam (Valium) and alprazolam (Xanax); panic disorder could be controlled quite well with Xanax; bipolar disorder was treated with lithium; and the hallucinatory disorders continued to respond well to Thorazine and newer generations of antipsychotic drugs. The age of the magic pills had dawned, in which the biochemical roots of many psychiatric disorders could be targeted with highly specific molecules. Moreover, the treatments tended to work for long periods of time. With the exception of Valium and Xanax, none of the drugs seemed to produce tolerance or addiction. People stayed on Prozac, lithium, and Thorazine for years without a return of symptoms, although a certain percentage of patients found it beneficial to switch to substitute drugs over time.

Still, the majority of patients who sought mental health care continued to be treated with psychotherapy alone, even though multiple studies showed that most people improved faster and more thoroughly when they were treated with both medication and therapy. Therapists came to realize that once relieved of their neurochemical challenges, many patients still needed to learn how to live life anew. While a serotonin deficiency may have initially caused a person to be shy, phobic, and introverted, fixing the serotonin level did not automatically cause years of habituated introversion to fall away. The therapist needed to teach the patient how to live life in the absence of physiological barriers. In this sense, medication and therapy worked in conjunction to treat mental illness much the same way that prosthesis and rehabilitation aided an amputee. The amputee could not walk without the appropriate artificial limb, but generally he required extensive lessons in walking once he received the correct limb.

One of the broadest studies on the efficacy of both therapy and medication was conducted not in a laboratory setting, but by the magazine *Consumer Reports*, which in 1995 surveyed 4,000 readers who had sought help for mental illness. While the readers were not a good representation of the general American population—they tended to be wealthier and more highly educated than most of their compatriots—they did represent the full spectrum of emotional functioning. The results were highly encouraging. The majority were "highly satisfied" with their care, be it from a psychiatrist, a psychologist, a social worker, or a self-help group.[27] Patients found that therapists of all orientations were helpful, with special praise reserved for Alcoholics Anonymous. They found that both medication and therapy helped, although a surprisingly large number reported that therapy alone was as helpful as therapy with medication. Overall, nearly 70 percent felt that their emotional health had improved significantly with treatment, confirming the "two-thirds" hypothesis first formulated in the 1950s.

A few notable failures emerged. Patients who had sought help from non–mental health counselors—notably nonpsychiatrist physicians—did not fare as well. They were treated almost exclusively with drugs and tended not to be referred to mental health specialists later on, even when symptoms were not well controlled. The authors of the report noted that "if you begin treatment with your family doctor, that's where you're likely to stay," and encouraged readers to avail themselves of specialists who were more likely to combine therapy with medication.[28]

Most improvement took place early on in the therapeutic cycle, although there was some evidence that patients who stayed in therapy longer (beyond twenty-five sessions) did benefit somewhat from the extended treatment. While 50 percent improved within eleven weeks (at one session per week), another 25 percent improved after a year, suggesting that pressure from managed care companies to move patients quickly through therapy was probably undermining treatment. Patients improved with virtually all types of mental health providers, with the sole exception of self-described "marriage counselors." This largely un-regulated profession maintained few quality standards, and indeed in most states required no license. Pastoral counselors, by contrast, were deemed to be effective, as were social workers and psychologists. Philosophical orientation generally was irrelevant.

A few patients found cognitive-behavioral therapy to be particularly helpful. Patients suffering from OCD or specific phobias improved more rapidly under a CBT orientation than under an eclectic or psychodynamic one, and both types of patients benefited from the new SSRI drugs. Overall, though, the study confirmed earlier studies from the 1980s that found the characteristics and skills of the particular provider to be more important than his or her theoretical training or orientation. Essentially, everything worked, though nothing worked perfectly. Lester Luborsky of the University of Pennsylvania noted that the results confirmed the philosophy of the dodo bird in *Alice in Wonderland*: "Everyone has won and all must have prizes."[29]

Some career practitioners were unsettled by the successes wrought by the SSRIs. Therapists who had achieved impressive results over many years using therapy alone were startled when their most difficult-to-treat patients responded well to the drugs. One therapist described a patient suffering from OCD who, after two years in therapy, had hardly improved. After several weeks on Prozac, however, he improved so rapidly and completely that he declined to continue in therapy. The therapist wrote, "This patient's impressive response to medication and other patients' subsequent pharmacotherapeutic success temporarily caused me to question the efficacy of psychotherapy. Indeed, for the first few months after [the patient's] improvement, I questioned my role as a psychotherapist."[30] The therapist later realized that even as his patients improved on medication, those who remained in therapy tended to improve even more so, and stayed healthier for longer.

Psychotherapy has reached a certain stasis since the advent of the second generation of SSRI drugs in the late 1990s. While newer drugs continue to emerge from the research laboratories of the major pharmaceutical companies, none has achieved the breakthrough status of Prozac, Thorazine, or lithium. Newer drugs that selectively target active sites in the brain leave fewer residual side effects, but none has elicited the sort of profound leap in understanding mental illnesses as have previous drugs upon introduction. At the same time, psychotherapy has remained highly stable. Most therapists are now eclectic, although most lean toward one of the same three schools that have existed for over a half century: psychodynamic, interpersonal, and cognitive-behavioral. Psychiatrists have largely withdrawn from practicing therapy, while psychologists, social workers, and pastoral counselors continue to work in a large variety of settings. Alcoholics Anonymous has spawned multiple "anonymous" relations, including those for narcotics users, abused spouses, overeaters, and even workaholics. It continues to be the most successful venue in the world for treating alcoholism, and now has branches in virtually every country where alcohol is sold.

Freud's influence has waned but it has hardly disappeared. Millions of students of psychology, sociology, human relations, and intellectual history continue to study his opus and ponder his insights. Few serious mental health professionals turn to his works for clinical guidance, but many continue to cleave to his basic understandings of repression, the unconscious, ego development, and sexual instincts. He remains one of the most influential individuals in history, sharing his perch with Marx, Darwin, Jesus, Mohammed, and Einstein, and his place in the history of our efforts to understand ourselves and one another seems assured.

Afterword

Psychotherapy works. For all of the doubts expressed by skeptics over the decades, none can credibly discount the evidence emerging from numerous studies that patients emerge from therapy feeling better. A consistent two-thirds of patients improve after six months of therapy, consulting with therapists from every educational background and using every type of therapeutic approach.[1] And while many patients suffering psychic discomfort do improve on their own without therapy, they progress far more slowly and with higher rates of relapse. It is the difference between walking and driving; you *can* walk from coast to coast across the United States, but at a far slower pace, and with a far lower chance of succeeding, than if you drive.

The success of psychotherapy alone must be qualified, however. It works best with people who are not severely ill. Patients suffering from schizophrenia, bipolar disorder, and obsessive-compulsive disorder improve little with psychotherapy, although some do improve with psychotherapy used in conjunction with medication. In 1970, one dispassionate psychiatry researcher concluded that the most "reasonable" description of psychotherapy was that it was "moderately successful" in treating patients falling within a "relatively narrow range of the full spectrum of disorders."[2] And while both therapeutic technique and pharmacological interventions have improved over the past thirty years, the same can generally be said today.

Finding the right match between therapist and patient is critical to a successful therapeutic relationship, and it is part diagnostic accuracy, part chemistry, and part luck. Success has little to do with the type of training the therapist has undergone or his or her disciplinary orientation. Neither psychiatry nor psychology nor social work appears to have garnered technical superiority in dispensing therapy, and the precise terminal degree held appears to be nearly irrelevant. Moreover, the self-described philosophical approach of the therapist—psychodynamic, cognitive-behavioral, client-centered, or rational-emotive—seems to bear little on his or her ultimate success.[3]

What is important is empathy. The great preponderance of patients report the need to feel comfortable and understood by their therapist; empathy is the precursor to the trust upon which a productive therapeutic relationship is built. Far more important than a therapist's analytical brilliance and insight is his or her ability to connect with the patient, to understand the patient's concerns, and to put the patient at ease.[4] The therapist who sits stone-faced and aloof may grant the patient insight into his or her psyche and soul, but is unlikely to inspire confidence. Anthony Storr, a British psychiatrist, once commented that therapy should be "emotionally demanding," not just of the patients, but of the therapist. A therapist should be "somewhat drained" at the end of the day, or he probably accomplished little therapeutically.[5]

The exact mechanism by which therapy works has never precisely been established. Some therapies allow for greater insight into trauma and fears, some help to reorganize patients' thoughts, some help redirect their behaviors. Almost all, it seems, rely to some degree on actually *teaching* the patient a new set of skills or more productive thinking patterns, and thus more than anything the therapeutic relationship resembles that of tutor and pupil. We should not really be so surprised at the results of the famous Vanderbilt experiment in which distraught under-graduates improved after receiving therapy from untrained empathetic humanities professors—the professors were simply adapting their natural teaching mien to a slightly different pedagogical problem. This also explains the need for therapy to end, for the successful relationship is less one of peer support than pedantry; at some point the pupil has mastered the lesson. Countering the Freudian emphasis on prolonged treatment, which had become the standard in the 1960s, Bennet Olshaker, a psychiatrist in Washington, D.C., noted in the 1970s, "A good psychiatrist should be like a good parent; that is, he should eventually become dispensable."[6]

And Freud? Have his vaunted contributions really come to so little? Yes and no. On one hand, most of his detailed models of the structure of the psyche have seen dismissed; few serious students of psychology or the mental health sciences continue to refer to *ids* and *superegos*. Neurological and psychological research over the past three decades has effectively disproved many of his theories regarding repressed memories, infantile sexuality, and the general psychosocial developmental sequence that he posed as normal. Freud's complexes, phobias, yearnings, and instincts have largely been superceded. His sexual constructs are laughably archaic; his reductive and ideological views of society and social tensions are inconsistent with more modern and practical understandings of realpolitik and economic growth. More than ever, we understand Freud to be a product of his time; highly significant within the spectrum of intellectual history, but with little relevance to our best understandings of the human mind.

Yet Freud's presence continues. His notion of an unconscious, his reliance on talk, and his speculation about the biological underpinnings of some mental illness have all proved true. Moreover, his fundamental insight into the complexity of the human mind has been validated many times over, and his inclination to believe that the best path to gaining insight into that complexity is through a healer listening to a patient forms the basis of virtually all successful psychotherapy. Thomas Gutheil of Harvard Medical School pithily summed up Freud's beliefs: First, "there's a whole lot more to folks than meets the eye," and second, "keep your mouth shut and you might learn something."[7] That is, to help somebody in psychic distress, Freud taught us that there is no shortcut. People are complicated, and the therapist must take the time to tease out the complexities before he can help. We might all benefit from such insight in our everyday lives.

As for the organic nature of mental illness, we know much more than we did in Freud's time, yet we still have much to learn. Most mental disorders do have a chemical or physiological basis, and every day we get closer to understanding the precise neurochemical shortfalls or neuroelectrical abnormalities that cause particular psychic tics. The new medicines produced over the past half century have changed the shape of mental health care and promise to do more in the future. In this age of made-to-order psychopharmacology, however, psychotherapy still has an important role to play, for virtually all of the medications work best in conjunction with therapy. Patients cannot optimize their newly recalibrated brain chemistry without the personal tutorial in living life as a psychically healthy person that therapy provides.

At the same time, psychotherapy has proven to be only modestly successful in treating patients suffering from their own bouts of mismedication, with either alcohol or narcotics. These patients do need therapy, but of a particular sort uniquely suited to their own brands of illness. They, too, need to relearn how to live life, but seem able to do so only under the constant and overwhelming pressure of a highly judgmental and sanctimonious peer group—the empathetic individual therapist has little to offer. The good news is that the group therapy provided by AA and Narcotics Anonymous does help; the bad news is that a high percentage of these patients will never muster the strength to commit to such prolonged and painful life change. Psychotherapy, whether dispensed individually or in groups, can work only when the patient—the pupil—desires to learn. For the intransigent, hostile, and aloof patient, it has little to offer.

George Vaillant, perhaps the preeminent alcohol researcher of the past generation, ultimately understood the success of Alcoholics Anonymous to be based on a four-tiered foundation. Alcoholics needed (1) external supervision, (2) competing behaviors, (3) new love relationships, and (4) spiritual inspiration.[8] That is, the typical therapeutic relationship could not work for an alcoholic because it lacked the force of peer pressure, the ability to substitute one set of behaviors for another, the enticement of new friendships and new love relationships, and the promise of movement toward a higher good. While the absence of any one of these components greatly decreased the chance of success, Alcoholics Anonymous generally provided them all.

Psychotherapy works best when it leverages a patient's desire to participate more productively in the world around him, when the patient is genuinely committed to the difficult process of acquiring new, healthy psychic skills. To paraphrase Viktor Frankl, the Viennese-born psychiatrist who studied concentration camp survivors, the common trait in all emotionally healthy people is a desire to "get to work."[9] Those who choose to withdraw from the work of the world around them and to disengage from the tasks of life can neither heal nor experience true happiness. Even in the concentration camps, Frankl discovered, inmates who were somehow able to make themselves useful to their fellow inmates stood a higher chance of surviving, and a higher chance of achieving emotional recovery after liberation. By contrast, one of the most toxic effects of narcotics and alcohol abuse is the grotesque passivity it enforces upon addicts. Alcoholics and drug abusers destroy themselves by refusing to contribute to or to engage in life. They are the living dead.

And of the anti-psychiatrists? Besotted with their own rectitude, and above all mistrustful of organized authority, they prefer to protect patients' inalienable rights to be left untreated, rather than to induce them to "get to work." Their bizarre preference for fostering illness and compromised lives over a "minor league civil liberties goof" (in the words of popular novelist and psychologist Jonathan Kellerman) places them, if not exactly on the dark side, at least among the Neville Chamberlains of the psychological world.[10] These proponents of "peace in our time" are willing to surrender hope, standards, and the civic enterprise for the lure of psychic autonomy. They are not evil, but they may be unintentional catalysts of evil.

Psychotherapy has become mainstream. No longer the province of effete East Coast intellectuals passionately focused on their own self-knowledge, the practice has become less dogmatic and intimidating, more pragmatic and accessible. To a large degree William Menninger's vision has been achieved, with tens of thousands of licensed psychotherapists of all denominations ministering to a broad swath of Americans willing to shoulder the expense and effort to alleviate their own unhappiness. Psychoactive medications, far from drawing people from therapy, have actually pushed more people toward it as their success has fostered the understanding that mental illnesses are just that—illnesses. The acknowledged physical basis of social and emotional problems has removed some of the stigma from the enterprise, making it much more difficult to burden a depressive or phobic with the epithet "neurotic." A disease that responds to a drug must certainly be a *real* disease, and thus merits the attention of ordinary folks using whatever means may be at their disposal. Prozac has indeed been as much a diagnostic tool as a treatment, and Americans, as a result, have become more accurately diagnosed because of it.

Last, psychotherapy has been integrated into the uniquely American ethos of pragmatism. Our can-do nation, often skeptical of intellectualism and scholasticism, was unlikely to embrace an ideology born of fin-de-siècle European angst. The Jewish science of psychoanalysis, so foreign and distasteful to most Americans of the last century, has morphed into the eclectic therapy of twenty-first-century social workers, psychologists, and licensed therapists. Their goals are practical: greater emotional well-being, better social adjustment, happier marriages, and more productive lives. Few American would argue with these goals.

Acknowledgments

Thank you to my research assistants Samantha Ehrlich and Angela Mastria for help in tracking down articles and for wading through microfilm footage; to Robert Guinsler of Sterling Lord Literistic for his eternal optimism, warmth, and tenacity; and to Jessica Sindler at Gotham, who improved the manuscript in countless ways. Rick Willett copyedited the manuscript with a deft torch. Barbara Ward, the inter-library loan guru of Seton Hall's Walsh Library, is my unsung hero; without her this book would not exist. As always, thank you to Rozlyn for indulging my writing life.

Millburn, New Jersey
May 2008

Notes

Abbreviations used in Notes and Bibliography

AAP   American Academy of Psychoanalysis papers (Cornell Medical School, New York)

AAPSW   American Association of Psychiatric Social Work papers (University of Minnesota)

AGP   *Archives of General Psychiatry*

AJP   *American Journal of Psychiatry*

AJPH   *American Journal of Public Health*

AOA   American Orthopsychiatric Association papers (University of Minnesota)

AP   *American Psychologist*

APaA   American Psychoanalytic Association papers (Cornell Medical School, New York)

DHEW   Department of Health, Education, and Welfare

DHHS   Department of Health and Human Services

GAP   Group for the Advancement of Psychiatry papers (Cornell Medical School, New York)

JAMA   *Journal of the American Medical Association*

NASW   National Association of Social Workers papers (University of Minnesota)

NEJM   *New England Journal of Medicine*

PHS   Public Health Service

RC   Ralph Crowley papers (Cornell Medical School, New York)

PREFACE

1. Blaine Harden, "The Analyst," *Washington Post Magazine*, 11/22/81, p. 30.

2. Greer Williams, "He Made Psychiatry Respectable," *Saturday Evening Post*, 10/18/47, p. 32.

3. Paul Wender and Donald Klein, "The Promise of Biological Psychiatry," *Psychology Today*, February 1981, p. 28.

4. Peter Kramer, *Listening to Prozac* (New York: Viking, 1993), p. x.

5. Kenneth Appel, "Science, Psychiatry, Survival," *Science*, 11/26/48, p. 603.

6. Hans Strupp, "Psychotherapy Research and Practice: An Overview," in Sol Garfield and Allen Bergin, eds., *Handbook of Psychotherapy and Behavior Change: An Empirical Analysis* (New York: Wiley, 1978), p. 19.

CHAPTER I • FREUD

1. From the introduction to the 1926 edition of Freud's *Outline of Abnormal Psychology*, as quoted in David Shakow, "The Contributions of the Worcester State Hospital and Post-Hall Clark University to Psychoanalysis," in George Gifford, ed., *Psychoanalysis, Psychotherapy, and the New England Medical Scene, 1894–1944* (New York: Science History Publications, 1978), p. 31.

2. Myerson to Meyer, 11/30/37, as quoted in Gerald Grob, *The Inner World of American Psychiatry, 1890–1940, Selected Correspondence* (New Brunswick, Rutgers University Press, 1985), p. 133.

3. Karl Stern, "Religion and Psychiatry," *Commonweal*, 10/22/48, p. 30.

4. From Mesmer, *Reflections on the Discovery of Animal Magnetism* (1779), as quoted in Ralph Fuller, *Mesmerism and the American Cure of Souls* (Philadelphia: University of Pennsylvania Press, 1982), p. 5.

5. See Fuller for details of the nineteenth-century cult of Mesmer, particularly chapter 2.

6. Freud, *An Autobiographical Study, The Standard Edition of the Complete Works of Sigmund Freud,* James Strachey, ed. (London: Hogarth Press), volume XX, p. 16.

7. Ibid., p. 17.

8. Ibid., p. 20.

9. Notably, sexual ideas were much in the public ferment at the time of Freud's most productive work. Repressive Victorian mores had produced a sort of intellectual backlash, in which prominent psychologists such as Richard von Krafft-Ebing and Havelock Ellis wrote frequently of sex and sexual dysfunction. Indeed, Krafft-Ebing's monumental *Psychopathia Sexualis* reads as a sort of contemporary Kama Sutra of perversions and malfunctions. At least some historians, amused at the explicitness of the text, conjecture that it served as a sort of pornography of the time. See Gregory Zilboorg and George Henry, *A History of Medical Psychology* (New York: Norton, 1941), particularly chapter 11.

10. Later, Freud recognized that few analysts could become exposed to such intense transference feelings without themselves experiencing a counter-reaction, termed *countertransference.* This was not necessarily a problem, so long as the analyst recognized it and took care to contain it. Problems began when the analyst was no longer able to suppress the countertransference feelings and began to act on them, entering the patient's life as an intimate or lover.

11. Although Freud made sporadic efforts to treat schizophrenics through psychoanalysis, by the end of his life he admitted that the effort was futile, concluding that mental patients were "without the capacity for forming a positive transference." *Autobiographical Study*, p. 60.

12. Freud, *An Outline of Psycho-analysis* (1938), S.E., volume XXIII, p. 182.

13. See Adler, "Psychical Hermaphroditism in Life and in Neurosis," *Yearbook of Psycho-analysis and Psychopathology*, volume 2, 1910, p. 738.

14. Freud, *On the History of the Psycho-Analytic Movement*, S.E., volume XIV, p. 57.

15. Ibid., p. 60.

16. Ibid., pp. 57–58.

17. See Karl Popper, *The Logic of Scientific Discovery* (New York: Routledge, 1992) and Ian Hacking, *Representing and Intervening* (Cambridge: Cambridge University Press, 1982) for more on the definition of science. For a pithy introduction to

the sociology of science, see Thomas Kuhn, *The Structure of Scientific Revolutions* (Chicago: University of Chicago Press, 1962).

18. Freud, *An Autobiographical Study*, p. 52.

19. I believe J. K. Hall coined this phrase, though Henri Ellenberger publicized it by using it in the title of his comprehensive history of psychodynamic therapies. See J. K. Hall to Abraham Myerson, 6/1/38, in Grob, *The Inner World of American Psychiatry*, p. 135.

20. Zilboorg and Henry, *A History of Medical Psychology*, p. 503.

21. See David Shakow, "The Contributions of the Worcester State Hospital and Post-Hall Clark University to Psychoanalysis," in George Gifford, ed., *Psychoanalysis, Psychotherapy, and the New England Medical Scene, 1894–1944*.

22. Freud, *The Question of Lay Analysis* (1926), S.E., volume XX, p. 250.

23. Breuer and Freud, *Studies in Hysteria* (1895), S.E., volume II, p. 305.

24. See Karl Popper, *The Logic of Scientific Discovery* (1934), English edition (New York: Harper, 1965).

25. Myerson to Meyer, 11/30/37, in Grob, *The Inner World of American Psychiatry*, p. 133.

Chapter 2 • Orthodoxy and Pragmatism

1. See Hanna Segal, *Melanie Klein* (New York: Viking, 1980), particularly pp. 19–27, for a more detailed biography.

2. Melanie Klein, *The Psychoanalysis of Children* (1932) (New York: Delacorte, 1975), pp. 3–5.

3. Ibid., p. 7.

4. Ibid., p. 8.

5. Ibid., pp. 4–5.

6. Ibid., pp. 19–20.

7. Ibid., p. 21.

8. Ibid., pp. 38, 48.

9. Ibid., p. 51.

10. Segal, *Melanie Klein,* p. 26.

11. Urination and defecation, and bed-wetting in particular, seemed to fascinate many early Freudians. Two analysts based in New Haven, O. H. Mowrer and Willie Mae Mowrer, composed a lengthy dissertation on the implications of enuresis (bed-wetting), in which they claimed that it is "richly charged with pleasure-giving potentialities" and that it has the potential to become "highly libidinized." Mowrer and Mowrer, "Enuresis—A Method for Its Study and Treatment," *American Journal of Orthopsychiatry* (1938): 439.

12. Klein, *The Psychoanalysis of Children,* p. 3.

13. Franz Alexander and Sheldon Selesnick, *The History of Psychiatry* (New York: Harper and Row, 1966), p. 381.

14. As quoted in Elizabeth Young-Bruehl, *Anna Freud* (New York: Summit, 1988), p. 259.

15. See Laura Fermi, *Illustrious Immigrants: The Intellectual Migration from Europe, 1930–41* (Chicago: University of Chicago Press), especially chapter 4. Abraham Flexner, founding director of the Institute of Advanced Study, said of the émigré scholars, "We have tried to scatter them far and wide through Canada and the United States, so that they might infuse new life into struggling institutions and yet not block the path of young Americans bent on scholarly careers"; p. 73.

16. See Helen Swick Perry, *Psychiatrist of America: The Life of Harry Stack Sullivan* (Cambridge: Harvard University Press, 1982), particularly chapter 27, for a discussion on Meyer's views on the appropriate place of Freudian theory within psychiatry.

17. See Arthur David Robbins, "Harry Stack Sullivan: The Man or His Work?" c. 1980, unpublished paper in RC papers, box 2, folder 11, for more details on this period in Sullivan's life.

18. Leslie Farber, "Harry Stack Sullivan and the American Dream," *Times Literary Supplement,* 4/1/77, as quoted in ibid., p. 2.

19. See Alfred Stanton, "Sullivan's Conceptions," in Patrick Mullahy, ed., *The Contributions of Harry Stack Sullivan* (New York: Science House, 1967).

20. As quoted in Perry, *Psychiatrist of America,* p. 194.

21. Ibid., p. 194.

22. Ibid., p. 195.

23. As quoted in ibid., p. 230.

24. From unpublished lectures delivered at Chestnut Lodge, as quoted in Mary Julian White, "Sullivan and Treatment," in Patrick Mullahy, ed., *The Contributions of Harry Stack Sullivan,* p. 119.

25. Sullivan, *Personal Psychopathology* (New York: 1933), as quoted in Robbins, "Harry Stack Sullivan: The Man or His Work?" p. 30.

26. Sullivan, *The Interpersonal Theory of Psychiatry* (New York: Norton, 1953), p. 20.

27. Lawrence Kubie to Ralph Crowley, 3/1/71, RC papers, box 1, folder 7.

28. Ibid.

29. I'm grateful to Agnes N. O'Connell for her elegant synopsis of Horney's life and work in O'Connell and Nancy Russo, eds., *Women in Psychology: A Bio-Bibliographic Sourcebook* (Westport: Greenwood Press, 1990).

30. See Karen Horney, *Neurosis and Human Growth* (New York: Norton, 1950).

31. See Karen Horney, *Self-Analysis* (New York: Norton, 1942).

32. Literature on the early child guidance movement is somewhat thin. For a helpful overview, see James Whittaker, "Mental Hygiene Influences in Children's Institutions: Organization and Technology for Treatment," *Mental Hygiene* 55:4 (October 1971): 444–50.

33. See Steven J. Gould, *The Mismeasure of Man* (New York: Norton, 1981), for an extended account of the malicious side of psychometrics. See also David Horn, *The Criminal Body: Lombroso and the Anatomy of Deviance* (New York: Routledge, 2003).

34. See Jan Goldstein, *Console and Classify: The French Psychiatric Profession in the Nineteenth Century* (Chicago: University of Chicago Press, 2002), for an excellent discussion of the measuring impulse in nineteenth-century psychiatry. The gist was that accurate diagnosis (and prognosis) was a necessary precursor to treatment.

35. The two anecdotes are drawn from John Reisman, *The Development of Clinical Psychology* (New York: Appleton-Century-Crofts, 1966), p. 42.

36. The New York school later became the Columbia School of Social Work. For more on the genesis of psychiatric social work, see Helen Myrick, *Psychiatric Social Work: Its Nurture and Nature* (New York: National Committee for Mental Hygiene, 1929). Myrick, the president of the American Association of

Psychiatric Social Workers, took pains to note that psychiatric social work grew out of a "mental-hygiene approach," rather than a psychiatric one—p. 9.

37. George Stevenson and Geddes Smith, *Child Guidance Clinics: A Quarter Century of Development* (New York: Commonwealth Fund, 1934), pp. 57–58.

38. By 1927 there were 102 such clinics in the country, many funded by grants from the Harkness-endowed Commonwealth Fund. All used the team approach, and many drew on the newly minted psychiatric social workers whose training had been funded in large part from Commonwealth as well. See Lawson Lowrey and Geddes Smith, *The Institute for Child Guidance, 1927–1933* (New York: Commonwealth Fund, 1933).

39. Stevenson and Smith, *Child Guidance Clinics*, p. 55.

40. Ibid., p. 58.

41. All from ibid., pp. 96–97.

42. Ibid., p. 5.

43. William Burnham, *The Normal Mind* (New York: Appleton and Company, 1931), p. 1.

44. Moreno's two major works were *Who Shall Survive?* (New York: Beacon, 1953) and *The Sociometry Reader* (New York: Free Press, 1960).

45. Paul Hare, "Moreno's Sociometric Study at the Hudson School for Girls," *Journal of Group Psychotherapy, Psychodrama, and Sociometry* 45:1 (spring 1992).

46. Frederick Allen, "Therapeutic Work with Children," *American Journal of Orthopsychiatry* 4:2 (April 1934): 194.

47. Ibid., p. 200.

CHAPTER 3 • A CRYING NEED

1. "Mama's Boys," *Time,* 11/25/46, p. 80.

2. "Nervous in the Service," *Newsweek,* 11/25/46, p. 65.

3. William Menninger, "Psychiatric Experience in the War, 1941–1946," *American Journal of Psychiatry* (March 1947): 577.

4. Ibid., p. 578.

5. "Nervous in the Service," p. 66.

6. "Nerves in Combat," *Newsweek,* 9/9/46, p. 66.

7. Ibid.

8. Frank Trager, "Some Don't Wear the Purple Heart," *Nation,* 10/6/45, p. 335.

9. "Six Months Was Plenty," *Newsweek,* 10/8/45, p. 110.

10. See David Rothman, *The Discovery of the Asylum* (Boston: Little, Brown, 1971), for a good introduction to eighteenth- and early nineteenth-century insane asylums. For postwar mental health policy and statistics, as well as a detailed discussion of the effects of World War II medical experiences on postwar mental health policy, see Gerald Grob, *From Asylum to Community* (Princeton: Princeton University Press, 1991).

11. Greer Williams, "How Far Can We Safely Invade the Mind?" *Saturday Evening Post,* 5/25/46, p. 39.

12. As quoted in "Neuroses Out of Town," *Time,* 3/31/47, p. 27.

13. Lee Steiner, *Where Do People Take Their Troubles?* (Boston: Houghton Mifflin, 1945), as quoted in H. Meltzer, "The Place of Private Practice in Professional Psychology," in Bernard Lubin and Eugene Levitt, eds., *The Clinical Psychologist* (Chicago: Aldine, 1961), p. 216.

14. "Are You Always Worrying?" *Time,* 10/25/48, p. 68.

15. Ibid., p. 69.

16. Franz Alexander and Thomas French, *Psychoanalytic Therapy* (New York: Ronald Press, 1946), p. 11.

17. "Are You Always Worrying?" p. 71.

18. As quoted in "Talking Doctors," *Newsweek,* 11/18/46, p. 70.

19. Alexander and French, *Psychoanalytic Therapy,* p. 10.

20. Williams, "How Far Can We Safely Invade the Mind?" p. 57.

21. "Are You Always Worrying?" p. 70.

22. Rudolf Allers, "The Analyst and the Confessor," *Commonweal,* 8/27/48, p. 475.

23. Ibid., p. 71.

24. Williams, "How Far Can We Safely Invade the Mind?" p. 58.

25. "On Brain Waves," *Newsweek,* 6/10/46, p. 62.

26. A. E. Bennett, "Faulty Management of Psychiatric Syndromes Simulating Organic Disease," cited in Martin Gumpert, "Political Psychotherapy," *Nation,* 6/15/46, p. 719.

27. "Crise d'Asthenie en France," *Les Temps Modernes,* January 1946, as quoted in Gumpert, "Political Psychotherapy," p. 720.

28. Quoted in ibid.

29. Ibid.

30. "Nervous Nation," *Time,* 6/2/47, p. 74.

31. William Menninger, "Psychiatry Today," *Atlantic Monthly,* January 1948, pp. 67–68.

32. Martin Gumpert, "What to Do with Neurotics," *Nation,* 11/16/46, p. 553.

33. Carl Binger, "Why the Professor Fell Out of Bed," *Harper's Magazine,* October 1947, p. 338; and Menninger, "Psychiatry Today," p. 67; also Gumpert, "What to Do with Neurotics," p. 553.

34. And it would stay at 7 percent for decades, until it began to decline quite rapidly in the late 1970s. Frederick Sierles and Michael Alan Taylor, "Decline of U.S. Medical Student Career Choice of Psychiatry and What to Do About It," *American Journal of Psychiatry* 152:10 (October 1995): 1417.

35. See "A National Mental Health Program," *Science,* 8/15/47, for a nice synopsis of the bill.

36. Menninger, "Psychiatry Today," p. 68.

37. Frieda Fromm-Reichmann, *Principles of Intensive Psychotherapy* (Chicago: University of Chicago Press, 1950), p. 3.

38. Quoted in "Choosing a Psychiatrist," *Newsweek,* 8/25/47, p. 47.

39. All in William Menninger, "Psychiatric Experience in the War, 1941–1946," *American Journal of Psychiatry* 103 (March 1947): 583.

40. Ibid., p. 584.

41. Gumpert, "What to Do with Neurotics," p. 554.

42. Alexander and French, *Psychoanalytic Therapy,* p. 141.

43. Elizabeth Ross, "Military Psychiatric Social Work Participation in Group Therapy," AAPSW papers, box 71, folder 785, p. 4.

44. Clara Rabinowitz and Elizabeth Ross, "The Military Psychiatric Social Worker," *News Letter,* summer 1944, AAPSW papers, box 71, folder 785, p. 7.

45. "Urgent Red Cross Need for Psychiatric Social Workers," AAPSW papers, box 71, folder 778, summer 1945.

46. For an excellent history of early psychiatric social work, see Joseph Gabriel, "Mass-Producing the Individual: Mary C. Jarrett, Elmer E. Southard, and the Industrial Origins of Psychiatric Social Work," *Bulletin of the History of Medicine* 79 (2005).

47. "Smith's Social Workers," *Newsweek,* 6/21/48, p. 87.

48. See Hyman Lippman, "Historical Survey of Psychiatric Social Work," GAP papers, 38:7.

49. Adolf Meyer, "Objective Psychology or Psychobiology with Subordination of the Medically Useless Contrast of Mental and Physical," *JAMA* 65 (1915): 860, as quoted in Gabriel, "Mass-Producing the Individual," p. 433.

50. Leona Hambrecht, "Beyond a Decade," presented at the annual meeting of the AAPSW, AAPSW papers, 67:764, 1940, p. 1.

51. Mildred Scoville, "An Inquiry into the Status of Psychiatric Social Work," AAPSW papers, 69:764, June 1930, p. 1.

52. Sarah Swift, *Training in Psychiatric Social Work* (New York: Commonwealth Fund, 1934), p. 6.

53. Ibid., p. 9.

54. "Coordination of Work Between Psychiatrist and Psychiatric Social Worker," AAPSW papers, 69:763, p. 6.

55. "Minutes of the GAP Committee on Psychiatric Social Work," GAP papers, 36:7, 12/16/47, p. 4.

56. "GAP Committee on Psychiatric Social Work: Summary Discussion at Asbury Park," GAP papers, 36:7, November 9–11, 1947, p. 1.

57. "Social Work Therapy at the Southard School," 10/27/47, GAP papers, 37:1.

58. Marion Kenworthy and Porter Lee, *Mental Hygiene and Social Work* (New York: Commonwealth Fund, 1929), p. 168.

59. GAP, "The Psychiatric Social Worker in the Psychiatric Hospital," January 1949, GAP papers, 36:7, p. 2.

60. Hyman Lippman to Marion Kenworthy, 3/19/48, GAP papers, 37:1, p. 2.

61. Kenworthy and Lee, *Mental Hygiene and Social Work,* p. 250.

62. Sol Garfield, "Psychotherapy: A 40-Year Appraisal," *American Psychologist,* February 1981, p. 174.

63. Roy Wolford, "A Review of Psychology in VA Hospitals," *Journal of Counseling Psychology* 3:4 (1956): 243.

64. James Miller, "Clinical Psychology in the Veterans Administration," *American Psychologist* 1 (1946): 182.

65. Miller, "Clinical Psychology in the Veterans Administration," pp. 245–46.

66. A. T. Poffenberger, "The Training of a Clinical Psychologist," *Journal of Consulting Psychology* 2:1 (January–February 1938): 1.

67. *Training in Clinical Psychology* (New York: Prentice Hall, 1950), p. 151.

68. Robert Sears, "Clinical Training Facilities, 1947," *American Psychologist* 2 (1947): 201.

69. Laurence Shaffer, "The Problem of Psychotherapy," *American Psychologist* 2 (1947): 466.

70. Ibid.

71. Karl Menninger, *The Human Mind* (New York: Knopf, 1930), p. 8, as quoted in Simon Tulchin, "The Psychologist," in Lawson Lowrey and Victoria Sloane, eds., *Orthopsychiatry, 1923–1948* (New York: American Orthopsychiatric Association, 1950), p. 598.

72. Daniel Blain, "The Psychiatrist and the Psychologist," *American Journal of Psychiatry* (1946): 9.

73. William Menninger, "President's Page: Psychiatry and Psychology," *American Journal of Psychiatry* (1948): 389.

74. AMA Committee on Mental Health, *JAMA* (12/27/52), as quoted in "Psychiatrists and Psychologists Pose Question: Is Psychotherapy Medical Practice?" *Personnel and Guidance Journal* (May 1953): 544.

75. See ibid.

76. See Nolan Lewis, *Research in Dementia Praecox* (National Committee on Mental Hygiene, 1936), pp. 286–288.

77. "The Four Legs of Sanity," *Newsweek,* 4/21/47, p. 59.

78. Overholser to C. M. Hincks, 10/27/36, in Gerald Grob, ed., *The Inner World of American Psychiatry, 1890–1940* (New Brunswick: Rutgers University Press, 1985), p. 128; also ibid.

79. Jack Pressman, *Last Resort: Psychosurgery and the Limits of Medicine* (Cambridge: Cambridge University Press, 1998), p. 51.

80. Ibid., p. 54.

81. Quoted in ibid., p. 78.

82. Quoted in ibid, p. 341.

83. Ibid., p. 81.

84. "Mass Lobotomies," *Time,* 9/15/52, pp. 86–87.

85. Thomas McGehee, "The Anonymous Psychiatrist," *Atlantic Monthly,* October 1954, p. 24.

86. Franz Alexander and Sheldon Selesnick, *The History of Psychiatry* (New York: Harper and Row, 1966), p. 332.

CHAPTER 4 • THINKING

1. Carl Rogers, "A Process Conception of Psychotherapy," *American Psychology* 13 (1958): 143.

2. Ibid., p. 142.

3. "Person to Person," *Time,* 7/1/57, pp. 34 and 37.

4. Edward Joseph Shoben, Jr., "Psychotherapy as a Problem in Learning Theory," *Psychological Bulletin* 46 (1949): 370–71.

5. Carl Rogers, *Client-Centered Therapy* (Boston: Houghton Mifflin, 1951), p. 25.

6. Ibid., p. 35.

7. Rogers, "A Process Conception of Psychotherapy," p. 146.

8. Roy Jose DeCavalho, *The Founders of Humanistic Psychology* (Westport: Praeger, 1991), p. 21.

9. "Freud, Rogers, Ellis," *Christianity Today,* 12/11/81, p. 33.

10. "Person to Person," p. 34.

11. For a helpful synopsis of Maslow's writings, see DeCavalho, *The Founders of Humanistic Psychology,* pp. 19–21.

12. Allan Buss, "Humanistic Psychology as Liberal Ideology," *Journal of Humanistic Psychology* 19:3 (1979): 47.

13. Quoted in Bernard Baars, *The Cognitive Revolution in Psychology* (New York: Guilford Press, 1986), p. 41.

14. J. B. Watson and R. Rayner, "Conditioned Emotional Reactions," *Journal of Experimental Psychology* 3:1 (1920): 1–14.

15. Quoted in Baars, *The Cognitive Revolution in Psychology,* p. 43.

16. Quoted in ibid., p. 67.

17. H. J. Eysenck, "Learning Theory and Behavior Therapy," *Journal of Mental Sciences* 105 (1959): 61–75.

18. Ibid., p. 70.

19. Joseph Wolpe and Arnold Lazarus, *Behavior Therapy Techniques* (Oxford: Pergamon, 1966), p. 20.

20. P. J. Lang and B. G. Melamed, "Avoidance Conditioning Therapy of an Infant with Chronic Ruminative Vomiting," *Journal of Abnormal Psychology* 74 (1969): 1–8.

21. M. J. Raymond, "Case Fetishism Treated by Aversion Therapy," *British Medical Journal* 2 (1956): 855.

22. C. B. Blakemore, "The Application of Behavior Therapy to a Sexual Disorder," in Hans Eysenck, ed., *Experiments in Behavior Therapy* (New York: MacMillan, 1964), pp. 165–75.

23. T. Ayllon, "Intensive Treatment of Psychotic Behavior by Stimulus Satiation and Food Reinforcement," in Hans Eysenck, ed., *Experiments in Behavior Therapy,* pp. 213–23.

24. H. L. Freeman and D. C. Kendrick, "A Case of Cat Phobia," in Hans Eysenck, ed., *Experiments in Behavior Therapy,* pp. 51–61.

25. Ibid., p. 52.

26. Ibid.

27. Notably largactil, in the days before the invention of other tranquilizers. See D. Walton, "The Relevance of Learning Theory to the Treatment of an Obsessive-Compulsive State," in Hans Eysenck, ed., *Experiments in Behavior Therapy*, pp. 153–63.

28. K. Freund, "Some Problems in the Treatment of Homosexuality," in Hans Eysenck, ed., *Experiments in Behavior Therapy*, pp. 312–26.

29. From Keith Dobson and David Dozois, "Historical and Philosophical Bases of the Cognitive-Behavioral Therapies," in Keith Dobson, ed., *Handbook of Cognitive-Behavioral Therapies*, 2nd edition (New York: Guilford, 2001), p. 13.

30. Aaron Beck, "Cognitive Therapy: Nature and Relation to Behavior Therapy," *Behavior Therapy* 1 (1970): 186.

31. Albert Ellis, "Rational Psychotherapy," in Hans Eysenck, ed., *Experiments in Behavior Therapy*, p. 290.

32. Ibid., p. 288.

33. Ibid., p. 289.

34. Ibid., p. 290.

35. Ibid., pp. 292–93.

36. Ibid., p. 296.

37. Albert Ellis and Robert Harper, *A Guide to Rational Living* (Englewood Cliffs: Prentice-Hall, 1961), p. 37.

38. Ellis, "Rational Psychotherapy," pp. 305–6.

39. Raymond DiGiusepe and Bernard Raymond, "The Application of Rational-Emotive Theory and Therapy to School-Aged Children," *School Psychology Review* 19:3 (1990).

40. Ellis, "Rational Psychotherapy," p. 317.

41. Gene Marine, "Molecules and Mental Illness," *Nation*, 4/20/47, p. 338.

42. See Frank Beach, "Neural and Chemical Regulation of Behavior," in Harry Harlow and Clinton Woolsey, eds, *Biological and Biochemical Bases of Behavior* (Madison: University of Wisconsin Press, 1958), pp. 263–71.

43. "Mind v. Brain," *Time*, 5/31/48, p. 56.

44. See Peter Kramer, *Listening to Prozac* (New York: Viking, 1993), pp. 44–46, for details on the understanding that lithium brought to psychiatric disease modeling. Kramer discusses at length the history of psychiatrists using drugs as a means for validating the boundaries of mental disease states.

45. "Pills for Mental Illness?" *Time,* 11/8/54, p. 96.

46. David Healy, *The Psychopharmacologists* (London: Chapman and Hall, 1996), p. 241.

47. Donald Eldred, George Brooks et al., "The Rehabilitation of the Hospitalized Mentally Ill—the Vermont Story," *American Journal of Public Health* 52:1 (January 1962): 45.

48. Marine, "Molecules and Mental Illness," p. 338.

49. Anonymous, "A Psychiatrist's Choice," *Atlantic Monthly,* July 1954, p. 44.

50. Ibid., p. 45.

51. GAP, Committee on Medical Education, *The Preclinical Teaching of Psychiatry* (New York: GAP, 1962), p. 344.

52. Don Jackson, "Beware Ataraxes in the Attic," *New Republic,* 10/22/56, p. 22.

53. J. M. Bradford, "Correspondence," *New Republic,* 11/19/56, p. 31.

54. "Wonder Drugs and Mental Disorders," *Consumer Reports,* August 1955, p. 388.

55. H. Azima, "Drugs for the Mind," *Nation,* 7/21/56, p. 57.

56. "Molecular Chemistry of Mental Disease," *Science,* 10/19/56.

57. Wilford Cross, "Faith and Analysis," *New Republic,* 6/6/55, p. 25.

58. Nathan Hale, *Psychoanalytic Training: Young Americans Abroad* (New York: Oxford University Press, 1995), p. 305.

59. Clara Thompson, *Psychoanalysis: Evolution and Development* (New York: Hermitage House, 1950).

60. Quoted in Hale, *Psychoanalytic Training,* p. 305.

61. Ibid., p. 306.

62. "For the Psyche," *Time,* 9/2/46, p. 73.

63. As quoted in Allen Bergin and Michael Lambert, "The Evaluation of Therapeutic Outcomes," in Sol Garfield and Allen Bergin, eds., *Handbook of Psychotherapy and Behavioral Change,* 2nd edition (New York: Wiley, 1978), p. 141.

64. Jerome Frank, Lester Gliedman, Stanley Imber et al., "Why Patients Leave Psychotherapy," *Archives of Neurology and Psychiatry* 77 (1957): 286.

65. Hans Eysenck, "The Effects of Psychotherapy: An Evaluation," *Journal of Consulting Psychology* 16 (1952): 319–24.

66. See Allen Bergin and Michael Lambert, "The Evaluation of Therapeutic Outcomes," pp. 24–42.

67. Allen Bergin and Michael Lambert, "The Evaluation of Therapeutic Outcomes," p. 144.

68. Lester Luborsky, "Quantitative Research on Psychoanalytic Therapy," in Sol Garfield and Allen Bergin, eds., *Handbook of Psychotherapy and Behavioral Change,* 2nd ed., p. 337.

69. See Lester Luborsky, "The Patient's Personality and Psychotherapeutic Change," in Hans Strupp and Lester Luborsky, eds., *Research in Psychotherapy* (Washington, D.C.: American Psychological Association, 1961), pp. 120–21.

70. J. McV. Hunt, "Measuring Personality Change," in Hans Strupp and Lester Luborsky, eds., *Research in Psychotherapy,* p. 167.

71. Allen Bergin and Michael Lambert, "The Evaluation of Therapeutic Outcomes," p. 243.

Chapter 5 · Alcohol

1. Quoted in "Problem Drinking," *Time,* 1/31/49, p. 54.

2. Ralph Habas, "Drinking," *U.S. News & World Report,* 8/26/55, p. 111.

3. Quoted in C. Lester Walker, "What We Know About Drinking," *Harper's Magazine,* July 1950, p. 29.

4. Habas, "Drinking," p. 111.

5. "Drink, Drink, Drink," *America,* 5/21/55, p. 200.

6. Habas, "Drinking," p. 119.

7. Ibid., p. 120.

8. "Mrs. Drunkard," *Newsweek*, 3/8/48, p. 22.

9. "The Problem Drinker," *Time*, 12/22/57, p. 66.

10. Ibid.

11. Habas, "Drinking," p. 112.

12. C. Lester Walker, "What We Know About Drinking," p. 32.

13. See Charles Snyder, *Alcohol and the Jews* (New York: Free Press, 1958).

14. "It's Not That Drink," *Newsweek*, 10/28/57, p. 92.

15. For an excellent description of life on skid row in the 1950s, see Jerome Ellison, "The Shame of Skid Row," *Saturday Evening Post*, 10/18/52.

16. Colette Hunter, "Feature 'X'," *America*, 1/1/55, pp. 359–60.

17. Charles Crowe, "It Doesn't Make Sense?" *Christian Century*, 2/22/56, p. 239.

18. Ibid.

19. Ibid.

20. "The Drinkers," *Time*, 1/16/50, p. 40.

21. Elvin Jellinek, "What Shall We Do About Alcoholism?" *Vital Speeches of the Day*, 2/1/47, p. 252.

22. Ibid., p. 253.

23. Sidney Vogel, "Psychiatric Treatment of Alcoholism," *Annals of the American Academy of Political and Social Science*, January 1958, p. 99.

24. Ibid., p. 100.

25. Ibid.

26. George Thompson, "Psychiatry of Alcoholism," in George Thompson, ed., *Alcoholism* (New York: Basic Books, 1957), pp. 454–55.

27. "The Drinkers," p. 40.

28. "Life, Hope, and Meaning," *The Christian Century*, 4/10/57, p. 445.

29. Thompson, "Psychiatry of Alcoholism," p. 457.

30. Ibid., p. 456.

31. "The Alcoholic's Plight," *Newsweek*, 1/5/48, p. 46.

32. Ruth Fox and Peter Lyon, *Alcoholism: Its Scope, Cause, and Treatment* (New

York: Random House, 1956), quoted in John Ford, "Why Do They Drink?" *America,* 1/28/56, p. 483.

33. Vogel, "Psychiatric Treatment of Alcoholism," p. 103.

34. "The Alcoholic's Plight," p. 46.

35. W. W. Bauer, "Approval by Director, Bureau of Health Education of the American Medical Association," *U.S. News & World Report,* 8/26/55, p. 113.

36. Jean Sapin, "Social Work and Alcoholism," *Annals of the American Academy of Political and Social Science,* January 1958, p. 128.

37. "Life, Hope, and Meaning," p. 446.

38. See John Ford, "Coping with the Problem Drinker," *America,* 11/9/57, p. 165.

39. "A.A.: A Uniquely American Phenomenon," *Fortune,* February 1951, p. 99.

40. Jack Alexander, "The Drunkard's Best Friend," *Saturday Evening Post,* 4/1/50, p. 74.

41. Leslie Farber, "Blueplate Gospel," *New Republic,* 5/21/45, p. 716.

42. "Anonymous Ally," *Time,* 2/8/71.

43. Ford, "Coping with the Problem of the Drinker," p. 165.

44. "A.A.: A Uniquely American Phenomenon," p. 141.

45. Ibid.

46. Joseph Hirsh, *The Problem Drinker* (New York: Duell, Sloan, and Pearce, 1949), as excerpted in "Public Health and Social Aspects," in George Thompson, *Alcoholism* (New York: Basic Books, 1957), p. 69.

47. *U.S. News & World Report,* 10/2/53, p. 117.

48. Ibid., p. 116.

49. Ibid.

50. Wilburn Echols, "Here's Hope for Alcoholics," *Christian Century,* 11/25/47, p. 1452.

51. Ibid.

52. Harrison Trice, "Alcoholics Anonymous," *Annals of the Academy of Political and Social Science,* January 1958, p. 113.

53. There is much ill-willed debate over the founders of the discipline, and the

literature is inconsistent. See Esther Somerfeld-Ziskind, "Group Therapy," *Education,* January 1949, pp. 280–87.

54. J. L. Moreno, *The First Book on Group Psychotherapy,* 3rd edition (New York: Beacon House, 1957), p. vii.

55. Max Rosenbaum and Milton Berger, eds., *Group Psychotherapy and Group Function* (New York: Basic Books, 1963), p. 3.

56. Ibid., pp. 12–13.

57. Quoted in ibid., p. 13.

58. Jerome Frank, *Persuasion and Healing: A Comparative Study of Psychotherapy* (New York: Schocken, 1969), p. 176.

59. See Somerfeld-Ziskind, "Group Therapy," p. 283.

60. Frank, *Persuasion and Healing,* p. 183.

61. Moreno, *The First Book on Group Psychotherapy,* p. xi.

62. Hugh Mullan and Max Rosenbaum, *Group Psychotherapy: Theory and Practice* (New York: Free Press of Glencoe, 1962), p. 209.

63. Jung to Hans Illing, 1/26/55, reprinted in ibid., p. 184.

64. See Ruth Fox, "Modifications of Group Therapy for Alcoholics," AOA papers, 2:1965.

65. "Insulin for Alcoholism," *Newsweek,* 9/2/46, pp. 50-51.

66. C. Lester Walker, "What We Know About Drinking," p. 36.

67. Ibid.

68. See Fox, "Modifications of Group Therapy for Alcoholics," AOA papers, 2:1965, especially p. 3.

Chapter 6 • Psychological Society

1. See Ruth Falk, "Innovations in College Mental Health," *Mental Hygiene* 55:4 (October 1971): 451–55.

2. Ernest Havemann, "The Age of Psychology in the U.S.," *Life,* 1/7/57, p. 68.

3. Quoted in George Krupp, "Analyzing the Analysts," *Saturday Review,* 3/14/70, p. 27.

4. Havemann, "The Age of Psychology in the U.S.," p. 72.

5. Ibid., p. 75.

6. Judd Marmor, "Psychiatry and the Survival of Man," *Saturday Review,* 5/22/71, p. 18.

7. Ibid., pp. 18–19.

8. Quoted in Krupp, "Analyzing the Analysts," p. 28.

9. K. T. Erikson, "Notes on the Sociology of Deviance," in T. J. Scheff, ed., *Mental Illness and Social Processes* (New York: Harper and Row, 1967), as quoted in Richard Pasewark and Max Rardin, "Theoretical Models in Community Mental Health," *Mental Hygiene* 55:3 (July 1971): 361.

10. James Halliday, *Psychosocial Medicine: A Study of the Sick Society* (New York: Norton, 1948).

11. See William Whyte, *The Organization Man* (1956), revised and reprinted (Philadelphia: University of Pennsylvania Press, 2002).

12. As quoted in Thomas Scheff, *Being Mentally Ill: A Sociological Theory* (1969), reprinted (New York: Aldine, 1984), p. 160.

13. Ibid., p. 161.

14. See Morris Black and Leslie Rosenthal, "Changes in the Therapeutic Techniques in the Group Treatment of Delinquent Boys," AOA papers box 1, file 1963.

15. Marc Fried, "Social Problems and Psychopathology," in GAP, *Urban America and the Planning of Mental Health Services* (New York: GAP, 1964), p. 419.

16. Ibid., p. 420.

17. James Comer, "The Need Is Now," *Mental Hygiene,* winter 1973, p. 4.

18. Fried, "Social Problems and Psychopathology," p. 426.

19. See William Mitchell, "Fictive Siblings and the 'Unworthy' Child in Changing Rural Vermont," AOA papers, box 1, folder 1964.

20. Seymour Halleck, "Psychiatry and the Status Quo," *Archives of General Psychiatry* 19 (September 1968): 257–65.

21. "The Psychiatrist: Activist or Onlooker," *Mental Hygiene* 54:2 (April 1970): 191.

22. Ibid., p. 193.

23. Ibid., p. 194.

24. Richard Schwartz, "Psychiatry's Drift Away from Medicine," *American Journal of Psychiatry* 131:2 (February 1974): 132.

25. GAP, "The Social Responsibility of Psychiatry: A Statement of Orientation," APaA papers, RG11, "Committee for the Study of Social Issues," p. 1.

26. Ibid., p. 3.

27. See Robert Blank to George Gardner, APaA papers, RG11, Committee for the Study of Social Issues, 12/29/65.

28. GAP, *Psychiatric Aspects of School Integration* (New York: GAP, 1957).

29. Quoted in "Psychiatrists Report Gains Against Bias," *Christian Century,* 6/5/57, p. 700.

30. See "The Military Psychiatrist," *Time,* 7/27/70.

31. "The Mind: Science's Search for a Guide to Sanity," *Newsweek,* 10/24/55, p. 61.

32. Louis Reed, Evelyn Myers, and Patricia Scheidemandel, *Health Insurance and Psychiatric Care* (Washington: American Psychiatric Association, 1972), pp. 30–33.

33. Gerald Klerman, "The Psychiatric Revolution of the Past Twenty-five Years," in Walter Grove, ed., *Deviance and Mental Illness* (Beverly Hills: Sage, 1982), p. 192.

34. Ibid., p. 195.

35. Reed, Myers, and Scheidemandel, *Health Insurance and Psychiatric Care,* p. 13.

36. American Hospital Association: Advisory Panel on Financing Mental Health Care, *Financing Mental Health Care in the United States* (Rockville, Maryland: NIMH, 1972), p. 12.

37. Ibid., p. 5.

38. As quoted in David Musto, "Whatever Happened to Community Mental Health?" *Public Interest,* spring 1975, p. 55.

39. Quoted in ibid., p. 65.

40. Ibid., p. 55.

41. Joint Commission on Mental Illness and Health, *Action for Mental Health* (New York: Basic Books, 1961), p. v.

42. Ibid., pp. v–xvii.

43. Ibid., p. 40.

44. Advisory Panel on Financing Mental Health Care, *Financing Mental Health Care in the United States* (Chicago: American Hospital Association, 1974), p. 10.

45. Franklin Chu and Sharland Trotter, "The Fires of Irrelevance," *Mental Hygiene,* fall 1972, p. 8.

46. Rosalyn Bass, *CMHC Staffing: Who Minds the Store?* (Washington: NIMH, 1977), p. 2.

47. Constance Holden, "Community Mental Health Centers: Storefront Therapy and More," *Science,* 12/17/71, p. 1220.

48. Constance Holden, "Nader on Mental Health Centers: A Movement That Got Bogged Down," *Science*, 8/4/72, p. 413.

49. Mark Vonnegut, "Community Mental Health: Good Intentions Run Amok," *Harper's Magazine,* February 1975, p. 109.

50. Ibid., p. 110.

51. Ibid.

52. Walter Barton, "Psychiatry in Transition," *American Journal of Psychiatry* (July 1962): 4.

53. Constance Holden, "Community Mental Health Centers: Growing Movement Seeks Identity," *Science,* 12/10/71, p. 1110.

54. Steven Sharfstein, "Community Mental Health Centers: Returning to Basics," *American Journal of Psychiatry* 136:8 (August 1979): 1078.

55. Quoted in "Crackup in Mental Care," *Time,* 12/17/73, p. 74.

56. See ibid.

57. As quoted in Musto, "Whatever Happened to Community Mental Health?" p. 66.

58. Ibid., p. 69. Musto is quoting the Chu and Trotter report done for Ralph Nader here.

59. Helen Hershfield Avnet, *Psychiatric Insurance* (New York: GHI, 1962), p. 3.

60. Reed, Myers, and Scheidemandel, *Health Insurance and Psychiatric Care,* p. 62.

61. Advisory Panel on Financing Mental Health Care, *Financing Mental Health Care in the United States,* pp. 43 and 46.

62. Hershfield Avnet, *Psychiatric Insurance,* pp. 121–27.

63. Reed, Myers, and Scheidemandel, *Health Insurance and Psychiatric Care,* p. 62.

64. Nathan Hale, *The Rise and Crisis of Psychoanalysis in the United States* (New York: Oxford, 1995), p. 223.

65. Ibid., p. 222.

66. See ibid., p. 222; also Douglas Kirsner, *Unfree Associations: Inside Psychoanalytic Institutes* (London: Process Press, 2000), p. 22.

67. Kirsner, *Unfree Associations,* p. 22.

68. Hale, *The Rise and Crisis of Psychoanalysis in the United States,* p. 223.

69. Quoted in Eli Zaretsky, *Secrets of the Soul: A Social and Cultural History of Psychoanalysis* (New York: Knopf, 2004), p. 290.

70. Quoted in ibid., pp. 290, 292.

71. Martin Gross, *The Psychological Society* (New York: Random House, 1978), p. 146.

72. Jerome Frank, *Persuasion and Healing* (New York: Schocken, 1969), p. 15.

73. Franz Alexander, "The Dynamics of Psychotherapy in the Light of Learning Theory," *American Journal of Psychiatry* 120 (1963): 442.

74. Gross, *The Psychological Society,* p. 151.

75. Ad Hoc Committee on Scientific Activities, "Report," 12/14/66, APaA papers, RG 11, p. 2.

76. "Proceedings of the Workshop on the Relations Between Psychoanalytic and Psychiatric Training," 12/6/64, AAP papers, box 1, folder 7, p. 2.

77. John Briggs, "The Vicissitudes of the 'Shrink-Beat,'" 5/7/69, AAP papers, box 1, folder 9, p. 6.

78. Frieda Fromm-Reichmann, *Principles of Intensive Psychotherapy* (Chicago: University of Chicago Press, 1950), p. 11.

79. Ibid., p. 12.

80. Gross, *The Psychological Society,* p. 155.

81. Quoted in Edward Dolnick, *Madness on the Couch* (New York: Simon & Schuster, 1998), p. 90.

82. Ibid., p. 96.

83. Quoted in ibid., p. 117.

84. Ibid., p. 130.

85. Martin Grotjahn, "About the Relation Between Psychoanalytic Training and Psychoanalytic Therapy," APaP papers, RG11, May 1962, p. 3.

86. Quoted in Zaretsky, *Secrets of the Soul: A Social and Cultural History of Psychoanalysis,* p. 13.

87. Ibid.

88. Richard Schwartz, "Psychiatrists Drift Away from Medicine," *American Journal of Psychiatry* 131:2 (February 1974), p. 130.

89. Ibid.

90. Frank, *Persuasion and Healing,* p. 14.

91. Ibid., pp. 13–14.

92. Joseph Jaffe, "Position Statement on Psychoanalytic Research," AAP papers, box 1, folder 11, 1970, p. 2.

93. Ibid.

94. K. M. Colby, "Discussion of Papers on Therapists' Contribution" (1962), as quoted in Hans Strupp and Allen Bergin, "Some Empirical and Conceptual Bases for Coordinated Research in Psychotherapy," *International Journal of Psychiatry* 7:2 (February 1969): 72.

95. Quoted in "Freud Is Unfair," *Nation,* 8/2/47, p. 115.

96. Quoted in "Psychiatry and Faith," *Time,* 4/18/49, p. 80.

97. Fritz Kunkel, "How Much Truth Is There in Freud?" *Christian Century,* 10/20/48, p. 1107.

98. Waldo Frank, "Psychology and Religion," *Nation,* 1/16/54, p. 54.

99. Both quoted in Robert Morse, "Faith and Analysis," *New Republic,* 5/23/55, p. 22.

100. Karl Stern, "Psychoanalysis and Christianity," *Commonweal*, 9/2/55, p. 541.

101. Gregory Zilboorg, "Psychoanalysis and Religion," *Atlantic Monthly*, January 1949, p. 49.

102. See Harry McNeil, "Freudians and Catholics," *Commonweal*, 7/25/47, pp. 350–51.

103. Ibid., p. 353.

104. "Clergy and Mental Health," *America*, 4/24/54; also J. C. Barden, "Ministering to Emotions as Well as Spirit," *New York Times*, 9/28/90.

105. "Drawing the Line," *Newsweek*, 12/3/56, p. 97.

106. "The Mental Ministry," *Time*, 9/12/55.

107. W. George Scarlett, "The Clergyman's Role and Community Mental Health," *Mental Hygiene* 54:3 (July 1970): 378.

108. Jurgen Moltmann, *Theology of Hope* (New York: Harper and Row, 1965), as quoted in ibid., p. 380.

109. Quoted in Allen Bergin, "Psychotherapy and Religious Values," *Journal of Consulting and Clinical Psychology* 48:1 (1980): 101.

110. R. Hogan, "Interview," *APA Monitor*, April 1979, p. 4; quoted in ibid., p. 99.

111. "Mind and Spirit," *Newsweek*, 1/26/59, p. 62.

112. Anonymous, "Psychiatry and Spiritual Healing," *Atlantic Monthly*, August 1954, p. 43.

113. Quoted in Victor White, "The Analyst and the Confessor," *Commonweal*, 7/23/48, p. 349.

114. Edith Weigert, "I Have Never Met a Genuinely Irreligious Person," *New Republic*, 5/16/55, p. 19.

115. Marion Sanders, "Social Work: A Profession Chasing Its Tail," *Harper's Magazine*, March 1957, p. 56.

116. George Pikser, "The Essentiality of the Development of the Private Practice of Case Work," NASW papers, box 2, folder 17, 5/19/60, p. 1.

117. Herman Leon, Rena Schulman, Aaron Esman, "Professional Issues in the Training of Psychiatric Social Workers for Child Guidance Clinic Practice," AOA papers, box 1, folder 1963, 4/5/63, pp. 8–9.

118. Richard Cabot had remarked on the potential for social workers to provide private psychotherapy as early as 1919. See Mary Read, "A Review of Social Work Literature on Private Practice," NASW papers, box 2, folder 16, 1963.

119. Daniel Jennings, "Is Private Practice Merely a Self-Seeking Kind of Practice and Thus at Variance with the Ethics of the Profession?" NASW papers, box 2, folder 16, 1963, p. 2.

120. Saul Hofstein, "The Potential in Private Practice for the Profession of Social Work," NASW papers, box 2, folder 17, May 1962, p. 6.

121. Ibid.

122. Ibid., p. 11.

123. Pikser, "The Essentiality of the Development of the Private Practice of Case Work," p. 11.

124. Ibid., p. 12.

125. Walter Barton, "Perspectives and Prospects," GAP papers, box 53, folder 6, 11/11/66, p. 3.

126. "Notes Taken at the Meeting of GAP Committee on PSW: Asbury Park, New Jersey," GAP papers, box 36, folder 7, fall 1948, p. 2.

127. Damon Turner, "The Licensing Effort—Seven Years Later," *Social Work Journal,* April 1954, p. 69.

128. Council of State Governments, "A Study of State Legislation Licensing the Practice of Professions and Other Occupations," February 1955, p. 1.

CHAPTER 7 • NARCISSISM

1. Christopher Lasch, *The Culture of Narcissism* (New York: Norton, 1978).

2. Quoted in ibid., p. 5.

3. Ibid., p. 13.

4. Perry London, "From the Long Couch for the Sick to the Push Button for the Bored," *Psychology Today,* June 1974, p. 64.

5. Heinz Kohut, *The Analysis of Self* (New York: International Universities Press, 1971). Quoted in Susan Quinn, "Oedipus vs. Narcissus," *New York Times,* 6/30/81.

6. Herbert Fensterheim and Jean Baer, *Don't Say Yes When You Want to Say No* (New York: David McKay, 1975), p. 5.

7. Gerald Gurin, Joseph Veroff, and Sheila Feld, *Americans View Their Mental Health* (New York: Basic Books, 1960), p. 24.

8. Ibid., p. 25.

9. Gerald Klerman, "The Psychiatric Revolution of the Past Twenty-five Years," in Walter Grove, ed., *Deviance and Mental Illness* (Beverly Hills: Sage, 1982), p. 196.

10. "Test Your Own Sanity," *Saturday Evening Post,* October 1976, p. 16.

11. Anne David, "Effective Low Cost Aftercare," *Mental Hygiene* 55:3 (July 1971): 353.

12. Lasch, *The Culture of Narcissism,* p. 13.

13. Ibid., p. 14.

14. Robert Seidenberg, "Drug Advertising and Perception of Mental Illness," *Mental Hygiene* 55:1 (January 1971): 24.

15. "Company Shrink," *Newsweek,* 10/24/77, p. 96.

16. Seidenberg, "Drug Advertising and Perception of Mental Illness," p. 26.

17. Ibid., p. 27.

18. Ibid.

19. Rivero, "The Therapy Game: An Introduction to the Topic More Talked About Than Sex," *St. Louisan Magazine,* April 1977, as quoted in Sol Garfield, "Psychotherapy: A 40-Year Appraisal," *American Psychologist,* February 1981, p. 175.

20. James Bugental, *Challenges of Humanistic Psychology* (New York: McGraw-Hill, 1967), p. 7.

21. Ibid., p. 9.

22. Hans Strupp, "On the Basic Ingredients of Psychotherapy," *Journal of Consulting and Clinical Psychology* 41:1 (1973): 2.

23. Ibid., pp. 3, 4.

24. As quoted in Marvin Goldfried and Wendy Padawer, "Current Status and Future Directions in Psychotherapy," in Marvin Goldfried, ed., *Converging Themes in Psychotherapy* (New York: Springer, 1982), p. 10.

25. Ibid., p. 12. Goldfried was paraphrasing a comment made by Roy Grinker, a humanistic psychiatrist trained in psychoanalysis.

26. Kurt Goldstein, *The Organism* (Boston: Beacon Press, 1939).

27. Fritz Perls, Ralph Hefferline, and Paul Goodman, *Gestalt Therapy* (New York: Julian Press, 1951), p. 36.

28. Ibid., p. 40.

29. Fritz Perls, *Gestalt Therapy Verbatim,* John Stevens, ed. (Lafayette, California: Real People Press, 1969), p. 19.

30. Ibid., p. 11.

31. Fritz Perls, "Four Lectures," in Joen Fagan and Irma Lee Shepherd, eds., *Gestalt Therapy Now* (New York: Harper and Row, 1970), p. 14.

32. Joen Fagan and Irma Lee Shepherd, "Theory of Gestalt Therapy," in Joen Fagan and Irma Lee Shepherd, eds., *Gestalt Therapy Now,* p. 3.

33. Perls, Hefferline, and Goodman, *Gestalt Therapy,* p. 41.

34. Ibid.

35. Perls, *Gestalt Therapy Verbatim,* p. 4.

36. R. Bruce Sloan, Fred Staples et al., *Psychotherapy versus Behavior Therapy* (Cambridge, MA: Commonwealth Fund, 1975), p. 7.

37. On therapeutic relaxation, see Ernst Schmidhofer, "Mechanical Group Therapy," *Science,* 2/1/52, pp. 120–22.

38. On Morita therapy, see "Four-Walls Treatment," *Time,* 10/2/72.

39. "Latest Rage: Getting People to Tune Into Themselves," *U.S. News & World Report,* 2/16/76, p. 38.

40. Gurney Williams III, "Transcendental Meditation: Can It Fight Drug Abuse?" *Science Digest,* February 1972, p. 74.

41. Ibid., pp. 77–78.

42. Fensterheim and Baer, *Don't Say Yes When You Want to Say No,* p. 13.

43. Betty Crowther and Paul Pantleo, "Marathon Therapy and Changes in Attitude Toward Treatment and Behavior Ratings," *Mental Hygiene* 55:2 (April 1971): 165–70.

44. John Lee, "Therapy for Ethnics," *Time,* 3/15/82, p. 42.

45. "Of Two Minds," *Time,* 7/24/50, p. 64.

46. For an excellent early description of Dianetics, see "After Hours," *Harper's Magazine,* January 1951, pp. 101–103.

47. "Of Two Minds," p. 65.

48. "The Primal Screamer," *Newsweek,* 4/12/71.

49. "Ticklish Treatment," *Newsweek,* 7/30/73, p. 74.

50. Quoted in Richard Ofshe and Ethan Watters, *Making Monsters* (New York: Charles Scribner's Sons, 1994), p. 44.

51. Ibid., p. 17.

52. Ibid,. pp. 66–67.

53. Bryce Nelson, "Efforts Widen to Curb Sexual Abuse in Therapy," *New York Times,* 11/23/82.

54. Dava Sobel, "Sex Therapy: As Popularity Grows, Critics Question Whether It Works," *New York Times,* 11/4/80.

55. Jerome Frank, "Psychotherapy: The Restoration of Morale," *American Journal of Psychiatry* 131:3 (March 1974): 273.

56. "Poor Man's Psychoanalysis," *Newsweek,* 10/16/50, p. 59.

57. "Ticklish Treatment," p. 75.

58. Sol Garfield and Richard Kurtz "Clinical Psychologists in the 1970s," *American Psychologist* 31 (January 1976): 4.

59. Gerald Klerman, "The Psychiatric Revolution," in Walter Grove, ed., *Deviance and Mental Illness* (Beverly Hills: Sage, 1977), p. 195.

60. Quoted in Alfred Auerback, "The Anti–Mental Health Movement," *American Journal of Psychiatry* 120 (1963): 108.

61. See Phyllis Chesler, *Women and Madness* (New York: Doubleday, 1972). Quote from "Women on the Couch," *Time,* 1/22/73.

62. Suman Fernando, *Race and Culture in Psychiatry* (London: Croom Helm, 1988), p. 129. See also "White Racism: Report of Ad Hoc Committee on Social Issues," APsP papers, RG11, folder: "Committee on Social Problems."

63. Quoted in James Gordon, "Who Is Mad? Who Is Sane?" *Atlantic Monthly,* January 1971, p. 56.

64. See Peter Sedgwick, "Anti-Psychiatry from the Sixties to the Eighties," in Walter Grove, ed., *Deviance and Mental Illness* pp. 199–223.

65. David Cooper, *Psychiatry and Anti-Psychiatry* (New York: Ballantine, 1971), quoted in Roberta Wilhelm, "Man the Machine," *Society,* July–August 1973, p. 88.

66. Ibid., p. 90.

67. Richard Vatz and Lee Weinberg, eds., *Thomas Szasz: Primary Values and Major Contentions* (Buffalo: Prometheus Books, 1961), p. 10.

68. Ibid., p. 92.

69. Ibid., p. 78.

70. Thomas Szasz, "Power and Psychiatry," *Society,* May–June 1981, p. 16.

71. Vatz and Weinberg, eds., *Thomas Szasz: Primary Values and Major Contentions,* p. 87.

72. Ibid., p. 96.

73. Peter Breggin, *Toxic Psychiatry* (New York: St. Martin's Press, 1991), p. 344.

74. Ibid., p. 16.

75. Ibid., p. 17.

76. See Donald Templer, "Analyzing the Psychotherapist," *Mental Hygiene* 55:2 (April 1971); as well as Thomas Scheff, *Being Mentally Ill* (New York: Aldine, 1984). Scheff in particular points out that a psychiatrist's medical training prepares him predominantly to focus on "internal bodily states" rather than "social and psychological concerns," p. 172.

77. The groupings of outcomes are from Garfield, "Psychotherapy: A 40-Year Appraisal," *AP* 36 (1981): 180.

78. Ibid.

79. Ibid. For more on outcomes studies of psychoanalysis, see Helen Sargent, Lolafaye Coyne et al., "An Approach to the Quantitative Problems of Psychoanalytic Research," *Journal of Clinical Psychology* 23 (1967): 243–91.

80. "Task Panel Reports Submitted to the President's Commission on Mental Health" (Washington: GPO, 1978), p. 1752.

81. See "Congress Puts Psychotherapy on the Couch," *Economist,* 2/16/80, p. 95. Also, Hans Strupp, Ronald Fox, and Ken Lessler, *Patients View Their Psychotherapy* (Baltimore: Johns Hopkins Press, 1969), p. 135; also "Psychotherapy Faces Test of Worth," *Science,* January 1980, pp. 35–36.

82. Strupp, Fox, and Lessler, *Patients View Their Psychotherapy,* p. 21.

83. Ibid., p. 28.

84. "Task Panel Reports Submitted to the President's Commission on Mental Health," p. 1747.

85. Erica Goode, "Does Psychotherapy Work?" *U.S. News & World Report,* 5/24/93, p. 56.

86. Charles Krauthammer, "Public Policy at the Scientific Frontier: Assessing the Efficacy of Psychotherapy," 3/8/80, APaP papers, RG 11, folder: "Committee on Scientific Activities," p. 5.

87. Eliot Marshall, "Psychotherapy Works, but for Whom?" *Science,* 2/1/80, p. 506.

88. Ibid.

89. Ibid., p. 507.

90. "New Ways to Heal Disturbed Minds: Where Will It All Lead?" *U.S. News & World Report,* 2/16/76, p. 35.

91. Ibid.

CHAPTER 8 • NARCOTICS

1. "Drugs on Campus," *Newsweek,* 1/25/71, p. 52.

2. Robert DuPont, "Drugs, Alcoholism, and Women," *Vital Speeches of the Day,* 10/24/75, p. 141; also Robert DuPont, "Marijuana Is Far from 'Harmless,'" *Education Digest,* November 1981, p. 53.

3. "Drug Menace: How Serious: Interview with John Ingersoll, Director, Federal Bureau of Narcotics," *U. S. News & World Report,* 5/25/70, p. 38.

4. Ibid., p. 41.

5. DuPont, "Marijuana Is Far from 'Harmless,' " p. 54.

6. Ibid., p. 55.

7. Edward Bunker, "A Junkie View of the Quagmire," *Nation,* 6/25/77, pp. 785–86.

8. "Society Is Hooked," *Nation,* 1/24/72, p. 100.

9. Bunker, "A Junkie View of the Quagmire," p. 786.

10. Robert Steele, "Our Most Dangerous Epidemic," *Nation's Business,* July 1971, p. 46.

11. George McGovern, "Toward an End to Drug Use," *Vital Speeches,* 3/15/72, p. 324.

12. Ibid.

13. Quoted in Bunker, "A Junkie View of the Quagmire," p. 786.

14. "Children in Peril: 'Pushers' Are Selling Narcotics to Thousands of Teen-Agers," *Life,* 6/11/51, p. 116.

15. Marie Nyswander, *The Drug Addict as a Patient* (New York: Grune & Stratton, 1956), p. 2.

16. The best source on the United States' long effort to regulate narcotics use is David Musto, *The American Disease: The Origins of Narcotics Control,* 3rd ed. (New York: Oxford, 1999).

17. Ibid., p. 13.

18. Ibid., p. 1.

19. Herbert Brown, "A Short—and Horrible—Life," *Life,* 6/11/51, p. 126.

20. Art Linkletter, "Drug Abuse," *Vital Speeches,* 10/15/71, p. 23.

21. Mac Proctor, "Addiction, the Counter-Culture," *Nation,* 5/17/71, p. 623.

22. Samuel McCracken, "The Drugs of Habit and the Drugs of Belief," *Commentary,* 51:6 (June 1971): 45.

23. Ibid., p. 44.

24. Quoted in ibid., p. 49.

25. Proctor, "Addiction, the Counter-Culture," p. 624.

26. "Did Elvis Die from Drug Abuse?" *Newsweek,* 1/28/80, p. 35.

27. Linkletter, "Drug Abuse," p. 22.

28. George Gallup, "Alcoholism's Spreading Blight," *Christianity Today,* 9/18/81, p. 27.

29. Quoted in McCracken, "The Drugs of Habit and the Drugs of Believe," p. 49.

30. Donald Thorman, "A New Dope Peril?" *Catholic World,* March 1957, p. 447.

31. William Wyant, "Coming Home with a Habit," *Nation,* 7/5/71, p. 7.

32. Robert Steele, "Our Most Dangerous Epidemic," *Nation's Business,* July 1971, p. 46.

33. "The GI's Other Enemy: Heroin," *Newsweek,* 5/24/71, p. 26.

34. "Drugs on Campus," *Newsweek,* 1/25/71, p. 52.

35. "Drug Abuse: Now It's Downers," *U.S. News & World Report,* 12/27/71, p. 44.

36. "Toll of Alcoholism," *U.S. News & World Report,* 10/29/73, p. 46.

37. Ibid.

38. Robert Stout, "Teen-Age Alcoholism: An Alarming Trend," *Christian Century,* 11/1/78, p. 1048.

39. "The Drug Sickness: No Company Is Immune," *Nation's Business,* November 1972, p. 20.

40. "A Drug on the Market," *Newsweek,* 3/27/72, p. 90.

41. "Taking Drugs on the Job," *Newsweek,* 8/22/83, p. 55.

42. Ibid., p. 54.

43. Interview with Harry Johnson, "Drugs and Drinking in the Business World," *U.S. News & World Report,* 3/22/71, p. 71.

44. Robert Smith, "Confessions of an Alcoholic Executive," *Duns,* June 1972, p. 74.

45. "Three Weapons and One Flaw," *Life,* 6/11/51, p. 123.

46. "Latest Turn in Treatment of Drug Addicts," *U.S. News & World Report,* 9/11/72, p. 76.

47. U.S. Public Health Service, *Rehabilitation in Drug Addiction* (Washington, D.C.: PHS, 1963), p. vii.

48. Alfred Freedman, "Studying and Treating the Addict in and out of a City Hospital," 4/28/63, AOA papers, box 1, folder: 1963, p. 3.

49. Paul Good, "What Did I Do Wrong?" *Today's Health*, August 1973, p. 41.

50. Freedman, "Studying and Treating the Addict in and out of a City Hospital," p. 16.

51. See Musto, *The American Disease*, for more on nineteenth-century attitudes toward narcotics use.

52. See Caroline Jean Acker, *Creating the America Junkie* (Baltimore: Johns Hopkins Press, 2002), p. 141.

53. Elizabeth Rosenthal, "Addiction: Is It a Disease?" *Science Digest*, August 1983, p. 76.

54. Paul Verden and Daniel Shatterly, "Alcoholism Research and Resistance to Understanding the Compulsive Drinker," *Mental Hygiene* 55:3 (July 1971): 331.

55. Ibid., p. 332.

56. "Firewater Myths," *Science Digest*, April 1976, pp. 21–23.

57. W. Herbert, "Alcoholics' Odd Blood Suggests Genetic Disease," *Science News*, 124:12 (9/17/83).

58. "Alcoholism: On-the-Job Referrals Mean Early Detection, Treatment," *Science*, 1/26/73, p. 363.

59. Quoted in William McIlwain, "A Farewell to Alcohol," *Atlantic*, January 1972, pp. 32–33.

60. *Rehabilitation in Drug Addiction*, p. 13.

61. Ibid., p. 11.

62. Thorman, "A New Dope Peril?" p. 448.

63. Jerome Ellison, "These Drug Addicts Cure One Another," *Saturday Evening Post*, 8/7/54, p. 22.

64. Nyswander, *The Drug Addict as a Patient*, p. 129.

65. "Latest Turn in Treatment of Drug Addicts," *U.S. News & World Report*, 9/11/72, p. 77.

66. "The House on 92nd Street," *Newsweek*, 11/22/71, p. 115.

67. Proctor, "Addiction, The Counter-Culture," p. 626.

68. Ibid.

69. Ibid.

70. Ronald Moscowitz, "Leaving the Drug World Behind," *Education Digest*, May 1970, p. 6.

71. Cook, "What Did I Do Wrong?" p. 42.

72. Quoted in Paul Martin, "Is God at Gateway House?" *Christian Century*, 9/20/72, p. 934.

73. As quoted in David Musto and Pamela Korsmeyer, *The Quest for Drug Control* (New Haven: Yale, 2002), p. 85.

74. Edward Bunker, "A Junkie View of the Quagmire," *Nation*, 6/25/77, p. 788.

75. Quoted in "To Save Our Cities," *Newsweek*, 4/10/72, p. 96.

CHAPTER 9 • PSYCHOANALYSIS IN DECLINE

1. Nathan Hale, *Rise and Crisis of Psychoanalysis in the United States* (New York: Oxford, 1995), p. 302.

2. Hans Strupp (in discussion with Roy Grinker, Sr.), "Some Critical Comments on the Future of Psychoanalytic Therapy," in Marvin Goldfried, ed., *Converging Themes in Psychotherapy* (New York: Springer, 1982), p. 106.

3. Quoted in David Gelman, "Where Are the Patients?" *Newsweek*, 6/27/88, p. 62.

4. Hale, *Rise and Crisis of Psychoanalysis in the United States,* p. 303.

5. T. M. Luhrmann, *Of Two Minds* (New York: Knopf, 2000), p. 186.

6. Ibid., p. 183.

7. Gelman, "Where Are the Patients?" p. 62.

8. Hans Eysenck, *The Future of Psychiatry* (London: Methuen, 1975), p. 18.

9. Figures from Luhrmann, *Of Two Minds,* p. 185.

10. See Martin Gross, *The Psychological Society* (New York: Random House, 1978), p. 200.

11. Ibid., p. 201.

12. Ibid., pp. 201–2.

13. Four studies with similar outcomes were Denker (1947); Endicott and Endicott (1963); Wallace and Whyte (1959); and Giel, Knox, and Carstairs (1964); all cited in Eysenck, *The Future of Psychiatry,* p. 9.

14. G. L. Engel, "Some Obstacles to the Development of Research in Psychoanalysis," *Journal of the American Psychoanalytic Association* 16 (1968): 195–204.

15. Eysenck, *The Future of Psychiatry,* p. 9.

16. Ibid.

17. Gross, *The Psychological Society,* p. 218.

18. Ibid., p. 221. On breastfeeding, see William H. Sewell and Paul H. Mussen, "The Effects of Feeding, Weaning, and Scheduling Procedures on Childhood Adjustment and the Formation of Oral Symptoms," *Child Development* 23:3 (September 1952): 185–91.

19. Tom McGlashan, *Schizophrenia: Treatment and Outcome* (Washington, D.C.: American Psychiatric Association Press, 1989), as cited in Joel Paris, *The Fall of an Icon* (Toronto: University of Toronto Press, 2005), p. 30.

20. Philip May, *The Treatment of Schizophrenia* (New York: Science House, 1968), as cited in ibid., p. 32.

21. Lee Birk and Ann Brinkley-Birk, "Psychoanalysis and Behavior Therapy," *American Journal of Psychiatry* 131:5 (May 1974): 503.

22. Joseph Adelson, "Not Much Has Changed Since Freud," *New York Times,* 9/27/81.

23. "The Head Man," *Washington Post Magazine,* 8/7/83.

24. Blaine Harden, "The Analyst," *Washington Post Magazine,* 11/22/81.

25. Gross, *The Psychological Society,* p. 203.

26. Quoted in ibid., p. 204.

27. Gerald Klerman, "The Psychiatric Patient's Right to Effective Treatment: Implications of *Osheroff v. Chestnut Lodge,*" *American Journal of Psychiatry* 147:4 (April 1990): 412.

28. Ibid., p. 415.

29. Klerman's analysis drew critique, notably Alan Stone, "Law, Science, and Psychiatric Malpractice: A Response to Klerman's Indictment of Psychoanalytic Psychiatry," *American Journal of Psychiatry* 147:4 (April 1990). Stone argued that psychiatrists, like all physicians, rely to a good degree on personal judgment, which may or may not be consistent with outcomes research.

30. Edward Dolnick, *Madness on the Couch* (New York: Simon & Schuster, 1998), p. 152.

31. May published his work in *Treatment of Schizophrenia: A Comparative Study of Five Treatment Methods* (1969), nicely summarized in ibid., p. 161.

32. Aaron Beck and Steven Hollon, "Psychotherapy and Drug Therapy: Comparison and Combinations," in Sol Garfield and Allen Bergin, eds., *Handbook of Psychotherapy and Behavior Change,* 2nd ed. (New York: Wiley, 1978), pp. 445–60.

33. A. J. Rush, A. T. Beck, M. Kovacs, and S. D. Hollon, "Comparative Efficacy of Cognitive Therapy and Pharmacotherapy in the Treatment of Depressed Outpatients," *Cognitive Therapy and Research* 1 (1977).

34. Gerald Klerman, Alberto DiMascio et al., "Treatment of Depression by Drugs and Psychotherapy," *American Journal of Psychiatry* 131:2 (February 1974): 188.

35. Solomon Goldberg, Nina Schooler et al., "Prediction of Relapse in Schizophrenic Outpatients Treated by Drug and Sociotherapy," *Archives of General Psychiatry* 34 (February 1977).

36. Leslie Iversen, "Dopamine Receptors in the Brain," *Science,* 6/13/75; P. Seeman and T. Lee, "Antipsychotic Drugs: Direct Correlation Between Clinical Potency and Presynaptic Action on Dopamine Neurons," *Science,* 6/20/75; Sheldon Preskorn, George Irwin, et al., "Medical Therapies for Mood Disorders Alter the Blood–Brain Barrier," *Science,* 7/24/81.

37. Sandy Rovner, "New Light on Depression," *Washington Post,* 5/21/82.

38. See Vernon Mark, "A Psychosurgeon's Case for Psychosurgery," *Psychology Today,* July 1974, p. 29.

39. A synopsis of the development of Beck's thought can be found in Keith Dobson and David Dozois, "Historical and Philosophical Bases of the Cognitive-Behavioral Therapies," in Keith Dobson, ed., *Handbook of Cognitive-Behavioral Therapies,* 2nd ed. (New York: Guilford, 2001), chapter 1.

40. See Aaron Beck, *Cognitive Therapy and the Emotional Disorders* (New York: International Universities Press, 1976), pp. 92–94.

41. Ibid., p. 99.

42. Aaron Beck, *Depression: Clinical, Experimental, and Theoretical Aspects* (New York: Hoeber/Harper and Row, 1967), p. 3.

43. Aaron Beck, Gary Emery, and Ruth Greenberg, *Anxiety Disorders and Phobias* (New York: Basic Books, 1985), p. 171.

44. See, for example, Aaron Beck and Maria Kovacs, "A New, Fast Therapy for Depression," *Psychology Today,* January 1977, pp. 94–102; also Augustus Rush, Aaron Beck, Maria Kovacs, and Steven Hollon, "Comparative Efficacy of Cognitive Therapy and Pharmacotherapy in the Treatment of Depressed Outpatients," *Cognitive Therapy and Research* 1:1 (1977): 17–37. Also, "Kind Ears Help Some Depressed Patients," *Science News,* 12/2/89.

45. See, for example, R. Christopher Miller and Jeffrey Berman, "The Efficacy of Cognitive Behavior Therapies: A Quantitative Review of the Research Evidence," *Psychological Bulletin* 94:1 (1983): 39–53.

46. Keith Dobson, "A Meta-Analysis of the Efficacy of Cognitive Therapy for Depression," *Journal of Consulting and Clinical Psychology* 37:3 (1989): 414–19.

47. Darrell Smith, "Trends in Counseling and Psychotherapy," *American Psychologist* 37:7 (July 1982): 804.

48. See, for example, Gerald Koocher and Barbara Pedulla, "Current Practices in Child Psychotherapy," *Professional Psychology,* August 1977, p. 280.

49. John Norcross and Michael Wogan, "American Psychotherapists of Diverse Persuasions," *Professional Psychology: Research and Practice* 14:4 (1983): 531.

50. David Gelman and Mary Hager, "Psychotherapy in the '80s," *Newsweek,* 11/30/81, p. 70.

51. James Mann, *Time-Limited Psychotherapy* (Cambridge: Harvard University Press, 1973), p. x.

52. See Rudolph Wittenberg, "Short-Term Therapy," AOA papers, box 2, folder: 1965, January 1965.

53. Daniel Goleman, "Deadline for Change: Therapy in the Age of Reaganomics," *Psychology Today,* August 1981, p. 68.

54. Erica Goode, "Therapy for the '90s," *Science and Society,* 1/13/92, p. 55.

55. Dava Sobel, "A New and Controversial Short-Term Psychotherapy," *New York Times,* 11/21/82.

56. Emily Yoffe, "Dial P for Psychotherapy," *Newsweek,* 11/19/90, p. 72.

57. Allen Bergin, "The Evaluation of Therapeutic Outcomes," in Allen Bergin and Sol Garfield, eds., *Handbook of Psychotherapy and Behavior Change* (New York: Wiley, 1986), p. 241.

58. Bruce Bower, "Psychotherapy on Trial: Mixing Art with Science," *Science News,* 7/14/84, p. 29.

59. Lester Luborsky, Paul Crits-Christoph et al., "Do Therapists Vary Much in Their Success?" *American Journal of Orthopsychiatry* 56:4 (October 1986): 501–12.

60. See Philip Hilts, "Psychotherapy Put on Couch by Government," *Washington Post,* 9/14/80, p. A1.

61. George Albee, "Psychiatry's Human Resources: 20 Years Later," *Hospital and Community Psychiatry,* 30:11 (November 1979): 784.

62. Frederick Sierles and Michael Alan Taylor, "Decline of U.S. Medical Student Career Choice of Psychiatry and What to Do About It," *American Journal of Psychiatry* 152:10 (October 1995): 1420.

63. Ibid., p. 1421.

64. Albee, "Psychiatry's Human Resources," p. 785.

65. "Psychologists Get Direct Pay Ruling," *Science News,* 3/7/81, p. 10.

66. Patrick DeLeon, Raymond Folen et al., "The Case for Prescription Privileges," *Journal of Clinical Child Psychology* 20:3 (1991): 254.

67. Eliot Marshall, "Blue Shield as a Medical Cartel," *Science,* March 1981, p. 1402.

68. DeLeon and Folen, "The Case for Prescription Privileges," p. 264.

69. George Albee, "A Declaration of Independence for Psychology," *Ohio Psychologist,* June 1964, reprinted in Bernard Lubin and Eugene Levitt, eds., *The Clinical Psychologist* (Chicago: Aldine, 1961), p. 136.

70. Donald Peterson, "Twenty Years of Practitioner Training in Psychology," *American Psychologist,* 40:4 (April 1985): 441–51.

71. Quoted in John Norcross and James Prochaska, "A National Survey of Clinical Psychologists: Views on Training, Career Choice, and APA," *Clinical Psychologist* 35:4 (Summer 1982): 3.

72. Arnold Levin, "Is There a Role for Clinical Doctoral Education? Yes!" *Journal of Social Work Education,* 27:3 (Fall 1991).

73. See Ingeborg Oppenheimer, "When a Social Worker Turns Psychotherapist," *New York Times,* 12/8/81, p. A30.

CHAPTER 10 • BIOLOGY

1. David Gelman and Mary Hager, "Drugs vs. the Couch," *Newsweek,* 3/26/90, p. 42.

2. Quoted in Max Fink, *Electroshock* (New York: Oxford University Press, 1999), p. 4.

3. See Tanya Luhrmann, *Of Two Minds* (New York: Knopf, 2000), pp. 166–67.

4. See Gwen Broude, "Freudian Quack-up," *Weekly Standard,* 4/15/96, p. 12.

5. Laura Elliott, "Help for Your Head," *Washingtonian Magazine,* April 1998, p. 76.

6. Luhrmann, *Of Two Minds,* p. 101.

7. Quoted in Elliott, "Help for Your Head," p. 76.

8. See Geoffrey Cowley, Karen Springen et al., "The Promise of Prozac," *Newsweek,* 3/26/90, p. 38.

9. Ibid.

10. Interview with Jonathan Cole published in David Healy, *The Psychopharmacologists* (London: Chapman and Hall, 1996), p. 258.

11. Peter Kramer, *Listening to Prozac* (New York: Viking, 1993), p. x.

12. Ibid., p. xv.

13. Ibid., p. 320.

14. Quoted in Ashley Pettus, "Psychiatry by Prescription," *Harvard Magazine,* July–August 2006, p. 44.

15. Quoted in ibid., p. 38.

16. David Gelman, Jeanne Gordon et al., "Growing Pains for Shrinks," *Newsweek,* 12/14/87, p. 70.

17. Robert Wallerstein, "The Future of Psychotherapy," *Bulletin of the Menninger Clinic,* 55:4 (Fall 1991).

18. Stanley Lesse, "Psychiatrists! Don't Look Behind You! Someone May Be Catching Up!" *American Journal of Psychotherapy*, 44:4 (October 1990): 467.

19. Ibid.

20. Robyn Dawes, *House of Cards: Psychology and Psychotherapy Built on Myth* (New York: Free Press, 1994), pp. 16–17.

21. Ibid., p. 149.

22. See Wallerstein, "The Future of Psychotherapy."

23. Elliott, "Help for Your Head," p. 76.

24. "Psychotherapy Under the Knife," *U.S. News & World Report* 4/24/93, p. 64.

25. Melinda Beck and Debra Rosenberg, "Managing the Mind," *Newsweek,* 6/6/94, p. 30.

26. See Mark Schlesinger, Matt Wynia, and Deborah Cummins, "Some Distinctive Features of the Impact of Managed Care on Psychiatry," *Harvard Review of Psychiatry* 8:5 (November 2000): 216–30.

27. "Mental Health: Does Therapy Help?" *Consumer Reports,* November 1995, p. 734.

28. Ibid.

29. Quoted in Erica Goode and Betsy Wagner, "Does Psychotherapy Work?" *U.S. News & World Report,* 5/24/93, p. 56.

30. Joseph Hyland, "Integrating Psychotherapy and Pharmacotherapy," *Bulletin of the Menninger Clinic* 55:2 (Spring 1991).

Afterword

1. Jerome Frank, "Therapeutic Components of Psychotherapy," *Journal of Nervous and Mental Disease* 159:5 (1974): 338.

2. David Shapiro, "Mental Health Professionals' Hang-ups in Training Mental Health Counselors," *Mental Hygiene* 54:3 (July 1970): 365.

3. William Stiles, David Shapiro, and Robert Elliot, "Are All Psychotherapies Equivalent?" *American Psychologist,* February 1986, pp. 165–90.

4. John Reisman, "The Definition of Psychotherapy," *Mental Hygiene* 55:3 (July 1971): 415.

5. Howard Gardner, "Peering Over the Therapist's Shoulder," *New York Times,* 10/5/80.

6. David Hendin, "How to Pick a Psychoanalyst," *Science Digest,* January 1974, p. 14.

7. John Elson, "Is Freud Finished?" *Time,* 7/6/92.

8. George Vaillant, "Alcoholics Anonymous: Cure or Cult?" *Australian and New Zealand Journal of Psychiatry* 39 (2005): 431–36.

9. "Viktor Frankl," *The Economist,* 9/20/97.

10. Jonathan Kellerman, "Bedlam Revisited," *New York Times,* 4/23/07, p. A17.

Bibliography

BOOKS

Agras, W. S., A. E. Kazdin, and G. T. Wilson. *Behavior Therapy: Towards an Applied Clinical Science.* San Francisco: Freeman, 1979.

Aichorn, A. *Wayward Youth.* New York: Viking, 1925.

Albee, G. W., L. A. Bond, and T. Monsey, eds. *Improving Children's Lives: Global Perspectives on Prevention.* Newbury Park, CA: Sage, 1992.

Alexander, Franz. *The Medical Value of Psychoanalysis.* New York: Norton, 1932.

———. *Psychoanalysis and Psychotherapy.* New York: Norton, 1956.

Alexander, Franz, and T. French. *Psychoanalytic Therapy: Principles and Applications.* New York: Ronald Press, 1946.

Alexander, Franz and Sheldon Selesnick. *The History of Psychiatry: An Evaluation of Psychiatric Thought and Practice from Prehistoric Times to the Present.* New York: Harper and Row, 1966.

Allen, F. *Psychotherapy with Children.* New York: Norton, 1942.

Applebaum, S. A. *The Anatomy of Change: A Menninger Foundation Report on Testing the Effects of Psychotherapy.* New York: Plenum, 1977.

Arkowitz, H., and S. B. Messer, eds. *Psychoanalytic Therapy and Behavior Therapy: Is Integration Possible?* New York: Plenum, 1984.

Avnet, Helen. *Psychiatric Insurance: Financing Short-Term Ambulatory Treatment.* New York: Group Health Insurance, 1962.

Bandara, A. *Behavioristic Psychotherapy.* New York: Holt, Rinehart and Winston, 1963.

Beam, A. *Gracefully Insane: The Rise and Fall of America's Premier Mental Hospital.* New York: Public Affairs, 2001.

Beck, Aaron. *Cognitive Therapy and the Emotional Disorders.* 2nd edition. New York: Basic, 1986.

————. *Depression: Clinical, Experimental, and Theoretical Aspects.* New York: Hoeber, 1967.

Beck, A. T., and G. Emery. *Anxiety Disorders and Phobias: A Cognitive Perspective.* New York: Basic Books, 1985.

Beck, A. T., and A. Freeman. *Cognitive Therapy of Personality Disorders.* New York: Guilford, 1990.

Beck, Aaron, A. J. Rush et al. *Cognitive Therapy of Depression.* New York: Guilford, 1979.

Bergin, Allen. *Handbook of Psychotherapy and Behavior Change.* New York: Wiley, 1971.

Bergin, A. E., and H. H. Strupp. *Changing Frontiers in the Science of Psychotherapy.* Chicago: Aldine-Atherton, 1972.

Bion, W. R. *Experiences in Groups.* New York: Basic Books, 1961.

Boars, B. *The Cognitive Revolution in Psychology.* New York: Guilford, 1986.

Breggin, Peter. *Toxic Psychiatry.* New York: St. Martin's Press, 1991.

————. *The War Against Children.* New York: St. Martin's Press, 1999.

Breslow, Joel. *Mental Ills and Bodily Cures: Psychiatric Treatment in the First Half of the Twentieth Century.* Berkeley: University of California Press, 1997.

Brill, Leon. *Rehabilitation of Drug Addiction.* Washington, D.C.: GPO, 1963.

Bromberg, W. *The Mind of Man: The History of Psychotherapy and Psychoanalysis.* New York: Harper and Brothers, 1959.

Budman, S. H., ed. *Forms of Brief Therapy.* New York: Guilford, 1981.

Bugental, J., ed. *Challenges of Humanistic Psychology.* New York: McGraw-Hill, 1967.

Buhler, C., and M. Allen. *Introduction to Humanistic Psychology.* Monterey, CA: Brooks/Cole, 1972.

Burnham, John. *Psychoanalysis and American Medicine, 1894–1918.* New York: International Universities Press, 1967.

Burnham, W. H. *The Normal Mind.* New York: Appleton, 1924.

Burrow, Trigant. *A Search for Man's Sanity.* New York: Oxford University Press, 1958.

Burton, A. ed. *Psychotherapy of the Psychoses.* New York: Basic, 1961.

Bychowski, G. *Psychotherapy of Psychosis.* New York: Grune & Stratton, 1952.

Coppolillo, H. P. *Psychodynamic Psychotherapy with Children.* Madison, CT: International Universities Press, 1987.

Corsini, R. J. *Methods of Group Psychotherapy.* New York: McGraw-Hill, 1957.

Crossman, R. H., and D. Engerman, eds. *The God That Failed.* New York: Columbia University Press, 1955.

Davanloo, H. *Short-Term Dynamic Psychotherapy.* Vol. 1. New York: Jason Aronson, 1980.

Dawes, R. M. *House of Cards: Psychology and Psychotherapy Built on Myth.* New York: Free Press, 1994.

Dollard, J., and N. E. Miller. *Personality and Psychotherapy.* New York: McGraw-Hill, 1950.

Dolnick, E. *Madness on the Couch.* New York: Simon & Schuster, 1998.

Dunlap, K. *Habits: Their Making and Unmaking.* New York: Liveright, 1932.

Dyer, R. *Her Father's Daughter: The Work of Anna Freud.* New York: Jason Aronson, 1983.

Eagle, M. *Recent Developments in Psychoanalysis: A Critical Evaluation.* Cambridge, MA: Harvard University Press, 1987.

Ehrenwald, Jan. *From Medicine Man to Freud: A History of Psychotherapy.* New York: Dell, 1957.

Ellenberger, Henri. *The Discovery of the Unconscious.* New York: Basic Books, 1970.

Ellis, A., and R. A. Harper. *A Guide to Rational Living.* Englewood Cliffs, NJ: Prentice-Hall, 1961.

———. *A New Guide to Rational Living.* North Hollywood, CA: Wilshire, 1975.

Erwin, E. *Behavior Therapy: Scientific, Philosophical, and Moral Foundations.* New York: Cambridge University Press, 1978.

Eysenck, Hans Jurgen. *Behavior Therapy and the Neuroses.* London: Pergamon, 1960.

———. *Biological Basis of Personality.* Springfield, IL: Thomas, 1967.

———. *Effects of Psychotherapy.* New York: International Science Press, 1966.

———. *The Future of Psychiatry.* London: Methuen, 1975.

———. *Rebel with a Cause.* London: W. H. Allen, 1990.

Fagan, J., and I. L. Shepherd, eds. *Gestalt Therapy Now.* Palo Alto, CA: Science and Behavior Books, 1970.

Fairweather, G. W., ed. *Community Life for the Mentally Ill: An Alternative to Institutional Care.* Chicago: Aldine, 1969.

Fein, Rashi. *The Economics of Mental Illness.* New York: Basic Books, 1958.

Fenichel, O. *Ten Years of the Berlin Psychoanalytic Institute: 1920–1930.* Berlin: Berlin Psychoanalytic Institute, 1930.

Fensterheim, H., and J. Baer. *Don't Say Yes When You Want to Say No.* New York: Dell, 1975.

Fermi, L. *Illustrious Immigrants: The Intellectual Migration from Europe, 1930–1941.* Chicago: University of Chicago Press, 1971.

Fernando, S. *Mental Health, Race, and Culture.* New York: Palgrave, 2002.

———. *Race and Culture in Psychiatry.* London: Croom Helm, 1988.

Fine, R. *A History of Psychoanalysis.* New York: Columbia University Press, 1979.

Finger, Stanley. *Origins of Neuroscience.* New York: Oxford, 1993.

Fink, M. *Electroshock: Restoring the Mind.* New York: Oxford, 1999.

Foa, E. B., and P. M. G. Emmelkamp. *Failures in Behavior Therapy.* New York: Wiley, 1983.

Frank, J. D. *Persuasion and Healing: A Comparative Study of Psychotherapy.* Baltimore: Johns Hopkins, 1973.

Freud, Anna, and D. Burlingham. *Infants Without Families.* London: Allen and Unwin, 1944.

———. *War and Children.* New York: Medical War Books, 1943.

Freud, Sigmund. *Analysis Terminable and Interminable.* London: Hogarth, 1937.

———. *Analytic Therapy.* London: Hogarth Press, 1916.

———. *The Problem of Lay Analysis.* New York: Brentano's, 1927.

———. *The Question of Lay Analysis.* London: Hogarth Press, 1926.

Friedman, Lawrence. *Menninger: The Family and the Clinic.* New York: Knopf, 1990.

Fromm-Reichmann, F. *Principles of Intensive Psychotherapy.* Chicago: University of Chicago Press, 1950.

Fuller, R. *Mesmerism and the American Cure of Souls.* Philadelphia: University of Pennsylania Press, 1982.

Garfield, S. L., and A. E. Bergin, eds. *Handbook of Psychotherapy and Behavior Change.* New York: Wiley, 1978.

Gellner, Ernest. *The Psychoanalytic Movement, or the Cunning of Unreason.* London: Paladin, 1985.

Giorgi, A. *Psychology as a Human Science.* New York: Harper and Row, 1970.

Goldfried, M. R. *Converging Themes in Psychotherapy: Trends in Psychodynamic, Humanistic, and Behavioral Practice.* New York: Springer, 1982.

Goldstein, A. P. *Therapist-Patient Expectancies in Psychotherapy.* New York: Macmillan, 1962.

Goldstein, K. *The Organism: A Holistic Approach Derived from Pathological Data in Man.* New York: American Book, 1939.

Greenson, R. R. *The Technique and Practice of Psychoanalysis.* Vol. 1. New York: International Universities Press, 1967.

Grob, Gerald. *From Asylum to Community.* Princeton: Princeton University Press, 1991.

Gross, M. L. *The Psychological Society: A Critical Analysis of Psychiatry, Psychotherapy, Psychoanalysis, and the Psychological Revolution.* New York: Random House, 1978.

Gurin, G., J. Veroff, and S. Feld. *Americans View Their Mental Health.* New York: Basic Books, 1960.

Guze, S. *Why Psychiatry Is a Branch of Medicine.* New York: Oxford, 1992.

Hale, N. *Freud and the Americans.* New York: Oxford, 1971.

———. *The Rise and Crisis of Psychoanalysis.* New York: Oxford, 1995

Healy, D. *The Psychopharmacologists.* New York: Chapman and Hall, 1996.

———. *The Psychopharmacologists III.* London: Arnold, 2000.

Harlow, H., and C. F. Woolsley. *Biological and Biochemical Bases of Behavior.* Madison: University of Wisconsin, 1958.

Healy, D. *The Creation of Psychopharmacology*. Cambridge: Harvard, 2002.

Hill, David. *The Politics of Schizophrenia: Psychiatric Oppression in the United States.* Lanham, MD: University Press of America, 1983.

Hollingshead, A., and F. Redlich. *Social Class and Mental Illness.* New York: Wiley, 1950.

Holt, R. R., and L. Luborsky. *Personality Patterns of Psychiatrists.* New York: Basic Books, 1958.

Homans, G. C. *The Human Group.* New York: Harcourt, Brace, and World, 1950.

Horney, Karen. *Neurotic Personality of Our Time.* New York: Norton, 1937.

———. *Self-Analysis.* New York: Norton, 1942.

Horowitz, M. J. *Introduction to Psychodynamics.* New York: Basic Books, 1988.

Jackson, D., ed. *The Etiology of Schizophrenia.* New York: Basic Books, 1960.

Jacobson, E. *Progressive Relaxation.* Chicago: University of Chicago Press, 1929.

Johnson-Laird, P. N. *The Computer and the Mind: An Introduction to Cognitive Science.* Cambridge: Harvard, 1988.

Joint Commission on Mental Health. *Action for Mental Health.* New York: Basic Books, 1961.

Jones, M. *The Therapeutic Community: A New Treatment Method in Psychiatry.* New York: Basic Books, 1953.

Kamin, L. *The Science and Politics of IQ.* Potomac, MD: Erlbaum, 1974.

Kazdin, A. E. *Child Psychotherapy: Developing and Identifying Effective Treatments.* New York: Pergamon, 1988.

———. *History of Behavior Modification: Experimental Foundations of Contemporary Research.* Baltimore: University Park Press, 1978.

Kernberg, O. F., M. A. Selzer et al. *Psychodynamic Psychotherapy of Borderline Patients.* New York: Basic, 1989.

Kirsner, D. *Unfree Associations: Inside Psychoanalytic Institutes.* London: Process Press, 2000.

Klein, M. *The Psychoanalysis of Children.* New York: Delacorte, 1932.

Klerman, G. L., B. Rounsaville et al. *Interpersonal Psychotherapy of Depression.* New York: Basic, 1984.

Koffka, K. *Principles of Gestalt Psychology.* New York: Harcourt, Brace, 1935.

Kohut, H. *How Does Analysis Cure?* Chicago: University of Chicago Press, 1984.

————. *The Restoration of Self.* New York: International Universities Press, 1977.

Korman, M., ed. *Levels and Patterns of Professional Training in Psychology: Conference Proceedings, Vail, Colorado.* Washington, D.C.: American Psychological Association, 1976.

Kramer, P. *Listening to Prozac.* New York: Viking, 1993.

Kubie, L. S. *The Riggs Story: The Development of the Austen Riggs Center for the Study and Treatment of the Neuroses.* New York: Paul Hoeber, 1960.

————. *Symbol and Neurosis.* New York: International Universities Press, 1978.

Kupers, T. A. *Public Therapy: The Practice of Psychotherapy in the Public Mental Health Clinic.* New York: Free Press, 1981.

Langs, R. *The Psychotherapeutic Conspiracy.* New York: Jason Aronson, 1982.

————. *The Technique of Psychoanalytic Psychotherapy.* New York: Jason Aronson, 1973.

Lasch, Christopher. *The Culture of Narcissism.* New York: Norton, 1979.

————. *Haven in a Heartless World: The Family Besieged.* New York: Basic Books, 1977.

Leahey, T. *A History of Psychology: Main Currents in Psychological Thought.* Englewood Cliffs, NJ: Prentice Hall, 1987.

LeDoux, J. E. *Synaptic Self: How Our Brains Become Who We Are.* New York: Viking, 2002.

Levant, R. F., and J. M. Shlien. *Client-Centered Therapy and the Person-Centered Approach.* New York: Praeger, 1984.

Levine, Murray. *Helping Children: A Social History.* New York: Oxford, 1992.

————. *The History and Politics of Community Mental Health.* New York: Oxford, 1981.

Levine, Murray, and A. Levine. *A Social History of Helping Services.* New York: Appleton-Century-Crofts, 1970.

Lewinsohn, P. M., R. Munoz et al. *Control Your Depression.* Englewood Cliffs, NJ: Prentice Hall, 1986.

Lewis, Nolan. *Research in Dementia Praecox.* New York: NCMH, 1936.

————. *A Short History of Psychiatric Achievements.* New York: Norton, 1941.

Lietaer, G., J. Rombaurs, and R. Van Balen. *Client-Centered and Experiential Psychotherapy in the Nineties.* Leuven, Belgium: Leuven University Press, 1990.

Linehan, M. M. *Cognitive-Behavioral Treatment of Borderline Personality Disorder.* New York: Guilford, 1993.

Lowrey, L. G., and G. Smith. *The Institute for Child Guidance: 1927–1933.* New York: Commonwealth Fund, 1933.

Luborsky, L. *Principles of Psychoanalytic Psychotherapy: A Manual for Supportive-Expressive Treatment.* New York: Basic Books, 1984.

Luborsky, L., P. Crits-Christoph et al. *Who Will Benefit from Psychotherapy? Predicting Therapeutic Outcomes.* New York: Basic Books, 1988.

Luepnitz, D. *The Family Interpreted: Feminist Theory in Clinical Practice.* New York: Basic Books, 1988.

Luhrmann, T. M. *Of Two Minds: The Growing Disorder in American Psychiatry.* New York: Knopf, 2000.

Mace, C., S. Moorey, and B. Roberts. *Evidence in the Psychological Therapies: A Critical Guide for Practitioners.* London: Brunner-Routledge, 2001.

Macmillan, M. *Freud Evaluated.* Cambridge: MIT Press, 1997.

Mahoney, M. J. *Cognition and Behavior Modification.* Cambridge, MA: Ballinger, 1974.

Malan, D. H. *The Frontier of Brief Psychotherapy.* New York: Plenum, 1976.

Malcolm, J. *Psychoanalysis: The Impossible Profession.* New York: Vintage, 1982.

Mann, J. *Time-Limited Psychotherapy.* Cambridge, MA: Harvard, 1973.

Marmor, J. *Psychiatrists and Their Patients: A National Study of Private Office Practice.* Washington D.C.: Joint Information Service of the American Psychiatric Association and the National Association for Mental Health, 1975.

Masserman, J. H., ed. *Dynamic Psychiatry.* Philadelphia: W. B. Saunders, 1955.

———, ed. *Science and Psychoanalysis.* Vol. 7. New York: Grune & Stratton, 1964.

McGrath, William. *Freud's Discovery of Psychoanalysis: The Politics of Hysteria.* Ithaca: Cornell University Press, 1986.

Meichenbaum, D. H. *Cognitive-Behavior Modification.* New York: Plenum, 1977.

Meltzoff, J., and M. Kornreich. *Research in Psychotherapy.* New York: Atherton Press, 1970.

Menninger, R. W., and J. C. Nemiah. *American Psychiatry After World War II.* Washington: American Psychiatric Press, 2000.

Minuchin, S. *Families and Family Therapy.* Cambridge, MA: Harvard, 1974.

Moreno, J. L. *The First Book of Group Psychotherapy.* New York: Beacon House, 1957.

Mullan, H., and M. Rosenbaum. *Group Psychotherapy.* New York: Free Press, 1962.

Muncie, W. S. *Psychology and Psychiatry* St. Louis: Mosby, 1939.

Murphy, G. *Historical Introduction to Modern Psychology.* New York: Harcourt, Brace, 1949.

Nyswander, M. *The Drug Addict as a Patient.* New York: Grune & Stratton, 1956.

O'Connell, A. N., and N. F. Russo, eds. *Models of Achievement: Reflections of Eminent Women in Psychology.* New York: Columbia University Press, 1983.

Ofshe, R., and E. Watters. *Making Monsters: False Memories, Psychotherapy, and Sexual Hysteria.* New York: Scribner, 1994.

Orlinsky, D. E., and K. I. Howard. *Varieties of Psychotherapeutic Experience.* New York: Teachers College Press, 1975.

Ornsteink, P., ed. *The Season for the Self: Selected Writings of Heinz Kohut 1950–1978.* New York: International Universities Press, 1978.

Paris, Joel. *The Fall of an Icon: Psychoanalysis and Academic Psychiatry.* Toronto: University of Toronto Press, 2005.

Parrish, J., and M. Lieberman. *Toward a Model Plan for a Comprehensive Community-Based Mental Health System.* Rockville, MD: NIMH, 1977.

Perls, F. *Ego, Hunger, and Aggression: The Beginnings of Gestalt Therapy.* New York: Random House, 1969.

———. *Gestalt Approach and Eyewitness to Therapy.* New York: Science and Behavior Books, 1973.

———. *Gestalt Therapy Verbatim.* Moab, UT: Real People Press, 1969.

Perls, F., R. F. Hefferline, and P. Goodman. *Gestalt Therapy.* New York: Julian Press, 1951.

Perry, H. *Psychiatrist of America: The Life of Harry Stack Sullivan.* Cambridge, MA: Belknap Press, 1982.

Persons, J. B. *Cognitive Therapy in Practice: A Case Formulation Aproach.* New York: Norton, 1989.

Peterfreund, E. *The Process of Psychoanalytic Therapy.* Hillsdale, NJ: Analytic Press, 1983.

President's Commission on Mental Health. *Report to the President.* Washington D.C.: GPO, 1978.

Pressman, Jack. *Last Resort: Psychosurgery and the Limits of Medicine.* New York: Cambridge University Press, 1998.

Raimy, V. *Training in Clinical Psychology.* Englewood Cliffs, NJ: Prentice-Hall, 1950.

Reed, Louis, E. S. Myers, and Patricia Scheidemandel. *Health Insurance and Psychiatric Care.* Washington, D.C.: Brookings, 1972.

Reisman, J. M. *The Development of Clinical Psychology.* New York: Appleton-Century-Crofts, 1966.

———. *A History of Clinical Psychology.* New York: Irvington, 1976.

Resnick, C., C. Ashton, and C. Palley, eds. *The Health Care System and Drug Abuse Prevention.* Washington, D.C.: NIDA, 1981.

Richards, Barry. *Images of Freud: Cultural Responses to Psychoanalysis.* New York: St. Martin's Press, 1989.

Riess, B. F., ed. *New Directions in Mental Health.* New York: Grune & Stratton, 1968.

———. *Progress in Clinical Psychology.* New York: Grune & Stratton, 1964.

Robach, H., S. Abramowitz, and D. Strassberg. *Group Psychotherapy Research.* New York: Robert Krieger, 1979.

Rogers, C. *Client-Centered Therapy: Its Current Practice, Implications, and Theory.* Boston: Houghton Mifflin, 1951.

———. *The Clinical Treatment of the Problem Child.* Boston: Houghton Mifflin, 1942.

———. *Counseling and Psychotherapy: Newer Concepts in Practice.* Boston: Houghton Mifflin, 1942.

———. *On Becoming a Person.* Boston: Houghton Mifflin, 1961.

———. *On Encounter Groups.* New York: Harper and Row, 1973.

Rogers, C. R., and R. F. Dymond, eds. *Psychotherapy and Personality Change.* Chicago: University of Chicago Press, 1954.

Rogers, C. R., G. T. Gendlin et al., eds. *The Therapeutic Relationship and Its Impact: A Study of Schizophrenia.* Madison: University of Wisconsin Press, 1967.

Rosenbaum, M., and M. Berger. *Group Psychotherapy and Group Function.* New York: Basic Books, 1963.

Rothenberg, A. *The Creative Process of Psychotherapy.* New York: Norton, 1988.

Rubenstein, E. A., and M. B. Parloff. *Research in Psychotherapy.* Vol. 1. Washington, D.C.: American Psychological Association, 1959.

Ryan, W., ed. *Distress in the City: Essays on the Design and Administration of Urban Mental Health Services.* Cleveland: Case Western University Press, 1969.

Sackler, Arthur., ed. *The Great Physiodynamic Therapies in Psychiatry.* New York: Hoeber-Harper, 1956.

Safran, J. D., and Z. V. Segal. *Interpersonal Process in Cognitive Therapy.* New York: Basic Books, 1990.

Santostefano, S. *Cognitive Control Therapy with Children and Adolescents.* New York: Pergamon, 1985.

Scheff, Thomas. *Being Mentally Ill: A Sociological Theory.* London: Weidenfield and Nicolson, 1966.

Schlein, J. M. *Research in Psychotherapy.* Vol. III. Washington, D.C.: American Psychological Association, 1968.

Schorske, Carl. *Fin-de-Siècle Vienna: Politics and Culture.* New York: Knopf, 1980.

Schwartz, G. E., and J. Beatty, eds. *Biofeedback: Theory and Research.* New York: Academic Press, 1977.

Segal, H. *Introduction to the Works of Melanie Klein.* New York: Basic Books, 1980.

———. *Melanie Klein.* New York: Viking, 1979.

Shakow, D. *Clinical Psychology as a Science and Profession.* Chicago: Aldine, 1969.

Shorter, E. *A History of Psychiatry.* New York: Wiley, 1998.

Showalter, E. *Hystories.* New York: Columbia University Press, 1996.

Sifneos, P. E. *Short-Term Dynamic Psychotherapy: Evaluation and Technique.* New York: Plenum, 1979.

Singer, M. T. and J. Lalich. *Crazy Therapies: What Are They? Do They Work?* San Francisco: Jossey-Bass, 1996.

Skinner, B. F. *The Behavior of Organisms: An Experimental Analysis.* New York: Appleton-Century-Crofts, 1938.

———. *Beyond Freedom and Dignity.* New York: Knopf, 1972.

———. *Science and Human Behavior* New York: Macmillan, 1953.

———. *Walden Two.* New York: Macmillan, 1948.

Sloane, R. B. *Psychotherapy Versus Behavior Therapy.* Cambridge, MA: Harvard, 1975.

Smith, M. L., G. T. Glass, and T. I. Miller. *The Benefits of Psychotherapy.* Baltimore: Johns Hopkins University Press, 1980.

Spiegler, M. D. *Contemporary Behavioral Therapy.* Palo Alto, CA: Mayfield, 1983.

Stevenson, G., and G. Smith. *Child Guidance Clinics: A Quarter Century of Development.* New York: Commonwealth Fund, 1934.

Strupp, H. H. *Psychotherapists in Action: Explorations of the Therapist's Contribution to the Treatment Process.* New York: Grune & Stratton, 1960.

Strupp, H. H., and J. L. Binder. *Psychotherapy in a New Key.* New York: Basic Books, 1984.

Strupp, H. H., R. E. Fox, and K. Lesser. *Patients View Their Psychotherapy.* Baltimore: Johns Hopkins University Press, 1969.

Strupp, H. H., S. W. Hadley, and B. Gomes-Schwartz. *Psychotherapy for Better or Worse: An Analysis of the Problem of Negative Effects.* New York: Jason Aronson, 1977.

Strupp, H. H., and L. Luborsky, eds. *Research in Psychotherapy.* Vol. 2. Washington, D.C.: American Psychological Association, 1962.

Sullivan, H. S. *The Interpersonal Theory of Psychiatry.* New York: Norton, 1953.

————. *The Psychiatric Interview.* New York: Norton, 1954.

Swazey, Judith. *Chlorpromazine in Psychiatry: A Study of Therapeutic Intervention.* Cambridge, MA: Harvard University Press, 1974.

Szasz, Thomas. *The Myth of Mental Illness: Foundations of a Theory of Personal Conduct.* New York: Hoeber-Harper, 1964.

Thompson, George N., ed. *Alcoholism.* New York: Basic, 1957.

Uhr, L. M., and J. G. Miller, eds. *Drugs and Behavior.* New York: Wiley, 1960.

Ullmann, L. P., and L. Krasner, eds. *Case Studies in Behavior Modification.* New York: Holt, Rinehart and Winston, 1965.

Valenstein, Eliot. *Great and Desperate Cures: The Rise and Decline of Psychosurgery and Other Radical Treatments for Mental Illness.* New York: Basic, 1986.

Vaughan, S. *The Talking Cure: The Science Behind Psychotherapy.* New York: G. P. Putnam's Sons, 1997.

Veroff, J., R. A. Kulka, and E. Douvan. *Mental Health in America: Patterns of Help-Seeking from 1957 to 1976.* New York: Basic Books, 1981.

Wachtel, P. *The Poverty of Affluence: A Psychological Portrait of the American Way of Life.* Philadelphia: New Society, 1989.

————. *Psychoanalysis and Behavior Therapy: Toward an Integration.* New York: Basic Books, 1977.

Waelder, R. *Basic Theory of Psychoanalysis.* New York: International Universities Press, 1960.

Wallerstein, R. S. *Forty-two Lives in Treatment: A Study of Psychoanalysis and Psychotherapy.* New York: Guilford, 1986.

———. *Hospital Treatment of Alcoholism.* New York: Basic Books, 1957.

Wampold, E. *The Great Psychotherapy Debate: Models, Methods, and Findings.* Mahwah, NJ: Erlbaum Associates, 2001.

Waskow, I. E., and M. B. Parloff, eds. *Psychotherapy Change Measures: Report of the Clinical Research Branch Outcome Measures Project.* Washington, D.C.: GPO, 1975.

Webster, S. *Why Freud Was Wrong.* New York: Basic, 1995.

Weiss, J., and H. Sampson. *The Psychoanalytic Process: Theory, Clinical Observations, and Empirical Research.* New York: Guilford, 1986.

Wells, R. A., and V. J. Biannetti, eds. *Handbook of Brief Psychotherapies.* New York: Plenum, 1990.

Whitaker, D. C., and M. A. Lieberman. *Psychotherapy Through the Group Process.* New York: Atherton, 1964.

Wikler, A. *The Relation of Psychiatry to Pharmacology.* Baltimore: Williams & Wilkins, 1957.

Winnicott, D. *The Child, the Family, and the Outside World.* New York: Penguin, 1964.

Wolf, A., and E. K. Schwartz. *Psychoanalysis in Groups.* New York: Grune & Stratton, 1962.

Wolpe, J. *The Practice of Behavior Therapy.* New York: Pergamon, 1973.

———. *Psychotherapy by Reciprocal Inhibition.* Stanford: Stanford University Press, 1958.

Wortis, J., ed. *Recent Advances in Biological Psychiatry.* New York: Grune & Stratton, 1960.

Young-Bruehl, E. *Anna Freud.* New York: Summit Books, 1988.

Zilboorg, Gregory. *History of Medical Psychology.* New York: Norton, 1941.

———. *Mind, Medicine, and Man.* New York: Harcourt, Brace, 1943.

ARTICLES

Adams, D. B. "The Future Roles of Psychotherapy in the Medical-Surgical Arena." *Psychotherapy* 29 (1992).

Albee, G. "Does Including Psychotherapy in Health Insurance Represent a Subsidy to the Rich from the Poor?" *AP* 32 (1977): 719–21.

———. "Psychiatry's Human Resources: 20 Years Later." *Hospital and Community Psychiatry* 30:11 (1979): 783–86.

Alexander, F. "The Dynamics of Psychotherapy in Light of Learning Theory." *AJP* 120 (1963): 440–48.

Allen, F. "Therapeutic Work with Children." *American Journal of Orthopsychiatry* 4 (1934): 193–202.

Altman, I. "Centripetal and Centrifugal Trends in Psychology." *AP* 42 (1987): 1058–69.

American Psychological Association. "Report of the Committee on Clinical Psychology." *Psychological Bulletin* 42 (1945): 724–25.

Anthony, W. A., and A. Blanch. "Research on Community Support Services: What Have We Learned?" *Psychosocial Rehabilitation Journal* 12:3 (1989): 55–82.

APA Committee on Training in Clinical Psychology. "Recommended Graduate Training Program in Clinical Psychology." *AP* (1947): 539–58.

Ash, E. "Issues Faced by the VA Psychology Training Program in Its Early Development." *Clinical Psychologist* 21 (1968): 121–23.

———. "The Veterans Administration Psychology Training Program." *Clinical Psychologist* 21 (1968): 67–69.

Auerback, Alfred. "The Anti–Mental Health Movement." *AJP* 120 (1963): 105–11.

Babcock, H. H. "Integrative Psychotherapy: Collaborative Aspects of Behavioral and Psychodynamic Therapies." *Psychiatric Annals* 18 (1988): 271–72.

Ballenger, J. C., G. D. Burrows et al. "Alprazolam in Panic Disorder and Agoraphobia." *AGP* 45 (1988): 423–28.

Barker, Lewellys. "Psychotherapy—A Modern Medical Science." *American Scholar* 11 (1942): 201–7.

Barlow, D. H., M. G. Craske et al. "Behavioral Treatment of Panic Disorder." *Behavior Therapy* 20 (1989): 261–82.

Barton, Walter. "Psychiatry in Transition." *AJP* 119 (1962): 1–15.

Bataille, G. G. "Psychotherapy and Community Support: Community Mental Health Systems in Transition." *New Directions in Mental Health Services* 46 (1990): 9–18.

Bateson, G., D. Jackson et al. "Toward a Theory of Schizophrenia." *Behavioral Science* 1 (1956): 251–55.

Beck, Aaron. "Cognitive Therapy as the Integrative Therapy." *Journal of Psychotherapy Integration* 1 (1991): 191–98.

———. "Cognitive Therapy: Nature and Relation to Behavior Therapy." *Behavior Therapy* 1 (1970): 184–200.

Becker, Alvin, N. M. Murphy, and M. Greenblatt. "Recent Advances in Community Psychiatry." *NEJM* 272 (1965): 621–26 and 674–79.

Beckham, E. E. "Psychotherapy of Depression at the Crossroads: Directions for the 1990s." *Clinical Psychology Review* 10 (1990): 207–28.

Beitman, B. D. "Why I Am an Integrationist (Not an Eclectic)." *British Journal of Guidance and Counselling* 17 (1989): 259–73.

Beitman, B. D., M. R. Goldfried, and J. C. Norcross. "The Movement Toward Integrating the Psychotherapies: An Overview." *AJP* 146 (1989): 138–47.

Bergin, A. E. "Psychotherapy and Religious Values." *Journal of Consulting and Clinical Psychology* 48 (1980): 95–105.

———. "Values and Religious Issues in Psychotherapy and Mental Health." *AP* 46 (1991): 394–403.

Beutler, L. E., D. C. Mohr et al. "Looking for Differential Treatment Effects: Cross Cultural Predictors of Differential Therapeutic Efficacy." *Journal of Psychotherapy Integration* 1 (1991): 121–41.

Bibring, E. "Psychoanalysts and Dynamic Psychotherapists." *Journal of the American Psychoanalytic Association* 2 (1954): 762.

Bickman, L. "Graduate Education in Psychology." *AP* 42 (1987): 1041–47.

Birk, L. and A. Brinkley-Birk. "Psychoanalysis and Behavior Therapy." *AJP* 131 (1974): 499–510.

Blain, Daniel. "The Psychiatrist and the Psychologist." *Journal of Clinical Psychology* 3 (1947): 4–10.

Blum, Jeffrey, and Fritz Redlich. "Mental Health Practitioners: Old Stereotypes and New Realities." *AGP* 37 (1980): 1253.

Bozarth, J. D. "The Evolution of Carl Rogers as a Therapist." *Person-Centered Review* 5 (1990): 387–93.

Bradford, D. T. and M. H. Spero, eds. "Psychotherapy and Religion." *Psychotherapy* 27:1 (1990).

Brown, Bertram. "The Life of Psychiatry." *AJP* 133 (1976): 492.

Bullard, Dexter. "The Organization of Psychoanalytic Procedure in the Hospital." *Journal of Nervous and Mental Disease* 91 (1940): 697–703.

Bunney, W. E. "Drug Therapy and Psychobiological Research Advances in the Psychoses in the Past." *AJP* 135 (1978): supp. 8–17.

Burnham, J. C. "On the Origins of Behaviorism." *Journal of the History of Behavioral Sciences* 4 (1968): 143–51.

———. "The Struggle Between Physicians and Paramedical Personnel in American Psychiatry." *Journal of the History of Medicine and the Allied Sciences* 29 (1974): 93–106.

Burns, S. M., P. H. DeLeon et al. "Psychotropic Medication: A New Technique for Psychology?" *Psychotherapy: Theory, Research, Practice, and Training* 25 (1988): 508–15.

Burrow, T. "The Group Method of Analysis." *Psychoanalytic Review* 19 (1927): 268–80.

Buss, A. "The Emerging Field of the Sociology of Psychological Knowledge." *American Psychologist* 30 (1975): 988–1002.

———. "Humanistic Psychology as Liberal Ideology." *Journal of Humanistic Psychology* 19 (1979): 43–55.

Catalano, R., and D. Dooley. "Health Effects of Economic Instability: A Test of Economic Stress Hypothesis." *Journal of Health and Social Behavior* 24 (1983): 46–60.

Catell, R. B., and L. B. Luborsky. "P-Technique Demonstrated as a New Clinical Method for Determining Peronality Structure." *Journal of General Psychology* 42 (1950): 3–24.

Cautela, J. "The Shaping of Behavior Therapy: An Historical Perspective." *Behavior Therapist* 13 (1990): 211–12.

Chipman, A. "Meeting Managed Care: An Identity and Value Crisis of Therapists." *AJP* 49 (1995): 558–67.

Conway, J. B. "Differences Among Clinical Psychologists: Scientists, Practitioners, and Scientist-Practitioners." *Professional Psychology: Research and Practice* 19 (1988): 642–55.

Cooper, A. M. "Concepts of Therapeutic Effectiveness in Psychoanalysis: A Historical Review." *Psychoanalytic Inquiry* 9 (1989): 4–25.

Corsini, R., and B. Rosenberg. "Mechanisms of Group Psychotherapy." *Journal of Abnormal and Social Psychology* 51 (1955): 406–11.

Craighead, W. E. "A Brief Clinical History of Cognitive-Behavior Therapy with Children." *School Psychology Review* 11 (1982): 5–13.

Crane, L. "A Plea for the Training of Professional Psychologists." *Journal of Abnormal and Social Psychology* 20 (1925): 228–33.

Cray, Ed. "Enemies of Mental Health." *Nation*, 4/8/61, pp. 3–4.

Cummings, N. A. "The Dismantling of Our Health System." *AP* 41 (1986): 426–31.

Dain, Norman. "Critics and Dissenters: Reflections on Anti-Psychiatry in the United States." *Journal of the History of Behavioral Sciences* 25 (1989): 3–25.

DeLeon, P. H., R. A. Folen et al. "The Case for Prescription Privileges: A Logical Evolution of Professional Practice." *Journal of Clinical Child Psychology* 20 (1991): 254–67.

DeLeon, P. H., R. E. Fox, and S. R. Graham. "Prescription Privileges: Psychology's Next Frontier?" *AP* 46 (1991): 384–93.

Dember, W. N. "Motivation and the Cognitive Revolution." *AP* 29 (1974): 161–68.

Deschin, Celia. "How Can Social Work Make a Major Contribution to Psychiatric Theory?" *Journal of Psychiatric Social Work* 20 (1950): 43–52.

Dithelm, O. "Obituary of Adolf Meyer." *AJP* 107 (1950): 78.

Dobson, K. S. "A Meta-Analysis of the Efficacy of Cognitive Therapy for Depression." *Journal of Consulting and Clinical Psychology* 57 (1989): 414–19.

Dunham, Warren. "Community Psychiatry: The Newest Therapeutic Bandwagon." *AGP* 12 (1965): 303–13.

Dworkin, R. J., and G. L. Adams. "Retention of Hispanics in Public Sector Mental Health Services." *Community Mental Health Journal* 23:3 (1987): 204–16.

Eisenberg, L. "The Past 50 Years of Child and Adolescent Psychiatry: A Personal Memoir." *Journal of the American Academy of Child and Adolescent Psychiatry* 40 (2001): 743–48.

———. "Past, Present, and Future of Psychiatry: Personal Reflections." *Canadian Journal of Psychiatry* 42 (1997): 705–13.

Eldred, Donald, G. W. Brooks et al. "The Rehabilitation of the Hospitalized Mentally Ill—The Vermont Story." *AJPH* 52 (1962): 39–46.

Elkin, I., M. B. Parloff et al. "NIMH Treatment of Depression Collaborative Research Program." *AGP* 42 (1985): 305–16.

Elkin, I., M. T. Shea et al. "NIMH Mental Health Treatment of Depression Collaborative Research Program: General Effectiveness of Treatments." *AGP* 46 (1989): 971–83.

Endicott, J., R. Spitzer et. al. "The Global Assessment Scale." *AGP* 33 (1976): 766–71.

Ervin, Frank. "Biological Intervention Technologies and Social Control." *American Behavioral Scientist* 18 (1975): 617–35.

Evidence-Based Medicine Working Group. "Evidence-Based Medicine: A New Approach to Teaching the Practice of Medicine." *JAMA* 268 (1992): 2420–25.

Ewalt, Jack and P. L. "History of the Community Psychiatry Movement." *AJP* 126 (1969): 51.

Eysenck, H. "The Effects of Psychotherapy: An Evaluation." *Journal of Consulting Psychology* 16 (1952): 319–24.

———. "Learning Theory and Behavior Therapy." *Journal of Mental Science* 195 (1959): 61–75.

———. "A Mish-mash of Theories." *International Journal of Psychiatry* 9 (1970): 140–46.

Fink, Paul, and S. P. Weinstein. "Whatever Happened to Psychiatry? The Deprofessionalization of Community Mental Health Centers." *AJP* 136 (1979): 406–9.

Fiske, D. W., H. F. Hunt et al. "Planning of Research on Effectiveness of Psychotherapy." *AGP* 22 (1970): 22–32.

Fox, R. E. "Building a Profession That Is Safe for Practitioners." *Psychotherapy in Private Practice* 4 (1986): 3–12.

Frank, G. "The Boulder Model: History, Rationale, and Critique." *Professional Psychology: Research and Practice* 15 (1984): 417–35.

Frank, J. D. "Psychotherapy: The Restoration of Morale." *AJP* 131 (1974): 271–74.

———. "Therapeutic Components of Psychotherapy: A 25-Year Progress Report of Research." *Journal of Nervous and Mental Disease* 159 (1974): 325–42.

Frank, J. D., L. H. Gliedman et al. "Why Patients Leave Psychotherapy." *Archives of Neurology and Psychiatry* 77 (1957): 283–99.

Franks, C. M. "Behavior Therapy and AABT: Personal Recollections, Conceptions, and Misconceptions." *Behavior Therapist* 10 (1987): 171–74.

French, T. M. "Interrelations Between Psychoanalysis and the Experimental Work of Pavlov." *AJP* 89 (1933): 1165–1203.

Gabbard, G. O. "Empirical Evidence and Psychotherapy: A Growing Scientific Base." *AJP* 158 (2001): 1–3.

Gabbard, G. O., J. G. Gunderson, and P. Fonagy. "The Place of Psychoanalytic Treatments Within Psychiatry." *AGP* 59 (2002): 505–10.

Garfield, S. L. "Basic Ingredients or Common Factors in Psychotherapy." *Journal of Consulting and Clinical Psychology* 41 (1973): 9–12.

———. "The Effectivenesss of Psychotherapy: The Perennial Controversy." *Professional Psychology* 14 (1983): 35–43.

———. "Evaluating the Psychotherapies." *Behavior Therapy* 12 (1981): 295–307.

———. "Psychotherapy: A 40-Year Appraisal." *AP* 36 (1981): 174-83.

Garfield, S. L., and R. Kurtz. "Clinical Psychologists in the 1970s." *AP* 31 (1976): 1–9.

Gedo, E. "Some Difficulties of Psychotherapeutic Practice." *AGP* 1 (1959): 3–6.

Gergen, K. "The Social Constructionist Movement in Modern Psychology." *AP* 40 (1985): 266–75.

Gill, M. M. "Psychoanalysis and Exploratory Psychotherapy." *Journal of the American Psychoanalytic Association* 2 (1954): 771–97.

———. "Psychoanalysis and Psychotherapy: A Revision." *International Review of Psychoanalysis* 11 (1984): 161–79.

Giorgi, A. "The Crisis of Humanistic Psychology." *Humanistic Psychologist* 15 (1987): 5–20.

Goldberg, S. C., N. R. Schooler et al. "Prediction of Relapse in Schizophrenic Outpatients Treated by Drug and Sociotherapy." *AGP* 34 (1977): 171–84.

Goldfried, M. R. "On the History of Psychotherapeutic Integration." *Behavior Therapy* 13 (1982): 572–93.

Goldfried, M. R., L. S. Greenberg, and C. Marmor. "Individual Psychotherapy: Process and Outcome." *Annual Review of Psychology* 41 (1990): 659–88.

Goldiamond, I. "Self-Control Procedures in Personal Behavior Problems." *Psychological Reports* 17 (1965): 851–68.

Goode, William. "Encroachment, Charlatanism, and the Emerging Profession: Psychology, Sociology, and Medicine." *American Sociological Review* 25 (1960): 902–14.

Gregg, A. "A Critique of Psychiatry." *AJP* 101 (1944): 290.

Gudnerson, J. G., and G. O. Grabbard. "Making the Case for Psychoanalytic Therapies in the Current Psychiatric Environment." *Journal of the American Psychoanalytic Association* 47 (1999): 679–704.

Guthrie, M., et al. "Tayside-Fife Clinical Trial of Cognitive-Behavioural Therapy for Medication Resistant Psychotic Symptoms." *British Journal of Psychiatry* 182 (2003): 303–11.

Guze, S. B. "Biological Psychiatry: Is There Any Other Kind?" *Psychological Medicine* 19 (1989): 315–23.

Haaga, D. A. "A Review of the Common Principles Approach to the Integration of Psychotherapies." *Cognitive Therapy and Research* 10 (1986): 527–38.

Hadden, Samuel. "Historic Background to Group Psychotherapy." *International Journal of Group Psychotherapy* 5 (1955): 324–33.

Haigh, G. "Defensive Behavior in Client-Centered Therapy." *Journal of Consulting Psychology* 13 (1949): 181–89.

Halleck, Seymour. "Psychiatry and the Status Quo: A Political Analysis of Psychiatric Practice." *AGP* 19 (1968): 257–65.

Hamburg, D. A., G. L. Bibring et al. "Report of the Ad Hoc Committee on Central Fact-Gathering Data of the American Psychoanalytic Association." *Journal of the American Psychoanalytic Association* 15 (1967): 841–61.

Harms, E. "At the Cradle of Child Psychiatry." *American Journal of Orthopsychiatry* 30 (1960): 187.

———. "Origins and Early History of Electrotherapy and Electroshock." *AJP* 12 (1955): 933.

Hartman, J. "Small Group Methods of Personal Change." *Annual Review of Psychology* 37 (1979): 453–76.

Havens, L., and J. Frank. "Review of Psychoanalysis and Interpersonal Psychiatry." *AJP* 127 (1971): 1704–5.

Hellersberg, E. F. "Child's Growth in Play Therapy." *American Journal of Psychotherapy* 9 (1955): 484–502.

Henry, Charlotte. "Growing Pains in Psychiatric Social Work." *Journal of Psychiatric Social Work* 17 (1947–48): 8–90.

Hoch, P. "Drugs and Psychotherapy." *AJP* 116 (1959): 305.

Hogarty, G. E., and S. Flesher "Practice Principles of Cognitive Enhancement Therapy for Schizophrenia." *Schizophrenia Bulletin* 25 (1999): 693–708.

Hollister, L. "Drugs in Emotional Disorders, Past and Present." *Annals of Internal Medicine* 51 (1955): 1032.

Holzman, P. S. "On the Trail of the Genetics and Pathophysiology of Schizophrenia." *Psychiatry* 59 (1996): 117–27.

Horenstein, D., B. K. Houston, and D. S. Holmes. "Clients', Therapists', and Judges' Evaluation of Psychotherapy." *Counseling Psychology* 20 (1973): 149–50.

Howard, K. I., S. M. Kopta et al. "The Dose-Effect Relationship in Psychotherapy." *AP* 41 (1986): 159–64.

Hug-Hellmuth, H. "On the Technique of Child Analysis." *International Journal of Psychoanalysis* 2 (1921): 287–305.

Jones, H. S. "The Applications of Conditioning and Learning Techniques to the Treatment of a Psychiatric Patient." *Journal of Abnormal and Social Psychology* 52 (1956): 414–20.

———. "The Treatment of Personality Disorders in a Therapeutic Community." *Psychiatry* 20 (1957): 212–13.

Jones, E. E., J. D. Cumming, and M. J. Horowitz. "Another Look at the Nonspecific Hypothesis of Therapeutic Effectiveness." *Journal of Clinical and Consulting Psychology* 56 (1988): 48–55.

Kandel, E. R. "Biology and the Future of Psychoanalysis: A New Intellectual Framework for Psychiatry Revisited. *AJP* 156 (1999): 505–24.

———. "A New Intellectual Framework for Psychiatry." *AJP* 155 (1998): 457–69.

Kendall, P. C. "Integration: Behavior Therapy and Other Schools of Thought." *Behavior Therapy* 13 (1982): 559–71.

Kendall, P. C., J. Reber et al. "Cognitive-Behavioral Treatment of Conduct-Disordered Children." *Cognitive Therapy and Research* 14 (1990): 279–97.

Kernberg, O. F., C. S. Bernstein et al. "Psychotherapy and Psychoanalysis: Final Report of the Menninger Foundation's Psychotherapy Research Project." *Bulletin of the Menninger Clinic* 36 (1972): 1–276.

Kessler, R. "Stress, Social Status, and Psychological Distress." *Journal of Health and Social Behavior* 20 (1979): 259–72.

Klein, Melanie. "The Psychoanalytic Play Technique." *American Journal of Orthopsychiatry* 25 (1955): 223.

Klein, M., A. T. Dittman et al. "Behavior Therapy: Observations and Reflections." *Journal of Consulting and Clinical Psychology* 33 (1969): 259–66.

Klerman, G. L. "The Psychiatric Patient's Right to Effective Treatment: Implications of Osheroff v. Chestnut Lodge." *AJP* 147 (1990): 409–18.

Klerman, G. L., and A. DiMascio et al. "Treatment of Depression by Drugs and Psychotherapy." *AJP* 131 (1974): 186–91.

Klosko, J. S., D. H. Barlow et al. "A Comparison of Alprazolam and Behavior Therapy in the Treatment of Panic Disorder." *Journal of Consulting and Clinical Psychology* 58 (1990): 77–84.

Knight, R. P. "Management and Psychotherapy of the Borderline Schizophrenic Patient." *Bulletin of the Menninger Clinic* 17 (1953): 139–50.

———. "The Psychodynamics of Chronic Alcoholism." *Journal of Nervous and Mental Disorders* 86 (1937): 538.

Koocher, G. P., and B. M. Pedulla. "Current Practices in Child Psychotherapy." *Professional Psychology* 8 (1977): 275–87.

Kosoff, E. H., and H. S. Singer. "Tourette Syndrome: Clinical Characteristics and Current Management Practices." *Paediatric Drugs* 3 (2001): 355–63.

Krasner, L. "Behavior Therapy." *Annual Review of Psychology* 22 (1971): 483–532.

———. "Mary Cover Jones: A Legend in Her Own Time." *Behavior Therapist* 11 (1988): 101–2.

Kubie, L. S. "Medical Responsibility for Training in Clinical Psychology." *Journal of the Association of American Medical Colleges* 23 (1948): 100–7.

———. "The Pros and Cons of a New Profession." *Texas Reports on Biology and Medicine* 12 (1954): 692–737.

Langsley, Donald. "The Community Mental Health Center: Does it Treat Patients?" *Hospital and Community Psychiatry* 31 (1980): 815–19.

Lazarus, A. A. "New Methods in Psychotherapy: A Case Study." *South African Medical Journal* 32 (1958): 600–64.

———. "Why I Am an Eclectic (Not an Integrationist)." *British Journal of Guidance and Counselling* 19 (1989): 248–58.

Lazell, E. W. "The Group Treatment of Dementia Praecox." *Psychoanalytic Review* 8 (1921): 168–79.

Lehmann, H. E. "The Future of Psychiatry: Progress—Mutation—or Self-Destruct?" *Canadian Journal of Psychiatry* 31 (1986): 362–67.

Levis, D. "Integration of Behavior Therapy with Dynamic Psychiatry: A Marriage with a High Probability of Ending in Divorce." *Behavior Therapy* 1 (1970): 531–37.

Levitt, E. E. "Psychotherapy with Children: A Further Evaluation." *Behavior Research and Therapy* 1 (1963): 45–51.

———. "The Results of Psychotherapy with Children: An Evaluation." *Journal of Consulting Psychology* 21 (1957): 189–96.

Lewin, K. "Frontiers in Group Dynamics: Concept, Method, and Theory in Social Science." *Human Relations* 1 (1947): 5–40.

Lewinsohn, P. M., and G. Atwood. "Depression: A Clinical Approach. The Case of Mrs. G." *Psychotherapy: Theory, Research, and Practice* 6 (1969): 166–71.

Lewinsohn, P. M., L. Teri, and M. Hautzinger. "Training Clinical Psychologists for Work with Older Adults." *Professional Psychology: Research and Practice* 15 (1984): 187–202.

Lewinsohn, P. M., and M. D. Tilson. "Psychotherapy Services for Older Adults: Innovative Roles for Clinical Geropsychologists." *Gerontology and Geriatrics Education* 7 (1988): 111–23.

London, P., and M. Palmer. "The Integrative Trend in Psychotherapy in Historical Context." *Psychiatric Annals* 18 (1988): 273–79.

Long, T. "The V.A. Guidance Program." *Personnel and Guidance Journal* 31 (1952): 104–7.

Luborsky, L. "Clinicians' Judgments of Mental Health: A Proposed Scale." *AGP* 7 (1962): 407–17.

———. "Research Can Now Affect Clinical Practice—a Happy Turnaround." *Clinical Psychologist* 40 (1987): 56–60.

Luborsky, L., P. Crits-Christoph et al. "Do Therapists Vary Much in Their Success? Findings from Four Outcome Studies." *American Journal of Orthopsychiatry* 56 (1986): 501–12.

Mahoney, M., and T. Gabriel. "Essential Tensions in Psychology: Longitudinal Data on Cognitive and Behavioral Ideologies." *Journal of Cognitive Psychotherapy* 4 (1990): 5–21.

———. "Psychotherapy and the Cognitive Sciences." *Journal of Cognitive Psychotherapy* 1 (1987): 39–59.

Marcus, S. C., A. P. Suarez et al. "Trends in Psychiatric Practice, 1988–98." *Psychiatric Services* 52 (2001): 732–35.

Marin, P. "The New Narcissism." *Harper's Magazine,* October 1975, p. 45.

Marsh, L. C. "Group Therapy and the Psychiatric Clinic." *Journal of Nervous and Mental Disease* 82 (1935): 381–92.

Marshall, E. "Psychotherapy Works, but for Whom?" *Science,* 2/1/80, pp. 506–8.

Martin, L., K. Saperson, and B. Maddigan. "Residency Training: Challenges and Opportunities in Preparing Trainees for the 21st Century." *Canadian Journal of Psychiatry* 48 (2003): 225–31.

Masserman, Jules. "Faith and Delusion in Psychotherapy." *AJP* 110 (1953): 324–33.

McGlashan, T. H. "The Prediction of Outcome in Chronic Schizophrenia." *AGP* 43 (1986): 167–76.

McHugh, P. R. "The Death of Freud and the Rebirth of Psychiatry." *Weekly Standard Magazine,* 7/17/00.

McNeilly, C. L., and K. I. Howard. "The Effects of Psychotherapy: A Reevaluation Based on Dosage." *Psychotherapy Research* 1 (1991): 74–78.

Menninger, William. "Psychiatric Experience in the War, 1941–46." *AJP* 103 (1947): 577–86.

———. "Psychiatry and Psychology." *AJP* 105 (1948): 390.

———. "The Relationship of Clinical Psychology and Psychiatry." *AP* 5 (1950): 3–15.

Meredith, N. "Testing the Talking Cure." *Science,* 1986, pp. 30–37.

Messer, S. B. "Integrating Psychoanalytic and Behavior Therapy: Limitations, Possibilities, and Trade-offs." *British Journal of Clinical Psychology* 22 (1983): 131–32.

Miller, J. G. "Clinical Psychology in the Veterans Administration." *AP* 1 (1946): 181–89.

Miller, R. C., and J. S. Berman. "The Efficacy of Cognitive Behavior Therapies: A Quantitative Review of the Research Evidence." *Psychological Bulletin* 94 (1983): 39–53.

Mowrer, O. H., and W. M. Mowrer. "Enuresis: A Method for Its Study and Treatment." *American Journal of Orthopsychiatry* 8 (1938): 436–59.

Murphy, G. "Psychology Serving Society." *Survey Graphic* 37 (1948): 12–15.

Murray, N. E. "A Dynamic Synthesis of Analytic and Behavioral Approaches to Symptoms." *AJP* 30 (1976): 561–69.

Musto, David. "What Happened to 'Community Mental Health'?" *Public Interest,* spring 1975.

Myers, J., M. Weissman et al. "Six Month Prevalence of Psychiatric Disorders in Three Communities." *AGP* 41 (1984): 959–67.

Norcross, J. C., and J. O. Prochaska. "A National Survey of Clinical Psychologists: Affiliations and Orientations." *The Clinical Psychologist* 35 (1982): 1–6.

Norcross, J. C., and M. Wogan "American Psychotherapists of Diverse Persuasions: Characteristics, Theories, Practices, and Clients." *Professional Psychology: Research and Practice* 14 (1983): 529–39.

Olfson, M., S. C. Marcus et al. "National Trends in the Use of Outpatient Psychotherapy." *AJP* 159 (2002): 1914–20.

Orlinsky, D. E., and K. I. Howard. "A Generic Model of Psychotherapy." *Journal of Integrative and Eclectic Psychotherapy* 6 (1987): 6–27.

Paris, J. "Evidence-Based Psychiatry: What It Is and What It Isn't." *Canadian Psychiatric Association Bulletin* 34 (2002): 32–34.

Parloff, M. B. "Psychotherapy Evidence and Reimbursement Decisions: Bambi Meets Godzilla." *AJP* 139 (1982): 718–29.

Pauling, Linus. "Orthomolecular Psychiatry." *Science* 4/19/68, pp. 265–71.

Peterson, D. R. "Twenty Years of Practitioner Training in Psychology." *AP* 40 (1985): 441–51.

Pfeffer, A. Z. "Follow-up Study of a Satisfactory Analysis." *Journal of the American Psychoanalytic Association* 9 (1961): 698–718.

———. "A Procedure for Evaluating the Results of Psychoanalysis: A Preliminary Report." *Journal of the American Psychoanalytic Association* 7 (1959): 418–44.

Poffenberger, A. T. "The Training of a Clinical Psychologist." *Journal of Consulting Psychology* 2 (1938): 1–6.

Prilleltensky, I. "On the Social and Political Implications of Cognitive Psychology." *Journal of Mind and Behavior* 11 (1990): 127–36.

Prochaska, J. O., and J. C. Norcross. "The Future of Psychotherapy: A Delphi Poll." *Professional Psychology* 13 (1982): 620–27.

Prochaska, J. O., J. S. Rossi, and N. S. Wilcox. "Change Process and Psychotherapy Outcome in Integrative Case Research." *Journal of Psychotherapy Integration* 1 (1991): 103–20.

Pulver, Sydney. "Survey of Psychoanalytic Practice." *Journal of the American Psychoanalytic Association* 26 (1978): 621.

Rabinowitz, Clara, and E. H. Ross. "The Military Psychiatric Social Worker."

Newsletter of the American Association of Psychiatric Social Workers 14 (1944): 14–26.

Rado, S. "The Psychic Effects of Intoxicants: An Attempt to Evolve a Psychoanalytic Theory of Morbid Cravings." *International Journal of Psychoanalysis* 7 (1929): 396.

Rangel, L. "Similarities and Differences Between Psychoanalysis and Dynamic Psychotherapy." *Journal of the American Psychoanalytic Association* 2 (1954): 734–44.

Raskin, N. J. "An Analysis of Six Parallel Studies of the Therapeutic Process." *Journal of Consulting Psychology* 13 (1949): 206–20.

Rhoads, J. M. "Combinations and Synthesis of Psychotherapies." *Annals of Psychiatry* 18 (1988): 280–87.

Riess, B. F. "Changes in Patient Income Concomitant with Psychotherapy." *Journal of Consulting Psychology* 31 (1967).

Roberts, Leigh. "Expanding Role of the Psychiatrist in the Community." *Diseases of the Nervous System* 26 (1965): 147–55.

Rogers, C. R. "The Necessary and Sufficient Conditions for Therapeutic Personality Change." *Journal of Consulting Psychology* 21 (1957): 95–103.

———. "A Process of Conception of Psychotherapy." *AP* 13 (1958): 142–49.

Roger, C., N. J. Raskin et al. "A Coordinated Research in Psychotherapy." *Journal of Consulting Psychology* 13 (1949): 149–220.

Rogers, C. R., and B. F. Skinner. "Some Issues Concerning the Control of Human Behavior." *Science* 124 (1956): 1057–66.

Rosenzweig, S. "Some Implicit Common Factors in Diverse Methods in Psychotherapy." *American Journal of Orthopsychiatry* 6 (1936): 412–15.

Rush, A. J., A. T. Beck et al. "Comparative Efficacy of Cognitive Therapy and Pharmacotherapy in the Treatment of Depressed Outpatients." *Cognitive Therapy and Research* 1 (1977): 17–37.

Sampson, E. E. "Psychology and the American Ideal." *AP* 36 (1981): 730–43.

Sargent, H. D., H. C. Modlin et al. "The Psychotherapy Research Project of the Menninger Foundation. Second Report." *Bulletin of the Menninger Clinic* 22 (1958): 148–66.

———. "The Psychotherapy Research Project of the Menninger Foundation. Third Report." *Bulletin of the Menninger Clinic* 24 (1960): 157–216.

Sargent, H. D., L. Coyne et al. "An Approach to Quantitative Problems of Psychoanalytic Research." *Journal of Clinical Psychology* 23 (1967): 243–91.

Schachter, J., and L. Luborsky. "Who's Afraid of Psychoanalytic Research? Analysts' Attitudes Towards Reading Clinical Versus Empirical Research Papers." *International Journal of Psycho-Analysis* 79 (1998): 965–69.

Schlesinger, M., M. Wynia, and D. Cummins. "Some Distinctive Features of the Impact of Managed Care on Psychiatry." *Harvard Review of Psychiatry* 8 (2000): 216–49.

Schou, M., and P. C. Baastrup. "Lithium Treatment of Manic-Depressive Disorder: Dosage and Control." *JAMA* 201 (1967): 696–98.

Schwartz, E. K. "A Psychoanalytic Approach to the Mental Health Team." *American Imago* 15 (1958): 437–51.

Schwartz, Richard. "Psychiatry's Drift Away from Medicine." *AJP* 131 (1974): 129–33.

Sears, R. R. "Clinical Training Facilities: Report of the Committee on Graduate and Professional Training." *AP* 2 (1947): 199–206.

Seeman, J. A. "A Study of the Process of Nondirective Therapy." *Journal of Consulting Psychology* 13 (1949): 157–69.

Shaffer, L. F. "The Problem of Psychotherapy." *AP* 2 (1947): 459–67.

Shakow, D. "An Internship Year for Psychologists." *Journal of Consulting Psychology* 2 (1938): 73–76.

Sharfstein, S. "Community Mental Health Centers: Returning to Basics." *AJP* 136 (1979): 1077–79.

———. "Medicaid Cutbacks and Block Grants: Crisis of Opportunity for Community Mental Health?" *AJP* 139 (1982): 466–70.

Sharfstein, S., H. Eist et al. "The Impact of Third-Party Payment Cutbacks on the Private Practice of Psychiatry." *Hospital and Community Psychiatry* 35 (1984): 478–81.

Shaw, F. J. "Some Postulates Concerning Psychotherapy." *Journal of Consulting Psychology* 12 (1948): 426–31.

Shoben, E. J. "Psychotherapy as a Problem in Learning Theory." *Psychological Bulletin* 46 (1949): 366–92.

Sierles, F. S., and M. A. Taylor. "Decline of U.S. Medical Student Career Choice of Psychiatry and What to Do About It." *AJP* 152 (1995): 1416–26.

Silverman, L. H. "Some Psychoanalytic Considerations of Non-Psychoanalytic Therapies: On Aproaches and Related Issues." *Psychotherapy: Theory, Research, Practice* 11 (1974): 298–305.

Smith, D. "Trends in Counseling and Psychotherapy." *AP* 37 (1982): 802–9.

Spence, D. P. "The Hermeneutic Turn: Soft Science or Loyal Opposition?" *Psychoanalytic Dialogues* 3 (1993): 1–10.

Spitz, H. "Contemporary Trends in Group Psychotherapy." *Hospital and Community Psychiatry* 35 (1984): 132–42.

Stein, D. J. "Obsessive-Compulsive Disorder." *Lancet* 360 (2002): 397–405.

Stevenson, Ian. "Tranquilizers and the Mind." *Harper's Magazine,* August 1957, pp. 21–27.

Stiles, W. G., D. A. Shapiro, and R. Elliot. "Are All Psychotherapies Equivalent?" *AP* 41 (1986): 165–80.

Stone, A. A. "Law, Science, and Psychiatric Malpractice: A Response to Klerman's Indictment of Psychoanalytic Psychiatry." *AJP* 147 (1990): 419–27.

———. "Where Will Psychoanalysis Survive?" *Harvard Magazine,* January–February 1997, pp. 34–39.

Strupp, H. H. "On the Basic Ingredients of Psychotherapy." *Journal of Consulting and Clinical Psychology* 41 (1973): 1–8.

Strupp, H. H., and A. E. Bergin. "Some Empirical and Conceptual Bases for Coordinated Research in Psychotherapy." *International Journal of Psychiatry* 7 (1969): 18–90.

Talbott, John. "Why Psychiatrists Leave the Public Sector." *Hospital and Community Psychiatry* 30 (1979): 778–82.

Wachtel, P. L. "What Can Dynamic Therapies Contribute to Behavior Therapy?" *Behavior Therapy* 13 (1982): 594–609.

Wallerstein, R. S. "Assessment of Structural Change in Psychoanalytic Therapy and Research." *Journal of the American Psychoanalytic Association* 36 (suppl.) (1988): 241–61.

———. "One Psychoanalysis or Many?" *International Journal of Psychoanalysis* 69 (1988): 5–21.

———. "Psychoanalysis and Psychotherapy: An Historical Perspective." *International Journal of Psychoanalysis* 70:4 (1990): 563–92.

Wampold, B. E., G. W. Mondin et al. "A Meta-Analysis of Outcome Studies

Comparing Bona-Fide Psychotherapies: Empirically, 'All Must Have Prizes.'" *Psychological Bulletin* 122 (1997): 203–15.

Weithorn, L. A. "Mental Hospitalization of Troublesome Youth: An Analysis of Skyrocketing Admission Rates." *Stanford Law Review* 40 (1988): 773–838.

Weitzman, B. "Behavior Therapy and Psychotherapy." *Psychological Review* 74 (1967): 300–17.

Wender, L. "The Dynamics of Group Psychotherapy and Its Applications." *Journal of Nervous and Mental Disease* 84:1 (1936): 54–60.

Wilder, Joseph. "Facts and Figures on Psychotherapy." *Journal of Clinical Psychopathalogy and Psychotherapy* 7 (1945): 311–47.

———. "Twenty-five Years of the Association for the Advancement of Psychotherapy." *American Journal of Psychotherapy* 18 (1964): 452–57.

Willis, J., and D. Giles. "Behaviorism in the Twentieth Century: What We Have Here Is a Failure to Communicate." *Behavior Therapy* 9 (1978): 15–27.

Wilson, G. T. "Psychotherapy Process and Procedure: The Behavioral Mandate." *Behavior Therapy* 13 (1982): 291–312.

Winslow, Walter. "The Changing Role of Psychiatrists in Community Mental Health Centers." *AJP* 136 (1979): 24–27.

Witmer, L. "Retrospect and Prospect: An Editorial." *Psychological Clinic* 2 (1909): 1–4.

Wolford, R. A. "A Review of Psychology in VA Hospitals." *Journal of Counseling Psychology* 3 (1956): 243–48.

Wolpe, J. "Behavior Therapy Versus Psychoanalysis: Therapeutic and Social Implications." *AP* 36 (1981): 159–64.

Wolpe, J. and S. Rachman. "Psychoanalytic 'Evidence': A Critique Based on Freud's Case of Little Hans." *Journal of Nervous and Mental Disease* 131 (August 1960): 135–48.

Woodworth, R. S. "The Future of Clinical Psychology." *Journal of Consulting Psychology* 1 (1937): 4–5.

Woolfolk, R. L., and F. C. Richardson. "Behavior Therapy and the Ideology of Modernity." *AP* 39 (1984): 777–86.

Wright, W. W. "Results Obtained by the Intensive Use of Bromides in Functional Psychoses." *AJP* 5 (1926): 365.

Yates, A. J. "Behavior Therapy and Psychodynamic Therapy: Basic Conflicts or Reconciliation or Integration." *British Journal of Clinical Psychology* 22 (1983): 107–25.

Yontef, G. M. "The Future of Gestalt Therapy: A Symposium." *Gestalt Journal* 4 (1981): 7–11.

Zimet, C. N. "Managed Care Is Here and Is Not Going Away." *Psychotherapy Bulletin* 25:4 (1991): 21–22.

"Report of the Committee on the Role of Psychiatric Social Worker as Caseworker or Therapist." *Journal of Psychiatric Social Work* 19 (1950): 87–90.

BOOK CHAPTERS

Allen, F. "The Philadelphia Child Guidance Clinic." In L. Lowrey and V. Sloane, eds. *Orthopsychiatry, 1923–1948.* New York: American Orthopsychiatry Association, 1948.

Arkowitz, H., and M. T. Hannah. "Cognitive, Behavioral, and Psychodynamic Therapies: Converging or Diverging Pathways to Change." In A. Freeman, K. Simon et al., eds. *Comprehensive Handbook of Cognitive Therapy.* New York: Plenum, 1989.

Axline, V. "The Eight Basic Principles." In M. R. Haworth, ed. *Child Psychotherapy.* New York: Basic Books, 1964.

Beck, A. T. "Cognitive Approaches to Panic Disorder: Theory and Therapy." In S. Rachman and J. D. Maser, eds. *Panic: Psychological Perspectives.* Hillsdale, NJ: Erlbaum, 1988.

Burnham, John. "Psychology and Counseling: Convergence into a Profession." In Nathan Hatch, ed. *The Professions in American History.* Notre Dame, IN: University of Notre Dame Press, 1988.

Clark, D. M. "A Cognitive Model of Panic Attacks." In S. Rachman and J. D. Maser, eds. *Panic: Psychological Perspectives.* Hillsdale, NJ: Erlbaum, 1988.

Curtis, H. C. "The Concept of Therapeutic Alliance: Implications for the 'Widening Scope.'" In H. Blum, ed. *Psychoanalytic Explorations of Technique.* New York: International Universities Press, 1980.

Danziger, K. "The Social Origins of Modern Psychology." In A. Buss, ed. *Psychology in Social Context.* New York: Irvington, 1979.

DeLeon, P. H., and B. R. Vandenbos. "Psychotherapy Reimbursement in Federal Programs: Political Factors." In G. R. Vandenbos, ed. *Psychotherapy: Practice, Research, Policy.* Beverly Hills, CA: Sage, 1980b

Dobson, K. S., and L. Block. "Historical and Philosophical Bases of the Cognitive-Behavioral Therapies." In K. S. Dobson, ed. *Handbook of Cognitive-Behavioral Therapies.* New York: Guilford, 1988.

Ellis, A. "History of Cognition in Psychotherapy." In A. Freeman, K. M. Simon et al., eds. *Comprehensive Handbook of Cognitive Therapy.* New York: Plenum, 1989.

Emmelkamp, P. M. G., and E. B. Foa. "The Study of Failures." In E. B. Foa and P. M. G. Emmelkamp, eds. *Failures in Behavior Therapy.* New York: Wiley, 1983.

Eysenck, H. J. "Learning Theory and Behavior Therapy." In H. J. Eysenck, ed. *Behavior Therapy and the Neuroses.* London: Pergamon, 1960.

Frank, J. D. "Therapeutic Components Shared by All Psychotherapies." In J. H. Harvey and M. M. Parks, eds. *The Master Lecture Series.* Vol. 1. *Psychotherapy Research and Behavior Change.* Washington, D.C.: American Psychological Association, 1982.

Franks, C. M. "Behavior Therapy and Its Pavlovian Origins." In C. M. Franks, ed. *Behavior Therapy: Appraisal and Status.* New York: McGraw-Hill, 1969.

———. "Behavior Therapy: An Overview." In C. M. Franks, G. T. Wilson et al. *Reviews of Behavior Therapy: Theory and Practice.* New York: Guilford, 1990.

Freud, Anna. "A Short History of Child Analysis." In *The Psychoanalytic Study of the Child.* Vol. 21. New York: International Universities Press, 1966.

Furumoto, L. "Shared Knowledge: The Experimentalists 1904–1929." In J. G. Morawski, ed. *The Rise of Experimentation in American Psychology.* New Haven: Yale, 1988.

Glenn, J. "An Overview of Child Analytic Technique." In J. Glenn, ed. *Child Analysis and Therapy.* New York: Jason Aronson, 1978.

Goldfried, M. R., and W. Padawer. "Current Status and Future Directions in Psychotherapy." In M. R. Goldfried, ed. *Converging Themes in Psychotherapy.* New York: Springer, 1982.

Goldfried, M. R., and J. D. Safran. "Future Directions in Psychotherapy Integration." In J. C. Norcross, ed. *Handbook of Eclectic Psychotherapy.* New York: Brunner/Mazel, 1986.

Healy, W., and A. Bronner. "The Child Guidance Clinic: Birth and Growth of an Idea." In L. Lowrey and V. Sloane, eds. *Orthopsychiatry, 1923–1948.* New York: American Orthopsychiatry Association, 1948.

Hildreth, J. D. "Psychology's Relation with Psychiatry: A Summary Report." In B. Lubin and E. E. Levitt, eds. *The Clinical Psychologist: Background, Roles, and Functions.* New York: Aldine, 1967.

Himwich, H. E. "Effect of Shock Treatment on the Brain." In Paul Hoeber, ed. *Biology of Mental Disease.* New York: MMF, 1952.

Hollon, S. D., and A. T. Beck. "Research on Cognitive Therapies." In S. L. Garfield and A. E. Bergin, eds. *Handbook of Psychotherapy and Behavior Change.* New York: Wiley, 1986.

Illing, H. A. "Jung on the Present Trends in Group Psychotherapy." In M. Rosenbaum and M. Berger, eds. *Group Psychotherapy and Group Function.* New York: Basic Books, 1963.

Kendall, P. C., and K. M. Bemis. "Thought and Action in Psychotherapy: The Cognitive Behavioral Approaches." In M. Hersen, A. E. Kasdin, and A. S. Bellak, eds. *The Clinical Psychology Handbook.* Elmsford, NY: Pergamon, 1983.

Kovel, J. "The American Mental Health Industry." In D. Inglesby, ed. *Critical Psychiatry: The Politics of Mental Health.* New York: Random House, 1980.

Krasner, L. "Behavior Therapy: On Roots, Contexts, and Growth." In G. T. Wilson and C. M. Franks, eds. *Contemporary Behavior Therapy: Conceptual and Empirical Foundations.* New York: Guilford, 1982.

Lambert, M. J., D. A. Shapiro, and A. E. Bergin. "The Effectiveness of Psychotherapy." In S. L. Garfield and A. E. Bergin, eds. *Handbook of Psychotherapy and Behavior Change.* 3rd edition. New York: Wiley, 1986.

Leahy, R. "Cognitive Therapy: Current Problems and Future Directions." In R. L. Leahy and E. T. Dowd, eds. *Clinical Advances in Cognitive Psychotherapy: Theory and Application.* New York: Springer, 2002.

Levenson, E. "The Interpersonal (Sullivanian) Model." In A. Rothstein, ed. *Models of the Mind.* New York: International Universities Press, 1985.

Levin, M. "The Impact of Psychoanalysis on Training in Psychiatry." In F. Alexander and H. Ross, eds. *Twenty Years of Psychoanalysis.* New York: Norton, 1953.

Lietaer, G. "The Client-Centered Approach After the Wisconsin Project." In G. Lietaer, J. Rombauts, and R. Van Balen, eds. *Client-Centered and Experiential Psychotherapy in the Nineties.* Leuven, Belgium: Leuven University Press, 1990.

Mahoney, M. J. "The Cognitive Sciences and Psychotherapy: Patterns in a Developing Relationship." In K. S. Dobson, ed. *Handbook of Cognitive-Behavioral Therapies*. New York: Guilford, 1988.

Menninger, K. "The Contributions of Psychoanalysis to American Psychiatry." In B. H. Hall, ed. *A Psychiatrist's World*. New York: Viking, 1959.

O'Connell, A. N. "Karen Horney: Theorist in Psychoanalysis and Feminine Psychology." In A. N. O'Connell and N. F. Russo, eds. *Eminent Women in Psychology*. New York: Human Sciences Press, 1980.

———. "Karen Horney." In A. N. O'Connell and N. F. Russo, eds. *Women in Psychology: A Bio-Bibliographic Sourcebook*. Westport, CT: Greenwood, 1990.

Orlinsky, D. E., and K. I. Howard. "The Psychological Interior of Psychotherapy: Explorations with the Therapy Session Reports." In L. S. Greenberg and W. M. Pinsof, eds. *The Psychotherapeutic Process: A Research Handbook*. New York: Guilford, 1987.

Peterson, D. R. "Professional Program in an Academic Psychology Department." In E. L. Hoch, A. O. Ross, and C. L. Winder, eds. *Professional Preparation of Clinical Psychologists*. Washington, D.C.: American Psychological Association, 1966.

Rodnick, E. H. "Comments on the 'Boulder' Model." In E. L. Hoch, A. O. Ross, and C. L. Winder, eds. *Professional Preparation of Clinical Psychologists*. Washington, D.C.: American Psychological Association, 1966.

Schacht, T. E. "The Varieties of Integrative Experience." In H. Arkowitz and S. B. Messer, eds. *Psychoanalytic Therapy and Behavior Therapy: Is Integration Possible?* New York: Plenum, 1984.

Sharfstein, S., J. E. C. Turner, and H. W. Clark. "Financing Issues in the Delivery of Services to the Chronically Mentally Ill and Disabled." In J. Talbot, ed. *The Chronic Mental Patients*. Washington, D.C.: American Psychiatric Association, 1978.

Sears, R. R. "Experimental Analysis of Psychoanalytic Phenomena." In J. McV. Hunt, ed. *Personality and the Behavior Disorders*. New York: Ronald Press, 1944.

Sedgwick, Peter. "Anti-Psychiatry from the Sixties to the Eighties." In Walter Gove, ed. *Deviance and Mental Illness*. Beverly Hills: Sage, 1982.

Seidenfield, M. A. "Clinical Psychology." In R. S. Anderson, ed. *Neuropsychiatry in World War II*. Vol. 1, *Zone of Interior*. Washington, D.C.: Office of the Surgeon General, 1966.

Silberschatz, G. "Testing Pathogenic Beliefs." In *The Psychoanalytic Process: Theory, Clinical Observations, and Empirical Research.* New York: Guilford, 1986.

Silberschatz, G., J. T. Curtis et al. "Research on the Process of Change in Psychotherapy." In L. Beutler and M. Crago, eds. *International Psychotherapy Research Programs.* Washington, D.C.: American Psychological Association, 1991.

Strupp, H. H., T. E. Schacht et al. "Problem-Treatment-Outcome Congruence: A Principle Whose Time Has Come." In H. Dahl, H. Kachele, and H. Thoma, eds. *Psychoanalytic Process Research Strategies.* New York: Springer-Verlag, 1988.

GOVERNMENT DOCUMENTS

Bass, Rosalyn. *CMHC Staffing: Who Minds the Store?* DHEW doc. 78-686, 1978.

Goldston, Stephen, ed. *Concepts of Community Psychiatry: A Framework for Training.* PHS doc. 1319, 1965.

Kramer, Morton. *Facts Needed to Assess Public Health and Social Problems in the Widespread Use of Tranquilizing Drugs.* PHS doc. 486, 1956.

———. *Psychiatric Services and the Changing Institutional Scene.* DHEW doc. 77-433, 1977.

Lerman, Paul. *Deinstitutionalization: A Cross-Problem Analysis.* DHHS doc. 81-987, 1981.

Levine, Daniel and D. R. *The Cost of Mental Illness—1971.* DHEW doc. 76-265, 1975.

NCMHI. *Mental Health Benefits of Medicare and Medicaid.* PHS doc. 1505, 1969.

NIMH. *Financing Mental Health Care in the United States: A Study of Assessment of Issues and Arrangements.* DHEW doc. 73-9117, 1973.

———. *Private Funds for Mental Health.* PHS doc. 1985, 1969.

———. *The Treatment of Psychiatric Disorders with Insulin 1936–1960.* PHS doc. 941, 1962.

Index

Abraham, Karl, 11, 20, 30
Action for Mental Health (Joint
    Commission on Mental Illness
    and Health), 141–142
Adler, Alfred, 1, 11, 12, 229
Advice columns, 132–133
Alcohol and alcoholism, xiii, 109–131,
    188–189
  accidents and, 114–115
  aversion therapy, 129–131, 140
  causes of alcoholism, 115–118,
    130
  costs of, 110, 113–115
  disease theories of, 208–210
  ethnic groups and, 112
  female drinking, xiii, 109–131
  genetic basis of, 210
  social drinkers, 210
  teenage use, 203–204
  in workplace, 111, 205–206
Alcoholics Anonymous (AA), xiv, 118–
    124, 129, 131, 140, 169, 178, 186,
    189, 212, 213, 215, 252, 254, 258,
    259
Alexander, Franz, 1, 49, 57, 75, 150–
    151

Alexander, Jack, 119, 120
Alienation, 130, 174
Allen, Frederick, 41–42
Allers, Rudolf, 50
Allis-Chalmers, 111
Alprazolam, 251
American Association of Psychiatric
    Social Workers, 60
American Association of Social
    Workers, 166
American Institute for Psychoanalysis,
    31
American Journal of Psychiatry, 56
American Orthopsychiatric Association
    (AOA), 41
American Psychiatric Association,
    53, 98, 100, 141, 148,
    218
American Psychoanalytic Association,
    18, 125, 153, 218–220
American Psychological Association,
    66, 231, 237
American Red Cross, 58
Analysis of Self, The (Kohut),
    167
Antabus, 130

Anthropology, 34, 36

Antidepressant medications, 70, 97, 101, 170, 193, 194, 223–226, 240, 242–244, 250

Antipsychotic medications, 70, 170, 251

Anxiety, 8–9, 28, 29, 72, 88, 101–102, 225, 226, 228–229, 251

Appel, John, 45

Appel, Kenneth, xiv

Are You Considering Psychoanalysis? (Horney), 49

Assertion therapy, 178

Aversion therapy, 84–86, 129–131, 140

Azima, Heller, 101

Balin, Daniel, 69

Barbiturates, 140, 203, 204

Barton, Walter, 144

Bauer, W. W., 117–118

Beck, Aaron, 90, 228–230

Behaviorism, 82–89, 94

Benson, Herbert, 178

Berlin Psychoanalytic Society, 23, 30

Bini, Lucino, 71

Biological psychiatry, xii–xiii, 225–227, 236, 240–254

Bipolar disorder, xiii, 225, 226, 251, 255

Blank, Robert, 137

Block, Marvin, 110

Bloom, Floyd, 209

Blue Shield, 145, 237

Boisen, Anton, 159

Bowman, Karl, 52

Brain research, 96–97, 241

Breggin, Peter, 187

Breuer, Josef, 5–6, 9

Briggs, John, 152

Brill, Abraham, 11, 16, 35

Brooks, George, 98

Brown, Herbert, 198–199

Buber, Martin, 202

Buchman, Frank, 120

Bugental, James, 172

Buhler, Charlotte, 116

Bunker, Edward, 197

Burlingame, Charles, 71–72

Burnham, William, 38

Burrow, Trigant, 124–125

Buss, Allan, 81

Cade, John, 97

Caterpillar Tractor Company, 111

Catharsis, x, 63

Cerletti, Ugo, 71

Cheaper by the Dozen (Gilbreth), 125

Chesler, Phyllis, 185

Chestnut Lodge, 221–224, 227

Child analytic techniques, 20–23

Child guidance movement, 32–38, 66, 80

Childhood experiences, xi, 6–7, 31, 32, 181–182

Chlorpromazine, 97–98, 101, 107

Church of Scientology, 171

Clergy
   drug problem and, 202, 212
   informal therapy and, 106–107
   psychotherapy and, xiv, 50, 156–161

Clergy and Mental Health (National Association for Mental Health), 158

Client-centered therapy, 76–80, 172

Client-Centered Therapy (Rogers), 78

Clinical psychology (*see* Psychology)

Cobbs, Price, 179

Cocaine, 196, 208

Codeine, 198

Cognitive behavioral therapy (CBT), 94, 153, 228, 232, 253, 254
Cognitive therapy, advances in, 228–231
Cohen, Sidney, 203
Colby, K. M., 155
Cold War, 134
Cole, Jonathan, 242
Comer, James, 136
Commonwealth Fund, 37–38
Community Mental Health Centers Act of 1963, 142
Community mental health centers (CMHCs), 139–145
Cooke, Elliot, 45
Cooper, David, 185–187
Cough suppressants and elixirs, 198, 208
Counter-transference, 29
Crowe, Charles, 114

Dawes, Robyn, 247
Deinstitutionalization, 142–145
Delta-9-tetrahydrocannabinol (THC), 196
Denker, Peter, 56, 57, 104
Depression, xiii, 8–9, 52, 71, 88, 188, 223–226, 228–229, 250–251
Dershimer, Frederick, 51
Desrosiers, Norman, 210
Deutch, Albert, 140
Dianetics, 171, 179–180
Diazepam, 251
Divided Self, The (Laing), 185
Divorce, 115, 136, 202
Dolnick, Edward, 225
Dopamine, 227, 241
Dream theory, 7, 12
Drinking (see Alcohol and alcoholism)

Drug use and addiction, xiii, 140, 142, 188, 195–217, 259 (see also specific drugs)
    advertising, 171
    in armed forces, 203
    culture of, 200–204
    disease theories of, 208–209
    incidence of, 195, 198
    juvenile, 203–204, 208
    life of addict, 198–199
    personality of addict, 211–212
    religion and, 215–217
    treatment programs, 206–217
    white collar, 204–206
Drugs (see Medications)
Dunn, Richard, 216
DuPont, Robert, 196

Eclecticism, 231, 254, 261
Ego, 7–8, 79
Ego and the Id, The (Freud), 7
Eisenberg, Leon, 183
Eitingon, Hans, 11
Ellis, Albert, 89–95, 163, 228
Emertine, 129
Emetics, 84, 85, 87, 88, 129
Encounter groups, 177–179
Endocrine system, 96
Engel, George, 220
Engrams, 180
Enlightenment philosophy, 13
Erb, Wilhelm, 4
Erhard, Werner, 171, 178
Erickson, K. T., 134
EST (Erhard Seminars Training), xiv, 171, 178
Ethnotherapy, 179
Exodus House, New York, 214
Eysenck, Hans, 83–84, 105–106, 219–221, 223

Farber, Leslie, 26, 119
Federal Bureau of Narcotics, 198
Felix, Robert, 100, 145, 207
Female drinking, 110–111
Fenichel, Otto, 104
Fensterheim, Herbert, 168, 178
Ferenczi, Sándor, 11, 20, 25
Fishbein, Morris, 183
Ford Foundation, 102
Fox, Ruth, 117
Frank, Jerome, 126, 154, 183, 191, 192
Frankl, Viktor, 259
Free association, ix, xi, 9–10, 12, 17–18, 36, 77–78
Freeman, Walter, 73
Freud, Anna, 23
Freud, Sigmund, ix, 1–18, 55, 63, 72, 91, 133, 134, 150, 155, 156, 181, 219, 239, 254, 257–258
Freudian theory
    orthodoxy and, 19–25, 36, 37, 69, 148–155
    pragmatism and, 25–32, 36–41, 63, 174
Fromm, Erich, 31, 36, 81
Fromm-Reichmann, Frieda, 55, 57, 152–153
Frontal lobes of brain, 72

Ganglion cells, 96
Gardner, George, 137
Garfield, Sol, 66, 190
Gateway House, Chicago, 216
General Motors Corporation, 204
Genetics, 208–210
Geographic mobility, 168
Gestalt therapy, 174–176
Gestalt Therapy (Perls, Hefferline, and Goodman), 174–175
Gibson, Jim, 215

Gibson, Robert, 193
Gilbreth, Frank, 125
Giordano, Joseph, 179
Glenmullen, Joseph, 244
Glover, Edward, 103
Goldberg, Solomon, 226
Goldfried, Marvin, 174
Goldstein, Kurt, 174
Goodall, Jane, 221
Goodman, Paul, 174–175
Greaves, Donald, 231
Greenberg, Joanne, 221–222
Gregg, Alan, 50
Gross, Martin, 150, 152, 223
Grotjahn, Martin, 153
Group for the Advancement of Psychiatry (GAP), 62, 63, 100, 135, 137–138, 165
Group therapy, 212, 217, 258
    beginnings of, 124–125
    Hawthorne study, 125
    issues addressed by, 127
    psychodrama, 38, 127
    sociometry, 38–41
Guilt, role of, 157–159
Gumpert, Martin, 52, 53
Gutheil, Thomas, 258

Habas, Ralph, 110
Hale, Nathan, 148
Halikas, James, 242
Hall, G. Stanley, 14, 15
Halliday, James, 134
Hambrecht, Leona, 60
Hare, Paul, 40
Havemann, Ernest, 133
Hawley, Paul, 66–67
Hawthorne study, 125
Health insurance, 145–148, 237
    managed care, 247–250

Hefferline, Ralph, 174–175
Hendrick, Ives, 150
Heroin, 195, 197, 199, 201, 203, 204, 208, 214, 217
Hersh, Stephen, 249
Hippocampus, 241
Hirsh, Joseph, 109, 121–122
Hoarding behavior, 86
Hogan, Robert, 160
Holmes, David, 181
Homosexuality, 7, 22, 26, 87–88
Horney, Karen, 1, 30–32, 34, 36, 42, 49, 62, 63, 81, 163, 228, 234
Hougan, Jim, 167
How to Live Without Liquor (Habas), 110
Hubbard, L. Ron, 171, 179
Humanism, 27, 30, 31, 76–83, 136, 153, 163, 172–175, 230, 231
Huxley, Aldous, 201
Hypnosis, 2–6, 9

I Never Promised You a Rose Garden (Greenberg), 221
Id, 7, 12, 79, 257
Imipramine, 97
Incest, 181–182
Infantile psychosexual development, 7, 23, 25, 28, 29, 221, 257
Inferiority complexes, 48
Informal therapy, 106–107
Ingersoll, John, 196
Institutes of Religion and Health, 158
Insulin comas, 99
Insulin therapy, 227
Intelligence tests, 65, 69
Interpersonal psychology, 25–29, 31, 72, 126, 163, 254
Interpersonal Theory of Psychology, The (Sullivan), 28–29

Interpretation of Dreams, The (Freud), 7
Iproniazid, 97, 107
Irving, David, ix

Jaffe, Joseph, 154–155
James, William, 64
Janov, Arthur, 180
Jarrett, Mary, 58
Jelliffe, Smith Ely, 14
Jellinek, Elvin, 114, 130
Jennings, Daniel, 163
Johnson, Virginia, 182, 183
Joint Commission on Mental Illness and Health, 141
Jones, Ernest, 11, 24
Jung, Carl, 1, 11, 12, 124, 128, 160–161

Kazin, Alfred, 150
Kellerman, Joseph, 260
Kemper, Edmund, 145
Kennedy, John F., 141
Kenworthy, Marion, 62–64
Kirsner, Douglas, 149
Klein, Donald, xii
Klein, Judith, 179
Klein, Melanie, 1, 20–24, 28
Kleinman, Arthur, 244
Klerman, Gerald, 139, 168, 184, 224–226
Kline, Nathan, 194, 223
Kohut, Heinz, 167
Kolb, Lawrence, 208
Korgeski, Gregory, 249
Kramer, Peter, xii, 242–243
Krauthammer, Charles, 192
Kubie, Lawrence, 103–104
Kuhn, Thomas, 24
Kunkel, Fritz, 156
Kurzweil, Edith, 150

Lacan, Jacques, 233
Laing, Ronald (R. D.), 134, 185–187
Lasch, Christopher, 167, 169
Lazarus, Arnold, 84
Lazell, Edward, 124
Lennon, John, 180
Leucotomy, 72, 73
Levine, Irving, 179
Lewin, Kurt, 125
Lidz, Ted, 153
Lifton, Robert Jay, 138
Light therapy, 227
Ling, Paul, 249
Linkletter, Art, 199–201
Listening to Prozac (Kramer), 242–243
Lithium, 97, 193–194, 240, 251, 254
Lobotomy, 73–74, 99, 107, 108
London, Perry, 167
Low, Abraham, 124
LSD, 196, 200, 201, 203
Luborsky, Lester, 234, 253
Luhrmann, Tanya, 219
Lyon, Peter, 117

Managed care, 247–250
Mann, James, 232
Marijuana, 195–197, 199–201, 203, 204
Marine, Gene, 96
Mark, Vernon, 227
Marmor, Judd, 134
Marsh, L. Cody, 124
Marshall, Eliot, 237
Maslow, Abraham, 80–81, 191
Massage, 177
Masters, William, 182, 183
Mature Mind, The (Overstreet), 133
May, Philip, 222, 225
Mayo, Elton, 125
McCracken, Samuel, 200–201
McDougall, William, 2

McGlashan, Tom, 222
McGovern, George, 197
McNeil, Harry, 158
Mechanic, H. S., 134
Medicaid, 142, 146
Medical training, 16, 53–56, 139, 236
Medicare, 146, 190
Medications (see also specific drugs)
    biological psychiatry, xii–xiii, 225–
        227, 236, 240–254
    breakthrough, 97–102, 107, 193–194
Meditation, 177, 178
Meduna, Ladislas, 71
Menninger, Karl, 69, 110
Menninger, William, 44, 49, 50, 52, 53,
    55–56, 69, 260
Menninger Foundation, 189, 220
Menninger Psychiatry Clinic, Topeka,
    Kansas, 44, 55, 56, 227
Mesmer, Franz Anton, 2–3
Mesmerism, 2–3
Meta-analysis, 105, 106
Methadone treatment, 216, 217
Methamphetamine ("speed"), 195–196,
    204
Meyer, Adolf, 2, 14–16, 18, 24–25, 42,
    59
Michels, Robert, 219
Mielcarek, Henry, 111
Military, U.S., 43–46, 52, 58, 64, 136,
    138, 203
Miltown, 100, 107
Moltmann, Jurgen, 159
Moniz, Egas, 72
Monoamine oxidase inhibitors
    (MAOIs), 97, 225, 240, 250
Moore, Arnold, 137
Moreno, Jacob Levy, 38–41, 124, 127,
    178
Morita therapy, 178

Morphine, 195, 216

Motivation and Personality (Maslow), 81

Mullan, Hugh, 127–128

Musto, David, 141

Myerson, Abraham, 2, 18, 102–103

Narcissism, 167–194

Narcotics abuse (*see* Drug use and addiction)

Narcotics Anonymous, xiv, 212–213, 258

National Association for Mental Health, 158

National Association of Social Workers, 166

National Health Advisory Council, 54

National Institute of Alcohol Abuse and Alcoholism, 204

National Institute of Mental Health (NIMH), 74, 148, 150, 170, 216

National Mental Health Act of 1946, 54, 74

Needs, hierarchy of, 81

Neilson, William Allan, 59

Neuroimaging, 241

Neuroleptic drugs, xii, 97–98, 101, 225–227, 240, 251, 254

New York Psychoanalytic Institute, 16, 31, 149

New York School of Social Work, 34, 59

New York State Training School for Girls, 38–41

Newman, Robert, 217

Norepinephrine, 227, 241

Nyswander, Marie, 198, 213

Oberndorf, Clarence, 103–104

Obsessive-compulsive disorder (OCD), 250, 253, 255

Oedipus complex, x, 7, 21, 28, 56, 221

Olshaker, Bennet, 257

Ono, Yoko, 180

Operant conditioning, 83

Opium, 197–199, 208

Organicists, 95–96, 99–100

Organism, The (Goldstein), 174

Orthodoxy, 19–25, 36, 37, 69, 148–155

Osheroff, Rafael, 223–224

Osheroff vs. Chestnut Lodge (1982), 223–224

Outcomes studies, 103–108, 189–194

Outline of Psychoanalysis, An (Freud), 10–11

Overholser, Winfred, 71–72

Overstreet, Harry, 133

Oxford Movement, 120

Panic disorder, 187

Past-lives therapy, 179

Pastoral counseling, 158–159, 253, 254

Pastors (*see* Clergy)

Pauling, Linus, 98, 102

Pavlov, Ivan, 82

Paxil, 250

Peace of the Soul (Sheen), 156

Peale, Norman Vincent, 133

Penis envy, ix

Perls, Fritz, 174–176

Perls, Laura, 174

Perry, Helen Swick, 27

Pharmaceutical companies, 187

Phenothiazines, 224

Phobias, xiii, 86–87, 253

Pikser, George, 162

Play therapy, 20

Politics of Experience, The (Laing), 185

Popper, Karl, 17

Poverty, 134–137

Power of Positive Thinking, The (Peale), 133

Pragmatism, 25–32, 36–41, 63, 173–174, 260–261

Pratt, John Hersey, 124

Prefrontal cortex, 72, 241

Presley, Elvis, 201

Pressman, Jack, 72

Primal scream therapy, xiv, 177, 179, 180

Problem Drinker, The (Hirsh), 109

Proctor, Max, 201, 214–215

Prozac, xii–xiii, 242–244, 250, 251, 253, 254, 260

Prozac Backlash (Glenmullen), 244

Psychiatric activism, 137–138

Psychiatric Aspects of School Integration (GAP), 138

Psychiatry, 14–16, 28, 41
  biological, xii–xiii, 225–227, 236, 240–254
  criticism of, 184–189
  decline of, 235–236, 244–246
  distinguished from psychology, 68–70, 74
  drug addiction and, 206–207
  organic approach and, 99–100
  pharmacologic practices and, 244–245
  research, 74
  shock therapy and psychosurgery and, 70–74
  social work (*see* Social work)
  training and, 53–57, 70, 100, 138–139, 235–236
  U.S. Army and, 43–46, 52, 58, 64

Psycho-Analytical Congress, 11

Psychoanalysis
  cost of, x, 219–220
  in decline, x, 153–155, 218–224, 227, 236, 239
  Freudian theory, 4–18
  guilt and, 157–158
  legacy of, x–xi
  length of treatment, 103, 150–151, 154, 231–232
  medicalization of, 16
  outcomes research, 189–190
  professional arrogance and, 151–152
  training, 148–149, 154, 219

Psychodrama, 38, 127

Psychodynamic psychotherapy, xi, 190, 229, 230, 254

Psychological literature, 132–133

Psychology, 14, 153
  distinguished from psychiatric social work, 67–68
  distinguished from psychiatry, 68–70, 74
  growth of, 235, 236–237
  interpersonal, 25–29, 31, 72, 126, 163, 254
  prescription privileges and, 245–246
  Rorschach personality test and, 65–66, 247
  training and, 65, 67, 68, 70, 236, 237–238, 246–247
  World War II and, 64

Psychometrics, 32–33

Psychoneuroses, 43, 45–46, 52, 58

Psychopathology of Everyday Life, The (Freud), 7

Psychopharmacology (*see* Medications)

Psychosocial Medicine: A Study of the Sick Society (Halliday), 134

Psychosurgery, 70, 72–74, 227

Psychotherapy, (*see also* Psychiatry; Psychology; Social work)
  acceptance of, 47–48, 52
  behaviorism, 82–89, 94

biological psychiatry and (*see* Biological psychiatry)

challenges to, xii

child guidance movement and, 35–37

clergy and, xiv, 50, 156–161

community mental health centers (CMHCs) and, 139–145

cost of, 80, 146, 147

deinstitutionalization and, 142–145

drug addiction and, 207, 217

familiarity with, 48–49

group (*see* Group therapy)

guilt and, 157–159

health insurance and, 145–148

humanism, 27, 30, 31, 76–83, 136, 153, 163, 172–175, 230, 231

length of treatment, 231–233

managed care and, 249–250

multiplying therapies, 177–184

outcomes studies, 103–108, 189–194

practitioners of, xi, xii, 146

psychodynamic, xi, 190, 229, 230, 254

qualities of therapist, 234, 256

religion and, 155–161

skepticism about, 49–51

success of, xi, 255–256, 258

thinking, 89–95

workplace programs, 170

Putnam, James Jackson, 14, 15, 35

Racism, 33, 134, 135, 138, 179

Rangell, Leo, 153–154

Rank, Otto, 11

Rational emotive therapy (RET), 94–95, 153, 163, 228

Rayner, Rosalie, 82

Realistic psychotherapy, 36

Rebirthing therapy, xiv, 177, 179

Recapture therapies, 179–181

Reciprocal inhibition therapy, 86–87

Recovered memories, 177, 181–182

Relationship therapy, 136

Relaxation therapies, 177–178

Religion

drug use and addiction and, 215–217

psychotherapy and, 155–161

Repression, x, xi, 6, 8–10, 12, 29, 48, 63, 181, 221, 257

Reserpine, xii, 97–98, 101, 225

Roberts, William, 157

Rogers, Carl, 27, 66, 76–80, 82, 125, 136, 160, 163, 172

Rogow, Arnold, 132

Rolf, Anna, 178

Rolfing therapy, 178

Rorschach, Hermann, 66

Rorschach personality test, 65–66, 247

Rosenbaum, Max, 127–128

Rubin, Jerry, 170

Russell, Richard, 135

Russell Sage Foundation, 58

Sachs, Hanns, 12

Sakel, Manfred, 71

Salvation Army, 169, 212

Sanders, Marion, 161

Sapir, Edward, 126

Saturday Evening Post, 48, 119, 120, 169

Scarlett, George, 159

Scheff, Thomas, 135

Schizophrenia, 71–73, 96, 98, 101, 152–153, 185–188, 221–222, 225–227, 255

School integration, 138

Schwartz, Bertha, 111

Schwartz, Richard, 137

Science, 13, 19, 24

Scoville, Mildred, 60

Sechrest, Lee, 246–247

Selective serotonin reuptake inhibitors (SSRIs), 250–251, 253

Self-actualization theory, 81, 191

Self-love, philosophy of, 79

Seliger, Robert, 111, 114, 116

Serotonin, 241, 242, 251

Sex fetishism, 85–86

Sex hormones, 96

Sex therapy, 182–183

Sexual latency period, 7, 31

Sexuality, x, 7, 20–23, 156

Shaffer, Laurence, 68

Shainess, Natalie, 185

Shame of the States (Deutch), 140

Shapiro, Arthur, 220

Sharfstein, Steven, 144

Shatterly, Daniel, 209

Sheen, Fulton, 50, 156

Shell shock, 43, 45–46, 52, 58

Sheppard Pratt Hospital, Maryland, 25, 27, 29

Shinfuku, Noatake, 178

Shoben, Edward, Jr., 78

Shock therapy, 70–72, 74, 84–86, 87, 99, 187, 227, 240–241

Sick society, image of, 134–137, 168

Skinner, B. F., 83

Smith, Robert, 119, 120

SmithKline, 98

Social psychology, 27–29

Social work, 37, 58–64, 153, 161–166
    distinguished from psychology, 67–68
    gender imbalance in, 163–164
    growth of, 235, 238–239
    licensure and, 165–166
    malaise and ambivalence in, 161, 163
    private practice, 162–165
    training, 162, 166, 238–239

Sociology, 34

Sociometry, 38–41

Southard, Elmer, 58

Standard Edition (Freud), 4

Stanford–Binet intelligence test, 65

State mental hospitals, 140, 141, 143, 144

Steele, Robert Hampton, 203

Steiner, Lee, 48

Stern, Karl, 2, 157

Stimulus satiation therapy, 86

Storr, Anthony, 256

Strecker, E. A., 46

Strupp, Hans, xv, 173, 218

Studies in Hysteria (Freud and Breuer), 6

Sullivan, Harry Stack, 1, 25–32, 34, 36, 42, 62, 63, 72, 103, 125, 126, 163, 174, 178, 234

Summer, William, 109

Superego, 7, 79, 257

Swift, Sarah, 61

Switkes, Daniel, 138

Szasz, Thomas, 185–187

Tavistock Institute, London, 232

Testosterone, 96

Thinking, 89–95

Thomas, John, 110

Thompson, Clara, 25, 28, 31, 103

Thompson, George, 114, 116

Thorazine, xii, 98, 225, 227, 240, 251, 254

Thorman, Donald, 202, 212

Three Essays on a Theory of Sexuality (Freud), 7

Tietze, Trude, 153

Tillich, Paul, 157, 160

Toxic Psychiatry (Breggin), 187

Tranquilizers, 97–98, 100, 101, 107, 140–141, 170, 187, 240

Transcendental meditation (TM), 177, 178

Transference, 10, 12, 29, 42, 63, 101–102

Tricyclic antidepressants, 223–225, 240, 242, 250

Unconscious, x, 6–7, 10, 13, 30, 31, 36, 63, 72, 102, 186, 257

U.S. armed forces, 43–46, 52, 58, 64, 136, 138, 203

Upjohn, 187

Vaillant, George, 206, 259

Valium, xii, 251

VandenBos, Gary, 192

Verden, Paul, 209

Veterans Administration (VA), 44, 54, 55, 66–67, 146

Vienna Psycho-Analytical Society, 11

Vietnam War, 138, 203

Vogel, Sidney, 115, 117

Vonachen, Harold, 111

Vonnegut, Mark, 143

Watson, John, 82, 83

Wechsler-Bellevue intelligence test, 65

Wehr, Thomas, 241

Weigert, Edith, 161

Weinstock, Harry, 220

Wellbutrin, xii

Western Electric Company, Hawthorne, Illinois, 125

Where Do People Take Their Troubles? (Steiner), 48

White, William Alanson, 25

Whyte, William, 134

Wilder, Joseph, 104

Williams, Greer, 50–51

Williams, Roger, 117

Wilson, Bill, 119–120

Winkelman, Nathan, 96

Witmer, Lightner, 32–35

Wolfe, Tom, 17

Wolpe, Joseph, 84

Women and Madness (Chesler), 185

Workplace
    alcohol use in, 111
    drug use in, 204–206
    therapy programs in, 170

World War I, 45–46

World War II, 43–46, 51–52, 54, 58, 64, 115

Xanax, xii, 187, 251

Yoga, 177

Youngdahl, Luther, 114

Z-therapy, 179, 180–181

Zaslow, Robert, 180–181

Zen, 177

Zibloorg, Gregory, 158

Zoloft, 250